One National Family

One National Family

*Texas, Mexico, and the Making of the Modern United States,
1820–1867*

SARAH K. M. RODRÍGUEZ

Johns Hopkins University Press
Baltimore

Published in Cooperation with the William P. Clements Center for Southwest Studies, Southern Methodist University

© 2024 Johns Hopkins University Press
All rights reserved. Published 2024
Printed in the United States of America on acid-free paper

2 4 6 8 9 7 5 3 1

Johns Hopkins University Press
2715 North Charles Street
Baltimore, Maryland 21218
www.press.jhu.edu

Library of Congress Cataloging-in-Publication Data is available.
A catalog record for this book is available from the British Library.

ISBN 978-1-4214-4944-9 (hardcover)
ISBN 978-1-4214-4945-6 (ebook)

Special discounts are available for bulk purchases of this book. For more information, please contact Special Sales at specialsales@jh.edu.

CONTENTS

Map vi

Introduction 1

PART I

1 The Greatest Nation on Earth 15

2 Land, Loyalty, and Identity in the Trans-Mississippi Corridor 43

3 Slavery, Federalism, and Mexico's First Civil War 71

4 Anti-national and Contemptible Intrigues 103

PART II

5 Toward a Single National Truth 143

6 Sovereignty, Secession, and the Decline of the Old Federalism 178

7 Ayutla, Antislavery, and the Rise of the New Liberalism 210

8 The Birth of Two Nations 237

Epilogue 269

Notes 277
Index 325

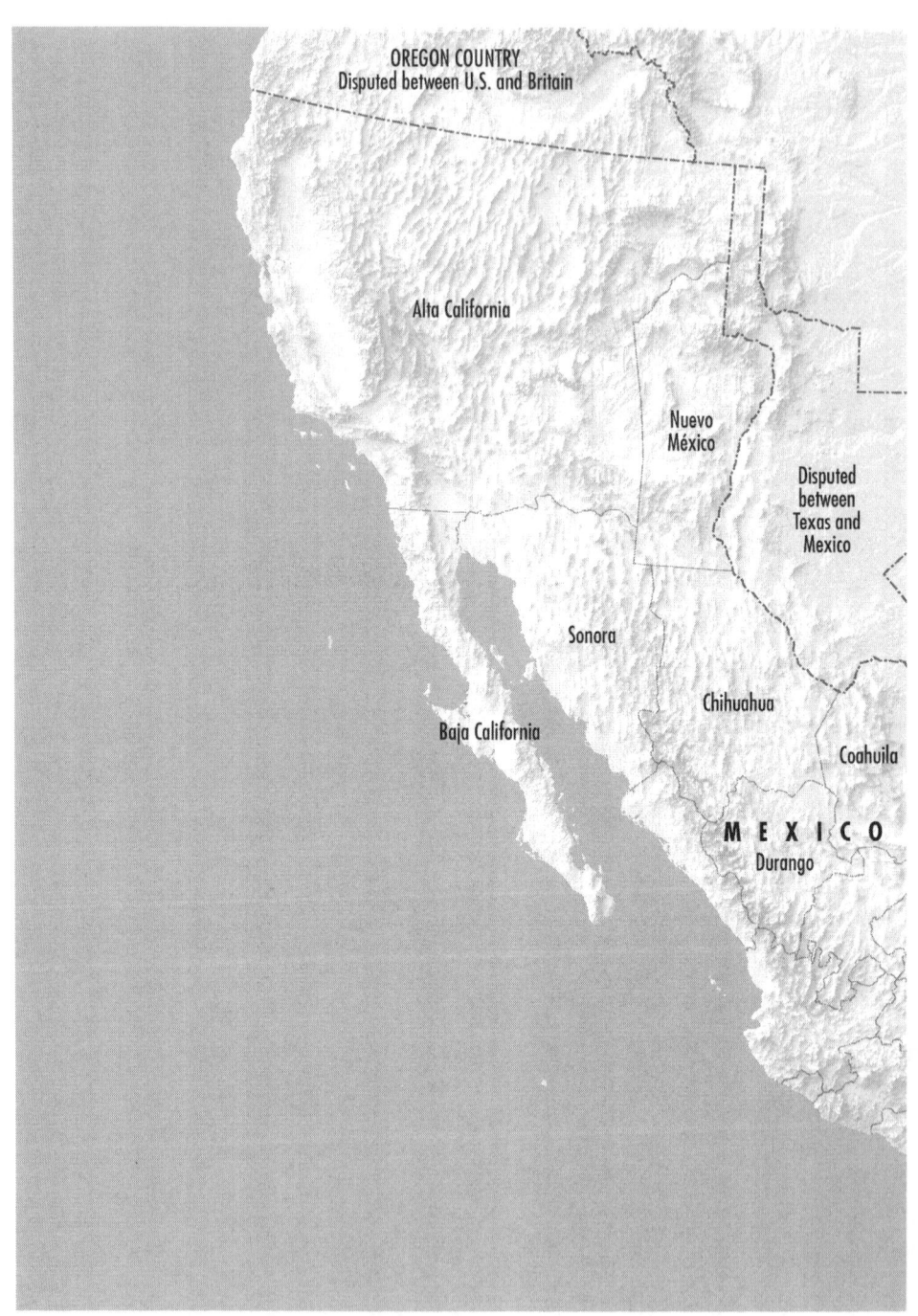

Texas and surrounding territory, ca. 1841
Map by Glen Pawelski, Mapping Specialists, Ltd.

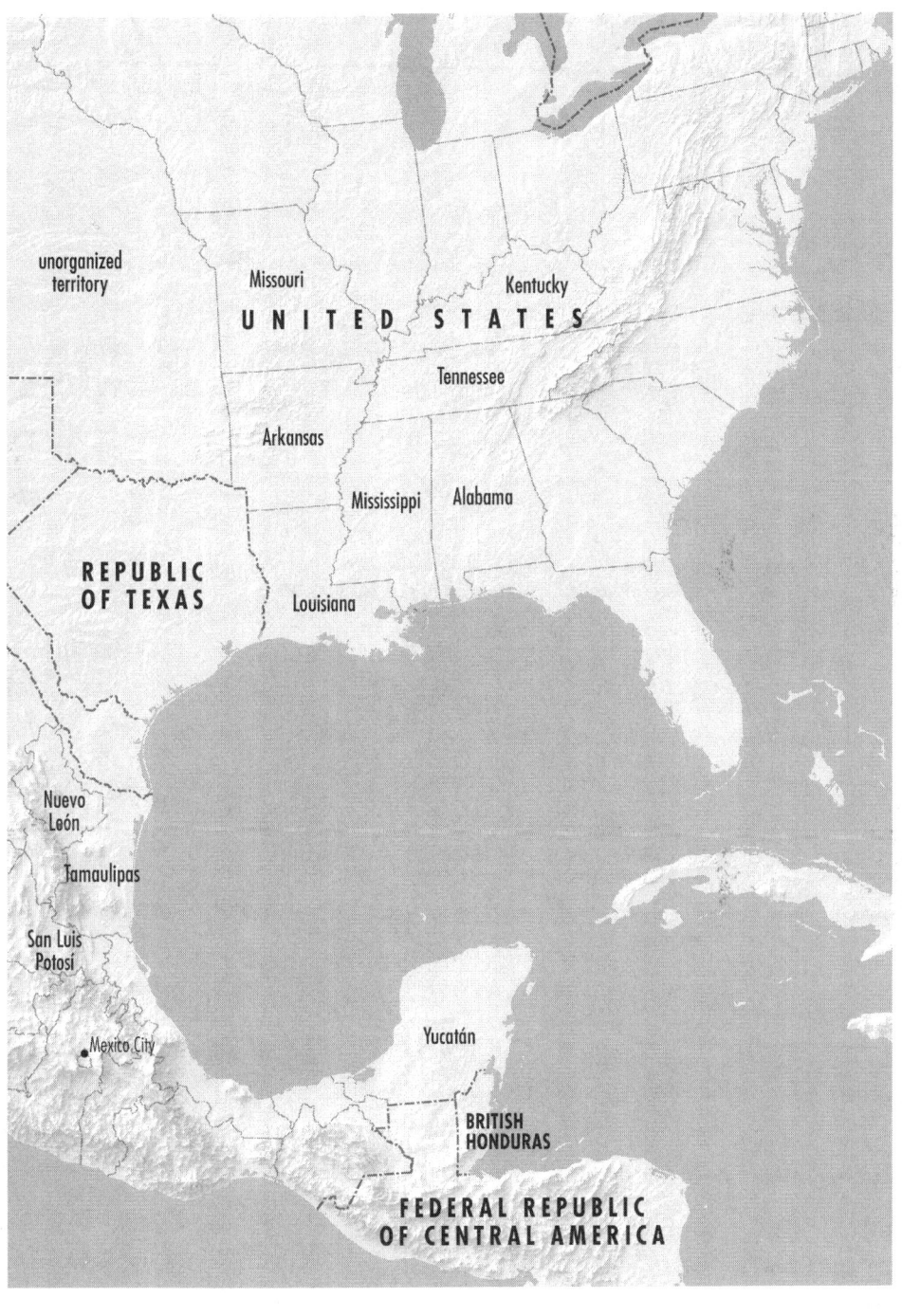

One National Family

Introduction

Shortly after negotiating the 1819 treaty that ceded Florida to the United States, the Spanish envoy Luis de Onís y González-Vera published one of the earliest foreign impressions of the United States to warn the Spanish-speaking world of its territorial ambitions. Onís predicted many future seizures by the republic, which seemed to equate power with territorial size and viewed itself as "destined to one day be the most sublime colossus of human power."[1] US leaders at the time, more laudatory of their republic than Onís, anticipated the same or similar outcomes.[2] Few of them, however, shared the second part of the minister's prediction although it was just as prescient. Despite the likely expansion of the United States, Onís felt confident that the country was doomed. Its people's commercialism, individualism, and self-interest presented a shaky basis for a nation, and its federal constitution sowed the seeds of "discord and disillusion." Onís anticipated that the United States would continue to expand before eventually collapsing, a casualty of its own ambition. Indeed, some four decades later, and only eleven years after formally acquiring nearly half of Mexico's territory in one of the largest land seizures in modern history, the United States would rupture from within.

This book reconsiders the causes and consequences of one stage of the United States' dramatic rise to continental dominance in the mid-nineteenth century—

the secession of Texas from Mexico and its subsequent annexation to the United States. It also makes two related claims. The first is that this phase of US expansion was characterized by a profound political irony: it flowed from US failures and Mexican viability, and Mexican federalism, long blamed for the country's disintegration and instability,[3] was precisely what attracted thousands of US immigrants to Mexican Texas and formed the basis of their loyalty to that country. The second is that the loss of Texas and eventually half of Mexico's territory to the United States prompted Mexicans to recognize the limits of their federal system sooner than their US counterparts recognized the limits of their own.

Even before independence, Anglo-American political tradition had presumed an association between small government, economic self-sufficiency, and personal autonomy.[4] Yet, for many Anglo-Americans—especially those in the western districts and territories of the United States—the country's founding betrayed this association, beginning with its adoption of the 1787 constitutional settlement.[5] Meanwhile, Mexico's comparatively weak fiscal structure, ample land, and apparently more thorough commitment to state sovereignty and local autonomy made it an appealing alternative to the disillusioned US agrarians who settled there in the wake of the 1819 economic crisis.[6] Thousands of them renounced their US citizenship and declared their loyalty to Mexico, insisting it was the only place where they could truly be American. Yet, if Mexico's political system was a strength in the 1820s, it would become the source of conflict and secession by the 1830s.[7] Perceiving the need to centralize power in the wake of foreign encroachment, Native raids, and economic underdevelopment, Mexicans, under the leadership of General Antonio López de Santa Anna, replaced their lauded federalist Constitution of 1824 with a form that exceeded even the 1787 US document in its centralism. The move prompted a federalist revolt that began in the Mexican interior before sweeping north and getting Texas involved. Anglo-Texans joined the resistance late, at the behest of Mexican federalists, and their call for independence came only after Southern interests refused to supply arms and resources unless the Texans separated from Mexico. Until the secession of eleven slave states from the United States twenty-five years later, the Texas rebellion of 1836 represented the most dramatic and enduring separatist movement to emerge on the North American continent in the nineteenth century.

By 1845, two competing political visions had emerged on the continent. One promoted centrifugalism, territorial expansion, and racial hierarchy, while the other advocated centralism, containment, and antislavery. Texas, which remained a functionally, if not legitimately, independent republic for nearly a decade, served as an ally and model for the former, inspiring a series of autonomist agrarian movements that stretched from Yucatán to Oregon. Prescribing to a version of this vision that departed only in its efforts to harness federal power to sectional aims, were slaveholders in the US South,[8] many of whom pushed for the US annexation of Texas. Meanwhile, Whigs in the United States joined Mexican centralists by dismissing US expansion as a plot to extend slavery and compromise the union. Most Whigs, however, also celebrated Texas as a symbol of the inherent superiority of Anglo-American institutions and a critical stage in what they hoped would become a continent populated by Anglo-inspired and -dominated republics. By the 1840s, it looked as if that vision might come to fruition as numerous Anglo polities cropped up in the wake of the Texas rebellion. Although each polity was distinct in its own way, they all shared with Texans a disillusionment with the US republic, though not its founding principles, which they hoped to perfect as part of separate and autonomous polities. Eventually, however, Texas's conflicts with Native powers, continued vulnerability to Mexican invasion, and lack of revenue would lead to popular support for annexation to the United States despite the hopes of some that Texas would one day constitute its own continental empire.[9] When Texas ultimately joined the United States in 1845, it provided an opportunity for proslavery interests in the South to launch an invasion of Mexico premised on the idea that the United States represented the sole guarantor of republican self-determination on the continent in terms that denied Anglo settlers' early attraction to and investment in Mexico and cast that country as a decidedly failed republic undeserving of its own land and sovereignty.[10]

While Mexicans of nearly all political persuasions had concluded by 1850 that Mexico needed a more robust central government capable of remedying the challenges associated with sovereignty, territoriality, and inequality, leaders in the United States, especially Democrats, insisted that their republic's weak federal structure was precisely what had contributed to its prosperity and expansion. So firm was their belief in the Anglo-American capacity for self-rule and decentralized governance that they insisted it could solve the most pressing issue to follow the war—whether the institution of slavery should be permitted to extend into the western territories, including those seized from Mexico.[11] When proslavery Southerners proved more committed to the institution's growth than to popular sovereignty,[12] they would draw from the same compact theory that the Texans had. As the US political system surrendered to the forces of centrifugalism, Mexicans moved toward a new liberal order.[13] The Constitution of 1857 embodied nearly all the elements of a modern state—federal supremacy, territorial inalienability, and racial equality. The United States, of course, would eventually integrate these elements into its constitution, but not until well after Mexico had, and after defeating the slaveholding South in one of the bloodiest conflicts of the modern age. Indeed, by 1860 both republics would find themselves confronting similar struggles against hierarchical, antidemocratic, imperial regimes. Although the administration of Abraham Lincoln was initially slow to offer support to that of President Benito Juárez, the two leaders eventually formed a successful alliance whose victory guaranteed the rise of two modern, liberal nation-states on the North American continent.

State of the Scholarship

This book begins in Texas, the only polity to secede from both Mexico and the United States. Long understood as the story of independent, freedom-loving Anglo-American frontiersmen fighting an oppressive Mexican dictatorship,[14] the history of the 1830s Texas rebellion and the events that led to it have undergone a generation of revisionist history, much of it aimed at integrating the perspectives of Native, Mexican, and Black inhabitants.[15] An even more recent body of scholarship points to the role of capitalism and slavery in the settlement, development, and eventual integration of the western part of the North American continent, in particular Texas, into the United States.[16] While such studies have contributed immensely to understanding the factors behind US expansion, they also implicitly confirm it as the story of US forces and institutions pushing westward. Another body of scholarship, on early Texas settlers, challenges the assumption that they had an interest in facilitating US expansion and argues instead that they prescribed to alternative, and often more flexible or pragmatic, forms of nationalism.[17] This book contributes to this third body of work by arguing that the settlers' attraction to Mexico was rooted in their belief that Mexico was a country of unique promise and potential in large part *because* of its political system. It takes settlers' commitment and testaments of loyalty to Mexico more seriously than any previous study, and in so doing, necessitates reconsideration of early Mexican viability and its appeal more broadly.

Meanwhile, a parallel body of scholarship points to the role that Native powers played in weakening Mexico's hold on its far northern region and priming it for US acquisition.[18] As crucial as such studies are to reconsiderations of Native power, they also tend to confirm that early Mexico's efforts at nation-building were largely a failure. It is a difficult assumption to dispute. The First

Mexican Republic (1824–1835) suffered from profound and persistent economic problems stemming from its relatively late entrance into the world of Atlantic capitalism, its ineffectual or nonexistent fiscal state, and its routinely being threatened by various foreign powers, including the United States.[19] During Mexico's first four decades of independence, it cycled through as many constitutions, experienced only one peaceful transference of power—the first one— and faced nearly uninterrupted political upheaval and revolution.[20] It is, therefore, unsurprising that until recently scholars of Mexico had mostly dismissed its early period as one characterized by national disintegration and institutional failure. That said, this "disorder thesis" ignores that the United States experienced a rupture in the mid-eighteenth century far more profound than anything that Mexico had undergone up to that point.[21] As the last twenty years of scholarship in the field of early US history has shown, the country was also plagued by violence, rebellion, and institutional failure.[22] Unlike in Mexico, however, most of this violence was not in the realm of formal politics, but was directed at people of color in the form of enslavement or forced removal.

Furthermore, the rebellion in the US South far exceeded in scope and purpose any of the numerous internal revolts that plagued early Mexico. Although frequently referred to as secessionist, none of the autonomist movements of 1830s or 1840s Mexico ultimately aspired to permanent and complete separation from it. The one exception, of course, was Texas, which would secede from the United States as well. In short, neither of the two North American republics was particularly strong or durable during this period, and both would end up redefining their politics, constitutions, and very identity before emerging as modern nations. Indeed, this book owes much to the recent scholarship on early Mexican politics, especially early Mexican conservatism.[23] The First Mexican Republic and the subsequent twenty years have long been called the "Age of Santa Anna" and for good reason. No one was arguably more influential in shaping the course of Mexican politics than the storied general who ruled the republic eleven times. Santa Anna is commonly understood to have been a product of Mexico's propensity for regional strongmen, a powerful symbol of its supposedly failed democracy, a self-proclaimed dictator, political opportunist, and pedophilic philanderer.[24] He was all of these things, but his administration was one of the first, not just in Mexico but on the North American continent, to articulate and realize a modern conception of national sovereignty and majoritarian democracy, and as such, it informed modern political governance in Mexico. Not only that, but santanistas shared many of the same political ideas as the Whigs.[25] Mexican conservatives' conception of a uniform, composite, and bounded polity was not far removed from the views of men like John Quincy Adams and Francis Lieber.[26]

Indeed, another major aim of this book is to place Texas more firmly within the national histories of early Mexico and the United States. The events that occurred there in the 1820s and 1830s need to be considered as extensions of political and social trends in both countries, not exceptions to them. The Texas rebellion itself is still largely presented as the outcome of American restiveness rather than an extension of Mexican politics. US immigrants' expressions of fealty to Mexico and its constitution, though numerous, are dismissed as insincere or pragmatic. Historians often point to their continued self-identification as "American," displays of US symbols, and claims to the Anglo republic's revolutionary heritage as evidence that their commitment to Mexico was half-hearted at best.[27] In fact, their behavior was entirely typical of immigrant communities the world over. Declaring political fealty to one country does not necessitate shedding one's former identity. For many of these men and women, identity and nation were separate, as they were for many people in the late eighteenth and early nineteenth century.[28] These immigrants were drawn to Mexico precisely because they believed it was better suited to the pursuit of their American identity. As much as events in Texas were an extension of the South's westward-facing cotton empire, they were also the result of agrarians' disillusion with US politics and government that emerged soon after the republic's founding.

Early US immigrants to Mexico were attracted to that country as much for its political institutions as its cheap, fertile land and opportunity for economic prosperity. Indeed, as far as they were concerned, Mexico's political and economic appeal were inseparable. For years, historians of the Texas rebellion have debated whether slavery or federalism played a role in Texans' decision to secede from Mexico,[29] overlooking the fact that, especially by the 1830s, these two systems were intimately linked. Slaveholders in both the United States and Mexico had effectively co-opted federalism and states' rights in defense of their institution.[30] Yet, a study that acknowledges federalism's role in secession should not be confused with one that argues that it was its cause. The US South's rebellion distinguished itself from the Mexican rebellions in both its motivation and aim. Indeed, as revealed by the simmering dispute over the Fugitive Slave Act of 1850, Southerners were willing to betray their attested commitment to states' rights whenever it collided with slavery. Yet, the Mexican autonomist movements of the 1840s and the South's secession did resemble one another in their means. Southerners harnessed their states' rights theory to a specifically proslavery interpretation of the Constitution to argue that they had the right to enjoy the protection of their slave property in the western territories, a position confirmed by the Supreme Court's devastating decision in *Dred Scott v. Sandford (1857)*. When it became clear that Northern Democrats did not agree and would not support a Southern effort to codify such a position, Southerners returned to federalism yet again to justify their leaving the union altogether. The relationship between slavery and federalism is indeed a complicated one. The two forces evolved in parallel, often overlapping and intersecting, but federalism is also rooted in early modern conceptions of republicanism that, although problematic from a democratic standpoint, were not always associated with slavery. This study aims to track the complicated evolution of federalism, a system that even today is often associated with self-determination and democracy. Thus, the defeat of radical federalism became a crucial stage on the journey to modern nationhood for both Mexico and the United States.

Because the Texas rebellion represented a confluence of forces that emanated from both Mexico and the United States, it is the ideal vantage point from which to draw important conclusions regarding the comparative political experiences and nation-building processes of both republics. To date, no comprehensive comparative political history of the United States and Mexico has been published in English.[31] While this study does not deign to attempt as much, it does take steps in that direction by examining how each republic addressed and ultimately resolved questions related to federalism, sovereignty, territoriality, race, slavery, identity, and democracy. As such, it makes an important contribution to a growing body of work that attempts to expand the geographical and chronological boundaries of the United States' War of the Rebellion.[32] As this study hopes to show, that conflict represented a collision of two opposing republican visions that slowly emerged in North America. The vision committed to state sovereignty, territorial impermanency, and racial hierarchy, although its proponents lost the war, represented a powerful alternative emanating from the continent's core and a formidable challenge to the modernizing and democratizing efforts of both the United States and Mexico.

Structure and Chapters

This book is divided into two parts. The first part focuses on Texas, where the story of the US and Mexican journeys from early republics to modern nation-states began and ended. By the late eighteenth century, suspicion of centralized authority had emerged as a powerful political impulse among colonial subjects in both Spain and the British Empire and continued long after the independence of Mexico and the United States, with both attempting to strike a balance between local autonomy and federal power strong enough to unite their diverse and sprawling young republics. Chapter 1 argues that by the 1820s, economic panic in the United States had prompted widespread hostility toward the federal government, with many citizens, especially those in the west, believing that their country had betrayed its founding promise to secure and protect the economic and political autonomy of its white male citizens. What historians have traditionally understood as Mexico's chief weakness—its commitment to an unobtrusive central government and strong local autonomy—is in fact what attracted so many norteamericano settlers to Mexico and compelled them to become citizens. Rather than their testaments of fealty to Mexico being pragmatic or sycophantic, it is more likely that they were sincere given what is known about the comparative weakness of US nationalism at that time and the relative appeal and promise of Mexico.

Chapter 2 explores the extent and nature of the northern settlers' relationship to Mexico, arguing that for many of them, identity and nation functioned as distinct entities. Being American more often meant prescribing to a set of principles associated with economic self-sufficiency, land proprietorship, and small government, which by the 1820s could be more readily secured on the northern Mexican frontier, where land was plentiful and cheap, war with indigenous communities was encouraged or ignored by authorities, and a federal presence was largely absent. Far from Mexican citizenship being a betrayal of the settlers' American identity, it was in fact foundational to it. The immigrants represented a specific thread of previously anti-federalist thought that shared a general distrust of overly centralized authority and frequently decried the "aristocracy," but nonetheless embraced and promoted social order and uniformity. This formed as much of the basis for early settlers' commitment to preserving and protecting Mexico as did their belief that Mexico was better equipped to deliver on the promises of economic autonomy and local authority. This commitment to social uniformity informed their surprising acceptance, and at times even vocal defense, of Mexico's establishment clause, recognizing Roman Catholicism as the state-sanctioned religion. Despite the settlers' suspicions that the clause suppressed the kind of free thinking that many deemed essential to republicanism, it nonetheless quelled the social disharmony and "fanaticism" that plagued the United States.

Chapter 3 aims to place the critical period leading up to Texas's secession within the context of shifting national politics in Mexico and the United States by arguing that the ascendence of popular federalism in both places, beginning in 1828 with the elections of Vicente Guerrero and Andrew Jackson, respectively, not only reflected a similar trend, but had a profound impact on the political and social dynamics of Texas's borderlands. Both presidents tested the limits of their executive power and asserted a direct relationship with the nation's people in terms that alarmed strict federalists. They also both worked to secure land and serve the economic interests of their respective constituents. For Guerrero, this meant championing the rights of indigenous communities and confirming Mexico's commitment to emancipation. For Jackson, it meant championing the rights of Anglo-American men, often by seizing land from indigenous groups and helping to expand slavery's domain. Jackson's election mitigated some of the very grievances that had pushed so many US agrarians to move to the Texas borderlands and formed the basis of their loyalty to Mexico. Meanwhile, Guerrero's presidency signaled a departure from Mexico's earlier federalist commitment in the service of egalitarian ends. This was especially the case in 1829, when Guerrero issued a national emancipationist decree that threatened the growing presence of chattel slavery in Texas. Yet, Texan leaders and their Tejano allies continued to rely on the Mexican Constitution of 1824 as their bulwark against abolitionist encroachment, demonstrating an enduring faith in Mexican institutions and their compatibility with Southern slavery.

Mexico's relationship with Texas began to sour in 1834 as the republic turned away from federalism. Much of this was in response to fears that the Anglo settlers in Texas might follow the example of their slaveholding US counterparts, who were then seizing on states' rights theory, specifically nullification, to protect proslavery interests from unfavorable congressional legislation like the tariff. Such actions, commonly understood as paving the way for secession, alarmed both Mexican and US nationalists, raised Mexican leaders' awareness of increasingly restive forces in Texas, and likely informed the decision of Santa Anna to respond to a wave of popular demands for a new constitutional convention. Though supported by many Mexicans, the decision to discard the 1824 constitution prompted a series of federalist revolts throughout Mexico, the one in Texas among them. Contrary to popular opinion, Texans joined the federalist resistance late and at the behest of federalist allies elsewhere in Mexico. Texans initially demanded the reinstatement of the Constitution of 1824, but their later decision to instead pursue independence opened the door to intervention from proslavery interests in New Orleans, a city that in addition to forming the nexus of republican radicalism for decades had more recently become the epicenter of the US cotton economy. Wealthy slave interests contributed to the rebellion on the condition that Texas declare independence from Mexico and, in so doing, lent their voices to the appeals of a nascent pro-independence movement in Texas composed of more recent US arrivals, who had emerged in opposition to the "old settlers."

Chapter 4 departs from most studies of the Texas rebellion by challenging views on the Mexican centralist response in arguing that Santa Anna's regime drew on the same principles of majoritarian democracy, federal supremacy, and territorial sovereignty as those expressed by opponents of South Carolina's nullification of tariffs. As such, santanistas not only rejected the antidemocratic and antistatist theories that proslavery Southerners in the United States were then embracing, but they also laid the groundwork for the modern liberal state that both republics would ultimately embrace.

Part II broadens the book's geographical and theoretical scope by examining how questions around federalism, sovereignty, and democracy continued to plague Mexico and the United States at the national level, while highlighting the centrality of Texas to these debates. Chapter 5 argues that the ten years between the Texas rebellion and the 1846 US invasion of Mexico was one of profound geopolitical competition and contingency as two distinct visions of North American republicanism emerged on the continent. Ultimately, however, competition for Texas would prompt federalists in both countries to reconsider their relationship to the state. Mexican "*puro*" (pure) federalists—among them Mariano Otero, Manuel Crescencio Rejón, and Valentín Gómez Farías, leader of the Mexican resistance and an early supporter of the Texas rebellion—combined an enduring commitment to state and local autonomy with aspirations for a diverse, democratic, and sovereign republic. In short, they aimed to use federalism to unite and secure. Meanwhile, in the United States, proslavery Southerners would begin to abandon their historic commitment to federalism in their efforts to harness federal power to proslavery interests like the annexation of Texas and, ultimately, the US invasion of Mexico. They attempted to reconcile these two counter impulses and defend themselves against accusations of hypocrisy by recasting early Anglo settlers of Texas as willing agents of US expansion in terms that simplified or denied their Mexican citizenship.

The United States' dramatic defeat of Mexico in 1848 constituted not only a national humiliation, but also a reckoning. As chapter 6 argues, the need for a strong central government capable of unifying and defending Mexican territory from further aggression became evident to nearly all members of the Mexican political class by 1850, as federalists discarded their earlier resistance to consolidation and called for a more uniform society with sovereignty residing indisputably in the people. Meanwhile, back in the United States, national leaders would move in the opposite direction as the Mexican cession catapulted questions around slavery and sovereignty to the forefront of national debate. Yet, many US leaders, unlike their Mexican counterparts, insisted that a commitment to localism could resolve sectional fissures over whether slavery should be permitted to extend into western territories by simply leaving it to white settler communities to decide by the ballot. Southern Democrats, however, knowing that they lacked the numerical power to sway such elections and historically hostile to popular democracy, harnessed states' rights theory to a proslavery interpretation of the constitution to insist that Congress had an obligation to protect their human property in the territories.

While the Southern states surrendered to the forces of slavery and centrifugalism, in Mexico and the northern United States, liberalism, equality, and nationalism were taking hold. Chapter 7 compares the rise of Mexican liberalism as embodied by the Reforma generation and the Constitution of 1857, a document that contained many of the lessons of the recent war with the United States, to that of the new Republican Party. Both movements rejected systems of unfree labor, concentrated wealth, and inequality. Interestingly, Lincoln would draw from a similar theory of territorial inalienability in denying the legitimacy of southern secession as Mexican liberals had in rejecting the Treaty of Guadalupe Hidalgo. Republicans, however, although thoroughly rejecting the expansionist aims of the proslavery South and especially its earlier assault on Mexico, mostly failed to recognize the extent to which their ideas were shared or reflected in the new Mexican regime or the way in which the sectional divide then plaguing the United States was akin to the one that had divided Mexico. The one group that did understand this, not surprisingly, were Texans, who drew a direct comparison between their recent struggles with Mexico and their ultimate decision to secede from the United States for many of the same reasons.

Chapter 8 compares the civil conflicts that had consumed both countries by 1862. In Mexico, the members of Juárez's party, which included many authors of the 1857 constitution, found themselves having to defend the republic against Mexican conservatives aligned with Maximilian I's French imperial regime. In the United States, the new Lincoln administration found itself at war with a Confederate state born from the same anxieties that contributed to the rise of the Second Mexican Empire (1864–1867). Both Juárez and Lincoln characterized their respective conflicts as representing an existential struggle—one between the forces of aristocracy and democracy, slavery and equality, sovereignty and empire—a confrontation that would have ramifications for the entire continent. Yet, in many respects, the fissures that characterized the Mexican civil war were less significant than those that characterized the simultaneous conflict in the north, for both liberals and imperialists wanted to see Mexico become a modern, prosperous, and viable nation capable of defending its territory from further encroachment by the United States. Nevertheless, the similarities between these two conflicts were immediately evident to Mexican liberals, who solicited Lincoln's assistance in defeating the French emperor even before his inauguration. The Republican administration, however, viewed the dispute as primarily a domestic one until late 1863, when it finally formally recognized the Juárez regime and agreed to aid it in its war with France. Ultimately, both regimes would have to defeat the residue of federalism before they could emerge as modern, bounded nation-states and claim their shared dominance of the North American continent.

In conclusion are a few notes on the text: All translations of Spanish sources are those of the author, unless otherwise indicated. Quotations from nineteenth-century sources have been adjusted to maintain grammatical consistency and according to the standards of modern capitalization. In addition, contemporary spellings have been retained, and no emphases have been added. Concerning documentation from archives in Mexico City, *legajo* has been translated as "volume," *expediente* as "file," and *caja* as "box."

PART ONE

CHAPTER ONE

The Greatest Nation on Earth

In the summer of 1822, William Walker, a recent immigrant from the United States to the Mexican province of Texas, penned a letter to a relative back home. "It seems as if providence designs this world to outshine the balance of the earth, in every respect," wrote the Mississippi native. "Her streams, her mountains, her soil, her men, her politics, all, allure on great scales—nothing small or contracted on her whole construction." Walker predicted that the "spire" of Mexico's "political fabric" would be "seen as a mirror to the civilized world" and concluded, "With these and a thousand other advantages I repeat that Mexico cannot fail, under the influence of a wise and liberal government, to become the greatest nation on earth."[1] Others who were acquainted with the recently independent Mexican Empire had little reason to doubt his prediction. While the United States had remained a marginal outpost of Great Britain for most of the seventeenth and eighteenth centuries, New Spain had claimed most of the North American continent. The United States may have doubled its size a quarter of a century after independence and gained control of the continent's most important river network and port, but Mexico remained the largest independent polity in the Western Hemisphere after Brazil, and one of the largest in the world. It encompassed two million square miles that stretched from present-day Costa Rica to Northern California. Strategically nestled between the Atlantic and Pacific Oceans, Mexico possessed all manner of climate and topography, natural resources, and a population three times larger than that of the United States at its independence.[2]

In a country so vast and diverse, it is easy to understand why republican governance represented such a challenge and why scholars have long argued that Mexico's weak federal structure was to blame for the decades of political instability, social conflict, and economic underdevelopment that characterized its first four decades.[3] Meanwhile, scholars of US colonization have long assumed that men like Walker were attracted to Mexico for its cheap land, rich natural resources and not much else. For many of these early immigrants, however, Mexico's form of government was just as appealing. Indeed, the Constitution of 1824, with its commitment to decentralized authority and local autonomy, embodied the very principles that had defined the Anglo-American political tradition since the eighteenth century.[4] Although rightly blamed for the many challenges that plagued the young republic, Mexico's early federal structure constituted one of the many sources of attraction for settlers from the United States like Walker. In addition to being highly mobile, some of these individuals had lived under Spanish jurisdiction, in Missouri or Louisiana, and had long benefitted from the open, porous boundaries and interethnic exchange that characterized the late eighteenth-century borderlands. They therefore demonstrated a flexible and contingent nationalism, often more influenced by pragmatics than ideology.[5] If they shared one thing in common with most Mexican republicans, however, it was a desire to discard the centralized governing structures that had characterized the European monarchies from which they had claimed independence.

Indeed, the framers of both republics engaged in intense debates regarding the scope, purpose, and aim of federal power that often pitted those committed to weak central authority and strong local autonomy against those who argued for greater centralization and limited democracy. While the terms of this debate were strikingly similar in both countries, their eventual outcomes differed. The Anglo-American republic embraced independence earlier as a bankrupt, vulnerable, and loosely connected alliance of sovereign states with few unifying characteristics. These factors, as well as many of the framers' desire to keep the colonial social order intact, resulted in a system that while honoring state sovereignty in many matters was nonetheless designed to strengthen federal power when it came to fiscal and military affairs.[6] Meanwhile, Mexico initially opted for monarchical empire under a constitution modeled after Spain's 1812 governing document,[7] but its founders swiftly abandoned this system in favor of a federalist model committed to allowing the individual states considerable control over their internal affairs. Thus, the early colonization of Mexican Texas was in many ways an extension of the very Anglo-American hostility to centralized authority that fueled US independence and contributed to many Americans' subsequent frustration with their central government. What Mexican framers forged, though it ultimately weakened their republic in the long term, was precisely what attracted so many norteamericanos to Mexican Texas and formed the basis of their loyalty to that country.

The United States: "A great mass of disaffection"

For much of the seventeenth century, the British colonies' distance from the metropole and relatively peripheral status permitted a climate of political autonomy and economic latitude. Unlike Ireland or the West Indies, North American British subjects enjoyed considerable self-governance, access to land, exemption from taxation, and legislative independence.[8] So when the crown initiated a series of reform policies designed to centralize and consolidate its power around the middle of the eighteenth century, it ignited a debate about the relationship between metropole and periphery and contributed to a general suspicion of centralized power that reached its apex in the decade just before independence.[9] Crucial to these debates was an assumption about the relationship between liberty and power, two elements presumably in opposition but no less essential to good governance.[10] The best central government was believed to be small and unobtrusive.[11] Such views intensified in the wake of extensive tax legislation passed after the Seven Years' War and a prohibitive land policy designed to mitigate conflict between western settlers and Natives. Opponents of the British excise system argued that it violated the precept of divided sovereignty and colonial autonomy that had come to define imperial governance over the past century and violated colonists' natural rights since they did not enjoy representation in Parliament.[12]

Yet, the same grievances that had fueled independence soon characterized many former colonists' relationship with their new government. For ordinary citizens, independence represented only the first stage in what they hoped would become a more thorough restructuring of the social order, particularly regarding land accessibility. As early as 1776, restive white men and women, previously contained by Britain's prohibitive settlement policies, began to stream over the Appalachian range and, in most cases, attempted to establish their own independent states.[13] By late 1782, Congress was receiving reports from the general at Fort Pitt, in western Pennsylvania, that people "in great numbers" were "flocking over the Ohio into what has hitherto been called Indian country" and "beyond the western line thereof."[14] Many of these frontier settlers shared an idealized agrarianism that viewed small-scale land proprietorship as the key to personal autonomy, social stability, and political autonomy,[15] but they also complained of a lack of representation.[16] Not long after the republic's founding, many feared its dissolution. One observer noted that the possibility "of a separation of the federal union into *two parts*. . . was [a] matter of frequent discussion."[17] From the perspective of those most committed to decentralized governance, this might not have been such a bad thing. Thomas Jefferson, in fact, had initially envisioned a series of Anglo-American republics occupying the continent, rather than just one,[18] but the geopolitical realities of the moment belied such possibilities. Many feared that such autonomous polities would be more vulnerable to European interference or threat, not an unfounded suspicion. With few trade partners and largely isolated from the rest of the Atlantic world, unity was critical to the economic and political survival of the republic.

Yet, just a few years after gaining independence, US leaders faced a set of challenges like those of their imperial predecessors.[19] Efforts to impose taxation were met with widespread and occasionally violent protest. Rebels insisted that their actions represented a mere extension of the revolution's aim to dismantle long-standing hierarchies and equalize society, but political and economic elites argued that they constituted a form of anarchy that if left unchecked threatened the republic's survival and even a return to British control.[20] Their concerns were aggravated by a federal structure that appeared impotent in the face of such disorder. The first framing document of the United States, the Articles of Confederation, privileged state sovereignty and limited federal power to international affairs, interstate relations, and territorial governance. Such an arrangement seemed fitting for a republic composed of thirteen formerly autonomous colonies, but it proved woefully inadequate following independence, especially when states began to express sectional divisions of their own or to channel the grievances of their more radical constituents.[21] Separatist impulses emerged among restive populations in remote areas underserved by the new government and at the state level, usually among representatives and local elites who sensed the impeding threat to their power and insisted that the variable interests of the states and regions were far too diverse to share membership in one republic.[22]

Thus, the fifty-five men who gathered in Philadelphia in the summer of 1787 aimed to design a new federal structure that would allow national leaders to exercise direct control over citizens, instill obedience, suppress conflict, and demand loyalty. Considering the profound social and economic crisis the country faced, some even pondered if a republican form of government was suited to their new country.²³ From the floor of the Constitutional Convention, Alexander Hamilton bluntly expressed doubt that a "republican govt. could be established" over such a vast territory. While most framers found Hamilton's suggestion of a return to monarchical rule unrealistic and undesirable, they seemed to agree with his assertion that the "extent of the country, is the strongest argument in favor of an energetic government; for any other can certainly never preserve the Union."²⁴ But opponents of this view cited political philosophers like Montesquieu to insist that most governing should remain at the state level, where the "interest of the public good is easier perceived, better understood, and more within the reach of every citizen." In a lengthy article published under the pseudonym Brutus, advocates of this view explained that the republic's vast territory and variety of climates, economies, interests, habits, laws, and customs made a single legislature impractical if not dangerous. It would not only be "too numerous to act with any care or decision," but also be "composed of such heterogenous and discordant principles" as to rarely find consensus.²⁵

What ultimately emerged was a document that could best be described as fiscally strong but democratically weak. Its authors sought to preserve, rather than transform, the preexisting social order and place a check on the most revolutionary and egalitarian impulses of the previous decade while also empowering the federal government to address what they perceived to be the most pressing national issues. The 1787 settlement empowered the federal government to lay and collect taxes, form a standing army, and suppress rebellion and it left to the states most other matters affecting the daily lives of citizens, including and perhaps most significantly, slavery.²⁶ Indeed, the document remained conspicuously silent on the issue due to its divisive quality. Revealingly, however, the few clauses addressing the institution did so in ways that protected the rights of slaveholders. Extraterritoriality would become a lynchpin of sectionalism by the 1850s, but at the time it was adopted, national leaders viewed it as essential to the kind of regional concession that they believed necessary for national cohesion.²⁷ Despite the claims of progressive historians that the constitution dramatically undermined state sovereignty in the wake of the political and economic crisis of the 1780s, the framers were revealingly selective in their reconceptualization of it. They deliberately sought to shield the federal government from the popular will through institutions like the Senate and Electoral College, and they made congressional districts intentionally large and representatives few to guarantee that only the most prominent men be elected to office.²⁸

Unsurprisingly, criticism of the proposed new system was swift and unalloyed. Opponents, or antifederalists as they were known, accused the framers of empowering economic and political elites at the expense of ordinary Americans and undermining the federal compact. "Instead of being thirteen republics, under a federal head," wrote the so-called Federal Farmer, the new plan was "clearly designed to make us one consolidated government." The system threatened to create a central government, the seat of which rested "more than three hundred miles from" many of its citizens, possessed all the "essential powers" of governance, and made "those of the states a mere shadow of power."[29] Virginia's George Mason put it most bluntly, predicting that the proposed government would "produce a monarchy, or a corrupt abusive aristocracy."[30] Perhaps Patrick Henry best summed up the antifederalist position when he warned that overconcentration would fuel the very problem the framers had hoped to avoid: "If you make the citizens of this country agree to become the subjects of one great consolidated empire of America, your government will not have sufficient energy to keep them together."[31]

Federalists responded by insisting that the envisioned system was necessary to address the most pressing needs of a republic whose citizens, despite their geographical and regional differences, shared a set of national interests. As James Madison explained, the system did not eclipse state sovereignty so much as create a "dual system," in which the federal and state powers shared governing responsibilities and cooperated to suppress the more dangerous impulses of a national majority. According to Madison, under the proposed plan, federal and state governments would cooperate to check the overconcentration of power at the top as well as at the bottom. Like most of the other framers, he considered the gravest threat to the Union to be the "superior force of an interested and overbearing majority."[32]

Not too long after the US Constitution's ratification, George Washington's second administration would have the opportunity to test the new system. In 1794 a group of farmers in western Pennsylvania called for limits on land speculation, insisting that the financial burdens of the young republic ought to be laid at the feet of the republic's "men of fortune." The Pennsylvania Regulation of 1794 was, in fact, a continuation of the same set of ideas that had spurred the separatist and egalitarian movements of the 1780s, including the inalienable right of citizens to "alter or abolish" their government. Unlike those protests, however, the 1787 settlement enabled Congress to assemble the militias of surrounding states and bring a swift end to a "treasonous" rebellion, insisting that any concession would undermine the legitimacy of the republic and that of the new administration.[33]

Obedience and fealty are not the same and, as antifederalists had predicted, the newly empowered central government managed to alienate many of its citizens by appearing to undermine the very democratic ideals on which it had been founded. For the framers, the revolution was over—independence had been accomplished and a republic established—but their new document offered little for the thousands of ordinary American men who seized land, attacked tax collectors, and burned courthouses, many of them still locked in relations of economic dependency.[34] Indeed, as historians have aptly observed, the purpose of the Constitution was to limit democracy, not expand it.[35] Not a single clause empowered Congress to abolish slavery, redistribute property, enact debt relief legislation, or guarantee voting rights. As such, the framers had effectively shielded the federal government from the most democratic impulses of the age and tactfully avoided its most divisive issues.

Despite the conservative thrust of the founding document, the federal government moved to institute systems designed to address some of the grievances of frontier agrarians. Thomas Jefferson believed that the solution to the social pressures plaguing the young republic lay in facilitating land acquisition in the west and populating the republic with economically and politically autonomous agrarians. Despite his own commitment to an unobtrusive central government, Jefferson believed that the republic had a responsibility to secure land from Natives and facilitate its distribution to white settlers before stepping aside and allowing the states to take over local governance. As chairman of a committee on territorial management, he advanced a comprehensive program whereby territories recently ceded to Congress by the eastern states would be surveyed, divided into uniform plots, and sold at market value. The plan was designed to make land acquisition both more equitable and affordable, yet it offered nothing to impoverished squatters and departed from colonial precedent in failing to offer a right of preemption. Furthermore, it placed no prohibition on the amount of land that could be acquired by any one party, thereby facilitating speculation.[36]

In short, the federal policies of the 1780s and 1790s merely aggravated the very tensions they aimed to remedy. As president, Washington was certainly aware of the persistent division that characterized the country when he left office in 1796. In his departing address, he attempted to rekindle a withering sense of national loyalty by reminding his citizens of "the immense value of your national union to collective and individual happiness" and urged them to "[discountenance] whatever may suggest even a suspicion that [the union] can in any event be abandoned."[37] Yet, for the first several decades of the republic's existence, disgruntled western citizens unable to secure land, or indebted as a result of their efforts to do so, echoed the claims of the Carolinian antifederalist John Taylor, who criticized what he deemed as an unholy alliance between the legislature and a "powerful faction" of bankers, investors, and speculators who had redirected the government toward "principles dangerous to the rights and interests of the community."[38]

Despite Washington's appeals, ordinary Americans were beginning to wonder whether their interests might be better served beyond the confines of their new republic. During the late eighteenth century, the Spanish-controlled Louisiana Territory was an area of fluid borders and overlapping powers. The framers' fear that some of these powers might take advantage of the centrifugal forces then plaguing the nation were not unfounded.[39] Having helped the United States secure its independence from Britain, by the 1790s the Spanish Empire now feared its encroachment as land-hungry US settlers began moving into Spanish Louisiana, a region that encompassed the Mississippi River's western basin from New Orleans to where the Rocky Mountains met the Canadian border.[40] Rather than securing its borders against the encroachers, however, Spanish officials decided to take advantage of the United States' domestic troubles and entice thousands of US citizens to settle the Lower Mississippi Valley with the promise of two hundred acres for small households and seven hundred for larger ones. They would grant legal title to the lands after the immigrant settlers had shown themselves capable of occupying and cultivating it for at least four years, and settlers could purchase the land outright after ten years. This system favored poorer people by allowing them to accrue profits from the land before purchasing it. It also discouraged speculation by requiring that purchasers live on and work the land.[41] For many disillusioned westerners, Spanish imperial policies appeared better suited to deliver on the promises of their own late republican revolution than the United States did. Here was a system better designed to privilege occupancy and avoid speculation. In addition to living on and developing their land, every head of household had to swear allegiance to the crown and promise to defend the province against "whatsoever enemy might attempt to invade it." The settlers were not required to convert to Catholicism, but they could not openly practice any other faith.

Access to the Mississippi River and the port at New Orleans were also crucial incentives for westerners. Madison himself had acknowledged that the chief limitation to the United States' settlement of the trans-Mississippi west was the lack of an artery that would allow farmers to get their produce to market. Spain offered a solution for the agrarians. Americans who swore allegiance to the crown would enjoy the same rights and privileges as other Spaniards and could sell their goods and produce in New Orleans free from all duties and taxes.[42] Spain also allowed settlers to keep their human property as long as they abided by the Siete Partidas, a collection of laws that, among other things, protected the enslaved and their families from abuse, permitted manumission, and recognized the enslaved as human beings with certain inalienable rights, including the right to testify in court.[43]

That so many US citizens were willing to abandon their new republic to live as Spanish subjects reveals the extent of their disillusionment with their own republican experiment. It also reveals that under certain circumstances, the Spanish monarchy was better able to deliver on at least some of the revolutionary promise of the recent Anglo-American struggle for independence. Anglo-American subjects of Spain might not have been able to elect their political leaders or openly practice their faith, but their ability to own their own land free of onerous taxation and governmental intrusion seemed to be enough to entice them.

Not only were alienated settlers leaving the United States to settle in Spanish territory, some of them were also contemplating secession, especially those who already claimed large tracts of land in the west but were finding it difficult to obtain legal title or secure it and a market for their goods. If Spain could help them accomplish these things, then they were willing "to preserve their independence from the American republic" and form an alliance with the crown.[44] Such efforts would eventually come to an end in 1800, when the Spanish, to offset their worsening financial situation and condense their empire, transferred Louisiana back to the French, who then sold it to the United States. For Jefferson, the purchase represented a critical stage in his own dream of establishing a yeoman's republican empire, but for the thousands of US immigrants who had settled there, it represented a return to the country they had rejected.

"To remain in this country . . . I could not submit": Moses Austin and the Panic of 1819

At first glance, Moses Austin and his son Stephen seem unlikely candidates for the economic hardship and political disaffection that drove so many Americans to turn their backs on the United States in the late eighteenth and early nineteenth centuries. Born into a family of middling New England traders and farmers, Moses expected to lead a comfortable life after independence. Ambitious and enthusiastic, he relocated his family in 1789 to western Virginia, where he had purchased title to a lead mining operation. While thousands of ordinary Americans attacked the postindependence social order, Moses was determined to succeed in it. He successfully petitioned Congress to enact a protective tariff on lead and secured a lucrative contract with the state of Virginia to assist in constructing its new capitol. Unfortunately, the Austins had borrowed heavily to purchase the mines and, before long, found themselves looking longingly toward Spanish Louisiana, the location of the greatest known lead deposits on the continent. By 1810 the family had established a successful operation in Mine á Breton, Missouri. After welcoming impending war with Great Britain as good for business, however, the Austins once again found themselves bankrupt. The War of 1812 devastated the region, draining it of money and labor. With virtually no banking institutions in the territory, the Austins had to rely, as so many other westerners did, on private creditors.[45] Yet, they remained optimistic.

As aspiring frontier entrepreneurs, the Austins well understood the value of federal patronage. In 1815, the twenty-two-year-old Stephen managed to win a seat in the territorial legislature, from which he lobbied for infrastructure projects and federal recognition of land claims. Missouri had been the site of some of the most contested land disputes in the west, making Moses keenly aware of the concerns of Missouri squatters. He supported measures delaying eviction proclamations as well as those designed to protect local industry, such as his own, and secure federal funding for development projects. Aware of the territory's need for a viable financial institution, Moses had partnered with several other local businessmen to establish the Bank of St. Louis in 1814. With the war's conclusion the following year, demand for western lands in Missouri skyrocketed, making the need for a territorial bank even more crucial, and the father and son hoped to use Stephen's position in the legislature as political leverage to secure a federal charter. The other lawmakers argued that their push constituted a conflict of interest and voted to award the charter to the Austin's rival, the Bank of Missouri. Matters worsened for the Austins when the US Treasury selected that bank as the depository for the proceeds of public land sales.[46]

At this point, Stephen determined to pursue the one occupation at which it seemed impossible to fail—territorial land speculation. With a loan from the Bank of St. Louis, he purchased an interest in an Arkansas parcel on the Red River in anticipation of the federal government soon making the land available for white settlement.[47] This might have been the beginning of the family's economic recovery had the United States not experienced its worst financial crisis since independence in 1819. The Bank of the United States was supposed to function as the federal government's financial and regulatory agent. In addition to overseeing tax collection and paying the government's debts, it was responsible with regulating the lending practices of state and local institutions like the Bank of St. Louis. Following the 1815 peace treaty with the British, however, the national bank significantly loosened its regulatory practices to facilitate settlement of the trans-Mississippi west, thereby permitting, and even encouraging, the over issuance of loans to western farmers and speculators. When European demand for US goods leveled off several years later and demand for land plummeted, the bank responded by suddenly recalling its loans, forcing thousands of debtors into bankruptcy and foreclosure. The contraction was worse in the west, where lending had been the most liberal. There, the panic took hold earlier and lasted longer than anywhere else in the country. As Missouri legislator Thomas Hart Benton put it, "All the flourishing cities of the West are mortgaged to this money power. . . They are in the jaws of the monster! A lump of butter in the mouth of a dog! One gulp, one swallow, and all is gone!"[48]

The Austins were prime targets of the financial collapse, having borrowed and speculated extensively. As Stephen scrambled to borrow from private creditors to fund his Arkansas land scheme, the Bank of St. Louis filed a credit claim for $9,000. Moses assumed responsibility for the debt, but no sooner had he done so than the struggling bank demanded he repay $15,000 that he had borrowed earlier against the Mine à Breton property. By now, the only thing that kept the Austin family from complete financial ruin was Stephen's $9,000 investment in Arkansas land, made entirely on credit. When the panic finally reached Missouri in the fall of 1819, the Austins became the target of numerous creditors who had won civil judgments in Missouri after the judiciary struck down nearly all forms of debtor relief, and the family began losing property to foreclosure. What is more, Moses struggled to sell his Missouri property, which he had mortgaged to the now insolvent Bank of St. Louis.[49]

For Stephen and Moses Austin, the events of 1819 and 1820 seemed to confirm the accusations of American men with whom they had, until now, shared little in common. Moses, once a firm supporter and hopeful recipient of federal patronage, attacked the national government in terms that would have rung familiar to an eighteenth-century regulator.[50] After the Jefferson County sheriff besieged his home in pursuance of his numerous debts, Moses declared to fellow residents, "When our rights are invaded it is of no consequence to the citizen or subject whether it comes by the hand of an emperor king or demon in office under republic. They are alike destructive of all security to person and property."[51] Moses now believed that he could no longer rely on his government's guarantee of "civil and religious liberties" and perceived what men less fortunate than he had long complained of—a distant federal government unwilling or unable to meet the needs and interests of western settlers. He was also prepared to adopt their remedy. As he explained in his correspondence to a relative the following year, *"As I am, ruined in this* [country], I found nothing I could do would bring back my property again, and to remain in a Country where I had enjoyed *wealth* in a state of *poverty* I could not submit."[52] Moses' words reflect the longstanding relationship between economic prosperity and political featly that eighteenth-century Anglo-Americans held dear and the related belief that the government's primary responsibility was to secure or at least facilitate the economic happiness of its people. If the US government failed to do so, there was little reason to remain in the country.

Moses might not have been so willing to renounce the country of his birth had things not looked more promising farther south. Like many frontier Anglo-Americans, he had followed events surrounding the Mexican independence movement since its inception in 1810. He first proposed the idea of establishing an Anglo colony in Texas in 1819, following the signing that year of the Adams-Onís Treaty, the United States–New Spain border agreement that confirmed Spain's possession of Texas and thus helped pave the way for the authorization of Spanish land grants in the region.[53] In February 1820, Moses requested a copy of the passport that Spanish authorities had issued him in 1797 when he moved to Missouri to establish a lead mine. With passport in hand, Moses set off for Texas at the age of fifty-eight with fifty dollars, a horse, a mule, and an enslaved man named Richmond. They were all borrowed.[54]

Mexico: "Not to be despotically commanded"

Despite the disaffection, discord, and threat of dissolution that accompanied US independence, it is Mexico's birth that has earned the moniker of the "unfortunate revolution." Scholars have long emphasized the economic decline, social conflict and political chaos that followed independence from Spain, dismissing its early political structures and institutions as inherently flawed and insufficiently revolutionary.[55] Yet it was precisely these structures and institutions that attracted many members of the first wave of settlers from the United States, including the Austin family. Mexico was not even independent when Moses Austin initially asked for permission to settle its far northern province in December 1820, and it was not the first time that he had sought to live under the Spanish crown. Austin first obtained a Spanish passport in 1797 and settled in Saint Louis, one of many disaffected US settlers to do so. By 1820 not only had he had experience living in the Spanish Empire, but he cited the Spanish political system as the primary impulse behind his decision to immigrate yet again, stating that "in view of the new system of government adopted by Spain" he "resolved upon applying for authorization to settle this province."[56]

Austin was most likely referring to a series of reforms first instituted as part of the 1812 Cádiz Constitution. When Napoleon invaded Spain in 1808 and forced its young king, Fernando VII, to abdicate, the event created a vacuum and supplied an opportunity for the renewed autonomy of the colonies. As it so happened, Spanish imperial law provided for just such a crisis, stipulating that in the absence of the king, sovereignty should transfer to the provinces. Throughout the empire, local governing bodies, or juntas, were established to rule in the king's absence.[57] The need for a coordinated defense against the French prompted the establishment of the Junta Central in Aranjuez. Originally composed of representatives from provinces across the peninsula, in January 1809, the Junta Central decided to expand its membership to include representatives from the New World. This was the first time that Spanish American representatives were included in the imperial government, effectively acknowledging their equal status with the *peninsulares*, and prompting a number of questions regarding Spain's relationship to the Americas.[58]

One year later, in response to widespread demand, the Junta Central called for the election of a permanent Cortes, or legislature, composed of elected representatives from across the empire. Almost as soon as the Cortes convened in September, the Spanish American deputies issued a series of demands for greater representation and local autonomy to counter the centralizing tendencies of the Bourbon reforms. Their chief advocate was Miguel Ramos Arizpe, a Coahuilan priest and sole representative of the Eastern Interior Provinces, a recently designated administrative unit that included Texas, Coahuila, Nuevo León, and Nuevo Santander. In an appeal for greater regional representation, Arizpe described his region as having long suffered under administrative neglect, incompetence, and over-consolidation because of its relative remoteness. Specifically, Arizpe cited the absence of local governing bodies. In that regard, he argued that the provinces were controlled by "arbitrary" governors, many of them military men, who enjoyed protection "from any responsibility whatever for their actions." Such a system, he insisted, fostered "despotism" and violated the empire's principles of limited and constitutional monarchy. As a remedy, Arizpe called for the establishment in each province of an "*executive council* or a *provincial deputation*" composed of men elected from the community itself and each enjoying a direct relationship with the monarch. This, Arizpe insisted, was consistent with the principles of the monarchy and indeed formed the very basis of the Cortes themselves. At the core of this system of government rested the principles of local autonomy and popular sovereignty then sweeping the Atlantic. "Each community is an association of freemen who are united[,] not to be despotically commanded by the strongest," declared Arizpe, "but by one or more prudent men, capable of being fathers of the republic."[59]

The American demands resulted in a fundamental restructuring of the Spanish Empire and contributed significantly to a new constitution established on the principles of local sovereignty, representative government, and free enterprise. The Cádiz Constitution of 1812 limited the monarchy and clerical privilege, abolished viceroyalties and the Inquisition, introduced freedom of the press, and extended citizenship to all men—except those of African descent. Finally, it dramatically decentralized power by creating provincial deputations consisting of locally elected members.[60] In so doing, it went further than any other European power, including Britain, in extending democracy to its American territories.[61]

In June 1813, British, Spanish, and Portuguese forces finally managed to handily defeat the French, on the plains of northern Spain. By March, Fernando VII was back on the throne, and anyone hoping that he would honor the Cádiz reforms was sorely disappointed. Responding to the advice of his conservative advisers, the king declared the Cortes illegal and abolished its Cádiz Constitution; he imprisoned Arizpe, as well as many of the other delegates. In Mexico, Spanish authorities promptly set to work reversing the reformist efforts of the past several years. Recently elected officials were dismissed, and their reforms cancelled or nullified. A year later, from a stronghold in Apatzingán, a group of autonomist rebels, whose movement had initially coalesced in 1809 under the leadership of a priest from the Bajía named Miguel Hidalgo, issued a new constitution modeled directly after the Cádiz document with one critical exception: It declared Mexico independent from Spain.[62]

The independence movement would stumble along for the next five years—plagued by internecine conflict between its political and military factions and lacking credible leadership—until the spring of 1820, when Fernando VII finally succumbed to the demands of the constitutionalists. After several failed *pronunciamientos,* a call for the reinstitution of the 1812 constitution by Rafael del Riego, commander of the Asturias regiment, garnered enough sustained and widespread support that the king finally capitulated in March 1820.[63] As the Cortes reconvened for the first time since its dissolution in 1813, Arizpe and his Mexican co-delegates, José Mariano Michelena and Lucas Alamán, proposed that the colonies be transformed into a collection of "confederative commonwealths," each with its own governing body and an executive appointed by the king. The Cortes flatly rejected the proposal. Given the viceroyalty's pattern of refusing to institute constitutional reforms, many of the Spanish Americans feared that their recent victory would mean little change for Mexico.

More than a decade of unceasing conflict had taken its toll on Mexico's economy, infrastructure, and people, however, leaving royalists and rebels alike war-weary and eager for an end to the violence. Thus, while the Cortes in Spain was rejecting the Mexican delegates' appeal for greater autonomy, in Mexico a thirty-seven-year-old royalist colonel named Augustín de Iturbide proposed an alliance with the rebel leader Vicente Guerrero, and on February 24 issued his Plan de Iguala, which he had crafted as a compromise of sorts between Mexico's various factions. Mexico would remain a Catholic country to the exclusion of all other faiths, and the clergy would retain their property and privilege. Mexico would also be fully independent from Spain and ruled by a constitutional monarchy. Significantly, article 12 placed sovereignty in the people, declaring "all of the inhabitants of the empire" official members of the body politic.[64] Although the plan, like the independence movement itself, lacked a clear ideology, it contained enough modifications to satisfy most people for the time being. The combined strength of Guerrero and Iturbide's armies, the sudden refusal of many Mexicans to pay taxes to or cooperate with the royalists, and the sweeping popularity of the Plan de Iguala all made independence look eminent. As the rebels approached Mexico City in August, having already captured nearly all of Mexico's major towns, Viceroy Juan O'Donojú assessed the situation and requested to meet with Iturbide in Veracruz. In the bucolic city of Córdoba, nestled in the foothills of the volcanic Pico de Orizaba, the two men signed a treaty formally recognizing Mexico's independence from Spain on 23 August 1821.[65]

Many Americans greeted news of Mexico's independence with excitement and optimism about its beauty, natural resources, and political and economic potential, largely due to what they had read about the country in the work of foreign travelers, the most noted of whom was the Prussian explorer Alexander von Humboldt, whose *Political Essay on the Kingdom of New Spain* (1810), stemmed from his 1803/4 tour of the viceroyalty. Mexico, with its diverse climate and topography, Humboldt wrote, was perfectly suited for expanding the cultivation of commodities like tobacco, cotton, and sugar. He likewise reported on the extent of Mexico's precious metals, which, especially in the case of silver, far exceeded that available in Europe. These resources were made all the more valuable by the nearly impenetrable topography in which they were found, which although responsible for the colony's primitive transportation system, nonetheless shielded it from foreign incursion. Humboldt observed, "With respect to Mexico proper, there is scarcely a country on the globe of which the military defense is more favored by the configuration of the ground."[66]

Humboldt's work no doubt informed the cautious optimism with which frontier newspapers greeted independence. "The fertility of [Mexican] soil is astonishing," reported the *Arkansas Gazette* in October 1822, "and the fields are covered with harvests which exceed in their produce, by twenty-fold, the corn fields of Europe." The paper claimed that Mexico produced twice as much wheat as the United States and "in any actual dearth" could feed the whole population of Great Britain.[67] The *St. Louis Enquirer* called Mexico's capital "one of the finest cities built by Europeans in either hemisphere. There does not exist a city equal to Mexico for the elegance, regularity, and breadth of the streets." Its market presented a "plane of immense commerce, and the shops display a profusion of gold, and silver, and jewels." The paper concluded that Mexico City's "majesty" surpassed that of Lima, Philadelphia, Paris, Rome, and Naples. Such praise was merited. The three-hundred-year-old metropolis had been built on top of the Aztec capital of Tenochtitlán and was home to 120,000 inhabitants. It had served as the political, commercial, and administrative center of the Spanish Empire and the capital of New Spain. It was impressive not only for its wide, brilliantly illuminated streets and remarkable architecture—perhaps best exemplified by its imposing national palace—but also for its strategic placement on an isthmus with ready access to both the Atlantic and Pacific Oceans.[68]

It was not just Mexico's economic potential that excited them. Noting the violence of Mexico's independence struggle and still unstable political climate, the *Arkansas Gazette* nonetheless deemed Mexico's a "most extraordinary revolution," welcoming it to the "*great family* of the new world."[69] Even more notably, the paper praised Mexico's founders for managing to achieve "equality of rights for all persons, Indians, Mulattos, and Negroes, as well as whites," and celebrated their remarkable ability to accomplish a revolution that "united all interests, and promised to all; to the soldiery promotion, to the priests their authority over souls, to the titles their titled, to the merchants commerce, and to the various classes of laborers, liberty."[70] Regarding the form of government that followed independence, the *St. Louis Enquirer* observed, "The condition of the country, and the inhabitants is probably such, as to have rendered it expedient to adopt a monarchical form of government." The paper warned its audience of the dangers that too rapid a transition to a republic could entail, reminding them of what happened to a "more enlightened people"—the French—"in their rapid transition from despotism to a republic." Its editors went on to praise Mexico's "gradual regeneration" as evidence of a "cautious and enlightened policy," informed more by a fear of "aiming at too much to defeat all, than any hostility to a republican form of government."[71] As for Iturbide himself, whom Congress later claimed to have been reluctant to assume the presidency, despite his significant popularity and election,[72] the *Enquirer* declared him to be "of the highest encomium," possessing "moderation, disinterestedness, and heroism." Similarly, *Le Courrier de la Louisiane* called Iturbide a "man of extraordinary talents and acquirements."[73] Newspapers from Nashville to New Orleans reported on events in Mexico as part of a wave of interest in and sympathy with Spanish American independence that represented a departure from past characterizations of the Spanish-speaking world as despotic and backward.[74] Some newspapers even published the Plan of Iguala.[75] *Le Courriere* predicted that Mexican independence "will be of more importance to the United States than all the rest of Spanish America," because of its proximity, and that Pensacola "will become an emporium of far greater consequence than is generally anticipated by our citizens."[76] In March 1822, Congress announced its recognition of Mexico along with several other South American nations. The event garnered widespread enthusiasm across the west. "Nothing has occurred in the administration of our national government for some years, which has given us a pleasure so intense as the message of the president recommending a recognition of the Republics in South America and the Empire of Mexico," reported the *Frankfort (KY) Argus*. "On the [w]hole we consider this act the most glorious which has been performed by our government since the adoption of our constitution, the most salutary in its influence and the most important in its consequences."[77] Those consequences were just beginning to become evident to the disillusioned citizens of the trans-Mississippi west.

Texas: "Sure promises of future greatness"

Moses Austin was not the first *norteamericano* to attempt to establish himself in Texas. Throughout the late eighteenth and early nineteenth centuries, Native groups, Anglo colonists, and Spanish-speaking residents formed extensive networks and communities through land ownership, commerce, politics, and marriage in the province. While Spanish officials often feared that the Anglo presence would compromise their hold on the northern frontier, the region's inhabitants welcomed *norteamericanos* who offered valuable goods and skills.[78] In the 1810s, Texan officials began arguing that increased settlement and a strong militia were required to establish territorial integrity when policies designed to exclude foreigners from settling or inhabiting the region were at their zenith as a result of rumored territorial aggression on the part of the United States and Napoleon. "All indicates a very considerable upturning if this province is not attended to," bemoaned Nemesio Salcedo, commander general of the internal provinces of New Spain, in June 1812. "How the cares and troubles of this province daily increase." Salcedo predicted, "Their continued succession will alone show the evidence of their reality."[79] Increased population, he and others insisted, was the only remedy. Manuel Sambrano, senior commandant general at Nacogdoches, expressed confidence that men of means would settle the region "for the advantage of finding a good sale for their produce and grains, provided they find themselves protected properly." Settlement was not, however, possible, he insisted, without an aggressive and relentless war against the region's Natives, namely the Comanche, who since the mid-eighteenth century had been raiding ranches and settlements in the north, forming perhaps the greatest obstacle to the Spanish presence there.[80] One of independent Mexico's first legislative endeavors was to adopt a liberal immigration policy that invited foreigners to settle in small communities along the northern frontier if they promised to help develop and settle the region. This empresario system is what allowed the Austins to establish their colony of three hundred families along the Brazos River.[81] After years of watching the region languish in the face of administrative neglect, political turmoil, and ethnic conflict, Governor Antonio Martínez concluded that Moses Austin "was a man of honesty and formality, and that the proposal he is making is, in my opinion, the only which is bound to provide for the increase and prosperity of this province."[82]

Initially, Stephen Austin had little intention of joining his father in Mexico. He had fled to New Orleans and tried to rebuild his fortune there in the wake of his bankruptcy and the country's economic collapse during the Panic of 1819. In the summer of 1821, the younger Austin received news that his father, who had secured a land grant to settle three hundred US families along the Brazos River, had passed away in Missouri shortly after returning from a brief trip to Texas. Moses Austin's last wish was that his son "go on in the business in the same way he would have done had not sickness and oh dreadful to think of perhaps death" not prevented him from doing so himself.[83] Stephen could not ignore his father's dying wish, especially if it promised more opportunity for land speculation, a habit of which he was not yet cured. That fall he departed for Natchitoches to take claim of the land that his father had applied for and received from the Spanish. Determined to fulfill his father's request, he quickly began recruiting additional colonists.[84]

Despite the younger Austin's initial reluctance to emigrate, he appeared to have been pleasantly surprised by what he encountered in Texas, where, he believed, more promising conditions existed for ambitious immigrants like himself. In a letter to prospective settlers intended for publication in the *Arkansas Gazette*, he explained, "The constitution of Spain is in full operation at those provinces and recent accounts state that the beneficial effects of it are already perceptible." The precious metal mines were back in full operation and producing more than they had under the Spanish. Money was "more abundant," trade restrictions had been lifted, and the "restrictive system" regarding foreign immigration "superseded by the most liberal encouragement."[85] Indeed, Stephen envisioned Texas as a place where he and thousands of disillusioned American agrarians like him could start over. "Should you yet meet with any farmers of good character or mechanics, who wish to emigrate to this fine country and participate in the advantages secured to my father by this grant you will oblige them," he wrote to his cousin James.[86] New Spain not only promised rich resources, but also made it possible for immigrants to benefit from them.

Interestingly, Mexico's chosen form of government, a constitutional monarchy, prompted little criticism from Austin. Indeed, US agrarians had been expressing disillusion with the United States since its founding and were no doubt curious to see what a reformed Spanish imperial system had to offer them that the United States could not. "[Y]ou must not be frightened at the name of the imperial government," Austin wrote to his cousin. "You like myself have lived under a monarchy, when Louisiana belonged to Spain [,] and I think we lived as happy then as under the government of the United States." This is not to say that Austin viewed imperial monarchy as a superior form of government. He simply viewed it as the best government for Mexico at that time and one that he himself could live under. What he could not live under was the system that characterized the United States. "A central republic is the worst gov't in the world," Austin wrote, "for all the power will be in the hands of a few men in Mexico and instead of a republic it will in effect be an aristocracy which is worse than a monarchy, for in it we shall have 100 tyrants instead of one."[87] Austin's words echoed the complaints of a generation of disgruntled Anglo-American agrarians, and he did not have to look far to find others who felt similarly. "There are hundreds on the way and *thousands* ready to go if one word of encouragement could now be had from you," wrote James Hawkins, Austin's friend and former business partner, just months after Mexico had gained its independence from Spain. "You and your colony excite more interest than the assembled sages of the nation."[88] Another prospective colonist wrote, "All those who once experienced the gratuity of the Spanish government (a thing I never have done), speaks, generally, in favor of it with a few exceptions of social inconveniences."[89] Indeed, Austin had little reason to doubt that his colony would soon be full of former US citizens. "I can assure you that a great number of families will move from this state, and from other states," wrote James Bryan, Austin's brother-in-law. "I have no doubt that the colony will be filled up in twelve months."[90]

At least some immigrants seem to have shared Austin's opinion regarding the Mexican political system. While perhaps not ideal, it was not bad either and certainly an improvement over what many perceived as the failed republic of the north. Although William Walker conceded to his father that he was less than pleased with the form of government that Mexico had adopted, it being "a limited monarchy," he nonetheless cautioned, "It is perhaps better that the [transition to a republic] should be gradual. I think the policy of Mexico at this time, is practically good."[91] Above all, Mexico had promise. Austin assured Hawkins, "The nation possesses great resources, and its vast and successful effort for independence combined with the general harmony which at this time prevails, furnish, I think, sure pledges of future greatness and prosperity."[92] With independence achieved, no matter what political course Mexico took, Austin and his associates believed that it held special appeal to the thousands of struggling agrarians in the United States. "The prospects of the farmer and planter were never more promising in any country, than in this, at the present time," Austin wrote. "Whatever be the collision arising from difference in opinion as to the course this government should pursue[,] it is gradually gaining strength, and will, I trust, ultimately secure the end of all government, the happiness of the people."[93] Such happiness, at least for the time being, appeared more readily secured under a Mexican monarchy than an Anglo-American republic.

"Prospects of freedom, happiness, and prosperity": From Monarchy to Republic

Yet, Mexico would not remain a constitutional monarchy for long. As happened in the United States, competing visions for Mexico's future emerged soon after independence. Confusion and disagreement over how power should be distributed and shared between the emperor and Constituent Congress emerged almost immediately. When the congress attempted to appoint a new Council of Regency in an effort to dilute Iturbide's control and guard against absolutism in late 1822, the latter accused the body of abusing its own power and moved to dissolve the legislature by force.[94] Believing Mexico's new leader to be in direct violation of the very principles that had sparked the independence movement, the provinces began to rebel a few months later with a series of pronunciamientos. These documents, modeled after the Plan de Iguala, were unofficial demands, usually issued by local leaders and designed to "forcefully negotiate" with the central government. Much like the Anglo-American Regulations of the 1790s, pronunciamientos would be utilized countless times during the first republican period (1824–1835) to remove unpopular national leaders, demand a change in the political system, or simply draw attention to the grievances of a particular community or region. Unlike the Regulations, however, Mexico's pronunciamientos proved to be both more successful and enduring. Hundreds of them were issued during the first four decades of Mexican independence, often collectively and usually by local leaders to assert their authority and voice the demands of their constituents. Frequently dismissed as an example of Mexican political disorder, pronunciamientos often functioned as the most effective means of popular political expression and more often complemented rather than undermined official political institutions.[95]

The first pronunciamiento after Mexican independence, the Plan de Casa Mata (1823), accused Iturbide of behaving like a dictator. It was issued by Antonio López de Santa Anna, a young captain from Veracruz whom the emperor had earlier relieved from his post for voicing opposition to his high-handed leadership style. The document, endorsed by numerous provincial elites, neither called for Iturbide's removal nor for the establishment of a republic, but rather for the election of a new congress by locally controlled provincial deputations. Sensing the plan's broad support, his own unpreparedness for the position of monarch, and the opposition he would likely face if he remained head of state, Iturbide decided to summon congress and abdicate the throne on 19 March 1823.[96]

Newspapers in the United States reported on events in Mexico approvingly and optimistically. In the fall of 1822, the *New York Spectator* reported, "That the Mexicans understand, and are attached to the principles of liberty, we have every reason to believe," citing Iturbide's actions as evidence of the strength of republican sentiment in the country. "Everything, therefore, connected with the affairs of Mexico, tends to show, that the overthrow of Iturbide, and the establishment of a republican government in that country, are events which ere long will assuredly happen."[97] The kind of "wise and liberal" government that William Walker had hoped for seemed to be coming to fruition.[98]

When Mexican leaders gathered to discuss their new form of government in the spring of 1823, however, they confronted the same ideological fissures that had divided the United States decades earlier. The central question concerned where sovereignty should reside.⁹⁹ For the provinces, the answer seemed clear.¹⁰⁰ Continuing the same tradition they had established during the Napoleonic war, provincial deputations eagerly asserted their autonomy. The first and perhaps most dramatic move came from Guadalajara in May 1823. The year before, the Captain General Luis Quintanar had called on Guadalajarans to accept Iturbide as head of state and honor the historic moment of Mexico's independence by observing "good order and harmony."¹⁰¹ Now he joined with the locally elected leadership in dissolving Guadalajara's "social pact" with the central Mexican government, declaring itself a sovereign power and asserting that it would establish relations with the other states on the principles of "fraternity and confederation." The authors went on to state that it was time for the provinces to declare "their natural rights" as free, sovereign and independent entities "without there being between them . . . the slightest inequality."¹⁰² Before long Coahuila, Nuevo León, Nuevo Santander, Oaxaca, Texas, Yucatán, and Zacatecas had all followed suit, with some adjoining states expressing the intention of forming separate confederations.¹⁰³ Significantly, these pronunciamientos did not call for separation or secession, but merely threatened such if congress failed to comply with their demands. The authors of the Guadalajara document even offered to comply with national elections. Nonetheless, like US leaders in the 1780s, leaders in Mexico City began to fear that their country was on the verge of disintegration. Civil war appeared likely by late July, when the Supreme Executive Authority, the interim body installed after Iturbide's abdication, dispatched troops to Guadalajara and Zacatecas. By mid-August, however, Congress had recommended amnesty for the rebellious provinces and called for a new round of elections. A new congress composed of locally elected representatives from the provinces convened in October.¹⁰⁴

On January 1, 1824, the *Kentucky Gazette* had reported that the convention called to form a new Mexican government was composed of some of the best and most "liberal minds" in Mexico.¹⁰⁵ As in the United States, however, Mexican framers were deeply divided. The wave of pronunciamientos the previous year had made it clear that they wanted a republic, but what kind? Whereas in the US context, where the call for stronger federal authority amid widespread social conflict and a worsening fiscal crisis, had prompted delegates to the Constitutional Convention to reject the earlier system of confederation, most of the Mexican delegates to the Constituent Congress were established provincial leaders who had struggled for decades to gain greater autonomy from Spain and now called for unmitigated state sovereignty. Miquel Ramos Arizpe called for a system of shared or dual sovereignty and composed an outline of it, the Acta Constitutiva (1824), the first article of which declared, "The Mexican nation is composed of the provinces." Such language was understood to confirm that the provinces, soon to be states, would enter the union voluntarily and that their representatives constituted its government.[106] Article 6 asserted that the states were "independent, free, and sovereign . . . in that which exclusively concerns their administration and interior government."[107] All of this would have satisfied early proponents of state sovereignty and a decentralized federal structure, yet article 3 made it clear that "sovereignty resides radically and essentially in the nation" which possesses "the exclusive right" to adopt "by means of its representatives the form of government" deemed essential to its "conservation and greater prosperity."[108] This article functioned effectively as a supremacy clause, clarifying that sovereignty rested ultimately with the federal legislature.

Regardless, some delegates expressed doubt about the propriety of dual sovereignty for a country like Mexico. Servando Teresa de Mier insisted that Mexico's long history of revolution and relative lack of experience with self-governance necessitated that more power be granted to the federal government than the Acta Constitutiva allowed. Although his views resembled those of federalists in the United States, in a published speech, the esteemed priest laid out his case for why Mexicans should avoid modeling their republic after their northern neighbor, whose union was formed from thirteen virtually self-governing colonies. He noted that Mexicans had just emerged from "300 years under the yoke of an absolute monarch" and had hardly "succeeded, to take a step without stumbling in the unknown study of freedom." According to Mier, "We [Mexicans] are like children who have hardly removed the girdles, or slaves who have just been released from their chains." Mier's characterization of norteamericanos as "homogeneous, industrious, enlightened and full of social virtue" was certainly more generous than most framers would have described them, but Mier was correct at least in observing that Mexicans had less experience in self-rule than their northern counterparts.[109]

New Spain had functioned as the center of Spanish America for centuries and, as such, had experienced far greater political and administrative oversight than the Anglo colonies. It was also true, however, that long before Mexican independence, the empire had been in the process of reform, much of which had been driven by provincial leaders now eager to finally assert their autonomy. Regardless, Mier's concerns at the time echoed the view of many Spanish republicans, who believed that their people required a model more in line with what the Venezuelan liberator Simón Bolívar had envisioned a decade earlier. The system should shield the federal leadership from the people even more than the US model allowed and concentrate power in the hands of a white, educated, urban elite with the experience and nationalist perspective necessary to guide the young republic. Whatever specific form of government Mexico ultimately adopted, Mier felt it needed to guarantee "union," permit "force," and allow the "majority of energy to be dedicated to governance."[110]

Mier and his supporters advocated a system perhaps best described as moderated federalism. Their views closely resembled those of US federalists, who advocated a government that could check the will of a majority presumed to be unsuited to self-government and that lacked nationalist sentiment or orientation.[111] Lucas Alamán, an esteemed scientist from Guanajuato who would become one of Mexico's foremost conservative leaders, called for a constitution that could "ensure our happiness and consolidate our independence."[112] His views closely resembled those of Hamilton and other nationalists who expressed little or no concern for state sovereignty and might have even preferred monarchy. Alamán, a former member of the original Constituent Congress, later dissolved by Iturbide, had been particularly disturbed by the provinces' actions. In an earlier circular, in which he had rebuked the authors of the Plan de Casa Mata, he asserted, "There can be only one power in the nation, and only the supreme government can wield it." He went on to warn, "To create another, separate [power] tends openly towards violation of the constitution, to division, and to anarchy." He also accused Santa Anna and his supporters of trying to usurp legitimate power.[113] Alamán believed that Mexico's national sovereignty was transcendent, supreme, indivisible, and permanent. He also believed that a general failure to acknowledge such would lead directly to anarchy and disintegration. As such, he believed in a fundamental compact between the people of a nation and their central government, not an arrangement to be mediated or compromised by the states. In a letter to Quintanar, he asserted bluntly that the "pretext of popular sovereignty" by which Guadalajara had asserted its sovereignty was "very much misapplied." Sovereignty, Alamán insisted, "resides solely in the nation."[114] Thus, he departed sharply from the "dual sovereignty" views of men like Madison and Arizpe, believing, as Hamilton did, that the national government was the only legitimate representative of the people. In the US context, however, few men had been willing to assert this position as firmly as Alamán in Mexico.

On the opposite end of the political spectrum were "confederalists," who questioned whether the Acta Constitutiva went far enough in granting sovereignty to the states and disputed the claims of Mexican centralists like Alamán that independence had merely transferred sovereignty from one imperial government to another. They insisted instead that the crisis of 1808 had effectively dissolved the preexisting national apparatus and transferred sovereignty to the provinces. There was no central Mexican government then and, with Iturbide's abdication, there effectively was none now. The most articulate spokesman for this view was Valentín Gómez Farías, who asserted that the "provinces are separated and going to unite . . . because lacking a fundamental pact, there is certainly no such union."[115] Like similarly minded thinkers in the United States, Mexican opponents of overcentralization would consistently point to their country's vast territory, complicated topography, and remarkable diversity to argue that any form of government other than one that acknowledged the ultimate sovereignty of the states was inappropriate. If such elements can be said to characterize the United States at its founding, then they certainly characterized early Mexico as well. Mexican proponents of radical state sovereignty argued that an overly robust national government would unfairly subject the remote regions to the same kind of marginalization and neglect they had suffered under the crown.[116]

As in the United States, the debate ultimately rendered a compromise. Mexico's 1824 federal constitution awarded states full autonomy over internal matters, while granting the federal government control over interstate and international affairs under a system that resembled the Articles of Confederation more than the 1787 constitutional settlement. The framers adopted Arizpe's Acta Constitutiva with a slight reordering of its articles. The third article, which stated that sovereignty resided "radically and essentially in the nation," became the first. While historians have tended to interpret the 1824 compromise as a net loss for the proponents of state sovereignty because it did not go as far as many had hoped in privileging that system, it granted the federal government far less immediate interventionist power than its US counterpart. When it came to taxation, for example, state compliance was voluntary.[117] Likewise, states were to have full authority over the regulation, arming, and control of local militias, while the central government maintained its own military presence in most states and provinces.[118] Although the Mexican constitution embodied the customary separation of powers, widespread suspicion of executive authority rendered a legislature empowered with the ability to elect and remove the president and to oversee the appointment of ministers of state.[119]

Whereas the US Constitution was fiscally strong but democratically weak, Mexico's was fiscally weak and democratically strong, especially given that the 1824 document contained none of the accommodations to slaveholding interests that the 1787 settlement did; the institution had been abolished by the Spanish years earlier. That said, neither republic empowered its federal legislature to protect or extend individual rights, and although slavery was technically illegal in Mexico, other forms of forced labor proliferated. Yet, the Mexican document did not grant the practitioners of any such system inflated representation, though it did call on states to "return the fugitives of other states to their just claimants, or otherwise compensate the interested party." Indeed, the lack of fundamentally divisive issues like slavery meant that Mexican framers were able to adopt a system that more honestly reflected the Montesquieuian concept of dual sovereignty.[120] Scholars have often criticized the 1824 document for creating confusion around where sovereignty ultimately rested, but the United States' framing document possessed no less ambiguity on this matter, although it would not become evident until much later. Perhaps the most concise distinctions concern who wrote the document and for what purpose. Mexico's first republic was established by provincial elites—who were more suspicious of centralized authority than they were of each other and eager to assert their autonomy and welcome foreign investment—and largely in the absence of widescale social rebellion by a landless agrarian majority. The United States was established precisely in response to such disorder and by elites deeply divided among themselves on questions well beyond sovereignty but eager to harness federal power to serve their economic interests and shield their isolated republic from foreign aggressors.

Mexico's decision not to copy the Anglo republic's fiscal and military state coupled with its more thorough, if somewhat untested, commitment to state sovereignty, undoubtedly contributed to its appeal to men like the Austins—onetime provincial elites themselves who had found their power and fortune hindered by the very centralized fiscal structure that they had once attempted to utilize. As for Stephen Austin and his small cohort of US colonists, they could not have been more thrilled with the direction of Mexican politics, which, more than anything before it, solidified their loyalty to their adopted country. In a formal proclamation issued to the "fellow citizens" of his colony on May 1, 1825, Austin declared, "I am convinced that there is not a breast amongst you that will not palpitate with exultation and delight at the prospects of freedom, happiness, and prosperity which the *federal republican system of government* presents to you." He went on to express full faith in every immigrant's ability to see their dreams realized if they only remained true and patient citizens of Mexico. "[N]o difficulty or embarrassment can or ever will arise unless produced by your own impatience or imprudence."[121] Indeed, by embracing a truly dual sovereignty system, Mexico's framers skillfully addressed the very fear that the Austins and so many other disillusioned norteamericanos like them had expressed—an overly robust central government controlled by distant interests. Thus, Mexico adopted what many of them considered the ideal form of government—a confederate republic explicitly established on the premise of dual sovereignty.

For Americans on the frontier, where newspapers had closely tracked events in Mexico for some time, the reporting of events continued to be optimistic. "Days of prosperity, of liberty, and concord," declared the *St. Louis Enquirer* had replaced "usurpation and despotism. Honour and praise to the valiant soldiers of the country!"[122] Several months later, it confirmed that "every part of the new political system was in regular and successful operation in Mexico."[123] Frontier Americans specifically looked forward to freer trade with their new "sister republic." The United States and Mexico were not only "neighboring powers, inhabitants of the same continent, their territories contiguous, and their settlements approximating to each other," they were now "two chief powers of the new world . . . standing at the head of a *cordon* of republics, which, stretching from pole to pole across the two Americas, are destined to make the last stand in defense of human liberty."[124]

Yet, Mexico's size, topography, diversity, underdevelopment, wealth disparity, and vulnerability to foreign invasion remained very real. No one was more aware of Mexico's unique promise and peril than its new leadership. Considering Mexico's recent political past, federalists could not deny the challenges their form of government presented. On October 24, 1824, President Guadalupe Victoria issued a manifesto like the one delivered by George Washington thirty years earlier. Joining the chorus of optimistic voices, the first president of the Mexico declared, "All appears to anticipate order, abundance, and prosperity." The federal constitution had supplied the "last hand to the beautiful edifice of Mexican society." He reassured citizens of Mexico's numerous benefits, including the "uniform march" of its states and the "progress being made in the first sources of our wealth." This, Victoria insisted, should give Mexicans every hope that the republic would not deteriorate during his administration. Yet, he was also cautious, urging "the appreciation and consideration of the authorities" and the "most strict observance of the public moral." Mexico's first president specifically referenced the "immortal Washington," similarly warning that "if the states do not leave to the General Congress the duty of exercising whatever functions are indubitably conferred to it," then "anarchy and confusion" would soon follow. Therefore, obedience to the "supreme power" was essential to national success and happiness. The president concluded by asserting that any action that may lead to the dissolution of the union should be considered "hostile" and "against liberty and independence."[125] Indeed, by the end of 1824, Mexico could be characterized as one of the most promising of the new Atlantic republics as well as one of the most perilous.

CHAPTER TWO

Land, Loyalty, and Identity in the Trans-Mississippi Corridor

Moses Austin had applied for and received an empresario contract from the Spanish government two years before his son Stephen penned a letter to the Mexican emperor Augustín I in May 1822, to "make a tender of my services, my loyalty, my fidelity" and disclaiming "all protection or dependence on my former government." Designed to facilitate the development and security of New Spain's far north, the empresario program granted land to small communities of foreign settlers if they promised to become Spanish subjects, convert to Catholicism, and settle the region. By the time Stephen wrote to the emperor, he had managed to recruit and settle several hundred US colonists along the Brazos River on a small tract of the land his father had acquired. He now sought to convince the new government to honor the contract his father had made with the Spanish so that the settlers could enjoy legal title to their land. Insisting that the "property," "prospects," and "future hopes of happiness" of himself and those who had settled with him were now "centered" in Mexico, Austin concluded his correspondence by asserting, "This is our adopted nation," and beseeching the emperor to accept them "as children of the great Mexican family."[1]

Since the founding of the United States, American agrarians had expressed frustration with their country's political and economic direction, and many had sought refuge in its neighbor to the west. By the 1820s, however, nothing seemed to compel them more than the desire for land. Austin and other Anglo-American men of the Jeffersonian generation viewed landownership as essential to economic prosperity, political autonomy, and social power. Yet, by the 1820s, widespread speculation in western territories, coupled with an unprecedented national economic crisis, the Panic of 1819, had made land acquisition virtually impossible for thousands of people and had driven numerous others into bankruptcy or financial ruin. Meanwhile, land was plentiful and cheap in newly independent Mexico, and unlike in the United States, Mexican officials seemed eager to help them secure it.[2]

Yet, despite Mexico's clear economic and political appeal to disillusioned US agrarians, historians of early Texas have been reticent to take declarations like Austin's seriously.[3] They cite settlers' continued identification with the United States and their general lackluster efforts to assimilate.[4] As studies of early American nationalism have revealed, members of Austin's generation tended to decouple identity and state, making it possible to continue to identify as both Anglo American *and* Mexican.[5] In fact, for Austin and his allies, Mexico was the only place where they could achieve the economic independence and political autonomy that they associated with their Anglo republican heritage. Mexican independence not only eased foreign immigration and land acquisition for US settlers, it enabled the political ascendance of a generation of post-independence Mexican liberals, men who shared with them a Jeffersonian vision of agrarian republicanism. Miguel Ramos Arizpe, Lorenzo de Zavala, and Tadeo Ortíz, some of the most noted members of this group, were admirers of the United States who hoped to import the skills and knowledge they believed necessary to transform Texas into a viable agro-industrial power. Arizpe, who laid the groundwork for Mexico's federal system with his Acta Constitutiva, also shared with the settlers the belief that local and state governments were the best equipped to make economic decisions for their communities, especially those on public land distribution. As such, he helped push for a policy more decentralized than the United States', and one specifically designed to ease land acquisition. In other words, they envisioned the very agrarian society that was becoming increasingly unattainable farther east.

A more nuanced understanding of US settlers' Mexican identity and loyalty is called for today. The same goes for explanations of Mexican leaders' motivation for inviting the settlers to their country. Mexican officials were neither negligent nor naïve. They knew exactly what they were doing, were almost certainly aware of conditions in the United States, and had every reason to take US settlers attested fealty to Mexico seriously.

Political economy was not the only arena where Mexican liberals and norteamericanos found common ground. Militias were considered critical to republican government in the United States as well as in Mexico. They functioned as an expression of community autonomy, national loyalty, and sometimes both. They served to check tyranny and to suppress internal rebellion. In the United States, however, the Constitution placed ultimate control of the militia under the authority of the executive branch; in Mexico, militias remained under the control of state and local authority, meaning that they served as a more effective expression of community sentiment. One might assume that when Anglo settlers mustered in defense of Mexico, their actions were an accurate expression of their fealty to that country. More surprising was their defense of Mexico's establishment clause. By the time Stephen Austin settled in Mexico, most US states had abandoned establishmentarianism, and anti-Catholic sentiment was ascendent. Yet, Austin and other immigrants defended Mexico's established faith using the same logic that many Mexicans did. That is, they understood it as crucial to reinforcing Mexican federalism by supplying a means of social unity across an otherwise diverse and fragmented republic. Indeed, as inheritors of a "middling" antifederalist tradition,[6] Austin and his followers viewed republican citizenship as a kind of social contract in which individuals alienated some of their personal liberties in exchange for certain rights and privileges from the state. For these men, surrendering religious freedom likely felt like a small price to pay for the guarantee of land and social power no longer available to them in the United States.

Yet, while generally the US colonists were largely united around the economic incentives that had attracted them to Mexico, they did not always agree on how to take advantage of them. While Austin and the other prominent members of the Anglo settler community with whom he formed close alliances and business partnerships remained loyal and dutiful Mexican citizens, less fortunate members of their larger community—those who struggled to secure land claims or gain Mexican citizenship—channeled the politics of the agrarian rebellions that swept across the eastern United States in the 1780s and 1790s by denouncing Mexican "despotism" and eventually demanding independence. They threatened to undermine Austin's carefully crafted relationship with state and federal authorities, but their actions also provided an opportunity for his colony to demonstrate their fealty to Mexico by swiftly suppressing the movement and evicting its participants.

Peopling

While the early United States didn't have enough land in the 1820s, Mexico had too much. The region between the Arkansas River and the Rio Grande was largely unseen by Europeans until the late seventeenth century and was populated by autonomous Native groups, including the Caddo, Coahuiltecan, Hasinai, Kadohadacho, Karankawa, and Natchidoches.[7] The immense size of Texas and its relative lack of navigable waterways hindered Spanish exploration until the 1680s, when the French explorer Sieur de La Salle mistakenly landed near present-day Matagorda Bay during a failed and ultimately disastrous search for the mouth of the Mississippi River.[8] La Salle's encounter was the first in a series of events that would lead to profound demographic and geopolitical transformations for the Southern Great Plains, then home to as many as thirty-three indigenous groups. His men—nearly all of whom ultimately perished, deserted, or joined the local Natives—ended up murdering him, leaving nothing but his remains and the ruins of their fort for the Spanish to find in 1689.

The French intrusion prompted Spanish authorities to focus their attention on securing Texas with a series of missions and presidios along its eastern coast,[9] but their efforts were less successful than they had been in New Mexico a century and a half earlier. According to one official, the mostly nomadic and seminomadic Eastern Plains tribes "refused to submit to the merciful yoke of the church" and largely ignored instructions to halt trade with the French, who by the 1750s were threatening to undermine Spanish efforts to settle and control the region.[10] When approximately 2,000 mounted Comanches pillaged and burned Santa Cruz de San Sabá, killing eight people and destroying the mission, it foreshadowed what would become a sustained practice of raiding Spanish communities to obtain goods that ultimately fueled a growing trade with the French and Americans to the east.[11] The Comanches would reshuffle the balance of power in the far north by the late eighteenth century, as the Apache and other groups found themselves marginalized and increasingly dependent on the Spanish missions, which continued to suffer from administrative isolation, lack of supplies, and persistent raiding.[12]

In the 1770s, France, in an effort to condense its overseas empire following the Seven Years' War, transferred its North American territories, which then contained the middle third of the North American continent from New Orleans to Canada, to the Spanish, effectively ending the two empires' rivalry on the continent and inspiring the Spanish crown to unleash a series of administrative reforms designed to integrate and secure Spanish dominance there. Concerned primarily with British and Russian imperial threats, administrative officials believed they could subdue Native groups and harness them to Spanish imperial aims if they abandoned their missionizing efforts and replaced them with increasing military pressure on the "pagan" Indians, alliance building, and trade and gift-giving.[13] Spain hoped that this new alliance might help secure its eastern border from the new imperial rival to the east.[14] In the 1780s, US traders, some of them with ties to known filibusters in the north, began venturing into Texas.[15] The lieutenant governor of the town of Nacogdoches, long a hotbed of foreign trade and other illicit activity on the border with Louisiana, was instructed to arrest "any foreigners existing, or who may hereafter introduce themselves among our friendly Indian nations."[16] The results were mixed. Raids continued, though less systematically than before, and around the presidios, nascent Spanish ranching communities emerged, some of which even traded with previously hostile Natives.

In 1804 Spanish anxieties concerning the United States were heightened yet again when Louisiana came under its control, and six years later, in 1810, on the heels of Napoleon's invasion of the Iberian Peninsula and conquest of Spain, an independence movement wracked New Spain. When the Cortes convened in 1812 and took the unprecedented move of soliciting input from local representatives throughout the empire, Arizpe, as a representative from New Spain, blamed the suboptimal state of the Eastern Interior Provinces on centuries of imperial neglect and mismanagement. "After so many years of abandonment," Texas contained "only three towns" and "five missions of native Indians of the region." Arizpe estimated the non-Indian population to be less than 3,000, most of whom struggled under administrative neglect and the constant threat of raids and foreign filibustering. Despite "poverty, wars, and epidemics of smallpox," the Comanches could "in a few days assemble many thousands of armed warriors." Their raids had hindered the settlement and development of Texas which, as Arizpe indicated, was especially unfortunate considering how much natural wealth the region possessed. The interior provinces' "vast extent," location, climate, and "most abundant and varied native products" made them "worthy of constituting by themselves one of the most extensive and richest empires of the universe."[17] If Spain wished to benefit from this peripheral region, it needed greater integration and increased population.[18] Arizpe insisted that this would not be a difficult task. The size, products, and "excellent seaports" of the internal provinces invited "millions of men to enrich themselves." Yet, the government had never instituted "effective measures" to attract them. To this end, Arizpe recommended a project designed to enhance the white population in Texas, insisting that such a policy constituted the "principal road to national prosperity."[19]

Arizpe's remarks did not go unheeded. The imperial government soon commenced a sustained effort to encourage former subjects of Spain then residing in Louisiana, now under US control, to relocate to Spanish Texas. Initially, authorities admitted only Spanish vassals wanting to escape the "harsh" rule of the United States, but before long, US residents with no previous relationship to Spain were expressing their interest in immigrating as well. Then, local pressure combined with the US decision to abandon all claims to Texas in the Adams-Onís Treaty (1819), establishing the United States–New Spain border, resulted in a sudden shift in Spanish policy. By July 1821, on the eve of Mexican independence, the Cortes, in response to pressure from Arizpe and others, determined to allow foreigners to settle on the public lands of Mexico's far north, so long as local officials exercised special vigilance when it came to norteamericanos.[20] It was this shift in policy that resulted in Moses Austin, a one-time resident of Spanish Louisiana, receiving a promised plot of land on the Brazos River to settle 300 Catholic families. Texas governor Antonio Martínez, who had an instinctive distrust of foreigners, claimed that "his suspicions were overcome by his desire to see Texas prosper and grow." A similar impulse likely prompted the governor to grant Austin's son Stephen a request for transference of that grant following his father's death.[21]

When Mexico gained independence from Spain in September, the question of colonization reemerged as some national leaders questioned the location of settlements, how seriously immigrants took their Catholic faith, and whether they were bothering to learn Spanish. Anastasio Bustamante, commandant general of the internal provinces, suggested that immigrants be required to establish themselves closer to Béxar so that they could remain "under the protection and observation of our government subject of course to our laws, and under terms that we prescribe." Permitting them to settle too far from the center of governmental power might compromise the security of the young empire by "paving the way for invasion."[22] As news of Mexico's independence from Spain reached places like Arkansas, Kentucky, Louisiana, and Missouri, interest in the colony grew. Austin determined that his best option for securing the colony was to travel to Mexico City and make his case to the new emperor directly. Arriving in the spring of 1822, Austin found himself in good company, having encountered several other norteamericanos seeking colonization contracts in Texas. They would all have to wait until the new congress formally declared Iturbide emperor on May 19, at which point Austin immediately set to work convincing the new government to affirm his contract. He couched his words in effusive praise for the empire and its leader, congratulating Iturbide "on the happy consummation of the independence of Mexico" and assuring him that his colonists looked to the Imperial Congress "as the pure fountain from whence those blessings are to flow."[23]

Despite Austin's supplications and his tactful appeal to Mexican leaders' interest in developing the far north, Bustamante remained skeptical.[24] Just days after Congress had its first session, however, Tadeo Ortíz de Ayala, former imperial commissioner to Guatemala, presented Iturbide with his *Statistical Resume of the Mexican Empire*. Ortíz echoed the optimism about Mexico's future characteristic of the time. The country's remarkable topography, along with its rich soil and diverse climate, appeared to make it ideal for the cultivation of various crops including corn, rice, potatoes, cotton, and cacao. Situated as it was, between the Atlantic and Pacific Oceans, and with extensive shorelines on both coasts, Ortíz confirmed that Mexico "appears destined to exercise great influence in the political events that agitate the great nations."[25] He also cautioned that Mexico's success would ultimately depend on its ability to populate the distant provinces of California, Durango, New Mexico, Sonora, and Texas.[26] Ortíz warned that the "descendants of the English," having already settled Louisiana and Missouri while that territory was controlled by the "impotent" Spanish Empire, now had their sights set on New Mexico and California. To guard against this threat, he urged greater commercial and political integration of the empire, clarification of the empire's northern boundary with the United States, and, perhaps counterintuitively, colonization of its far northern and southern provinces by norteamericanos themselves.[27]

Although the latter idea of populating a vulnerable region with inhabitants from a country with a demonstrated interest in absorbing that very territory seems nonsensical, or even dangerous, Ortíz's proposal hinged on a long-standing belief shared by many Mexican economic liberals as well as state and local officials in the far north—that the prosperity of these regions depended on the ability to attract and secure the loyalty of foreign colonists, chiefly from the United States, whose citizens had a demonstrated ability to transform fallow, uncultivated lands into profitable farms and plantations.[28] Some of the advocates fostered a reverence for an agrarian economy virtually indistinguishable from that of Jefferson himself. In 1775 Arizpe declared agriculture to be the "source of the true wealth of nations, the worthy occupation of man, the principal foundation of the most solid happiness of the citizen and the most secure wealth of the state." Regarding the Hispanic inhabitants of the northeastern provinces, he wrote that the "harvest and systematic cultivation of the soil, from which alone they derive their sustenance" had made them "truly inflexible to intrigue, virtuously steadfast, haters of tyranny and disorder, justly devoted to true liberty and naturally the most inclined to all the moral and political virtues."[29] Such characteristics, Arizpe implied, not only distinguished this population from many of their compatriots who lacked the same accessibility to independent land proprietorship, but it also implied that they were culturally more akin to norteamericanos.

Indeed, in the decades leading up to Mexican independence, residents of the far northern provinces, chiefly Texas, had formed economic and personal ties with Anglo-American traders and squatters, and like the US settlers of the trans-Mississippi west in the 1790s, many of them felt abandoned or at least underserved by their central government, whose administrative presence in its distant borderlands was nearly as weak as that of the young republic to its west.[30] Understanding the desire of many of these settlers to secure lands for themselves and their families, and likely aware of the economic crisis in the United States that was driving them to Texas, liberals like Arizpe and Ortíz believed that Mexico could make loyal citizens of them if it granted their request for Texas lands, thereby managing to secure and develop its most vulnerable province. Around the same time that Ortíz issued his report, Congress also received a report from the Committee on Foreign Affairs that similarly emphasized the vulnerability and promise of Mexico's "auxiliary provinces" and suggested that under the right circumstances, Veracruz might become the next Boston Harbor. The report concluded with a recommendation that the government immediately commence colonization of Texas with settlers from New Orleans, Europe, and the Mexican interior.[31]

Within months, the Mexican government received more than a dozen petitions for contracts to settle in Texas, including Austin's request to assume his father's earlier contract with the Spanish Empire and a proposal by Ortíz to settle 10,000 Irish and Canary Islanders in Texas. By the spring of 1823, Congress had approved a colonization plan designed to address the need to populate the eastern interior provinces and concerns about doing so with former inhabitants of the United States. It departed from the recommendations of Bustamante and the Congressional Committee of Foreign Affairs in permitting foreigners to both settle along the coast and to bring enslaved persons. Article 1 stipulates, "The government of the Mexican nation will protect the liberty, property and civil rights, of all foreigners, who profess the Roman Catholic apostolic religion, the established religion of the empire." The document went on to present clear terms on which land was to be distributed and maintained. Empresarios—those who introduce at least two hundred families—were to inform the executive "what branch of industry they proposed to follow, the property or resources they intend to introduce" and any other "particulars they may deem necessary." Immigrants were expected to immediately introduce themselves to the governing councils, ayuntamientos, of the towns in which they intended to settle "in conformity with the instructions of the executive" so that local officials "may designate the lands corresponding to them." The amount of land distributed was to be highly regulated according to the stated occupation of each colonist, usually either farming or raising stock. Settlers would be permitted to select plots in the order in which they arrived, with natives of Mexico getting the first pick. If empresarios failed to "populate and cultivate" the lands contracted to them within twelve years, then they would lose title, and if a colonist failed to cultivate the land after two years, it would be presumed that he had renounced his right to it, and the ayuntamiento could grant it to someone else. Colonists were exempt from all taxation of their products for six years and subjected to only "half tithes" for the six years following that.

Mexico finally had a colonization law and one that promised to populate the region with Mexican and Anglo inhabitants committed to its settlement and development. It called for considerable administrative oversight of the colonization project and sought to ensure fealty among foreign settlers by requiring them to not only adopt Mexican citizenship, but to also conform to its establishment clause. Furthermore, it guarded against distant land speculators by insisting that colonists cultivate their land within two years.[32]

After residing in Mexico for nearly a year, learning Spanish, and dutifully cultivating the patronage of prominent Mexico City liberals, Austin finally managed to secure executive approval for his contract. Yet, no sooner had he done so, than Iturbide's government was dissolved. With the transition to a republic and adoption of the Constitution of 1824, Mexican leaders were forced to revisit their colonization strategy. Most agreed that some form of the imperial colonization law, adopted just a year earlier, ought to form the basis of the new policy, but the question arose of who would oversee the colonization projects. Under Mexico's new federal system, control of public lands fell under the jurisdiction of state legislatures.[33] This was different from the US system, where the original states had surrendered their western territories to the federal government, putting Congress in charge of surveying, regulating, and selling public lands. Austin clearly preferred the Mexican system.

In the summer of 1823, as provincial leaders were issuing their pronunciamientos in favor of federalism, Austin drew up a sample constitution for his adopted country and sent copies to the provincial representatives of Guadalajara, where the federalist pronunciamiento wave had commenced, as well as neighboring Monterrey and to Arizpe in Coahuila. Article 20 carefully enumerated the rights of the provinces, which included cultivating and selling their own agricultural products, admitting foreign immigrants without restriction, and enjoying unmitigated control over all vacant lands within their boundaries, including the right to sell such property so long as it was not to a foreign power. The article so closely resembled Arizpe's own views on provincial autonomy that the two men likely authored the document together. Regardless, it embodied the localist sentiments of many northeastern leaders, who had long expressed frustration with the central government's administrative neglect and prohibitive immigration policies. It also echoed the pronunciamientos of federalist states like Jalisco and Yucatán, which also asserted that each state was sovereign and independent in matters affecting its population, commerce, agriculture, and industry.[34] Conversely, the article garnered the opposition of centralist writers, including Francisco Severo Maldonado, who called for nationalizing public lands and permitting the federal government to capitalize on their sales by funneling them into a national bank under a system more akin to that of the United States.[35] Adoption of the Constitution of 1824 guaranteed a land policy that confirmed state sovereignty, eased foreign immigration, and ultimately made lands far more attainable to norteamericano settlers than they had ever been previously. Mexico's National Colonization Law, issued in August of 1824, essentially left to state legislatures the right to dispose of their lands as they saw fit and to retain the profits of those lands. In so doing, it reversed a centuries long practice of centralized control of public lands and colonization, transferring it to local and state authorities with a vested interest in facilitating US colonization.

The law did not, however, resolve the question of Texas's status within the new republic. Since its population was so small, Arizpe proposed that Texas be united with Coahuila to form one state with its capital at Saltillo. Erasmo Seguín, the congressional representative from Texas, objected, not wanting to see Texas lose its autonomy to the more populous Coahuila. Believing that the population of Texas was too small to form a viable independent state, however, the provincial deputation voted to join Coahuila. Arizpe eventually managed to convince Seguín of the wisdom of a state composed of Texas and Coahuila, insisting that the only other alternative for Texas was adopting the "degrading" status of a federal territory. While such a status would enable Texas to rely on the superior resources of Mexico City, especially in matters related to frontier defense, Arizpe insisted nonetheless that territorial status would merely place Texas under the "iron grip" of a distant central government with little knowledge of the region or the needs of its inhabitants. A state government, even one dominated by *coahuillanos*, would be composed of men whose interests better aligned with their Tejano (Hispanic Texan), neighbors, would ease the process of colonization, and would likely shield or otherwise mitigate federal laws perceived to be obstructive to the economic interests of Texas, such as those against slavery and religious tolerance. Seguín eventually agreed to the arrangement—so long as it included a stipulation that allowed Texas the option of becoming a separate state once it had the population and resources to do so.[36] The state legislature also agreed to establish a department of Texas with political authority vested in a *jefe politico*, chief political officer, to be appointed by the governor with the approval of the state legislature.[37]

The colonization law of the new state of Coahuila y Téjas, issued the following year, departed from the national law by extending the length of foreigners' tax exemption to ten years after their arrival, instead of six, and providing for indemnification for settlers who mistakenly occupied and improved lands belonging to someone else. That said, it openly promoted assimilation of foreign settlers by forbidding settlement within twenty leagues of the United States and awarding twice the amount of land to foreigners who married Mexicans.[38] The law undoubtedly made land far more attainable to norteamericanos willing to relocate, adopt Mexican citizenship, and abide by the republic's laws. Whereas, the US Land Act of 1820 had priced land at $1.25 per acre and required immediate cash payment at a time when the country was experiencing a national banking crisis, in Mexico the head of a family could acquire as much as 4,428 acres (or one *sitio*) of grazing land and 177 acres (or one *labor*) of farming land for a modest fee that could be paid in installments over six years with the first payment not due until year four. All the foreign colonists needed to do was "prove their Christianity, morality, and good habits" and become naturalized Mexican citizens.[39]

While it is difficult to determine precisely what compelled hundreds of US citizens to immigrate to Texas during the 1820s, one can presume that Mexico's relatively liberal land policy, as opposed to the comparatively prohibitive one of the United States, was a significant factor. Of the 297 land grants that Austin managed to fill by mid-1825, most of them went to families or to single men like himself from such places as Arkansas, Kentucky, Louisiana, Missouri, and

Tennessee. Based on their place of origin, one might reasonably assume that many were victims of land speculation, economic panic, or squatter eviction. Such policies were certainly on the minds of a group of petitioners from Nacogdoches in 1824. Located on the border with Louisiana, the town was the site of numerous and competing land claims. The petitioners, all of whom appear to have been originally from the United States, cited the "healthfulness of the climate and the fertility of the soil, together with the pleasing hope of living under an independent and liberal government" as the reasons for them to "abandon our country, and seek another." Declaring "inequity in the distribution of land" to be the greatest misfortune that could befall a country" the petitioners clearly hoped to obtain from the Mexican republic what they had failed to gain in the United States. They cited "agrarian law" and may have also had the aims of Mexican liberals in mind when they asserted, "An exclusive right to the possession of the soil and its productions is the only agent that aids universally and constantly upon men and prompts human industry."[40]

It was not just land speculation, however, that pushed immigrants into the embrace of a recently independent Mexico. Robert Kuykendall, the first militia captain in Austin's colony, was involved in a lawsuit against the United States for remuneration for lands that had been confiscated for the purpose of Cherokee and Choctaw relocation. Beginning in 1808, the federal government had identified Arkansas Territory as a site for the relocation of eastern tribes and the project, initiated by President Thomas Jefferson, commenced soon after. References to the region as the "residue" of the Louisiana Purchase suggest that the US Congress was likely unaware of it being home to approximately 9,000 white inhabitants. Jefferson, however, was certainly not when he ordered the "depopulation" of its "loose settlements" to enable the "transfer of the southern Indians" to the territory. Instances of the US military forcibly removing white settlers to make way for Native tribes was certainly uncommon, if unprecedented, but in the Louisiana Territory it occurred during the first two decades of the nineteenth century.[41] Mary Crownover Rabb's family had similar grievances. Like the Kuykendalls, Rabb was originally from North Carolina, her husband's family from western Pennsylvania. The Rabbs had lived in the Ohio and Illinois Territories before settling briefly just west of the Red River. It was from there that in 1821 Mary Rabb's father-in-law, William Rabb, wrote a letter to the Spanish governor Antonio Martínez complaining that US officials in Miller County, Arkansas—from which white settlers were being relocated— were attempting to govern and collect "taxes" from the settlers of Pecan Point, just south of the Red River. Claiming that they were in Spanish territory, Rabb and others requested that Martínez respond by sending a commandant to assert Spanish authority and, in fact, to govern them. Rabb's letter was accompanied by a petition with about eighty signatures.[42] Likely not receiving a response or none that he liked, Rabb decided to move to Texas two years later. He was soon joined by his children and their families, including the recently married John and Mary Rabb. Both instances represent a profound departure from the way many US agrarians believed their federal government should function. The imposition of a degree of military rule in the Louisiana Territory, from which many early migrants to Texas originated, likely had the effect that General James Wilkinson warned it would—injuring their "amor propre" and exciting "seditious emotions."[43] It also likely deepened their animosity toward Native Americans.

Having lived in the trans-Mississippi West during the 1780s and 1790s, the settlers and their forebears had long competed with Natives for land, and many were well versed in an ideology that perceived those lands as vacant and unoccupied.[44] In fact, the eastern coast of Texas was then inhabited by approximately five hundred Karankawa, a semi-nomadic tribe whose members had resisted Spanish missionization for decades. By 1790 most had fled to the coast, pushed east by the Apache, thus bringing them into direct conflict with recent arrivals from the United States. As many of the early settlers initially set up homesteads along the Colorado River, the Karankawa frequently mistook their livestock as feral, occasionally hunting and killing cattle. Settlers often responded by transferring the animosity they had forged against tribes they had encountered further east to those they encountered in Mexico. This, in fact, was likely why northern Mexicans were eager to welcome them. For decades, Tejanos had considered themselves at war with Native raiders, compelling them to adopt an animosity toward Native Americans that resembled that of their Anglo counterparts and frequently brought them into conflict with national leaders, who did not view raids as a serious affront to Mexican sovereignty. Disputes with Mexico City over how best to respond to "los indios bárbaros" would continue for years, but by the 1820s Tejanos believed that they had a potential ally in their Anglo-American neighbors. This might have been the case had those neighbors settled farther west, where they were more likely to encounter Comanche and Kiowa raiders, but to the consternation of local and national officials, most of the Anglo settlements remained clustered along the eastern coast.

Although colonists were more than willing to avenge raids by local Natives, they were often reluctant to cooperate in coordinated attacks on more powerful tribes, with whom they were able to sustain peace. When the Comanche renewed their attacks on Tejano ranches and settlements in 1825, Austin responded to Mexican officials' orders to pursue and punish the raiders by informing them that his settlement was, unfortunately, "by no means well calculated to meet the commencement of a war."[45] He later asked that the settlers be permitted to "avail themselves of the friendly disposition of the Indians to remain Neutral," informing the commandant that "in consequence of the number of sick and the necessity of gathering our crops it would be impossible to commence hostilities at present." Austin and other colonists also seemed to fear that war with the "upper" Indians would stall migration to the colony.[46] Thus, colonists were strategic and selective about when and how they contributed to Mexico's efforts, defending its sovereignty when it suited them, but defending themselves when forced to choose between their adopted country and themselves.

Governing

In March 1825, a year that saw an explosion of immigration from the United States, Austin and his allies convinced the state legislature in Saltillo to turn the empresario system into state law. Having allocated his original three hundred land grants, Austin made a request for five hundred more the following month. "Application is made to me daily to receive and settle more families," he informed Texas governor Rafael González, some of which have already arrived here, others are on the road and have written to me."[47] The state government was happy to comply. In fact, it granted a total of twenty-five such contracts that year with only a few recipients managing to establish a permanent residence with sizeable communities in areas surrounding Austin's colony; the majority of attempts never came to fruition. The most determined and successful empresarios tended to be other norteamericanos, among them Robert Leftwich, Frost Thorn, Green De Witt and Haden Edwards.[48]

Coahuila y Téjas had been divided into a series of municipalities ruled by ayuntamientos, headed by an alcalde, who served as mayor, sheriff, and judge. The legislature in Saltillo, distracted with the responsibilities associated with establishing a new state government, was content to allow the colonies a significant degree of self-government and in fact requested that empresarios take care of whatever problems might arise under their jurisdiction themselves, so as not to burden their superiors.[49] Austin gladly complied. On June 24, 1824, he issued his first formal battalion orders "in conformity with the decree of the Superior Government of the Mexican nation" to constitute a militia.[50] The significance of militias to Anglo-American political tradition dates at the least to the seventeenth century, when most US citizens believed there was no better defense for a society than the armed strength of its own inhabitants.[51] Well after the institution had been denounced by some as inefficient and unreliable,[52] many in the United States continued to embrace the militia as an expression of local autonomy and representative self-government since compliance ultimately depended on community consensus.[53] Historians have long assumed that only in the Anglo world did the militia carry such an association,[54] but Spain's first constitution, the Cádiz Constitution of 1812, deemed the militia the most effective defense against monarchical absolutism, and the Spanish American republics would attempt to reestablish the institution in connection with the new definition of the body politic, often despite the continued existence of large, standing armies.[55] Perhaps nowhere else in Spanish America was the militia tradition as strong as in the Mexican north. Beginning as early as 1713 as part of the Spanish Empire's efforts to secure the region, the viceroy ordered landowners to form their own militias to help defend against Native and foreign incursions.[56] In 1772 the commandant general ordered that they receive formal military training from professional soldiers stationed at nearby presidios. Despite irregular pay and a constant lack of supplies, the *compañía volante* (volunteer company) enjoyed a certain prestige, and many settlers preferred that it, rather than the regular army, defend their municipality.[57] As nearby presidio soldiers integrated into neighboring communities, the militaristic culture of the region intensified, and a distinct identity began to emerge, one that Arizpe described as consisting of men who "serve not only as militiamen but even as common soldiers," demonstrating extreme "integrity, honor, and subordination."[58]

Militias were a well understood institution in both the Mexican and US republics. Yet, as calls to replace them with a more presumably efficient and reliable standing army erupted in the United States, by 1826 Mexico was disbanding its traditional cavalry and ordering citizens to form militia companies to operate under local command.[59] Austin received permission to "create a solid base of authority in his colonies" so long as he agreed to organize his colonists into a national militia force. He was appointed lieutenant colonel and granted full responsibility for maintaining "the good order[,] prosperity and defense" of his colonies.[60] Militia service was likely nothing new to most members of his colony. Not merely a way of life, it was also how most republican men defined, achieved, and secured their relationship to the state. Yet, as more and more immigrants flooded across the Sabine River, keeping track of them, and making sure they both adhered to the duties and received the benefits of Mexican citizenship, proved increasingly difficult in a region that had always suffered from a limited administrative presence. In February 1824, the same group of

Nacogdoches squatters who had requested title to their lands issued a second petition complaining that they wanted from "lack of any government" and that, as a result, "almost all this time they have been very unhappy not knowing their obligations as citizens of this government, and conversely those of the government towards its subjects." Far from wishing to evade the Mexican state, they pressed their eagerness "to conform in everything with the constitution of this government," including forming a militia "for the defense of the province in case of any invasion." They concluded that "as subjects" of Mexico, they took a "personal interest" in its "prosperity."[61] Until the government could process their claims, José Antonio Saucedo, the governor-appointed jefe político for Texas, advised them to listen with full "attention and confidence" to Colonel Austin "whose authority is from the supreme powers of the nation to which you now voluntarily belong."[62]

Not all the colonists expressed their frustrations so civilly. In 1825 Haden Edwards received a contract to settle eight hundred families in and around Nacogdoches. When he arrived there in September, he demanded that the current settlers produce titles to their land or face eviction to make way for his own colonists. In reference to the Edwards colony, however, Saucedo insisted that they had "arbitrarily established themselves" and threatened the rights of the "old residents." He further warned that if they attempted to "appropriate" the lands by force, it would jeopardize "any opportunity of being admitted as legal citizens."[63] On November 13, 1826, the commanding officer of the Nacogdoches militia, José Antonio Sepulveda, wrote to the political chief of Texas informing him that the "rebellious American rogues" associated with Edwards aimed to ally themselves with local Indians "to ensure their assistance in overthrowing the authorities of our government" and warned that Texas "would be lost to the country if the Almighty did not open the eyes of the Superior Government, and induce them to send troops for its protection."[64]

Tensions reached a climax during the election for alcalde, when battle lines were drawn between Samuel Norris, a representative of the old settlers, and the disgruntled faction, who supported Edwards' son-in-law, Chinchester Chaplin. When Norris's supporters declared Chaplin's election fraudulent because much of his support was drawn from individuals who had not yet gained Mexican citizenship, Chaplin seized the archives and assumed the duties of the alcalde. When Saucedo declared the election in favor of Norris and ordered Chaplin to step down, Chaplin declared that he only took orders from the state capital in Saltillo, dismissing Saucedo's authority. In July, Benjamin Edwards, Haden's brother, dismissed local officials' efforts as "incompatible with a republican government, and contrary to the fundamental principles of the constitution of the country." Benjamin Edwards seemed to suggest that his brother was the victim of arbitrary censure "without any inquiry into the truth or falsehood of the accusations" against him.[65] On November 22, the Edwards brothers and their allies seized Norris and Sepulveda and tried them for oppression and "corruption" in office. They were unable to convince state leaders, however, who ultimately sided with Norris. The military commander of Texas, Col. Mateo Ahumada, ultimately dismissed the Edwards faction as a "class of men who know no law but their rifle" and expressed his fear "that they will endeavor to render themselves independent of Mexico."[66] He was right.

Later that year, allied groups of Anglo settlers, Cherokees, and leaders of approximately twenty-seven other tribes launched a secessionist movement in Natchitoches, insisting that Mexico had "by repeated insults, outrages and oppressions" reduced the "white and red immigrants" of the United States of the North. They had been lured to Mexico "by promises most solemnly declared, and most vilely inforged," and that they now faced the "disagreeable alternative" of either submitting to an "faithless, and despotic government" for defending their inalienable rights.[67] In addition to casting aspersion on the republic, the Edwards faction reminded Nacogdoches residents, whose support they hoped to garner, that they were all "Americans in a foreign land" and compared their movement to the US war for independence. "Our fathers in their struggle for liberty contended against the giant of the world. We have to contend against a corrupt and imbecile government."[68]

Historians have interpreted the Fredonian rebellion, the first attempt by Texans to seceded from Mexico, as early evidence of the limits of Anglo American colonists' commitment to Mexico and their enduring identification with the United States. The rebellion, however, was also an extension of the separatist movements that swept the western United States in the decades following that republic's independence, when rebels lobbed the same accusations of despotism and tyranny at the government. Both expressed a sense of betrayal at their respective republic's inability to deliver on a set of economic and political promises and drew on the early republican right to "alter or abolish" a government unresponsive to the interests of its citizens. In this regard, the rebellion is evidence of the tenuous and contested state of national sovereignty in the late eighteenth and early nineteenth centuries as well as just one example of an agrarian populist radicalism that swept west from the Appalachian Mountains to the Southern Great Plains.

Unlike the agrarian revolts of the 1780s and 1790s, however, the Fredonian rebels self-consciously positioned themselves against a supposedly failed foreign power while simultaneously aligning themselves with Native Americans. Historians have correctly warned against perceiving the Fredonian event as an example of racial egalitarianism, however, because the Edwards brothers insisted that their newly independent republic would consist of two distinct halves—the northern part of Texas for the "red people" and the southern part for the "white people." Their decision to ally with the Cherokee was pragmatic. Another difference between the Fredonian and US agrarian revolts was the former's profound lack of popularity. One observer estimated that there "was not more than 30 Americans of the rebel party."[69] One resident of Nacogdoches explained later that the town had "been left entirely to the management of a few ignorant and designing men . . . who wished to show their power and acted with more tyranny than ever was, exercised under the king of Spain."[70]

Whereas the Fredonian rebellion demonstrated the limits of the Edwards' faction's commitment to Mexico, it also supplied a prime opportunity for Austin and his colonists to prove theirs. "I am compelled to say with all the frankness of an old friend that you are wrong," Austin wrote to one Buttil Thompson. "I cannot believe that you have so far lost your senses as to think of open opposition to the [Mexican] government." Yet it was not just Mexico these men had turned their backs on. "[N]either will I believe that you have so far forgotten the land of your birth and the proud name of *American*." For Austin, the rebels' decision to rebel against Mexico represented a betrayal of their Anglo-American identity, not a confirmation of it. Austin concluded his letter by encouraging the rebels to disband their militia and formally express their "entire submission and obedience to the [Mexican] government."[71] He reiterated this racialized condemnation in an address to the citizens of Victoria in which he denounced the Nacogdoches rebels as "infatuated madmen" who had "declared Independence and invited the Indians from Sabine to Rio Grande to join them and wage a war of murder, plunder, and desolation on the innocent inhabitants of the frontier." He then appealed to his audience "as men of honor, as Mexicans, and as Americans to do your duty" and join members of his own colony in suppressing the rebellion. Austin acknowledged that the men's interest as Americans sometimes conflicted with those of their adopted nation, but "in this instance they are the same" and reminded them of their "duty as *Mexicans*, to support and defend the government of our adoption, by whom we have been received with the kindness and liberality of an indulgent parent," their "duty as *men*, to suppress vice anarchy and Indian massacre," and their "duty as *Americans* to defend that proud name from the infamy which this Nacogdoches gang must cast upon if they are suffered to progress."[72] For Austin, American identity, Mexican nationality, and masculinity were complementary and mutually re-enforcing, not oppositional as the rebels portended.

In another correspondence, Austin again insisted that American and Mexican interests were the same: "As an American I feel a lively and warm interest in everything that concerns Americans, and as a Mexican I am bound by my duty, honor and every obligation that a man ought to hold sacred, to be faithful to this government and to the true interests of this nation."[73] His remarks seemed a clear departure not only from the Edwards faction's anti-Mexican sentiment, but also from its general anti-statism. Austin reminded settlers, "Without regular government, without law, what security have we for our persons, our property, our characters and all that we hold dear and sacred?" The answer was clear. The rights and privileges of a republican government could not be guaranteed if the integrity of the nation was violated, lest "we at once embark on the stormy ocean of anarchy, subject to . . . ruin and infamy."[74]

While the rebels saw themselves as Americans in a foreign land, Austin saw himself as an American at home in a land more committed to fulfilling American ideals than the United States. Granting that the rebels may have cause for grievance, he insisted nonetheless that they had "taken the wrong method of seeking redress." Furthermore, they were wrong to think that they would find any support among the other settlers. "The people of this colony are unanimous," insisted Austin, "I have not heard of one man who is not opposed to your violent measures and there is not one amongst us who will not freely take up arms to oppose you and sustain the Govt."[75] In his correspondence with Saucedo, Austin expressed sympathy toward the insurgents' original grievances, but renounced their ultimate actions. "From what I could learn of that occurrence, it would seem, that the principal cause was the hatred of these people [the Norris faction] and not any ill feelings against the Government." With a more impartial administrator, he assured Saucedo, "no difficulty need be apprehended on the part of the inhabitants."[76] Accompanying the letter was a formal "Resolution of Loyalty" from the inhabitants of his colony who had "no hesitation" in declaring that they viewed the actions of the Nacogdoches rebels, with the "most decided disapropriation." They further declared themselves "ready to rally around the standard of the Mexican nation and sustain its govt and authority by force of arms," asserting that they were gratified for the "favours" bestowed upon them by Mexico, that they had full faith in the government's "justice and magnanimity," and remained committed to the "defense of the liberty honor and rights of the Mexican nation."[77]

The district of Bravo issued a similar resolution, which declared, "We are Mexicans by adoption and as such are willing to turn out when called on to quell the enemies of the government." The petitioners offered their "services in support of said government on this or any similar occasion if required."[78] Dewitt's colony similarly resolved that "as adopted children they [the colonists themselves] have full confidence and faith in the equity, justice and liberality in the federal and state governments of their new parent" and they hoped that Mexico would distinguish "between the honest, industrious and peaceable American emigrants, and those of bad character, whom we consider as refugees and fugitives from justice." Like Austin, they renounced the insurgents' behavior as un-American and looked upon them "with contempt and disgust," insisting "they are unworthy of the character of Americans." They concluded by pledging their "lives" and "fortunes" to Mexico, "our much beloved and adopted country."[79]

On December 28, José Antonio Navarro, Texas's representative to Saltillo, announced to the citizens of Nacogdoches that, in response to their calls, the government would send its troops to maintain order. Mindful of the reaction that this might cause, he assured them that it was not an invasion and to dismiss reports to the contrary.[80] In fact, the colonists appeared to welcome Mexican troops and quickly formed a nearly two-hundred-man volunteer militia to assist them in suppressing the rebellion. The most convincing evidence of the general lack of support for the rebellion was the settlers' swift and organized, although ultimately anticlimactic, suppression of it. John Williams, commander of the volunteer militia, wrote, "As soon as the inhabitants were generally informed of the measure which had been taken to put down the rebellious party, they flocked to us from all quarters in defense of their country." Their patriotism "far surpassed my most sanguine expectation." Upon learning of the militia's approach, Edwards evidently fled across the border to the United States, at which point, a "party was dispatched in pursuit of them," but they only caught two. "The result of these just measures and fortunate reinforcements from different quarters, has, in my opinion, settled the fate of the rebellious party," concluded Williams. The next day, they were joined by a detachment under a Col. Bean and another from Austin's colony. "At this time there is every prospect of immediate tranquility in the neighborhood," Williams reported. One hundred eighty-seven men had enrolled as ready for duty and "manifested every disposition to serve their country."[81]

Richard Fields and one other insurgent leader were killed in the conflict, and the rest of the accomplices were taken prisoner and eventually expelled from the country. By the time the dust had settled over Nacogdoches, James Elijah Brown,

Austin's younger brother, reported that the insurgents were "treated with a degree of lenity by the Mexicans they had no right to expect from the nature of their crimes" and which "would not have been shewn them in their native country."[82] Rather than compromising Anglo immigrants' relationship with Mexico, the event cemented it by both allowing settlers to strengthen their ties to their adopted country through a mutually understood institution, a militia, and by exposing Mexican magnanimity.

On February 9, Nacogdoches loyalist, Samuel Kinney, wrote to Ahumada describing the situation in Nacogdoches following the rebellion. He relayed the request of the militia commander that an armed force continue to be kept in that quarter: "It also seems to be a general wish of the inhabitants here, that a portion at least, of the [Mexican] Troops should be quartered somewhere in that neighborhood." He also "delivered" nine individuals "charged with having belonged to the late faction." Kinney concluded by stating that he believed the recent rebellion to be "completely suppressed," but warned that "nevertheless as much confusion still exists," and recommended stationing troops "nearer the frontier than Nacogdoches" to "prevent any irruption from designing persons from the U.S. of the North." He concluded his letter with the customary "Union and Mexico."[83] By April 1827, Bustamante, the commandant general, reported that he was glad to hear that "complete tranquility" had been restored to the region and that the "honor of our government and the Mexican flag is still unsullied."[84] Yet, as Austin observed, the event exposed an unfortunate defect in the Anglo-American character. "Among the ignorant part of the Americans[,] independence means resistance and obstinacy right or wrong." Such an attribute, particularly common among "frontiersmen," set such men on a "violent course" toward both personal and political destruction.[85]

"The Roman Catholic is the religion of this nation"

In the summer of 1831, four years after the successful suppression of the Fredonian rebellion, at least one hundred members of Austin's colony gathered at Abner Kuykendall's ranch, about twenty miles north of San Felipe de Austin. They were there to be baptized and remarried as members of the Roman Catholic Church in accordance with Mexico's establishment clause. Mexican leaders had assigned Father Michael Muldoon, an Irish priest, to travel to the Anglo colonies and perform the necessary sacraments. The colonists themselves opted for a mass ceremony of sorts, perhaps for the sake of expediency. The experience must have been a strange one for late immigrants from a country where religious freedom was a founding precept and anti-Catholicism ascendent. Reports concur, however, that Muldoon's "sage appearance and seemingly good manners caused him to be kindly received by the colonists" as a "necessary evil which they could not well avoid." One individual tasked with organizing and facilitating the event stated that the brides and grooms "being used to married life did not feel that intense interest that is common for young expectants." Thus, they became "scattered and separated," creating a "complete hurly-burly" as lost spouses attempted to relocate one another. It took nearly an hour before all the participants were ready to commence their march to Kuykendall's property. One woman unable to find her husband was comforted by the assurance that given the present abundance of grooms, "she could certainly have another." The ceremony itself was followed by a "splendid barbeque" with "all the necessary exhilarating libations."[86] If the converts were resentful of their obligation, it was not evident. The relative lack of administrative and church presence in the far north meant that their commitment to Catholicism did not have to be thorough or complete or extend much beyond baptism and marriage.

By the early 1830s, nearly every one of the original thirteen states had disestablished their churches, leading to a proliferation and diversification of religious expression throughout the republic. In Mexico, however, Roman Catholicism was an important part of the independence movement and served to unite a racially, geographically, and politically diverse postindependence society. Scholars of the Spanish Empire and independent Mexico argue that it is a mistake to point to an establishment clause as evidence that a movement was insufficiently revolutionary. As one historian wrote of the Cádiz Constitution of 1812, limiting the power of the monarch was itself a radical move that did not necessitate a rejection of the church. In fact, pushing for religious tolerance in a society as deeply Catholic as New Spain might well have compromised the revolution's aims.[87] The same could be said for postindependence Mexico, where, as Brian Connaughton has argued, religion supplied a "metaphor of social unity" in an otherwise fractured and varied society with competing political visions. Catholicism was essential to the Mexican national identity that insurgent leaders, many of them priests, attempted to construct. They advanced a notion of a Mexican people whose purity of faith was what most distinguished them from *peninsulares* and often framed the independence movement as a crisis of religious legitimacy by pointing to the inability of King Fernando VII to stall secular impulses in Spain.[88] In this way, religion functioned to both build a sense of national unity and identity and bestow upon the new republic a sense of divine righteousness.

Given the United States' antiestablishmentarianism and general prejudice, one would expect US immigrants to react to Mexico's establishment clause with hostility. In fact, the immigrants demonstrated a sophisticated understanding of the centrality of Catholicism to Mexican society and politics, even going so far as to defend Mexican leaders' decision to adopt a state religion. Ira Ingram, perhaps the most vocal defender, explained to a relative back home that the country's framers had to indulge at least some of the "prejudices of the people" which, like "so many Gordian knots... must be untied." Confirming in a letter to his uncle, a Protestant minister back in the United States, that "the Roman Catholic is the religion, and the established religion of this government," Ingram went on to assert that such a law offered expatriated Americans freedom from the "shameless strife and animosities, too often the offspring of a well meant zeal" and "invariably the handmaid of intolerant fanaticism." Ingram seemed relieved that in Mexico there were "no ravings" and "no rompings of indecorious and indecent exhibitions under the cloak of religious assemblage" or "santuarys or pathetic by unholy intention." There were "no sanctuaries but private ones," where "all are perfectly free to worship as they please."[89]

Far from limiting religious expression, Ingram argued, Mexican policy enhanced it by stifling religious competition and animosity. "Why, then, it will be natural for you to enquire, have an established religion?" he continued. Because Mexico and its founders "knew no religion but the one they adopted." Ingram conceded that there were "a few really intelligent and liberal minded patriots" who preferred disestablishment, but they were "obliged to concede something to the physical mass of the nation" in order "to secure their political independence." Religion was their compromise, and an easy one at that: "A nation freed from the bondage of centuries, on the cheap condition of being permitted to retain a Name! Where is the patriotic citizen and philanthropist, who does not exclaim, on hearing this, Victory!"[90] Mexico's challenge, after all, had been to achieve a coherent, unified and peaceful country. An attempt "to overleap" might end up leading the people "captive to the temple of reform" and bringing on "the whole apparatus of war."[91] Ingram insisted that he would have made the same decision. "Yes, — with all my prejudice in favor of religious freedom ... I should have voted for the present constitution, persuaded that it was the best, all interests reconciled, and all predilections surrendered that the circumstances of the world permit." Besides, adopting Catholicism was a small price to pay for the privilege of "hav[ing] and daily enjoy[ing] more to create our deepest gratitude toward the Government of our adopted county, than any other people on earth."[92]

Austin himself largely concurred that the lack of establishment had rendered religious fervor and emotional excess in the United States.[93] In a letter to his sister, he expressed his strong distaste for the religious fervency associated with the Second Great Awakening and his own desire to make Texas a "little world of our own where neither the religious, political or *money-making* fanaticism, which are throwing the good people of our native country into all sorts of convulsions shall ever obtain admission?" Religious freedom, Austin believed, had led the "North American of the present day" to become a "*bundle of extremes.*"[94] This was particularly evident among the few unapologetically Methodist colonists who made their way to Texas and continued to practice their faith despite the religious strictures. "If [the Methodists] are kept out, or would remain quiet," a frustrated Austin wrote, "we shall succeed in getting a free toleration for all Religions," but a few "fanatic and imprudent preachers" were ruining the prospect.[95]

Given the commitment of Austin and his associates to social order, perhaps it should not be so surprising that they would embrace the capacity of an established faith to create at least the illusion of unity, solidarity, and obedience. When immigrants did occasionally express concern about Mexico's establishment clause,[96] Austin did little to allay their fears, and ultimately hundreds of Anglo- American immigrants made the decision to convert to Catholicism as a prerequisite to becoming Mexican citizens.[97] The general lack of concern regarding Mexican establishmentarianism likely had to do with the lack of a clerical presence in the far north, which sometimes contributed to a degree of secularity that scandalized more pious observers. When Father Mariano Sosa visited Béxar in 1810, for example, he complained of "numberless evils against religion, society, and good order," reporting that the majority of the region's residents were "dissolute, without morals nor Christianity." A few even seemed "to doubt or misbelieve the priests." Sosa was particularly shocked to learn that "fathers and daughters, brothers and sisters are living in the most damning intercourse." In addition to the lack of the church's presence, the padre cited the residents' extreme poverty as a factor contributing to their inability to construct "proper partitions" between the rooms of "parents and children" and to the tendency of married women to "sell their bodies."[98]

Yet, in 1821 Béxar residents joined their compatriots in swearing allegiance to their new nation and its Catholic faith in an elaborate ceremony in the town plaza. For most of the republic's inhabitants, being Mexican meant being Catholic even if it was also informed by a regional specificity that often meant avoiding certain obligations, such as mass and tithes. Even under Mexico's confederate system, which left it up to states to ultimately dictate the terms of colonization,

Coahuila y Téjas specifically stated that the rights and property of foreigners would only be honored if they became Catholics. By 1832 state legislators were demanding proof of every male immigrant's membership in the Roman Catholic Church.[99] Under such conditions, the striking lack of clergy created quite a predicament, prompting some colonists to engage in marriage by bond, in which they registered with the alcalde and then waited to have their marriages formalized when a priest came to town. Such logistical hurdles, however, did not deter immigrants from conforming to their adopted country's laws when they could. For example, those who could not make it to the mass ceremony at the Kuykendall ranch were careful to make other arrangements.[100]

To say the least, colonists understood and accepted their adopted country's terms of citizenship, as unfamiliar as they must have felt to them. This, of course, is not to say that they, like many of their Tejano neighbors, were enthusiastic or even dutiful Catholics. Nonetheless, although plenty of prospective immigrants expressed apprehension about the establishment clause, there is little evidence of opposition to it once they arrived in Mexico. Perhaps those who had the strongest reservations decided not to emigrate, or perhaps most were content to enjoy a kind of de facto religious freedom in which they were willing to conform publicly to Catholicism so long as they could practice their own faith in private. Others seemed more concerned with the economic cost, rather than the spiritual price, of established religion. "Will religious toleration be allowed the emigrants from the United States, so far as to be exempted from the payment of tithes to the established Church," asked one prospective settler, "and to think and act for themselves in matters of conscience? Provided they do not interfere with the Catholic religion?"[101]

All in all, immigrants demonstrated a surprising willingness to compromise, agreeing to become at least nominally Catholic. They must have figured it was worth it or perhaps the government guarantee of religious freedom not so essential. Some have argued that while demonstrating a surprising cultural flexibility, immigrants' decision to become nominally Catholic was ultimately a pragmatic one.[102] To the extent that Austin may have had reservations regarding Mexico's established church, he rarely expressed them, and he was unequivocal about ensuring that prospective immigrants understood what Mexican citizenship meant. "I wish the settlers to remember that the Roman Catholic is the religion of this nation," he wrote. "We must all be particular on this subject and respect the Catholic religion with all that attention due to its sacredness and to the laws of the land."[103]

Of course, in the United States, the main criticism of established religion was the deleterious effect that it supposedly had on the independence of thought and action, both considered so essential in a republican society. Austin himself expressed this concern in one noteworthy correspondence in which he expressed the suspicion that republicanism would never be embraced by the clergy, whom he called "miserable drones" and "enemies of liberty" and of "human happiness" and the "human race." He even expressed the fear that Mexicans might never be capable of sufficiently freeing themselves from clerical control to realize a successful republic. Assertions like these might be enough to compel a reassessment of Austin's investment in the Mexican political project were it not shared by noted Mexican liberals, who frequently pointed to the dangers of religious intolerance even as they acknowledged its benefits. Lorenzo de Zavala asserted in *Ensayo histórico de las revoluciones de México* (1831) that Mexico's laws hindered the very religiosity and morality that they were intended to foster, creating a uniformity of spirit and mind that was ultimately forced and artificial.[104] From 1830 to 1832, Zavala traveled extensively throughout the United States. Long an admirer of that country, he compared the Protestant religious ceremonies of the north to those of Mexico, "where the people take very little part in the religious feelings that should occupy them in those circumstances." Catholic worship, with its formalized Latin mass, recited "without coherence, without conscience, and without divine comfort," enjoyed little impact among its followers. Zavala particularly disapproved of the way the church emulated Europe and appeared to perpetuate its elitism. Of the United States, he wrote that "neither the general government nor that of the states intervenes," and "worship is entirely in the hands of the people." It was the democratic spirit of religion that Zavala admired most. Yet even he had to concur with Austin that the degree of religious fervor that characterized the American people bordered on "fanatic."[105]

In *Ensayo sobre tolerancia religiosa* (1831) the same year that Ingram penned his letters, Vicente Rocafuerte pondered why the Mexican republic "after ten years of independence and political thought" on the subject of liberty was still unable to seriously entertain the question of religious tolerance. "[W]hen will we ever arrive at a resolution to this important problem?"[106] Interestingly, Rocafuerte specifically attacked Mexico's establishment clause for the way in which, he believed, it deterred colonists from the north. "How much solicitude has the government maintained to colonize the state of Texas and the territories of the Californias? How many laws on the matter has Congress and the states passed concerning the matter? And what have they produced? Nothing." Not only did

Mexico's established religion present a problem for democracy, but it also impaired its national security. Like many Mexican liberals, including Zavala, Rocafuerte believed that colonization was essential to Mexico's sovereignty, but, he wrote, "Freedom of the faith is the basis of every system of colonization and so long as it is not established it is useless to waste time on occasional delusions."[107] Rocafuerte claimed that Mexican religious strictures had prevented past colonization efforts and would continue to do so in the future. It should be of more interest to Mexico that its territories become "robust, productive, and wealthy" than that they "prohibit Scottish and English protestants the exercise of their faith."[108] Citing the United States, Rocafuerte also believed that religious intolerance was incompatible with "morality" and the "development of human intelligence," just as "mercantile monopoly" conflicted with widespread "commerce and prosperity." He identified what he termed the "triple unity of political, religious, and commercial freedom" as essential to any well-functioning modern society and warned that if Mexico did not follow the path of the United States, it would "be delinquent to the eyes of prosperity," having rejected the "movement of the century."[109] That said, most of Mexico's political class, even most liberals, were ultimately reticent about pushing for religious freedom. Understanding its unifying capacity, they tended to limit their criticism to the vestiges of colonial rule that had concentrated land and wealth in the hands of the church, granted the clergy near exclusive control of education, and other practices that they believed hindered the intellectual and economic development of Mexicans.

Austin, perhaps due to his own awareness of this antiestablishment thread of Mexican republicanism, expressed optimism that the days of church omnipresence were numbered. "Mexico has recovered her civil liberty—she will soon assume her rights in full, and bursting the chains of superstition declare that *man has a right to think for himself.*"[110] Ingram, however, cautioned against embracing such a change too quickly, before the "mass of the nation" was ready. "[T]here is some reason to apprehend danger from doing, or attempting to do too much," he warned. "Perhaps there is more danger of this than that too little will be done." Forcing such a decision on a nation not yet prepared for such change could produce a "violent reaction" that could result in the "loss of everything."[111] Good leaders "must prepare innovation at a distance that it may not appear innovation." Ingram was careful to point out that such accommodation did not negate the possibility of future change. "If this has been done in Mexico then toleration will succeed," he assured his uncle, "because it will receive the popular sanction."¹¹² Ingram remained ever conscious of the challenges that Mexican lawmakers faced and insisted that Mexico's popular will should dictate its political course.

Ultimately, Mexican liberals and US colonists seemed to prefer something between what they perceived as the United States' religious anarchy and Mexico's religious determinacy. While acknowledging the social benefits of Mexico's establishment clause, they nonetheless viewed it as a profound barrier to free thought and economic success. Yet, as admirers of social order and uniformity, Austin and members of his cohort recognized that established religion played a role in Mexican society similar to that of the militia, by creating one of the few elements that bound citizens to one another and to their state. It could even be said that Mexico's establishment clause was what enabled it to embrace the very confederate system they so admired. As critical as Austin and his allies had been of US centralization and as much as their fealty to Mexico hinged on the extent to which it granted them relative autonomy, they nonetheless owed their livelihood and prosperity to the Mexican state. Other settlers felt differently. The Fredonian rebellion represented a different thread of US republicanism, one decidedly more restive, antistatist, and thoroughly dependent on the government's ability to meet the economic needs of its citizens. By 1827 the same "plebian populism" that had plagued national leaders in the United States in the decades following that republic's independence, had made its way to the Texas borderlands.¹¹³

CHAPTER THREE

Slavery, Federalism, and Mexico's First Civil War

In 1827, when Mexican officials finally turned their attention to formalizing their boundary with the United States, Juan Francisco de Azcarate, a councilman and former adviser to Emperor Augustín I, cautioned them to proceed with "appropriate delicacy" to avoid making the same mistake that Spain had with Florida by willfully surrendering territory to its avaricious neighbor, warning that the United States fostered an "immense ambition" for Mexican land. The northern republic may have made advances in technology, commerce, and agriculture, but it also suffered from an excessively cold and humid climate. In addition, it lacked the natural riches that abounded in Mexico.[1] His advice could not have been more prescient. The following year, 1828, the United States would elect as its president Andrew Jackson, a man whose expressed interest in acquiring Texas had been evident a decade earlier. Jackson ultimately failed to convince the Spanish to include Texas in the Florida purchase, but almost as soon as he became president, he began scheming to acquire it.

By 1830 Mexico and the United States would witness the ascendance of two transformative presidents: Vicente Guerrero and Andrew Jackson. Both were federalists and populists who redefined executive power by claiming to be the supreme representative of the people, especially the agrarian majorities of their respective republics. Their similarities largely ended there. The two men's policies, if not leadership style, differed significantly, and only one had expansionist aims on the other's republic. Jackson's ascendance understandably alarmed officials in Mexico City. They had begun to view the growing Anglo population in Texas with greater suspicion even though Stephen Austin and his allies responded with indifference to Jackson's election. Yet, by 1830, relations between US immigrants and their adopted country were more complicated than they had ever been as two competing visions for Mexico's economic future emerged soon after independence, mirroring the political divide evident at the republic's founding. One vision, advanced by most federalists, aimed to transform Mexico into an agrarian power capable of rivaling the US South. It called for free trade and unobtrusive federal oversight. The other vision, advanced by centralists and conservatives, prioritized industrial manufacturing, infrastructure development, tariffs, and centralized banking. Although eager to distinguish Mexico from its northern neighbor, proponents of the latter fostered a political and economic philosophy akin to that of US federalists like Alexander Hamilton. Undoubtedly adherents of the former vision, Anglo-Texans and their Mexican allies, worked tirelessly to transform Texas into the center of a Mexican agrarian empire. In this respect, according to Tadeo Ortíz, a liberal, a federalist, and a proponent of Texas colonization, Mexico's great challenge was how to match US productivity without the adoption of the one institution that made it possible, "because happily," as he pointed out, "we do not have a million and half slaves which we hold in bondage in contradiction to humanity and the rights of man."[2]

Over the course of Guerrero's eight-month presidency (1829), his policies would collide directly with the political and economic aspirations of most Anglo settlers and their Tejano allies, but none more so than his national emancipation decree issued in September 1829. The order was more symbolic than substantive, since there were few enslaved people in Mexico by that point, yet it had profound implications for US immigrants in Texas, a growing number of whom were slaveholders. Historians have rightly pointed to the slavery debates of 1829 and 1830 as a major contributor to the souring of relations between US immigrants and Mexico and for paving the way for the immigrants' secessionist rebellion years later. Yet, what is notable about these debates is the extent to which Austin and his Mexican allies relied on Mexican institutions in their efforts to mitigate antislavery policies. Their actions not only demonstrate an enduring faith in Mexico, but they also reveal an emerging relationship between slavery and federalism that was becoming increasingly evident in both countries.

Indeed, by 1830 slaveholders from Charleston to Béxar were effectively coopting the precepts of federalism and local rule to defend their institution from their respective central governments. That aside, the debates also revealed a growing division among federalists themselves. While the more populist, nationalist federalism of Guerrero and Jackson sought to harness federal power to the interest of agrarian majorities, others, including many slaveholders, viewed federalism as a means of concentrating power in the hands of local elites. This division would plague Mexican federalism for at least the next decade and pave the way for the rise of the first centralist regime in 1830. President Anastasio Bustamante's administration advanced a very different political and economic agenda for Mexico. This, combined with his violent overthrow of Guerrero and oppressive leadership style, prompted a widespread federalist resistance and civil war that eventually found its way to the Texas borderlands.

While it is easy to interpret the 1831 Anáhuac disturbance over the centralist government's efforts to enforce land distribution and import duties as a rehearsal for the Texas rebellion several years later, it was just as much an extension of the Mexican resistance movements that began in Veracruz in early 1831. The Texans' pronunciamiento, while prompted by local grievances with the policies of the new government, echoed the demands of federalist resistance movements in other parts of Mexico. As with slavery, Texans remained committed to resolving their disputes with Mexico City through Mexican institutional channels, specifically by appealing for a return to constitutional order.

A Tale of Two Presidents

For North American politics, 1829 was an important year. At first glance, Vicente Guerrero and Andrew Jackson had little in common. One was the first Afro-indigenous president of Mexico, the other an unapologetic slaveholder noted for Native removal. Yet, both men came from and owed their presidencies to agrarian majorities and, while ostensibly federalists themselves, their presidencies redefined executive power by asserting that they, as president, embodied ultimate representative authority.[3] Even more controversially, however, both men demonstrated a willingness to wield their executive power in ways that undermined states' sovereignty. The clearest example of this in Jackson's case was the nullification crisis, in which he flatly denied South Carolina's right to ignore a federal tariff on imported goods, even threatening to force compliance by marching federal troops to Charleston.[4] For Guerrero, it came in the form of a declaration of emergency powers that he issued following Spain's 1829 attempt to reestablish control over Mexico. The invasion lasted only six weeks, and merely confirmed Mexican independence, but it supplied the president with an opportunity to pass a series of emergency executive orders that ultimately defined his presidency.

Although the two men may have shared a similar leadership style, they differed profoundly in their conception of "the people." This was due in part to their personal backgrounds and proclivities, but it also stemmed from how their respective republics defined the body politic. For Jackson, the people represented small to middling farmers, artisans, and the growing ranks of urban wage earners whose experience with the economic transformations of the early antebellum age had been ambivalent at best.[5] Jackson in his speech on vetoing legislation approving the second charter of the Bank of the United States accused the institution of being "subversive to the rights of the states" and argued that it had placed an undue burden on westerners whose debt was chiefly "to the eastern and foreign stockholders." The speech might as well have been written by Austin himself. It was a regrettable truth, according to Jackson, "that the rich and powerful too often bend the acts of government to their selfish purposes." In vetoing the bank's charter, Jackson pledged to go "against any prostitution of our government to the advancement of the few against the expense of the many."[6] Yet, Jackson's egalitarianism was premised on the very racial and gender exclusions that had characterized the United States from its birth. When he spoke of the common man besought by privilege and greed, he spoke of the common white man, whose unquestioned entitlement to land and the potential for economic prosperity often came at the expense of Natives and enslaved Americans.[7] Jackson dismissed previous treaties signed between the eastern tribes and the federal government as violations of the very state sovereignty that he had pledged to protect and insisted that the lands would remain fallow and unproductive without being blessed by the industrious hands of white American men.[8]

For Guerrero, the people *were* the settled indigenous communities of Mexico who, although part of the formal body politic, lacked an effective means of self-representation in both the imperial and postindependence eras.[9] While both Jackson and Guerrero spoke in terms of a sovereign people whose identity transcended that of the states and enjoyed a direct relationship with the executive, only Guerrero used his authority to extend rights to marginalized members of the body politic. Only a few months after taking office, the Mexican president passed a series of executive decrees, perhaps the most notable being universal emancipation.[10] Although few enslaved people remained in Mexico by that point, the decree nonetheless positioned the president as the people's liberator, in addition to their leader, and made Mexico an assertively antislavery republic. His decrees were also an assertion of federal supremacy that departed from dominant conceptions of federalism and asserted an executive privilege that offended and alarmed local elites and even many of Guerrero's federalist allies.[11]

Although Jackson and Guerrero collided with state interests during their presidencies, only Guerrero would pay with his presidency and ultimately his life. His administration would last a mere eight months after he seized the office from his more moderate rival. In the election of September 1828, state representatives, alarmed by candidate Guerrero's radicalism, which included a plan to redistribute large, landed estates to indigenous communities,[12] abandoned him and selected his less popular and more moderate rival, Manuel Gómez Pedraza. Guerrero and his supporters dismissed the election, insisting that if it had been based on individual suffrage, rather than an indirect system that left it up to the state legislatures, he would have undoubtedly won. Within a matter of days, on 16 September 1828, they launched a pronunciamiento from the town of Perote calling for the election to be annulled and for Guerrero to replace Pedraza. After a subsequent revolt in the capital unleashed several days of rioting, Pedraza resigned and fled the country.[13]

It is easy to point to the questionable circumstances surrounding Guerrero's rise to the presidency as evidence of early Mexican institutional weakness and an unfortunate precedent that the country would follow for years. Jackson, who managed to stay in office far longer, and whose election was not shrouded in the same questionable legitimacy as Guerrero's, also exploited the institutional weaknesses of his own republic. Jackson directly violated the Constitution in his decision to overrule the Supreme Court in *Worcester v. Georgia* (1832), and many believed he exceeded his authority in vetoing the national bank legislation.[14] Thus, there is perhaps a better way to understand the relative success of these two presidents.

As Lorenzo de Zavala, Guerrero's secretary of finance, saw it, Guerrero and his followers aspired to "absolute equality" and "democratic liberty."[15] While Jackson's policies may have placed limits on the relative autonomy of South Carolina's legislators, they did not threaten their property or status. Jackson never discussed private wealth redistribution, abolition, or "absolute equality." He called for a more liberal land policy to facilitate the "speedy settlement" of public lands and promised to "afford to every American citizen of enterprise the opportunity of securing an independent freehold." But his policies hinged on the dispossession of the continent's non-Anglo peoples, not the United States' own landed white population.

Thus, Mexican liberals like Miguel Ramos Arizpe, Ortíz, and even Zavala ultimately recognized in Guerrero someone whose vision threatened not only their own status, but the success of the republic in general. Many of these men, while they may have shared the long-term vision of seeing Mexican society ultimately equalized and its indigenous communities made full-fledged political and economic contributors, they did not believe that day was anywhere near.[16] Rather, they embraced an economic vision more in line with that of the Jacksonians.

Ortíz wished to free Mexico from the remnants of its colonial past by following the examples of commodity exporters like Brazil, Cuba, and the US South. While serving as Mexican consul at Bordeaux during the 1820s, he penned a series of letters to his superiors in which he insisted that Mexico should follow the "model of the United States" and that Texas was the key to doing so.[17] Terming Texas "superior to any other province of the Empire" due to its "fertility" and "abundant waters," Ortíz called for prioritizing the development of its "agriculture, industry, and commerce." Texas was not only positioned to become the "mart of the commerce of the northern section of the republic," but it also constituted the "bulwark" of Mexico's defense. Ortíz noted, "The aforesaid advantages and the proximity of this country to the United States have long encouraged in that power the desire to possess it." He also believed, however, that increased immigration, both from the United States and Europe, could help develop and secure the region.[18] Ortíz laid down his vision for Mexico's economic prosperity in *México considerado como nación independiente y libre* (1832), the treatise in which he declared agriculture "the source of life, the material base of industry, and the inexhaustible foundation of trade—together the true wealth and real force of nations."[19] Given Mexico's natural riches and ideal climate, labor force, and free trade, Ortíz believed it could become one of the most prosperous republics in the world.

Even as Mexican liberals occasionally feared encroachment by the United States, they also expressed admiration for the ingenuity of norteamericanos themselves. "What aren't these people capable of?" José María Tornel mused in 1830 from his residence in Baltimore, where he served as Mexico's minister plenipotentiary.[20] The city, then the country's third largest, was a commercial and industrial hub with impressively large markets, steam-powered factories, brightly illuminated streets and theaters, and bridges of "solidity" and "elegance." Tornel was especially impressed with the speed with which Americans were able to lay track and imagined the immense distances they would soon cover. While spending his time socializing with the city's Catholic elite, many of whom resided in mansions on tree-lined streets of "unforgiveable grace and beauty," Tornel could not resist the tendency to make unfavorable comparisons to his own country and hoped that Mexico might learn something from these "prodigies of industry."[21] Zavala wrote of New Orleans, "There is not a city in the world that has the advantage of such extensive internal navigation." He marveled at Lowell, Massachusetts, which, having been a "forest ten years ago," now stood as a symbol of industry and progress. "Nowhere does the power of hard work and liberty make one feel so forcefully its beneficial effects than in the United States," Zavala remarked.[22]

Of course, the United States was hardly a beacon of liberty. Textile mills across the northeast hummed with southern cotton, almost all of it cultivated by enslaved workers. Banks extended credit to those looking to purchase land and human beings. Steamboats and railway cars transported cotton and enslaved people from the hinterland to New Orleans, the epicenter of the new southern economy. Southern cotton enabled the United States to pay off its foreign debt and fund its formidable infrastructure projects.[23] Indeed, the United States' command of slavery, combined with expropriation of indigenous land, is precisely what allowed the American South to become the world's largest cotton-producing region, fueling the country's technological, infrastructural, and commercial transformation by the 1830s.[24] This fact was not lost on most Mexican observers. Slavery was the only significant blemish on US society that Zavala detected. While he credited the Protestants of the north for being "more active, more industrious, and wealthier than Catholics," he nonetheless noted that only Catholic churches supplied "practical examples" of the Christian belief "that all men are children of God," and only in "a Catholic church" did "the black and the white, the slave and his master, the noble and the common man kneel before the same alter, and there is a temporary unawareness of all human distinctions." Meanwhile, the Protestant churches either excluded or fenced in their enslaved congregants, "so that even in the moment [of worship] they are obliged to feel their degraded condition."[25] Yet, while Zavala nonetheless failed to acknowledge the role that slavery played in fueling the very industriousness that he admired, Ortíz seemed to have a better grasp of the source of US economic success. As Ortíz noted, Mexico's campesinos were free but poor, and the country's great challenge was how to remedy the latter without sacrificing the former.[26] Indeed, for many Mexican liberals, there existed a fundamental tension between their desire to democratize Mexican society and their desire to develop it. Many of them ultimately opposed Guerrero's land reform policies, preferring to see communal holdings redistributed to individual owners.[27]

Almost as soon as Guerrero assumed power, he developed a series of reforms designed to jumpstart Mexico's economy, none of which garnered much support from his more moderate liberal allies. These included drastic cuts in spending, high tariffs, and a requirement that states contribute 30 percent of their total revenues to the federal government. The mastermind behind Guerrero's fiscal policies was his finance secretary, Zavala. Like Ortíz, Zavala believed that agricultural development was the key to Mexican prosperity, and like many liberals, he believed that the major obstacle was the church's monopolization of land.[28] That said, many liberals objected to Guerrero's executive privilege, especially when he used the Spanish invasion to declare emergency powers in violation of the constitution. His policies seemed to violate the very essence of federalism. For Guerrero, the ultimate unit of political representation was the municipality, not the states, but even more problematic was his assertion that the responsibility of the government was to "procure the widest possible benefits and apply them from the palace of the rich to the wooden shack of the humble laborer."[29] Guerrero called for a fundamental restructuring of society, but in doing so, he declared war on his own supporters. It had been members of the propertied middle class who brought Guerrero to power, not the disenfranchised communities he aimed to liberate. This was not the case for Jackson, who enjoyed the influence of a powerful political machine able to garner the support of the largest voting constituency in the country—landless white men.

Something else separated the two presidents. Jackson was a strong proponent of US exceptionalism. While commander of the Tennessee state militia, Jackson declared, "We are the free born sons of America; the citizens of the only republic now existing in the world; and the only people on earth who possess rights, liberty, and property."[30] Jackson not only redirected US federal power in the service of disillusioned American men like Austin and others, but he went even further to insist that the United States was the only country in the world that embodied the three principles, thereby justifying his expansionist aims, especially when it came to Texas. The general had long set his sights on the Mexican province, but as Texas began to fill with US citizens, his desire to claim it intensified.[31]

"The constitution is our shield and our arms": Texas's Proslavery Defensive

Given the factors that had compelled Austin to migrate to Mexico, it is not surprising that he revealed mild pleasure in Jackson's ascendance. "I have taken no great interest in the election," he reported on 4 March 1829, "tho I have no objection to see Jackson President." For Austin, the event suggested a return to the very democracy that he and others had accused the United States of having abandoned. He wrote to a correspondent in the United States, "Your govt is founded on the popular will—and agreeably to the principles on which it is based, whatever the people will, *is right*," his choice of a possessive pronoun indicating that his affiliation with Mexico remained unswayed.[32]

Not all the colonists were as optimistic about Jackson's administration. David G. Burnet called it the weakest and most inefficient that [the US] government had ever witnessed" and accused Jackson of "deplorable incompetency." Burnet concluded his letter, however, by asserting that he took "little active interest in US politics" and, "being a Coahuiatexanian," did not "feel authorized to meddle."[33] Austin also made it clear that his future rested firmly in Texas. Having "seen this continent from Connecticut to the city of Mexico," he could boldly assert that "as a country, taken in the general average, [Texas] is unequaled to any portion of North America," and "of more intrinsic value as a country than all the states of Louisiana[,] Mississippi, Alabama and Georgia and the territories of Florida and Arkansas." Of Mexico's current political climate, Austin was perhaps less sanguine, though still optimistic: "Our govt gets on very well, *All things considered* the federal system was an experiment and a very dangerous one for Mexico."[34]

It was a surprising statement considering what Austin had been through the previous year. Guerrero's emancipation decree had caused near panic in the Anglo colonies, but with the help of his Tejano allies, Austin had been able to secure an exemption for Texas. Regardless, the circumstances surrounding Guerrero's political rise and swift downfall must have given pause to the Anglo colonists, causing them to question the political viability of their adopted republic. Admitting, as Mexican leaders themselves did, that the "former habits and ideas" of the Mexican people had likely ill prepared them for republicanism, Austin predicted that "there must be some collisions for a while," but that "good will grow out of them; for they tend to illicit discussion and diffuse knowledge."[35] Although he supported Jackson's presidency generally, there is little to suggest that Austin felt encouraged by the new president's foreign policy. Austin termed the transference of Texas to the United States the "greatest misfortune that could befall Texas" because it would throw immigrants "upon the liberality of the Congress of the United States of the North." In a letter to a fellow colonist, Austin predicted that the United States had too much "magnanimity" to attempt to extend "its already unwieldy frame over the territory of its friend and sister republic."[36] Austin's federalism was one of small government and territorial containment, whereas Jackson's was one of executive action and expansion. Even after the United States had managed to elect a president explicitly committed to remedying the problems that had compelled Austin and so many others to flee it, most of them remained committed Mexicans with little interest of returning to their country of origin. Recognizing Texas's unique environmental, geographical, and political promise, they cooperated with local and state leaders to help turn the Mexican liberal economic dream into a reality.

Yet, doing so would prove difficult in a republic with a greater commitment to antislavery than its northern neighbor. Unlike in the United States, the Mexican independence movement had included the "abolition of slavery forever" among its initial demands.[37] Even after the more radical elements of the movement had been suppressed, Mexico's founders still sought to confirm abolition at independence. This elicited considerable resistance from Austin and his Tejano allies, who insisted that slavery's protection and preservation were necessary to attract the kinds of people best suited to develop the economy of Texas. After a series of lengthy debates, Mexican liberals convinced their colleagues to adopt a program of gradual emancipation, allowing Anglo immigrants to bring their human property so long as they agreed to liberate the children of enslaved parents when they turned fourteen. This practice, enshrined in the 1823 Colonization Law, conceded slavery's inhumanity and the shared desire of Mexican leaders to see it expunged from their republic altogether, while also acknowledging its supposed economic necessity.[38]

For a time, the compromise worked. Texas became an attractive destination for US slaveholders, and not only did the Mexican government look the other way when it came to slavery in the far north, but those who arrived with additional "servants" were able to render more of Texas's land productive. The most noted early Texas slaveholder was Jared Groce, who arrived in 1822 with ninety enslaved people. Born in Virginia in 1780, Groce had lived briefly in North Carolina before arriving in Alabama.[39] The details of his life and business ventures there are unknown. Perhaps he had gone bankrupt in the panic and was forced to abandon his land, or perhaps he merely wished to try his hand in Texas. Whatever the case, Groce's bondspeople allowed him to acquire a substantial headright from the Mexican government along the lower Brazos River, where he eventually established a cotton plantation that he called San Bernardo.[40]

Emperor Augustín I's abdication brought new challenges and uncertainties for the future of slavery in Mexico. Austin hoped to dissuade the imperial congress from issuing a blanket abolition decree in an 1823 petition in which he insisted that slave labor was necessary for bringing "civilization" to Texas.[41] Forced laborers were essential for "clearing the land and establishing their farms, which these colonists could not have affected without them."[42] While Congress issued a bill banning the "commerce and traffic in slaves," Austin and his Tejano allies interpreted the new law as a prohibition on the commercial slave trade, and therefore determined that it had no impact on colonists bringing their previously bought slaves to Texas.

The debates resulting in the Constitution of 1824 represented a new phase in Mexican politics and a new opportunity for Austin and his allies. Erasmo Seguín represented Texas in the national legislature and, along with his brother Juan Seguín, were two of the most noted and powerful *bexareños*. They came from a slaveholding family and saw in the possible adoption of US-style cotton production an unprecedented opportunity for Texas to escape the poverty and destitution that had long plagued it. At one point, Juan even traveled to New Orleans to learn about the cotton trade so that he might establish his own plantation in Texas.[43] Austin would form a powerful alliance with the Seguíns and other Tejano leaders who were far more invested in developing the Texas economy than in seeing Mexico fulfill its antislavery commitments.

Erasmo distinguished himself as an ardent defender of slavery during the constitutional debates, and his efforts were apparently successful. Despite the overwhelming antislavery sentiment in Mexico, the republic's first constitution, much like its US counterpart, made no mention of the institution, allowing some to believe that it fell under the purview of state sovereignty.[44] Yet, Austin and his allies would have to work just as hard to convince legislators in Saltillo to permit slavery in Texas. Although the liberals who dominated the legislature shared the same economic aspirations for northeastern Mexico as Austin and Seguín, they also shared a commitment to abolishing slavery. Article 13 of the new state constitution declared free "all the slaves who set foot on our soil." Its author, Manuel Carrillo, had been a leader in politics for years, was a known federalist, and supported US colonization. He could not, however, stomach slavery. Neither could Dionisio Elizondo, another liberal federalist for whom Texas's economic development was less important than ensuring the "universal rights of man."[45] There were others, of course, who felt differently.

It was not long before prominent Coahuilan liberals came forward in support of Seguín and Austin's position. These included José María and Augustín Viesca, brothers from Monclava, and the state governor, Victor Blanco, who wrote a lengthy address in opposition to article 13. These men not only believed that the need for economic development should outweigh any commitment to antislavery, but they also argued that emancipationist legislation like article 13 was unconstitutional since it violated property rights. As US newspapers reported that Mexico forbade the introduction of "negro property" and subjected the "persons so offending to the severest penalties,"⁴⁶ the Tejano proslavery contingent set to work lobbying the Saltillo legislature to make an exception for Texas. Their most potent weapon was federalism.

As the state legislature entered a lengthy debate on article 13, Blanco issued an address, the opening lines of which declared, "One of the great benefits of the federal system is the right or prerogative that states have to regulate their interior governance in the manner that most conforms to their particular circumstances." He proceeded to encourage the Saltillo lawmakers to consider the unique needs of their state in determining whether to admit slavery. Noting that the issue of slavery placed at odds two of the most fundamental rights—liberty and property—his most immediate concern was depopulation of the far north. The immediate abolition of slavery throughout the state, although consistent with "philanthropic ideas," would destroy the "the population, the property, and the agriculture" of a considerable portion of the state.⁴⁷

The Mexican liberals' defense of slavery was significant for two reasons. First, it welded federalist principles to proslavery interest. In this respect, it mirrored similar trends in the United States, where by 1830 appeals to states' rights had become southern slaveholders' weapon of choice when it came to combatting federal interference with the institution. Unlike in the United States, however, defenders of slavery in Mexico acknowledged the inherent contradiction between slavery and individual liberty. Slavery was an unfortunate necessity, not an inherent right as US slaveholders would soon argue. When Blanco spoke of "property," it was unclear whether he meant human property or the property that could be rendered from slave labor. As repugnant as many antislavery Saltillo liberals found the institution, few in fact were willing to enshrine emancipation in their state constitution. Even Elizondo conceded that forcing emancipation on the Anglo colonies would "bring tremendous ills upon the entire state." He ultimately called for a system of gradual emancipation designed to purge the institution "little by little over time."⁴⁸ Ultimately, state lawmakers altered the language of article 13 to declare that all individuals born in the state were born free, but that those already enslaved would remain so for the rest of their lives. The importation of slaves would be prohibited six months after the signing of the constitution.⁴⁹

At this juncture, Austin and his associates began to consider alternative measures for getting around Mexico's antislavery strictures. One way was to admit slaves as debt peons or indentured servants.⁵⁰ The abolition of Indian slavery in the late sixteenth century had merely paved the way for other means of compulsive labor. Chattel slavery might have been technically illegal, but slaveholders could take their human property before a notary public in the United States and draft a contract stipulating that the individual wished to accompany their master to Texas. Although technically not enslaved, a bondsperson would owe their master for the value plus the cost of travel, which they would theoretically pay with their labor. For several years, debt peonage served as the answer to slaveholders' qualms.[51] In practice, it functioned like the institution they were accustomed to, while offering an appealing way to avoid the slavery issue altogether. Furthermore, it appeared to ease the concerns of prospective settlers.[52] Such contracts were clearly designed to replicate slavery, typically binding servants for ninety-nine years and, in return, obligating owners to provide their bondspeople with "good and sufficient" meals, board, medicine, and "attention in case of sickness." Yet, as General Manuel Mier y Téran, head of the Mexican Boundary Commission, noted during his 1828 tour of Texas, in practice debt peonage functioned just like slavery.

For several years, Austin and his Tejano allies skirted Mexico's antislavery strictures without technically violating them while Austin worked to assuage the concerns of prospective settlers that relocating to Mexico meant losing their right to human property. The situation would change in September 1829, when Guerrero issued his blanket emancipation decree. The event revealed the extent to which Mexican liberals in Texas were willing to go to shield the institution. Ramón Músquiz, the political chief of San Antonio, simply refused to publish the decree in defiance of the president's order. Instead, he penned a letter to Augustín Viesca, now governor of Texas, requesting that he ask for an exemption, noting that the decree was unconstitutional because it violated article 8 of the Texas colonization law which promised foreigners who settled there "*security in their persons and their property.*"[53] Numerous members of the Tejano elite expressed their support for Texas slaveholders and outrage at the federal decree, but none more so than José Antonio Padilla, former Tejano secretary of state for Coahuila y Téjas, who pledged that he would "oppose with all my strength the publication and compliance of a law so tyrannical, cruel, illegal, and monstrous."[54] Meanwhile, Viesca addressed a lengthy letter to the minister of relations reminding him of Texas's exceptional circumstances and warning him in no uncertain terms that such a law, if put into effect, would surely ruin the state. While expressing admiration for the desire to liberate all men from a state of bondage, he asked, "What is the philanthropy of liberating men whose condition will be reduced to one even more obscure and barbaric." Likely referring to Britain and the United States, neither of which had yet abolished the institution, Viesca reminded his superiors that even the "most civilized nations on the planet have not been able to destroy the institution of slavery."[55]

Significantly, Tejanos consistently cited the Constitution of 1824, specifically its right to property. In doing so, they represented an emerging liberal defense of the institution. What is perhaps more surprising, however, is Austin's position. In a letter to John Durst, the *empresario* insisted that the best recourse for the people of Texas was to "represent to the government, through the ayuntamientos or some other channel, in a very respectful manner; that agreeably to the constitution and the colonization laws *all* their property is guaranteed to them without exception." Any other course was unnecessary, unjustified, and would likely only sour relations between Texas and the state and federal government. Convinced that Mexican institutions were fully equipped to resolve the slavery question in the colonists' favor, Austin insisted, "The constitution must be both our shield, and our arms, for under *it*, and with *it* we must constitutionally defend ourselves and our property." [56] Guerrero—deeply unpopular with the country's conservative elite and facing rebellion and Congress preparing to debate his removal—buckled to the Texans' demands and decreed that those Texas slaveholders who had already obtained a property contract with Mexico could keep their slaves.[57] Austin received warm congratulations from Músquiz for an accomplishment "of such importance for this department particularly and for your colony that was in eminent danger of being ruined."[58]

Although the concerns of Texas slaveholders might have been allayed by Guerrero's amendment, the emancipation decree itself emboldened the enslaved by signaling Mexican authorities' hostility to the institution and by providing them with a critical loophole with which to achieve manumission. Records indicate that by 1830, enslaved people knew that entering Mexico changed their legal status, and at least a few of them attempted to take advantage of Mexico's complicated legislation to secure their freedom. A man named Tomás Maque petitioned on behalf of himself and several others in 1830, requesting that they be set free because they surpassed the maximum age (fifty years) that Mexican law permitted one to be enslaved. It is unclear what happened to Maque's first petition, but two years later he petitioned again, this time claiming that his former owner was deceased and, being that he was on Mexican soil, he was technically free. The courts agreed and the alcalde of Béxar declared Macque "totally free" and that he may "enjoy the rights of freedom that the state constitution provides for all Mexicans."[59] In April 1932, Peter, a fugitive from Austin's colony, escaped to San Antonio with his son. The two appealed to the alcalde there, demanding their "protection" and "claiming the laws that favor them." According to the alcalde, Peter "demanded that he and his son be declared free and that the declaration of freedom be extended to include the rest of his family that was still held by his owner."[60] What the Mexican authorities found disconcerting was the way in which Peter's owner reacted—entering San Antonio and kidnapping the men before the courts could determine their status. Músquiz, who had worked so dutifully on behalf of Texan slaveholding interests, was irate at their disregard for Mexican authority. He ordered the immediate pursuit and arrest of Peter's abductors and claimed to be scandalized by their "audacity."[61] He further stated that their crime trampled over the laws of a "hospitable country" that had "received them in her bosom" and regarded them "as adoptive sons" only to have them "return the favour by making a mockery out of the authorities."[62] Mexican leaders like Músquiz were willing to aid slaveholders, understanding what their efforts could bring to Texas, but they also expected them to remain dutiful and lawful citizens in return and to rely on Mexican institutions to address their grievances.

While some colonists tested the limits of Mexican authority, Austin and his cohorts were as committed to Mexico as ever. Whatever economic development Texas gained by admitting slavery would be in the service of Mexico as much as Texas. J. Child, who had helped Austin establish his colony, claimed that Texas was "destined to become the strongest arm of the Mexican republic" and envisioned a "military lookout post at Fort Bolívar" and a "trading establishment at the head of the navigation on the Buffalo Bayou connecting these establishments with [Austin's] town on this side." Child even echoed Ortíz in calling for the settlement of both ethnic Mexicans and immigrants from the north as well as for more "foreign immigrants of good character and small capital with industrious habits." If the Mexican government did all this, he predicted, it would in just a few years "give a spur to commerce and agriculture" by enhancing land prices and converting the "drone like apathy" over the region "into the busy drum of the beehive come May."[63]

As historians have noted, Texas's exclusive trade relationship with the United States served to draw it commercially and economically closer to that country,[64] but this was not the ultimate outcome that most US immigrants anticipated or desired. They shared Ortíz's vision of Texas becoming a kind of economic and commercial nexus of the North American hemisphere, with Galveston replacing New Orleans as the chief Caribbean port of call and steamboats traversing the Rio Grande.[65] Nothing seemed to recommend Texas to US agrarians more than its superior soil, climate, and geography, all of which were ideal for the production of cotton, sugar, and the "other productions of Louisiana and Mississippi." Texas's pasturage was "certainly superior to anything I have ever seen in any country," declared Austin, and its location and terrain meant that growers and ranchers had ready access to ports in the Caribbean, Europe, and throughout Latin America, forgetting that many of these ports, principally Galveston, remained closed. "The facilities of interior navigation are considerable and susceptible of extensive improvements," he conceded, but "no country is better adapted for the cheap construction of country roads." Texas's harbors could not admit large vessels, but they were "sufficiently cheap for brigs and the smaller class of merchant ships." Additionally, Texas appeared to be more healthful than dank, overpopulated port cities like New Orleans, and its rivers "less liable to diseases than any river of the US below latitude 36."[66]

Texas's strategic location—nestled in the northwestern corner of the Gulf of Mexico and accessible from both the interior of the United States and Mexico as well as the Caribbean— positioned it to potentially become the hub of a commercial empire that encompassed the entire northwestern hemisphere. Austin wrote to his cousin, "I have it in contemplation to open a road direct from here to Paso del Norte, and Santa Fe," with the hope of redirecting trade to the Port of Galveston. He rightly observed the centrality of Texas to any trade network linking the Mexican interior with the United States. Austin noted, "The whole trade of the Chihuahua and Sonora and New Mexico regions must ultimately enter on one of the ports of Texas."[67]

It was not just Texas's natural advantages that appealed to US immigrants. As Texans, they made no secret of their hopes of replacing the South as the leader in cotton production and trade in the Western Hemisphere. The political climate in the US North at the time suggested that they might see their dream come true. The tariff on imported manufactured goods in 1828 presented a formidable obstacle to southern trade with Great Britain, and the South's loss was Texas's gain. Furthermore, with Mexico's liberal land policy and immigrants' exemption from taxation for the first seven years after migrating, "the means of subsistence here can be raised cheaper and no capital of consequence can be required at least for several years to procure land."[68]

Texans' dreams seemed temporarily dashed, however, when Mexico passed its own tariff, designed to remedy Mexico's sizeable national debt.[69] Though intended to boost domestic cotton production and textile manufacturing, the tariff threatened to adversely impact Texans, who still relied heavily on foreign trade, namely with the United States, for most of their necessities. Austin responded by insisting that free trade was essential for Texas to be "useful and rich by way of agriculture."⁷⁰ It coexisted with and in fact facilitated Texas's integration with the rest of Mexico. Arguing that lifting restrictions on international trade "was to the greater agricultural good of the entire country," he insisted that if his request was granted, Texas would surely become a "rich and important state for the great Mexican federation."⁷¹ On 8 September 1829, Austin wrote to President Guerrero directly, requesting permission to introduce all articles for the consumption of his colony free of duty and insisting that his suggestions "emanate from an ardent desire to see my country flourish."⁷² In a separate letter to Governor Viesca, he wrote that the "roadways and canals and the navigability of the rivers will improve in proportion to the wealth and prosperity of the people and the liberty of the government of the United States [of Mexico]." Meanwhile, Mexico's efforts to regulate and tax trade were not only unnecessary, Austin pointed out, but a hindrance to the nation's own enrichment. If the central government just got out of the way, Texans alone could bring on Mexico's market revolution. Austin spoke to the aspirations of Mexican leaders when he envisioned steamboats along the Rio Grande "carrying cotton and other products to the port of Matamoros." The fact that most of Mexico's rivers were unnavigable seemed inconsequential.⁷³

In 1829 Austin took it upon himself to make the first official map of Texas, which he promptly sent to Guerrero by way of Músquiz and Zavala, claiming that he did this service "for my adopted country in allegiance as a citizen" in order "to present our beloved Texas to the Mexicans and the rest of the world." Included was a lengthy set of explanatory notes indicating the need for more customs houses, the lack of which presented a considerable problem for the "infant" colonies. In the same letter, he emphasized that "Texas rightly belongs to Mexico" due to the "naturalness of its geographic location, of its commercial interests, and its products." He anticipated a day when Texas's trade with the United States of the North would cease, stating, "The commerce of Texas will not be nor should it be, with the United States of the North," but "with the neighboring and maritime states of Mexico, and with the islands, and Europe." Austin, at least in his correspondences with Mexican officials, saw Texas's dependence on northern trade as temporary, lasting only as long as it would take for Texas to develop its own internal economies. Austin therefore requested a few more years of unimpaired trade with the United States, "so as not to impede its progress and speed its development." Indeed, he envisioned a time when all the northern trade routes would lead to Matagorda or Béxar. Ultimately, St. Louis would be replaced by Matagorda, since "one look at the map of Texas" revealed that "the distance of this port to Santa Fe in New Mexico is less than to Saint Louis." Such a reorientation of the trade network would, of course, benefit Mexico, reducing the cost of transportation by containing it "within the territory of Mexico and by Mexican citizens."[74]

Yet, if Austin wished to convince Mexican leaders of Texas's potential economic contribution under the stewardship of an industrious Anglo population and liberal trade policies, he would also have to convince the Mexicans that they would acquiesce to government policies when necessary. Austin often found himself defending legislation to immigrants who insisted that the colonization law protected them from virtually all government imposition, no matter how innocuous. When the Guerrero administration finally passed a tariff, Austin reminded his colonists that they were in fact exempt from most taxes, noting that some taxation was necessary for the functioning of any republic. When colonists complained about a local census, he privately pondered how "strange and incredible" it was that "this measure should create discontent and misrepresentation" when it promised to secure "important privileges as native born Mexicans that some day or the other may be of the greatest advantage to them." He found himself consistently having to remind colonists that the benefits of Mexican citizenship came with responsibilities. When they objected to the state vagrancy law, he wrote that "all civilized countries" had such a law and blamed "disorderly and bad men" for instigating discontent. Austin later confided to a friend that the majority of his colonists seemed unable "to discriminate between a rigid and just execution of the laws and an abuse of them," and complained that Americans seemed to foster a unique "disposition to be suspicious and jealous of 'men in power.'"[75] Conceding that such feelings were justified when "guided by an enlightened judgment," the American people were "somewhat defective" in their ability to discriminate between when such protest was appropriate and when it was not.[76]

Ultimately, the very suspicion of centralized authority that had attracted so many norteamericanos to Texas would plague Mexico's best efforts at state building in the far north. Such conflicts also revealed the increasingly tenuous hold that Mexico had on its Anglo colonies, especially as its experiment in federalism began to falter. By 1829 Mexico was moving away from the federalist promised land that had attracted so many of Austin's generation. The Guerrero regime was both more democratic but also more activist than most immigrants believed was conducive to the kind of political economy that they hoped to see take hold in Texas. Conditions in the United States had changed as well. Jackson's ascendancy signaled the United States' renewed commitment to the interests of struggling agrarians and, while the US tariff complicated relations between Jackson and many of his core constituents, Mexico's promise was no longer as certain as it had once been. It was about to become even less so.

The Revolution of Jalapa and the Rise of Mexican Centralism

On 4 December 1829, Anastasio Bustamante, Guerrero's vice president and former commander general of the eastern interior provinces, issued the Plan de Jalapa from the barracks where he was overseeing a special army reserve unit in the aftermath of the Spanish invasion earlier in the year.[77] The plan never mentioned Guerrero by name, but its demand to remove "those public officials against whom public opinion had been expressed" was broadly understood to reference the president, whose decision to declare emergency powers and use them to pass a series of radical reforms, such as the federal emancipation decree and direct tax on income, had alienated the Mexican propertied class, conservative and liberal, alike. According to one anonymous note to the president, "The pronuncios continue to cry Long Live Centralism" and "Death to the Negro Guerrero!"[78] The plan itself accused Guerrero's regime of imposing "despotism" and creating "anarchy" and of having produced "general discontent in its failure to observe the law, in its administrative abuses, and in its loss of public confidence."[79] Indeed, opposition to Guerrero's emergency powers had arisen almost as soon as he declared them. Opponents insisted that they were in "direct opposition to the federative form of government" and state sovereignty.[80] Yet, while the rebels promised to "sustain the federal pact, respect the sovereignty of the states and conserve their indissoluble union," historians agree that the first two aims were insincere. The Plan de Jalapa ushered in Mexico's first centralist regime, led by Bustamante but largely overseen by Lucas Alamán.

Alamán had distinguished himself as an outspoken critic of state sovereignty as early as the constitutional debates of 1823 and 1824.[81] He was not only one of the first to declare that Mexican sovereignty ultimately rested in the nation, but he also warned of the danger of anarchy under an alternative system that failed to privilege a central power. Unlike many of his federalist counterparts, Alamán viewed centralism as a means of preventing despotism. "A firm union will be of the utmost moment to the peace and liberty of the states as a barrier against domestic faction and insurrection."[82] He fervently disagreed with the federalist argument that the Mexican republic effectively had no center, that it had dissolved in the political vacuum created first by the French invasion of Spain in 1808 and later by independence, and that sovereignty rested primarily in the provinces now becoming states. To this, he quipped that every government, "whatever its form" needed a center. How else could it ensure territorial defense, pay off the national debt, or conduct foreign relations? Rather than federalism, which he considered a foreign import, Alamán believed that Mexico needed a system more akin to that of Britain's Parliament. While still very much a supporter of the republic, he echoed Simón Bolívar's view that the people of Spanish America were far less prepared for self-governance than those of the United States and therefore required a very different form of government. Bolívar himself had called for a parliamentary system, replete with a hereditary senate. Alamán was less specific, but what is clear is that he adamantly disagreed with the radical federalist demand for universal suffrage and insisted that voting should be restricted to property owners.[83]

Alamán also advocated a very different economic path for Mexico. Born to a Guanajuato mining family, and having lived in Europe during Mexico's independence movement, he had served as Ortíz's superior during his years of foreign service and was the recipient of many of the correspondences in which Ortíz explained his agrarian vision for Mexico's future. Alamán, however, disagreed with his subordinate. An admirer of colonial institutions and eager to make the republic economically self-sufficient, he believed that the answer to Mexico's economic challenges was to promote industry. Industrialized manufacturing, Alamán thought, held the key to Mexico's most pressing problems, with the potential to draw its various indigenous communities into a national market economy, reduce its dependence on foreign manufacturers and contraband, increase its standard of living, and fuel domestic wealth accumulation. "To be rich and happy," he wrote, "the republic must have manufacturing, for without it her agriculture will remain reduced to a state of languor and poverty." Mexico's riches would pass to foreign ports, demonstrating "that the wealth does not belong to the peoples to whom nature conceded it."[84] Perhaps the primary benefit of an industrialized economy was its ability to integrate Mexico's vast territory and otherwise disparate population. If Mexican liberals fostered a Jeffersonian vision for their republic's future, then Alamán's was indisputable Hamiltonian. Likely aware of the first treasury secretary's report on manufacturers,[85] Alamán echoed the opinion that a strong manufacturing sector, even if regionally concentrated, provided the foundation for a strong agricultural sector, not the other way around. Manufacturers in one part of the country could supply rural populations in another with goods and, in turn, create a consumer base for agrarian products. In addition, manufacturing could supply the capital needed for large-scale national infrastructure and defense projects, something that Mexico sorely needed, especially in light of the recent Spanish invasion.

Much of Alamán's political views, however, were premised on the belief that

Mexico lacked, above all, a discernable national identity. The country's problem was not simply that of a failed state, but of a failed nation.[86] Federalism, which he considered a foreign import, weakened and divided Mexico by elevating local interests and concerns and antagonizing Hispanic colonial institutions like the church, which, Alamán believed, was the lodestar of Mexican identity. Undoubtedly fueling many of his concerns were the correspondences and reports of the Mexican Boundary Commission, tasked with surveying Texas's border with the United States. The commission—which arrived in Texas in 1828 and was headed by General Mier y Terán, who was also an esteemed Mexico City engineer—expressed alarm at the rapidly growing US population in Texas, many of whose members were squatting illegally along the border, skirting Mexican antislavery laws, and failing to pay customs duties. What the commissioners encountered in Texas did not leave them with much confidence that the border region could withstand territorial encroachment by the United States or any foreign power. Terán's co-commissioner, Jean-Louis Berlandier, noted that the military garrisons were sorely underfunded, and that Béxar resembled a "large village more than the municipal seat of a department" with "no paved street and no public building."[87] Lastly, the Tejano population, whom he called "wretched," were plagued by poverty, illiteracy, and laziness.[88] José María Sánchez, a military officer who accompanied Terán, had a similar impression of the region's Mexican inhabitants. Shocked at their ignorance, he noted that they seemed unaware "not only of the customs of our cities, but even of the occurrences of our revolution." Continued trade with the United States had led to the adoption of certain habits that rendered the inhabitants "not Mexicans except by birth, for they even speak Spanish with marked incorrectness."[89]

What most concerned the commissioners, however, was the rapidly growing size of the Anglo-American population, who "immigrate constantly, finding no one to prevent them," and who now occupied "practically all the eastern part Texas." Sánchez reported that with Mexico's weak administrative presence in the region, there was no one to stop these new arrivals from simply squatting wherever it suited them, "without either asking leave or going through any formality other than that of building their homes." Indeed, by the time of the commission's tour, Anglo colonists outnumbered Hispanic residents, almost three to one, and their number would continue to grow substantially over the next few years. Meanwhile, according to Sánchez, the Mexican population had been "reduced" to a few "wretched settlements," mostly in Bejar, Nacogdoches, and La Bahia de Espiritu Santo."[90] Terán feared that the inadequacies of the Tejanos might be just as evident to the Anglo settlers as they were to him, contributing to the Americans' lack of respect for Mexico as a whole. "I must disturb you in the same way I was disturbed to see the foreign colonists' attitude towards our nation," Terán wrote to Guerrero, informing him that "with the exception of a few who have travelled to our capital," most of the Anglo-Texans seemed to think that Mexico consisted of "nothing more than blacks and Indians, all of them ignorant." He even noted, "In some homes, where they have done me the favor of considering me an educated man, they have told me to my face that it could not be so unless I were French or Spanish."[91] It was not just that the situation in Texas did not bode well for Mexico's economy, but that it did not bode well for the state of Mexican nationality. The commissioners encountered men and women whom they did not recognize as Mexican, with whom they seemed to share little in common, and who lived among the former citizens of a republic with clear territorial ambitions of its own.

Terán cited one important exception to the colonists' general ignorance of their adopted country, noting that his observations "should not be understood as applying to the colony of Don Estében Austin, the only one where they try to understand and obey the laws of the country" and where "they have a notion of our republic and its government."[92] It was in Austin's colony that Terán claimed he and other commissioners were greeted by a woman and her daughter who "spoke Spanish well enough to be understood in conversation."[93] Berlandier reported, "The colony of San Felipe de Austin is the most remarkable and the richest in Texas." Like their Tejano neighbors, the Anglo residents of Austin's colony "had not as yet taken any part in the troubles which had agitated the country," and the commissioner proudly recalled how they had "banded together with Mexican troops and marched jointly to Nacogdoches to reestablish tranquility there" during the 1826/27 Fredonian rebellion, led by Haden Edwards.[94]

Not all the commissioners had the same impression of San Felipe de Austin or its empresario. Sánchez claimed that Austin, through his diplomatic actions, had "lulled the [Mexican] authorities into a sense of security," while working "diligently for his own ends." He described a brief stop at the home of Jared Groce, then the largest slave owner in Texas, who, despite his considerable wealth and comfortable home, did not offer them much hospitality and did not appear to speak any Spanish. "Perhaps [the Mexican government] does not realize the value of what it is about to lose," Sánchez warned, noting that if things did not change promptly, Texas would become "the prize of the ambitious North Americans."[95]

Yet, as Terán acknowledged, his country seemed to face a quandary. He and other leaders wanted to see Mexico's frontier settled and developed in a way that only norteamericanos seemed capable of doing. Most Mexicans, at least as far as he could tell, seemed loath to become farmers. "More than a century after it was colonized the region remains static," Berlandier noted, predicting, "it will never be covered with fields except in more active and hard-working hands."[96] And no matter how much credit Terán seemed willing to give Anglo settlers for their contribution, he simply could not take their allegiance to Mexico seriously. "If it is bad for a nation to have vacant lands and wilderness, it is worse without a doubt to have settlers who cannot abide by some of its laws and by the restrictions that [the nation] must place on commerce. They soon become discontented and thus prone to rebellion," he wrote. "Everything becomes graver still if those people have strong and indissoluble connections with a neighboring government."[97]

In a letter to the war department, Terán warned that Americans exercised a peculiar and inconspicuous form of imperialism that, if not checked, would "pull down" the entire Mexican federation. "The department of Texas is contiguous to the most avid nation in the world," he wrote. "The North Americans have conquered whatever territory adjoins them. In less than half a century they have become masters of extensive colonies which formerly belonged to Spain and France and of even more spacious territories from which have disappeared the former owners, the Indian tribes." Their ability to do so rested precisely on what he termed their "silent means"—the practice of settling sparsely populated regions belonging to other powers, and paving the way for eventual acquisition by their own state. "Instead of armies, battles, or invasions—which make a great noise and for the most part are unsuccessful—these men lay hand on means that, if considered one by one would be rejected as slow, ineffective, and at times, palpably absurd." Yet without a doubt, they were effective. Beginning with "adventurers and empresarios," who "take up their residence in the country, pretending that their location has no bearing upon the question of the government's claim," they then develop an "interest which complicates the political administration of the coveted territory; complaints, even threats, begin to be heard, working on the loyalty of the legitimate settlers, discrediting the efficiency of the existing authority and administration." This was precisely the stage at which Texas now found itself, and Terán warned that it would soon be followed by "diplomatic maneuvers." He concluded his letter by remarking that the population of Texas represented a "mixture of such strange and incoherent elements that no other like it exists in our entire federation." The foreigners were composed of "all kinds: fugitive criminals, honorable farmers, vagabonds, and ne'er do wells, laborers, etc." who "all go about with their constitution in their pocket, demanding their rights, and the authorities and functionaries that it provides."[98]

Not surprisingly, Texas became one of Alamán's first items of concern following his appointment as minister of interior and exterior relations under Bustamante. Alamán informed Congress on 8 February 1830 of his intention to reject the Jackson administration's offer to purchase Texas, citing all the ways in which the colonists had violated the laws and regulations laid down by the Mexican government. In terms reminiscent of Terán, he repeated the observation that "the United States has successively taken control, without attracting public attention, of everything that borders them" and thereby "come to be owners of extensive settlements belonging to various European powers and of even larger areas [once] possessed by Indian tribes."[99] Insisting that the province of Texas "now hardly belongs, in fact, to the Mexican confederacy,"[100] the minister encouraged Congress to consider the "urgency of taking prompt steps to prevent the shameful loss" of the territory. The result was the law passed on 6 April 1830, to strengthen the federal presence along the US-Mexican border. It placed a temporary prohibition on emigrants "from nations bordering on this republic" and settling "in the states or territory adjacent to their own nation." Perhaps most significantly, it ordered the government of every Mexican state to "strictly enforce" the federal colonization law and "prevent the further introduction of slaves."[101] Although the so-called Law of April 6 clearly targeted Texas, it was part of the regime's general efforts, spearheaded by Alamán, to centralize, integrate, and modernize Mexican economy and society. Many of Alamán's policies echoed those of his nationalist counterparts in the United States. His efforts to establish Mexico's first national bank, the Banco de Avío were likely inspired by Hamilton,[102] and his calls for a "proto-medical" council to establish hygiene and sanitation standards and for a "scientific establishment" dedicated to the study of Mexican "antiquity, industry, natural history, and botany" reflects the reformist and nationalizing efforts of John Quincy Adams.[103] Furthermore, Alamán was not alone in his perceived need for greater integration of the far north.

Ortíz, in correspondences with his superior, had called for a "more centralized, vigorous, and general power which can count upon greater coercive strength along with other wholesome improvements." Such control would enable "an orderly and progressive colonization system" that could direct "governmental and economic affairs through the intervention of local, political authorities that are independent of the states." Ortíz called for a stronger federal presence in the far north that could transcend state sovereignty and exercise direct authority over settlers. The "Mexican nation," he insisted, was "in a position to dominate the world," but it needed a "regular administration, the increase of its population, and the encouragement of elementary education, agriculture, industry and commerce to fulfill its destiny." Mexico had to find a means to strengthen the ties between citizen and state, especially among its settlers. Ortíz called for federal administrators to be sent into Texas with the task of administering land sales and supplying medical aid as well as the "necessary utensils for domestic and farming use." In return for these services and to "bind" settlers to the republic, the government would "cede to them its ownership, a fifth part of the land which they colonize by their own effort." Such an arrangement stood to benefit settlers by supplying them with the services and supplies necessary to establish themselves, and they would repay Mexico by helping to defend its borders against Indian and foreign incursion. Alamán and Ortíz may have held different visions when it came to Mexico's economic future, but they agreed on the need for a stronger central government, capable of integrating and governing its most vulnerable border territories.[104] For Alamán, however, these debates were not just about sparing Mexico from economic disaster or political anarchy. Indeed, he thought it faced an existential threat. In discarding Spanish rule, Mexicans had too swiftly shed their Hispanic identity—the only thing capable of uniting them, especially in the face of an increasingly aggressive United States. In his view, this rejection of the imperial institutional framework—the attacks on the church, the Spanish expulsion, etc.—constituted an attack on the most desirable and worthy traits of *mejicanidad*. Mexico was not just failing as a state, Alamán believed, Mexicans were failing as a people.[105]

There is little to suggest that the Anglo colonists interpreted the Law of April 6 as part of a larger effort to integrate and develop the Mexican economy. Instead, most interpreted it, and the Bustamante regime's policies generally, as an affront to their independence and a threat to their regional economy. Following the law's passage, and for the first time since the colony's establishment, Austin seemed to genuinely despair over its future, especially when officials in northeastern Mexico became far less willing to plead his case than they had been under Guerrero. Músquiz informed Austin bluntly that it was simply impossible, under the current state of political affairs, to do "anything to counteract the proposed law." Austin, afraid that the new law would sabotage his recruitment efforts, took matters into his own hands. In a letter to Bustamante, he warned that the object of the law "appears to be the complete destruction of all happiness and prosperity of this colony" and insisted that it was in violation of the preexisting colonization laws of the republic and the state of Coahuila y Téjas "which in direct and positive terms call for and encourage immigration."[106]

In a separate letter to Alamán, Austin sought to remind him that "it is doubtless well known to Y.E. that I am the first empresario who undertook to form a settlement in the wilderness of Texas" and that he had "succeeded fully" in redeeming a "considerable portion" of it from a "state of nature overrun by savages." Austin reiterated that his "maxim has always been and now is fidelity and gratitude to Mexico" and expressed confusion at the increasing sense of suspicion toward Anglo settlements, asserting that "the commercial and agricultural interests of Texas, will be more effectively promoted by remaining under this government than under any other." The colonists had been "faithful to this government since they entered this territory," he claimed, and wished "to remain Mexicans." The Law of April 6, however, would render those already on their way to Mexico "totally ruined" and create an "odium" that "would of necessity fall on the government that caused their ruin." Austin concluded by assuring Alamán that the immigrants he allowed to enter were "of the very best class" and that the "acquisition of that population would do more towards uniting Texas to Mexico and restoring order and tranquility than any measure that could be adopted."[107]

In Austin's letters to Mexican officials, he blamed Jackson's minister to Mexico, Joel Poinsett, for Mexican confusion and hostility and did what he could to distance himself from the intrigues of the Jackson cabinet. The empresario hardly minced words in his accusations. "For my part . . . I do not believe that it is in the interest of [T]exas to unite with the north."[108] His appeals were evidently successful. The government decided to lift the ban on future immigration to Austin's colony only. It continued to require, however, that all US traders pay 1 percent of their profits to the government.[109] In the summer of 1830, Austin and fellow colonist Samuel May Williams founded the *Mexican Citizen*. For the newspaper's motto, they chose "Mexico es mi patria" (Mexico is my country). The purpose, according to Austin, was to send the message "to people abroad 'we have a country and are proud of it, and we are ready and willing to defend her rights.'"[110]

By the beginning of 1831, it seemed that Anglo-Texan leaders had finally quelled the Bustamante regime's concerns. In fact, the kerfuffle over the April law ultimately did little to suppress immigration to Mexico from the United States, which jumped from approximately one thousand annually to around three thousand. A temporary lifting of the immigration restriction might have had something to do with this, or the decision to continue to allow only certain colonies, such as Austin's, to admit immigrants may have encouraged prospective immigrants to take advantage of such leniencies while they existed, perhaps fearing that they would disappear in the future.[111] Meanwhile, General Terán diligently set to work carrying out his new orders from Mexico City. He established military forts at Nacogdoches, Béxar and San Felipe, and one at the mouth of the Brazos that he called Velasco. He assigned Colonel David Bradburn, an immigrant from Kentucky, as overseer. Terán also established custom houses at Matamoros and Galveston, where he appointed George Fisher, another US immigrant, as officer. As the seven years during which immigrants were exempt from taxation began to expire, Terán ordered the collection of taxes on virtually all goods from the north.[112] By the start of 1831, Texans appeared to have developed a comfortable alliance with the new Mexican regime that largely complemented liberal aims for the development and integration of the region. While Alamán and other centralists undoubtedly remained wary, they could not deny the economic benefits that Anglo colonization had brought to the region and could potentially benefit Mexico as a whole. Yet, almost as soon as the new administration had implemented its policies, rebellion and political instability would strike again, and Texans would find themselves directly confronted by the fray of Mexico's political turmoil.

"Long live the republic, the constitution, and laws!": Mexico's First Civil War Comes to Texas

The Bustamante regime's economic policies were largely successful, managing to boost federal revenue and taking the first significant strides toward integrating the far north. Politically, however, his presidency was a disaster. While the administration never attempted to overthrow the Constitution of 1824 and justified its actions as necessary for the "reestablishment of constitutional order," its policies were widely understood to target federalism, centralize power under the new regime, and undermine democracy since they also targeted popularly supported legislatures and governors and sought to replace them with members of the upper class or, as they came to be known in Mexican political discourse, *hombres de bien*.[113] The assault was matched by an effort to drive the new administration's supporters from the country, crack down on the federalist press, and suppress the civic militias. According to at least one scholar, it constituted the "most extreme organized campaign of government persecution of political opponents since independence."[114] Unsurprisingly, it prompted a series of revolts, the most significant of which emerged in the south under the leadership of Guerrero, who bolstered his campaign with frequent appeals to the sovereignty of the people, specifically Mexico's rural majority, in ways that alarmed Mexican elites, both liberal and conservative.

In January 1832, Colonel Pedro Landero issued the Plan de Veracruz. Claiming to be motivated by a desire to chart a moderate course "between the two extremes," the Landero and his fellow authors affirmed their support for the constitution, called for the removal of those ministers "whom public opinion accuses of protecting centralism and tolerating the attacks committed against civil liberty and individual rights," and requested that General Antonio López de Santa Anna accept leadership of the pronunciamiento.[115] Santa Anna had been an outspoken federalist since the constitutional debates a decade earlier. Over the course of the following months, other Mexican states declared their support for Santa Anna as well, thereby launching what historians consider Mexico's first civil war. It was a particularly sanguinary struggle that reached nearly every corner of the republic.

In Texas, the conflict was manifested, not in bloodshed but in a series of disputes between federal and state agents over land claims and customs policy. In response to complaints from a group of colonists residing near Galveston Bay for a number of years without receiving formal land grants, the state of Coahuila y Téjas decided in March 1831 to appoint a land commissioner named Francisco Madero to meet with the colonists, survey their land, and issue them legal title.[116] When Terán, now commanding general of the Eastern Interior Provinces, caught wind of Madero's arrival in eastern Texas, he ordered Colonel Bradburn to arrest him for violating the federal decree. Madero, however, insisted that Bradburn worked for the state of Coahuila y Téjas and was therefore his subordinate, not Terán's.[117] It was a classic dispute between federal and state authorities that would simmer until it reached a boiling point in late 1831. Shortly after establishing a new customs house at Anáhuac, Bradburn demanded that all ships clear their papers there before departing. This required Brazos shippers to travel for several days to clear their passage before returning to their departure point at Velasco.[118]

In an angry letter to Bradburn in December, Austin called such regulations "utterly impracticable" and their execution practically impossible. "*You* know your native countrymen," he continued "and you also know that at this time the people have just causes and very many of them to complain." Austin warned that unless a more liberal system were adopted, "the country will be totally broken up and all commerce totally annihilated." Bradburn passed Austin's letter on to Terán, recommending that "the whole country lying within ten leagues of the coast" be placed "under martial law." If local authorities resisted, they would face "exemplary punishment."[119] The situation came to a head when the schooner *Sabine* attempted to run the blockade at Velasco, its captain having been unsuccessful in attempting to bribe a Mexican officer to allow his ship to pass without the necessary paperwork. The event prompted a brief skirmish and the arrest of the captain. Although the garrison commander soon complied with public demands to release him, those involved in the skirmish convened a public meeting the following day that culminated in raising funds for gunpowder and lead to send to Anahuac along with a group of men prepared to confront Bradburn.[120]

Terán was incensed when he heard the news of the simmering rebellion. "You want the government to adopt a more liberal policy, you should say what liberality you long for beyond that which you already receive," the general asserted in a reply to Austin, who, although denouncing the actions of the rebels, nonetheless echoed their complaints about the unreasonableness of Bradburn's actions. The collection of customs duties was a fair and nearly universal practice in the Americas, Terán insisted, adding, "Only in Brazoria is it believed that there is a reason for rebellion."[121] Not only did Terán refuse to alter the established policy or discipline Bradburn, but also dispatched Colonel Domingo Ugartechea and more than one hundred troops to reinforce Velasco.[122]

In mid-June, news of a federalist resurgence in the interior reached Texas. A pronunciamiento dated 27 April 1832 from Ignacio Inclán, commanding general of the Department of Mexico, had demanded a restoration of "constitutional order" and the reinstatement of Gómez Pedraza as the last constitutionally elected president. A wave of similar declarations followed, all of them notably moderate in their demands for a restoration of "order and tranquility."[123] Inclán's Plan de Lerma infused the federalist resistance with a renewed energy and inspired a series of similar calls that swept the republic. That spring, the Anahuac rebels attached their cause to the renewed federalist resistance. On June 13, the rebels held a meeting at Turtle Bayou, during which they drew up a seven-point plan that resembled the Lerma pronunciamiento in both tone and content. They expressed their "deepest regret" at the manner in which the "present dynasty" had determined to govern the republic with "repeated violations of the constitution." One week later, the citizens of Brazoria held a meeting in which they resolved "to place ourselves in the ranks of the supporters of the constitution," asserting that the present regime had "evinced a total disregard of the constitution of the country," "for the law," and an "entire prostration of the civil authority." They declared their support for the "highly talented and distinguished chieftain, Santa Anna" and his "manly resistance" to the current administration's "numberless encroachments . . . upon the constitution and laws of our adopted and beloved country" and pledged their "lives and fortunes" in support of his resistance.[124] The one-hundred-fifty strong then proceeded on to Velasco, where they anticipated a confrontation with federal authorities.[125] As tensions escalated, Williams implored citizens to appeal to Mexico City rather than take up arms. He and other more established colonists aimed to remain above the fray of Mexico's simmering conflict and counseled unconditional fealty to Mexico. Just as they had done for the Fredonian rebellion, Williams and Horatio Christman called on the local militia to help Mexican troops suppress their "poor, misguided fellow citizens" and ward off the evil "that threatens not only those who are unfortunately in arms, but ourselves because if the government be convinced that we are all in rebellion, by harvest time the colony will be filled with troops." Williams reminded colonists of the "sacrifices, bounties and benefits" of a government "that admitted and encouraged your settlement." Yet he also appealed to a shared sense of solidarity among the Anglo colonists. "Are you ready and willing to permit that your countryman, your friends, your kindred, and your brothers shall hurl defiance at that government, and destruction on your families." He encouraged loyal colonists to "unite as one man" and cause the rebels "to return to their home and to their duties."[126]

Yet, much of the federalist resistance, including that of the Texans, was fueled by an emerging ideology that separated nation and government. They accused Bradburn of having violated the rights "which we, as citizens of the Mexican republic, have considered as the rule of our civil conduct."[127] Furthermore, they framed their actions as an extension of the Mexican civil war, not a remote rebellion by a group of foreigners. Ugartechea reported that the rebels had indicated that their rebellion was in support of Santa Anna and his Plan of Veracruz and that they cried "'Long live the republic, the constitution, and laws! Long live the supreme government!'"[128]

Indeed, the rebels had consistently framed their demands in terms of defending Mexican federalism, but for representatives of the Bustamante regime and indeed for many of the more established members of the Anglo immigrant community, the rebellion represented something more ominous. At the very least, it suggested the conditionality of Anglo settlers' commitment to Mexico. What if the Constitution of 1824 was replaced by a system more assertively in line with centralist aims? What would that mean for Texas and its relationship with Mexico City? More importantly, what would it mean for this increasingly restive population of colonists that Austin and his allies now struggled to contain?

While the rate of immigration to Mexico increased after 1830, the very political system that had attracted US settlers to Mexico now seemed less secure, and even members of Austin's inner circle expressed less of the optimism that he had only eight years earlier. "I was not deceived in the country," wrote James Perry, Austin's brother-in-law and recent arrival to Texas, calling Texas "the garden of all North America" and predicting, "If full reliance could be placed in the stability of the government and permission for emigrants to settle here[,] it would soon be one of the most pleasing parts of the world."[129] Even as Mexican federalism appeared far less certain, however, members of Austin's generation expressed none of the concurrent Jacksonian interest in joining the United States. "They speak here of this matter [Texas's annexation] as one which in no wise concerns the present population [of Texas]," Ira Ingram, a member of Austin's colony, reported during a business trip to New Orleans, "and in fact, as though those now in peaceful occupation of the country, have neither rights nor impartialities to be invaded or consulted." Instead, the Jackson administration viewed Texans "like sheep and oxen, perfectly passive." Ingram went on to criticize the Jackson administration for its "national vanity," for viewing Texans "in no other light than a degraded species of property." Texans themselves "viewed the subject in a very different light."[130]

By the late summer of 1832, the complex and uncertain future of Texas politics was on full display at a public dinner in Matagorda. In a series of toasts, attendees both acknowledged Mexico's political instability and expressed hope for its peaceful resolution: "The republic of Mexico—Tho' not *first*, may she be the *last*, in the constellation of republics, in the new world," and "If there be a part where the *institutions* have made the men—there is another portion where the men have *yet* to *make* the institutions." Some toasted Texas's imminent admission into the Mexican union as a state, and some lifted their glasses "to the internal-improvement-fever of the *north*," expressing their hope that it might "cross the Sabine in a steamboat, . . . travel on a railroad to the waters of the Colorado," and "sweep the raft into the Bay of Matagorda." Others toasted to Santa Anna and to "The constitution of Mexico, and sovereignty of the states." Ingram wrapped up the exhaustive succession of toasts by honoring the settlers of Texas, who "have expelled the savage, subdued and planted the forest" so that "the enemies of their country, may read their future history."[131]

Yet, at that time, that future history was perhaps less certain than it had been eight years earlier. If one thing was clear by 1832, it is that Mexico was no longer the federalist promised land that had greeted US immigrants in 1824. Even if Anglo-Texans continued to declare fealty to Mexico and its constitution, leaders in Mexico City could not help but suspect that, if anything, their fealty was conditional. As norteamericanos and their human property filled the far northern province, Mexican leaders of varying political persuasions looked upon them with growing suspicion. By 1832 Texas was Mexico's promise and its peril. Its Anglo population seemed uniquely capable of enriching and developing its hereunto latent agricultural economy, but many wondered at what cost. This was undoubtedly the concern of Mexico City officials like Azcarate, who believed that the price of US colonization outweighed its benefits. Instead of welcoming these foreigners, Azcarate ironically suggested that Mexico take its nationalizing efforts even further than Alamán and his supporters had attempted. Mexico should construct an "antemural," a wall, along its northern border "to forever defend its national territory."[132]

CHAPTER FOUR

Anti-national and Contemptible Intrigues

In 1833 Ramón Músquiz, political chief of the Department of Texas, was nervous. The Mexican civil war continued to rage, but what concerned him ostensibly had little to do with Texas or Mexico. Thirteen hundred miles to the northeast, in South Carolina, a legislature controlled by slaveholders was attempting to nullify a federal tariff on imported goods. The event would prompt debates on sovereignty and federal authority in the United States in the decades leading up to the secession of eleven southern states from the Union. Músquiz believed that it could have implications for Mexico as well. The case for nullification was based on a compact theory that denied the Union's permanency, and if the southern states seceded over this or any other disagreement they might have with the federal government, Músquiz predicted, they were apt to pursue the "acquisition of Texas" to enlarge their territory and "gain greater wealth."[1] Músquiz was not alone in being worried. That same year, Tadeo Ortíz, in his capacity as commissioner of the Eastern Internal Provinces, reminded his superiors in Mexico City that most of the colonists in Texas were "natives of southern states" who "tend to divide the Anglo-American confederation." Their "anti-national and contemptible intrigues" threatened to do the same to Mexico.[2]

By 1833 Mexicans of all political persuasions were looking warily toward Texas, its Anglo settler population, and the system of government that had attracted them. Many, even some former federalists, were beginning to complain that the Constitution of 1824 was hindering their country's development and security. Perhaps the best evidence of the extent of the disillusionment with federalism was that Antonio López de Santa Anna himself would end up leading the centralist movement. The new regime's efforts to dramatically curtail state sovereignty, however, prompted a series of rebellions from peripheral states, of which Texas was just one.

Indeed, the Texas rebellion (1835–1836), would begin as a Mexican story and end as a southern one. It commenced, as so many contemporaneous Mexican federalist rebellions did, with a commitment to defend and uphold the 1824 constitution, but unlike the other movements, Texas was planned, supplied, and funded by moneyed interests in New Orleans. In many ways this made sense. The city had long been a center of republican agitation and had functioned as a home for numerous federalist exiles from Mexico. By the 1830s, it had also become the commercial center of a burgeoning regional cotton economy whose leaders were far less eager to see federalism return to Mexico than to see Texas breakaway from Mexico and join the United States as part of its rapidly expanding cotton empire. For the Texan rebels and their supporters in the United States, the rebellion represented a group of brave Americans fighting a war of independence against an oppressive tyrant, but for Mexican leaders, the rebellion represented a violation of national sovereignty, federal supremacy, and majoritarian democracy, not unlike the nullification effort in South Carolina.

Southern Radicalism and the Spector of Secession

Before secession came to Texas, it looked more likely to occur in the United States. As Mexicans began to recognize the dangers of unchecked federalism, defenders of slavery in the southern United States were seizing on it as the best means of protecting their institution from a national government that appeared increasingly committed to the precepts of majoritarian democracy. As the franchise extended among non-landholding white men during the antebellum period, slaveholders, who remained in the minority, began to fear what the consequences would mean for them.[3] They responded by attempting to consolidate power at the state level as the best means of shielding the institution of slavery from potential federal intervention. On its surface, the theory of states' rights appeared to build on a republican heritage, but as scholars of nullification have observed, adherents did not aim to use it as a vehicle for the expression of popular will so much as a means of concentrating representative power in the hands of local elites.[4] In this, they demonstrated the same antidemocratic impulses as

President Vicente Guerrero's federalist opponents. By the time of the nullification crisis, leaders in South Carolina had largely accomplished their aims by attaching stringent property requirements for office holding to guarantee that the state's slaveholding minority retained control of its legislature. In doing so, nullifiers adapted the more democratic precepts of localism that had characterized the republic for half a century and harnessed them to slavery's defense. That said, they did in fact draw on a specific thread of elite anti-federalism that viewed state governments as the best guarantors of individual rights, and they less often positioned themselves as counterpoints to the will of state majorities than as the only suitable leaders of those majorities.[5] They recalled the anti-centralism of men like James Madison and Thomas Jefferson, who themselves had employed nullification as a means of checking the John Adams administration's policies. Never mind that no constitutional amendment had been violated by the tariff and that nullification of it, unlike the attempted nullification of the Alien and Sedition Acts, benefited only one section of the country.[6] What most distinguished the nullifiers of the 1830s from those of a generation earlier, was their insistence that the federal government was a creature of the states, and the Union little more than a compact among them.[7]

This was the constitutional theory advanced by John C. Calhoun, who led the Palmetto State's nullification efforts in 1832. In the pamphlet *Exposition and Protest* (1828) Calhoun attacked the decision by Congress to impose a tariff on imports as "unconstitutional, unequal, and oppressive" to the South. The pamphlet was more than a protest, however. Its most important contribution was the way in which its author laid out his theory of dual sovereignty. Calhoun argued that unchecked majority rule inevitably led to anarchy, for which the only effective remedy was sovereignty of the states. Calhoun echoed Madison's claim that the US government consisted "of two distinct and independent governments"—the federal and state governments—each with its own "sole and separate powers." Where he departed from Madison's dual sovereignty thesis, however, was in his insistence that sovereignty resided ultimately "in the people of the states." This made the federal government a creature and instrument of the states alone and effectively denied the existence of a sovereign American people.[8] Calhoun never published the pamphlet, though he did circulate it among his allies, ensuring that his ideas permeated the southern political establishment.

Three years later, in a speech at Fort Hill, the senator's views on the relation between state and federal power found a public audience. Positioning his theories within the long tradition of republicanism, Calhoun began by asserting, "The question of the relation which the states and general government bear to each other is not one of recent origin." Repeating his claim that the "general government emanated from the people of the several states, forming distinct political communities," and not from "all of the people forming one aggregate political community," he then went on to insist, "The Constitution of the United States is, in fact, a compact, to which each state is a party." This, Calhoun asserted, was "the fundamental principle of our system" and "the only solid foundation" of the Union. It was, therefore, a "great error" to assume that the right of the majority to govern was "absolute and unlimited." The majority had no more right to rule over the minority than the minority a right to rule over the majority. This, Calhoun said, had been the intent of the Constitution's framers, who recognized "that such separate and dissimilar geographical interests" were "more liable to come into conflict" when ruled by a single supreme authority. The "naked question," according to Calhoun, was "whether ours is a federal or consolidated government . . . a government resting ultimately on the solid basis of the sovereignty of the States, or on the unrestrained will of a majority."[9]

Calhoun was able to make his claim because the 1787 constitutional settlement lacked a clause like article 1 of Mexican constitutions, which stated that sovereignty resided "essentially" in the nation. Yet, Calhoun's theories invited swift condemnation, most notably from Joseph Story, the Harvard law professor and Supreme Court justice who in his three-volume *Commentaries on the Constitution* insisted that the preamble indisputably placed sovereignty in the collective people of the United States, not their state governments. What is more, Article 6 clearly established the supremacy of federal laws. If the framers had intended the form of government that Calhoun described, then why did they discard the Articles of Confederation? Finally, the constitution clearly states that disputes between the states and the federal government were to be determined by the Supreme Court, a branch of the federal government.[10] Undeterred, the South Carolinians countered with Abel P. Upshur's *Brief Inquiry into the Nature and Character of Our Federal Government*. Repeating Calhoun's central argument, Upshur pointed to ratification and the amendment process as proof that it was the states, not some "aggregate" of the people, that had given the constitution life and legitimacy. Additionally, the constitution explicitly listed those powers which the states surrendered to the federal government and reserved all others for the states, including, he believed, the right to nullify federal law and secede from the Union. It was not unity the framers were attempting to accomplish, Upshur insisted, but autonomy within a union.[11]

The depth of Americans' disagreement over the question of whether the framers had created a confederacy of sovereignties, or a federal union governed by a central authority, was nowhere more evident than in the congressional debates of 1830 between Senators Daniel Webster of Massachusetts and Robert Y. Hayne of South Carolina. The immediate question at hand concerned whether ultimate control over public lands fell under state or federal authority. Hayne largely repeated Calhoun's view that "the very life of our system is the independence of the states," insisting that the constitution was therefore formed by the sanction of *the states*, given by each in its sovereign capacity" and, as such, "*there could be no tribunal above their authority.*" Webster denounced such a view as one that not only failed to acknowledge the benefits of union, but also its indissolubility. What was really at stake, according to the Massachusetts senator, was whether the federal government served as the agent of the states or of the people. Insisting on the latter, Webster argued that the nullifiers' theory arose "from a misconception as to the origin of this government and its true character. It is, sir, the people's Constitution, the people's government; made for the people, made by the people; and answerable to the people." The states were sovereign only "so far as their sovereignty is not affected by this supreme law." The state legislatures, however sovereign, were "not yet sovereign over the people."[12] Webster failed to convince the nullifiers, but his notion that sovereignty rested ultimately in the American people and that the federal government was not only their proper representative, but could function as a fundamentally positive and democratic force echoed the more democratic impulses of Guerrero and his supporters while highlighting a fundamental disagreement then emerging in both Mexico and the United States around where sovereignty ultimately rested.

Indeed, the nullification crisis was not just important for what it represented to the United States, but for the reaction it garnered among Mexican observers.[13] In February 1833, the editors of *El Fénix de la Libertad* wrote, "It is a rare occurrence that this periodical reports on events in the US," before going on to explain that they felt it nonetheless necessary to alert readers to some "grave occurrences" that might interest "the inhabitants of the new American republics." The editors of the liberal organ began by praising the United States for its federal system and then noted, "All human works are perishable, and the shiny look that this country presents can surely blur, if the union whose states constitute the force and respectability of this nation become aware of their various interests and break the confederative pact." This, the editors scoffed, was the essence of "the great revolution" taking place in South Carolina, "not because it does not have the same representation and the same privileges as the other states; not because the federal goverment has oppressed it or committed any great injustice," but because it had imposed a tariff on imported goods.[14] The following day *El*

Fénix published a second article praising President Andrew Jackson for his response: "The president explained that the existence of the Union would be impossible if one of the states took the right to annul the laws of the Union." Rejecting the fundamental presumption of the compact theory, they echoed Webster, asserting, "The colonies declared independence in common . . . and declared themselves as one nation in order to address internal affairs and all international relations." To say that a state could separate from the Union at will was "to say that the US is not a nation." The lesson for Mexico, which was just concluding its own civil war, was clear—reject the "far-fetched" and dangerous "pretensions" of South Carolina's leaders for the sake of preserving their own union.[15]

One week after *El Fénix* ran its story, *El Telégrafo* reprinted the same article, noting that nullification could be potentially detrimental to federalism in United States, the very key to its "grandeur."[16] Although clear admirers of their northern neighbor and of federalism, the two newspapers cautioned against the destructive tendencies of a system that, if unalloyed, could threaten order, prosperity, and the republic's very existence. As such, they represented the ascendance of a more modern, nationalist federalism that still aimed to honor state sovereignty without compromising national unity. As Músquiz's comments indicated, the interest in nullification didn't just spring from fears that Mexico might follow its example. Even if most Mexicans demonstrated greater prudence than their North American counterparts, nullification could still have profound consequences for their country.

The Push for Texas Statehood and the Rise of Popular Centralism
Given the direction of national politics in both Mexico and the United States, Texans could not have picked a worse time to push for statehood. When Stephen Austin arrived in Mexico City in the summer of 1833, he encountered not Santa Anna, who had been elected president after his overthrow of Bustamante's centralist regime the year before, but Vice President Valentín Gómez Farías, who had led the federalist resistance. At the time of the elections, Santa Anna had had little interest in running the country, which he had made clear in correspondence with Gómez Farías, who by arrangement then stepped in as acting head of state immediately after the election. Santa Anna retired to his country estate in Manga de Clavo. As vice president, and supported by a new Congress dominated by like-minded reformers, Gómez Farías pursued a program that rivaled that of Guerrero. He spoke of redistributing church property and attempted to abolish the clergy's immunity from civil prosecution through the colonial-era *fuero* system of independent clerical tribunals. He also attacked military priv-

ilege by transferring control of the commandants general to the states and strengthening civil militias.[17] Yet, when it came to managing federal territory, overseeing immigration, and other matters involved with securing and developing the republic, Gómez Farías was not that far removed from his centralist counterparts.[18] Furthermore, like many Mexican leaders, he was eager to impose order across the republic, believing that a restoration of state sovereignty when it came to military matters was the best means of doing so; in addition, he had grown particularly wary of the Texans.

Fueling Mexican concerns over the far north were the reports of officials like Tadeo Ortíz, who, after touring Texas in his capacity as Mexico City's official commissioner to the province, concluded that greater federal, not state, oversight was needed. Ortíz echoed General Manuel Mier y Terán's indictments of Mexico City: "Future generations will ask in surprise how the Constituent Congress, which gave life and being to districts of less political importance to the federal power . . . could sin against Texas . . . without realizing that they were compromising the integrity of the national territory and the future destinies of a vast empire." Ortíz noted that the "few honest men" in Texas were being "outdone" by a growing number of dishonest, lazy, and self-interested "vandals" and "criminals," mostly from the southern states, who were prone "to divide" whatever country they found themselves a part of. Such people threatened "to paralyze the nationalization of this region" and declare Texas independent. For this reason, he recommended separating Texas from Coahuila and transforming it into a territory "so that it may be distributed and peopled under the guidance and immediate supervision of the federal authorities." Then the Mexican government should oversee a "mixed colonization" composed of individuals from Mexico's interior, other Spanish American republics, Europe, and, not least of all, the displaced tribes of the United States. He suggested lifting Mexico's religious strictures so it could attract a more diverse group of immigrants and form a "chain of settlements" that connected Texas to New Mexico and the adjacent states, creating a "solid bulwark which will be connected with the center."[19]

Ortiz's comments represent the nationalist vision expressed by an increasing number of Mexican liberals by the 1830s. These men embodied the traditional federalist commitment to local rule in such matters as the militia, but they also believed that the federal government had an important role to play when it came to land redistribution, taxation, and border security. They believed in harnessing federal power to serve the needs and interests of Mexico's agrarian majority, and their commitment to federalism had more to do with weakening the military and the church as opposed to empowering regional elites.[20]

As the Mexican political class reached a consensus on the need to strengthen federal control and oversight of the far north, Texans were beginning to clamor for greater local autonomy. Their numbers had grown substantially since the arrival of the first US colonists. More recently, they had collided with the central government over a series of policies that were not likely to disappear under the new government headed by Santa Anna. These included taxing imported goods, among them cotton, and, even more critically, forbidding further immigration from the United States.[21] In April 1833, representatives from the Anglo colonies of Coahuila y Texas met in San Felipe to draft a formal petition requesting that the government admit Texas as a separate and independent state of the Mexican confederation under the Law of 7 May 1824, which allowed for Texas's eventual statehood.[22] They had good reason to believe that they would be successful. Texas, after all, had sided with Santa Anna in the recent civil war, and he was a known champion of federalism.

In fact, the demand for state government in Texas revealed a growing rift among Anglo-American settlers themselves. Austin and other well-established colonists, eager to remain above the fray of Mexico's recent political upheavals, found themselves increasingly at odds with a new generation of arrivals, many of whom, while expressing loyalty to Mexico in terms no less strident than the first generation of colonists, were far less eager to placate Mexican authorities. They also tended to resent the power and prominence that Austin exercised over Texas and its Anglo colonies as well as the special relationship he seemed to enjoy with Tejanos leaders.[23] No one seemed to better represent this new group than William H. Wharton, a thirty-three-year-old Tennessee lawyer with close personal connections to that state's political elite, including Andrew Jackson himself. After arriving in Texas in 1825 and swiftly marrying the daughter of Jared Groce, the largest enslaver in Texas and a member of Austin's colony, the couple returned to Tennessee, where Wharton continued his law practice before being lured back to Texas by the promise of land and a quick fortune.[24] In 1832 Wharton had participated in the Anáhuac rebellion against the onerous shipping regulations of Brigadier General Juan Davis Bradburn and in its aftermath had called for a convention to air grievances with Mexico City. Despite Músquiz's appeal that the delegates submit their complaints to the ayuntamiento for approval and submission to the state legislature, the colonists determined to hold their meeting without the proper sanction of local officials. San Antonio de Béxar? refused to send delegates, ensuring that the pronunciamiento would be exclusively from Texas's Anglo residents. Although Austin expressed reservations, he decided to attend the meeting, hoping to check its more restive elements.

The statement from the meeting was characteristic in that it confirmed the pronuncios' commitment to Mexico and their desire to see their country "remain united to the end of time." It then went on to demand a repeal of the Law of April 6 (1830), banning additional US immigrants, and a renewal of the tariff exemptions for Austin's colony. They concluded their appeals by requesting that Texas be permitted to separate from Coahuila and form its own state government per the 1824 state colonization law. Nowhere in the document was secession mentioned, although one attendee later complained that several delegates had been brazen enough to suggest it. The appeal for secession came from a minority faction and was not taken seriously. As the witness described it, such a proposition did not exist "in the mind of any man of common sense," nor did the colonists "want to belong to the United States of the North." They had "come to the country to participate of the benefits of the Mexican independence, and of their liberal policy in regard to land." Separation from Mexico would, according to this colonist, render Texans the "most oppressed people" and only invite the aggression of the Mexican government.[25]

Considering such reports and a promise from Músquiz to help the colonists in their reform efforts if they obeyed the law, Austin determined to deliver the demands to the ayuntamiento in Béxar, whose members, although declining to send delegates to the San Felipe convention, had echoed many of the Anglo settlers' demands in their own pronunciamiento issued in December. Both documents had called for an end to the Law of April 6, but had stopped short of a demand for statehood. This, however, was evidently not enough to placate the Wharton faction, who called for another convention that spring. This time they had reason to believe they might be more successful. By now, Santa Anna's federalist government, firmly in place under Gómez Farías's the leadership, had received reassurances from other Mexican federalists, namely Brigadier General José Antonio Mexía, who had met with the Anáhuac rebels in the immediate aftermath of the rebellion and was reassured of their Mexican loyalty. Yet, by the time the convention met for a second time, Wharton and his faction enjoyed the charismatic leadership of Sam Houston, who had only arrived from Tennessee a few months prior but had managed to get himself appointed to a committee to draft a state constitution for Texas.[26] The delegates, knowing that their demands would not be welcomed by authorities in either Béxar or the state capitol of Saltillo determined to solicit Mexico City directly. Austin, the only representative skilled and experienced enough in negotiating with federal authorities, was selected to travel to the capital of the republic. Ever since his colony's establishment, Austin had counseled patience and obedience, but this was becoming an increasingly tenuous position considering recent demographic and political changes. He therefore accepted the task, albeit with "great anxiety." In a letter to a nephew, Austin expressed his fear, stating, "The consequences of failure will no doubt be war." An armed conflict with Mexico would ruin the old settlers who had "earned what they have got too hard" and who, it seemed, now had more to fear from the newer elements of their own population "than from the whole Mexican nation."[27]

The timing could not have been worse for Austin. He arrived in Mexico City at in the summer of 1833, around the same time as Ortíz and his report advising the central government to strengthen oversight in Texas. It is unclear if Austin was aware of this when he presented his appeal to Gómez Farías. Calling Texas a "distinct" member of the "Mexican family," Austin insisted that his appeal came no less from "the duty and the interest of Texas to cement and strengthen its union with the Mexican confederation."[28] This was all par for the course for Austin, but toward the end of the document, he dared to state that, if denied, "self-preservation" would compel Texans to organize a local government "with or without the approbation of the general government." While Austin assured the administration that the measure did "not proceed from any hostile views to the permanent union of Texas with Mexico," to Gómez Farías it sounded like a secessionist threat.[29] He promptly put Austin in prison.

Ortíz would meet an even worse fate, coming down with cholera and dying not long thereafter.[30] The two commissioners sent in his stead to assess the situation in Texas were tasked with offering the colonists the "protection" they had requested and hearing their "complaints, requests, and aspirations."[31] The public instructions for one of the commissioners, Colonel Juan Nepomuceno Almonte, included dissuading settlers from demanding statehood and instead suggesting that Texas form a territory with its own elected deputation, thus allowing the central government to oversee matters there more effectively. Privately, Almonte was instructed to examine the colonists' "positions of defense" and their "opinions, resources, weapons, and support," to find out if "there are adherents of independence" and, if so, to exploit divisions between such individuals and those who "desire always to be united with Mexico." Finally, if he encountered any enslaved people who had been brought into Texas "in circumvention of the law," he was to inform them that they were in fact free "by the mere act of stepping onto" Mexican territory. He was also to inform "all nomadic tribes" that the government of Mexico "is prepared to admit them as an integral part of the federation," grant them land, assist them with arms, and "provide them every aid for agriculture and trade, as long as they make permanent settlements." Meanwhile, Almonte's co-commissioner, Colonel José María Díaz Noriega, was publicly instructed to head straight to Monclova, the state capital since 1833, to review the confusing morass of Texas colonization contracts and purchases and was privately instructed to remove "dangerous colonists" from Texas by offering to purchase their lands. The purpose of the commission, it appears, was to reestablish federal control and oversight of matters in Texas, particularly colonization and land distribution, garner the support and loyalty of its inhabitants, and gather information regarding potential unrest.[32]

Almonte's correspondences with Mexican officials were surprisingly optimistic. He confirmed that many of the Texas colonists were, in fact, law-abiding, loyal, and generally "interested in preserving the integrity of our Republic" since "under [the Mexican] government they hold vast lands that otherwise they would not have."[33] His ultimate report, however, cautioned against future immigration from the United States. He wrote, "Why do the inhabitants of one country emigrate to another if not to improve their fortunes? And do we believe that the foreigners who will come to Texas will do so only because that territory is Mexican? Certainly not." These men were compelled by their own "immediate interests," not the "political aims" of Mexico or any country, the colonel warned.[34] He further noted that poor frontier defense had resulted in squatters from the United States settling along the eastern boundary of Texas, only a few of them willing or able to learn Spanish, almost all of them ignorant or dismissive of Mexican laws, especially regarding slavery.[35] He offered a litany of suggestions for how to better secure the far north, including more troops, ceasing Anglo immigration, and a new colonization strategy that targeted ethnic Mexicans and Indian tribes, specifically those being displaced by the United States. Almonte believed that Mexico "could not place a more effective barrier to the ambitions of our neighbors" than those tribes, noting, "They are suffering from mistreatment by [the United States] and will never share their interests." Given the option of colonizing Texas with Anglo-Americans versus Native Americans, Mexico should undoubtedly choose the latter, Almonte suggested, stating, "we would gain nothing by giving more lands to foreigners." He also thought, however, that the government should legitimize the land possession of those who had already settled and demand the fulfillment of outstanding contracts or declare them void. Almonte also called for more customhouses along the border with the United States and a school of navigation at Galveston to help police the illegal traffic in slaves. Feeling the need to address the future status of Texas, the commissioner agreed with Ortíz that it should be given the status of a territory to allow the national government greater control and oversight.[36]

Yet, Almonte remained generally confident about conditions in Texas. After returning to Mexico City in December 1834 and delivering his report to Santa Anna, Almonte was able to reassure close Austin associate Samuel May Williams, a cotton merchant and Mexican loyalist, that "the president agrees with the politics conducted by the colonists at this time," and report on Austin's imminent release from prison. He also informed Williams that he would relay information about the outcome "regarding petitions of the communities to organize a government in Texas independent from that of Coahuila."[37] Mexico City was evidently interested in reaching a compromise with the colonists that would have allowed them some form of local rule under the territorial government. That same month, Austin was freed after serving nearly a year in prison. With calm in Texas and the confidence of Mexican officials evidently restored, Austin turned his attention to realizing his long-standing dream of turning Texas into a formidable and lucrative member of the Mexican family. "I hope that a dead calm will reign all over Texas for many years to come, and that there will be no more excitements of any kind." He assured one correspondent that "the dark days had passed," and insisted that "calm, a *dead calm*, is all that Texas needs." Instead of wrestling with national politics, Texans should focus on their own self-improvement. "Immigration—good crops—no party divisions" was the order of the day.[38]

Yet, events in Texas soon found themselves at the center of Mexican national politics again. Almonte's report embodied one of the most ambitious government plans for Texas's future. He echoed the views of previous commissioners when he called Texas "the most valuable possession of the republic" and added, "May God grant that our negligence may not be the cause for losing so precious a portion of our territory." Like so many Mexican leaders of his time, Almonte understood Texas to be both Mexico's greatest asset and its chief vulnerability. To avoid the negative consequences of the latter, Mexico had to assert its authority there. For years, Anglo-Texans had sung the praises of Mexican institutions and insisted that their interests aligned with those of their adopted republic, but had Mexican federalism truly benefited Mexico? While men like Almonte saw great promise and potential under the right circumstances, others saw federalism's greatest failure—evidence that a system that was faltering in the United States of the North would never work in Mexico.

Indeed, much had changed in Mexico City during Almonte's absence. The reformist efforts of Gómez Farías had prompted a new alliance of military officers and clergy and garnered support from conservative organs like *El Mosquito Mexicano*, which complained that federalism had turned the Mexican republic into a "theater of desolation and misfortune." The paper's editors bemoaned that the nation's two most important institutions—the military and the church—had become the "most hated and persecuted."[39] It blamed federalism's liberal immigration policies for compromising Mexican sovereignty.[40] Critics of federalism had one other advantage over Gómez Farías: access to Santa Anna. By the spring of 1834, after Gómez Farías had been in office for nearly a year, the general wrote him a strongly worded letter, urging him to practice more restraint and deference. Santa Anna reminded his vice president that although he had absented himself from the capital, he was still the president and that it was crucial that the executive appear united, lest political opinion turn against it. Gómez Farías defended his actions, however, and continued to ignore the president's directive. In May, José María Tornel, former member of the federalist resistance that had brought Santa Anna to power, and some of his close associates gathered in Cuernavaca to issue the first of a series of pronunciamientos critical of the recent reforms and of federalism generally, which they now blamed for the "chaos, confusion, and disorder" plaguing Mexico. Specifically, the plan called for a reversal of the policies enacted under Gómez Farías, removal of all deputies who supported the reforms, and the return of Santa Anna.[41] One week later, the Plan of Toluca spread from the republic's capital. Its author, Colonel José Vicente González's, demanded the salvation of "religion and true liberty." Claiming that Gómez Farías and his radical legislators represented a group of "abhorrent Jacobins," González called for an end to "all tyranny."[42]

More than three hundred similar pronunciamientos would be issued around the republic over the next several months, all of them rejecting federalism and identifying centralism as the form of government best suited to the needs and desires of the Mexican people.[43] Much of centralism's success in 1834 had to do with its popular support and that former federalists like Tornel had by then arrived at the conclusion that Mexico's reality demanded a new political system. As José María Bocanegra, a federalist statesman who served under Guerrero, noted years later, he had "become convinced, under the light of truth and experience" that "an abyss" existed between "the theory and the practice" of Mexican federalism, "between what is speculated and what is real." A decade of Mexican federalism had proven that the system offered no "truly national option." Reformed federalists joined their centralist counterparts in renouncing the system as "an attempt to blindly imitate" the United States "without making the necessary distinctions." They now called for the adoption of another form of government "more in tune with the people's needs, demands and customs." Federalism had served to weaken rather than strengthen Mexico.[44]

Meanwhile, the overwhelming success of centralist candidates in the 1835 election confirmed that many Mexicans agreed. The new Congress immediately nullified the reform laws passed by the proceeding government, while the conservative press ratcheted up its campaign denouncing the liberals and their policies.[45] Santa Anna, still a committed federalist, but one who understood well where his political future lay, took over leadership of the movement the following spring, expelled Gómez Farías, and dissolved Congress, setting in motion a series of events that would mark yet another civil rupture in Mexico's political fabric, but one that would render far greater consequences for Texas.

"To defend the Mexican constitution": Texas Joins the Federalist Resistance

The Gómez Farías family arrived in New Orleans in August 1835 after a particularly arduous journey. For nearly a year, the former vice president along with his wife, daughter, and three sons traveled throughout northern Mexico, hoping to eventually settle on some land that Augustín Viesca, governor of Coahuila y Texas, had set aside for them in the wake of the former vice president's expulsion from Mexico City. Gómez Farías had hoped to remain in Mexico. In a letter to interim president Miguel Barragán, his and Santa Anna's successor, he attempted to allay fears of his involvement in a "revolution in Texas which may cause the republic serious trouble." Gómez Farías reminded Barragán that not only had he opposed the "pretensions of Stephen F. Austin," but he had thrown the empresario in prison for entertaining the idea of pursuing statehood without going through the proper channels. After all, how much "prestige" could a man "who had not favored but opposed their desires have as the leader of their revolution?" Despite his continued reassurances, however, Gómez Farías was unable to convince Barragán that he posed no formidable threat and eventually determined that it was safest to leave Mexico altogether. Shortly after departing Matamoros for New Orleans aboard the schooner *Watchman* on August 15, a hurricane struck, capsizing the boat and throwing one of his sons overboard. The boy survived but *El Mosquito Mexicano* lamented that it had not been his father who was thrown overboard.[46]

The former vice president's choice of New Orleans was no surprise. The city had long been a destination for exiled republicans from all over the Western Hemisphere. It had also served as a launching point for most of the filibustering expeditions of the late eighteenth and early nineteenth centuries, including the Gutiérrez-Magee Expedition of 1812/13, and remained home to sizeable Spanish American and Caribbean expatriate populations, especially as Mexico's political climate worsened. In fact, not long after Gómez Farías's arrival, he encountered Brigadier General Mexía, a fellow federalist and former Veracruz customhouse officer who had recently begun speculating in Texas land near Nacogdoches and eagerly encouraged other Mexican liberals to follow his example.[47] It was during this time that Lorenzo de Zavala, Guerrero's vice president, formed the Galveston Bay and Texas Land Company, for which Mexía became the primary representative in Mexico City. It is unclear exactly how Mexía and the former vice president reunited, but when they did, they undoubtedly had much to talk about.

Centralists had dominated Congress after Santa Anna called elections in January 1835. After promptly nullifying the reform laws passed under Gómez Farías and placing civil militias under the control of army officers, Santa Anna decided to join the centralist revolution. It was a reluctant concession by one of federalism's most ardent defenders, but it reflected the turn in popular politics. While most of the historiography asserts that the general orchestrated or preempted the end of Mexico's first federal republic, in fact he was responding to widespread disillusionment with federalism. The hundreds of centralist pronunciamientos that rippled across the republic were evidence of this. Many of them echoed the words of centralist organs like *El Tiempo* which called for a "new order," insisting that federalism had made Mexico into little more than "An indigestible conglomeration of masses ... a multitude of states over a vast territory composed of some who wish to destroy it in one blow."[48] An editorial likely authored by Lucas Alamán, still a leading centralist intellectual, asserted that "the supreme power resides in the nation" and called for a special congress to be assembled to address the problems with the constitution.[49] *El Mosquito Mexicano* agreed. In June 1835, it printed the centralist Plan de Jalisco, asserting that the Constitution of 1824 had only brought "disorder and revolution" to Mexico, paving the way for the "tyrannical domination" of various factions. It denounced local and state governments for embracing the "inexact idea of sovereignty, liberty, and independence" and for forming "scandalous coalitions to declare war on their own union." Article six of the Jalisco pronunciamiento declared, "The form of government that should constitute our nation should be none other than a central republic."[50]

Indeed, over the next eighteen months, Congress would begin to dismantle the 1824 constitution and replace it with the so-called Constitución de las Siete Leyes (1836). The new charter dramatically undermined the political and financial autonomy of the states, reduced them to "departments" with federally appointed governors, and restricted voting to the wealthy.[51] These efforts did not go unopposed. As soon as Congress passed a bill ordering the discharge of local militias in March 1835, the governor of Zacatecas, Manuel González Cosío, announced, "The [state] government is awarded the faculty to make use of its civil militia to repulse any aggression that may be attempted against it."[52] Zacatecas would have its chance to do so, but not successfully. The following month, Santa Anna would launch a surprise attack in the middle of the night, and after a brief period of combat, his troops would level the state capital. Tornel would later remark, "The most persuasive proof that could be given that the federal system no longer suited the nation was that now not even [Santa Anna] himself wanted it."[53]

Santa Anna's swift suppression of the Zacatecas pronuncios in May guaranteed that any viable federalist resistance would have to come from peripheral regions or from abroad. This was a fact that Gómez Farías understood all too well. In fact, it was not long after his landing in New Orleans that he and Mexía began planning their two-pronged attempt to capture Santa Anna and reestablish federalism. The Constitution of 1824 would then be revised to allow for the confiscation of church property, secularization of all monasteries and convents, religious freedom, and redistribution of property.

Meanwhile, by the end of 1835, Coahuila y Texas remained the only federalist stronghold in Mexico, largely due to the determination of its federalist governor, Viesca, who had earlier assisted Anglo settlers in their efforts to shield Texas from Guerrero's emancipationist decree. Now he was appealing to the settlers for assistance. When the new commandant of the Eastern Interior Provinces, General Martín Perfecto Cos, attempted to replace Viesca with a federally appointed governor, he and his federalist allies established a separate state capital in Monclova. In April 1835, a mere two weeks after the new centralist Congress had mandated drastic reductions in the size of state militias, Viesca responded by setting up a war council and preparing to clash with Cos. The governor attempted to gain the support of the colonists by reminding them that the party in power "now was the same that had prohibited the emigration of North American colonists in 1830" and warned that if Texans did nothing, they would likely see a reinstatement of the Law of April 6.[54]

The Texans, however, were not eager to draw the attention of the new centralist leadership. Most hoped to wait out the political upheaval, evidently unaware of Congress's plans to abolish the 1824 constitution, which it would eventually do in another six months. Indeed, the Anglo colonies remained notably calm while federalist activity hummed along in New Orleans, where Zavala had joined his federalist allies. Recognizing the need for the Texans' support, Gómez Farías, Mexía, and Zavala sketched a preliminary plan that involved Zavala inciting rebellion from Texas and the other federalists coordinating an invasion at Tampico. Zavala arrived in early July with a lengthy address to Texas residents: So long as they remained faithful to the constitution, they would soon find federal troops at their doorsteps. Certain generals had "destroyed the federal constitution" in order "to be promoted to the presidency of the republic." Drawing on the same logic that had sparked the independence movement after the overthrow of the Spanish king, Zavala insisted that in the absence of a legitimate central government, the states were "left at liberty to act for themselves." While acknowledging the colonists' indebtedness to the "Supreme Government of Mexico," Zavala reminded them that "those governments are formed of the same men who are now persecuted, among whom I have the honor to count myself as one."[55]

Later that month, Austin himself, just back to Texas from Mexico City, called for a convention to discuss Zavala's recent appeal and a "question of the most vital importance."[56] He had hoped to remain out of the fray of Mexican politics, but Zavala's claims caused him concern. The 1824 constitution had been the inspiration for many to relocate to Mexico. It had functioned as the colonists' most effective tool against federal encroachment, especially when it came to slavery. If Mexico were to discard it, how would it affect Texans? His associates might be compelled to wait out the political maelstrom until things returned to normal, but what about the more restive elements of the population, especially those who had already expressed an interest in independence? In September, the ayuntamiento of San Felipe resolved to join the federalists in "support [of] the constitution of the Mexican republic of 1824, to which we have solemnly obligated ourselves," and recommended that each of the remaining jurisdictions elect a committee to meet in San Felipe.[57] The following month a circular appeared in the *Telegraph and Texas Register* reporting that "information of the most important and decisive character" had just been received from an "unquestionable authority" in Béxar, likely referring to Zavala's address. In response, Cos was planning an "immediate attack on the colonies" with five hundred of his troops. The newspaper cried, "They come to fasten down upon our necks the yoke, and to rivet upon our hands the manacles of a military servitude." It called on Texans to continue to insist on their rights under the constitution and "union with the Mexican confederation" as they organized the militia and arranged a concerted defense. "WAR is our only recourse," the circular declared, "there is no other remedy."[58] By the following week, *The Telegraph and Texas Register* published a petition from the Congress of Coahuila y Texas protesting "in the most solemn manner" any changes to the federal constitution and declaring that Texas's membership in the Mexican confederation rested on the "fundamental compact." Alongside the published petition were resolutions from various municipalities throughout Texas pledging their support of the 1824 constitution and promising to defend it.[59]

While Texans remained far from declaring independence that fall, the decision to join the resistance emboldened the pro-independence minority, who had first expressed their views during the statehood convention in 1833. Evidently, the issue was raised again at the San Felipe meeting in November 1835, but Texan leaders had resoundingly rejected it in favor of a "provisional government, upon the principles of the constitution of 1824." Yet, unlike the delegates who adopted the September resolution, the November 7 delegates implied a conditional allegiance to their adopted country, asserting that their membership in the Mexican confederation would remain only "so long as that nation is governed by the constitution and laws." They insisted that they were simply acting on their republican duty "to defend our unalienable rights against all who attempt to subvert our liberties." Accordingly, they offered their "support and assistance" to such members of the "Mexican confederacy as will take up arms against their military despotism."[60] One colonist even reported that he had a flag made "the colours, and their arrangement the same as the old one" with the phrase, "Constitution of 1824," displayed in the center.[61]

On 29 October 1835, Mexía informed the Texans that the expedition would be underway soon and that he had received letters of support from the federalist governor of Tamaulipas, who indicated that he and other "friends from the interior" would join Mexía as soon as he had taken Tampico. The expedition finally left New Orleans in November. One hundred and fifty well-armed men were on board, but just as they arrived at the mouth of the Pánuco River eight days later, a storm struck. As their schooner began taking on water, the men tossed their ammunition overboard. Once on shore, the expedition initially encountered little resistance, but soon got lost in the dense, tropical terrain. While they managed to capture the customhouse, they soon found themselves exhausted and lacking ammunition. When reinforcements from the interior failed to arrive, Mexía appealed to the Texans for assistance and relief. In accordance with the November 7 declaration, the provisional council agreed and issued another declaration reassuring Mexican federalists of their commitment "to sustain the republican principles of the Constitution of 1824."[62]

"Soley, simply, purely American"

By the end of 1835, the Texas rebellion was still ostensibly and officially an extension of the federalist resistance. *El Regenado* reported in December that most Texas colonists did not want war and speculated that Austin had been "seduced" by Zavala and Mexía,[63] but things looked very different to federal officials in Texas. In September, Almonte, still stationed there, received a letter from an American abolitionist named David Lee Child warning him that land speculators in the United States were responsible for instigating unrest in an effort "to plant slavery" in Texas. Child explained that intensifying abolitionist activity in the northern United States had served "to inflame the desire of southerners to possess" Texas. He concluded by encouraging Almonte to use the letter to "further the object we have in common—the preservation of the integrity of the Mexican republic." Child's assertions were not without merit.

In addition to functioning as a haven for Mexican federalists and a center of Spanish American revolutionary activity, New Orleans was also the commercial center of the South's burgeoning cotton economy. In fact, by the mid-1830s, the city could boast its own robust banking network and credit system and a rapidly rising class of American capitalists, speculators, and entrepreneurs, nearly all of them tied to the cotton trade.[64] It was members of this class who were likely the ones present at a meeting in September 1835 of federalists and a group of New Orleans businessmen. The latter likely knew little about Mexican federalism and, it is safe to say, their long-term aims differed markedly from those of Gómez Farías and Mexía. As the South's cotton empire began to push south and west beginning in the 1830s, cotton traders, land speculators, and prospective planters began looking hungrily toward Texas.

El Mosquito Mexicano was all too eager to point out the burgeoning quest for Texas in its report on the secret meeting between two of Mexico's most prominent federalist exiles and a group of Louisiana capitalists. The article, attributing information obtained from an intercepted letter between Mexía and one of his federalist allies in Mexico as the source, claimed that the norteamericanos present at the meeting had an expressed interest in acquiring Texas to annex it to Louisiana.[65] Permanent separation from Mexico was not something that interested the Mexican federalists, although threats of separation were not unheard of in federalist pronunciamientos dating back to 1823 and 1824. While none of these threats had ever culminated in actual secession efforts, the potential had existed since Mexico became a republic, and it is perhaps unsurprising that Mexican federalists, facing the most profound danger yet to their institutions, might entertain it.

According to *El Mosquito Mexicano*, Gómez Farías evidently stated at the meeting that the dismemberment should be "temporary," perhaps entailing a brief alliance with the southern US states if and when they "come to form one single federated union." Such a remark indicates that the former vice president was both aware of murmurings about a "Republic of the South" and perhaps sought to use it to his advantage even as he hoped for Texas's ultimate return to Mexico. He also reportedly disapproved of Mexía's strategy of promising Texas lands in exchange for monetary support from the Louisianan attendees. Mexía admonished his compatriot to "remain resolute" and leave the details of planning and funding of the expedition to him. Gómez Farías, not conversant in English, complied.[66] Before the participants sealed their resolutions, a final addendum was added, no doubt as a concession to the Louisianans. It called for a close alliance with the United States "especially those from Louisiana, who must be considered as brothers" and "who are to be allowed to enter [Mexico] freely without the need for passports."[67]

It is entirely possible that the editors of *El Mosquito Mexicano* were attempting to discredit the federalists by suggesting that they would entertain the idea of an independent republic composed of southern states and Texas. Regardless, the loss of Texas to the United States was a red herring for the Mexican centralists. The eventual plan significantly did not include an intention to permanently separate Texas from Mexico. Gómez Farías himself acknowledged that independence for Texas would be "painful" and that joining the United States would have compromised both his and Mexía's ambitions of returning to Mexico City. On the other hand, the aims of their Louisiana co-conspirators were slightly harder to discern. Mexía himself characterized them as men of means "interested in the freedom of mankind and in the welfare of the state of Louisiana," but their interest in Mexican federalism was likely secondary to their specific aim of preserving Texas's status as a region friendly if not indifferent to slavery. In addition to receiving favored status, the attendees wanted to make sure that "special care" be given to preventing "large numbers" of British expats from living in the republic and that the "English government have no influence over" the "new Mexican government."[68]

Fear that Britain would attempt to gain a foothold in North America in its efforts to undermine southern slavery was very real among southern slaveholders after the British Emancipation Act of 1833. That Britain might extend this campaign to North America itself was no doubt a motivating factor in the men's decision to support the Texans regardless of the political outcome of the rebellion. Once this British "clause" was added, the pact was sealed and signed by Gómez Farías, Mexía, and the thirty-seven other attendees, the names of whom the article failed to mention.[69]

By mid-October, just a few weeks after the plan to invade Tampico was finalized, the *New Orleans Bee* carried an announcement for a "meeting of the friends of Texas" to "deliberate on affairs of importance in relation to the country." The announcement came from Ambrose Calperthwaite Fulton, a twenty-five-year-old Quaker from Pennsylvania who "did not feel it right" when he heard about Austin's arrest and decided to organize a meeting to discuss how best to aid the Texans.[70] The meeting was the first of several that would bring together Mexican federalist supporters of the rebels, New Orleans business interests, and men willing to bear arms in a war that they had been conditioned to believe was akin to that of the Americans' war for independence in exchange for the promise of cheap land. The first of these meetings, which took place on the evening of October 12, was packed with men representing a cross-section of New Orleans society. Businessmen, immigrant dock workers, and Mexican exiles filled both floors of Thomas Banks's Arcade.

George Fisher, a former customhouse operator from Anáhuac and co-organizer of the meeting, spoke to the crowd at length, presenting a compelling exposé of Santa Anna's purported tyranny that was later reprinted in the *Bee*, including his government's censorship of the press, seizure of customhouse duties, and impending invasion of Texas, the last presumed federalist holdout. "The Liberals will sustain the Texans, if Texas sustain the Constitution of 1824," Fisher explained. "If Texas wins, then republicanism and constitutionality will triumph in Mexico; if not, then despotism."[71] While the Mexican federalists lent the meeting legitimacy, New Orleans businessmen like James Ramage, an inspector for the Louisiana Cotton Seed and Oil Factory, handled the logistics.[72] After Fisher spoke, Ramage and William Christy, a local attorney, advanced several resolutions, including a decision to offer "aid and support" to the Texans in their fight against Santa Anna, the formation of a committee "to communicate with and receive funds on behalf of the rebels," and the commencement of a list of volunteers for the Texans' cause. All the resolutions passed and as the meeting concluded, the "big men" began collecting names of recruits among attendees.

Although the leaders of the meeting had characterized the Texas struggle as motivated by the "same sacred cause which our fathers in '76 defended," many of the volunteers were likely motivated by promises of land. In addition to Christy and Ramage, the meeting's leaders included Thomas Banks, owner of Banks's Arcade and a prominent New Orleans real estate investor, and William Bogart, owner of one of the largest cotton shipping ventures in the city. Many of these men had likely been present at Gómez Farías and Mexías' gathering in September. Fisher would later insist that at the time of the arcade gathering, Texas *"did not war . . . against the Mexican nation, nor did it assume the hostile attitude of an independent state or nation."* Unlike the meetings of the previous month, this one had been led, organized, and attended almost exclusively by norteamericanos. Furthermore, none of the resolutions said anything about reestablishing Mexican federalism. As James Ramage later characterized it in a letter to Austin, the Banks's Arcade gathering, although ostensibly in support of the federalist cause, was nonetheless "solely, purely, simply American in all it parts."[73]

That the rebellion in Texas appeared to be swiftly turning into an unsanctioned US intervention fueled a series of editorials in *El Mosquito Mexicano* urging Mexicans to unite against the rapacious Americans who were undoubtedly behind the rebellion. By November, *El Anteojo* had picked up the story. Calling the Americans the "natural enemies" of Mexico, it declared that, despite the claims of Texans themselves, their movement was being fomented by foreigners eager to enrich themselves off Mexico's land. As events intensified over the next several months, the paper continued to point to the hypocrisy of the United States for claiming moral supremacy while violating the rights and sovereignty of its republican neighbor. Americans likely did not want all of Mexico, but they certainly wanted Texas, and they were chiefly motivated by a desire to extend slavery. This fact, the editors asserted, necessitated that the rest of Mexico, despite its political divisions, unite against the Texans and their US allies. Insisting that the Texas rebellion was "not the same" as previous federalist revolts in Mexico, the paper asserted that the desire of Austin to separate Texas from the rest of the Mexican territory had been known for some time and that it was the "disposition" of the citizens of the United States "to favor whichever pretension of the settlers would create the occasion to result in Texas not being a part of Mexico." If Mexicans had any "honor" or "love" for independence, it was necessary that they "unite to punish" the interlopers. It asked, "How can we tolerate a group of naturally arrogant people who have always held us in low regard and considered us inferior and threatened us with arms to impose the law which they desired?" Recalling the years of proslavery agitation and noncompliance with federal policy, the editors asserted that Texans had never really followed the constitution anyway, and now they claimed to be defending it? This was no domestic rebellion, but a "national" war that threatened to compromise the nation's honor.[74]

Meanwhile, the rebellion supplied an opportunity for that restive minority who had been calling for independence since the statehood conventions. By year's end, loyalists were beginning to express concern over growing anti-Mexican propaganda in Texas. "I fear if a stand is not taken against self dubed patriots all our labors in Texas are gone to the devil and me with it," warned Austin's friend and fellow colonist Thomas McKinney, after finding several pro-independence articles "written and published in favor of Independence by the same men over different signatures and finding none of our citizens opposing." McKinney claimed that he had in fact written to the publisher "in order to let it be known that we were not unanimous in that way of thinking and to get our citizens to reflect." After securing his promise that the editorial would appear in the next day's issue, he claimed the Wharton faction had suppressed the publication and "substituted a bag of stuff illy comporting with our present condition." McKinney feared that Texan politicians were yielding "to a wild unthinking faction."[75]

By the end of 1835, Anglo-Texan society was divided between war and peace parties. The latter mostly consisted of more-established settlers with more to lose by alienating the Mexican authorities. Their hesitancy to join the conflict would require its leaders to rely ever more heavily on resources and manpower from the Crescent City. On 14 November 1835, the *Telegraph and Texas Register* reported that $7,000 had been raised at a meeting in New Orleans "for the purpose of aiding and assisting" the Texans in their "very laudable struggle for liberty and the Constitution" and that one hundred volunteers from the United States, nearly half of them fully equipped, had pledged themselves to the cause.[76] As forces in Texas struggled to muster their militia, they would come to rely ever more on these recruits. "Hundreds of applications are daily making to join the rank," one recruiter reported, predicting, "This movement of ours here will be followed by similar ones thru' the whole valley of the Mississippi." The only concern was "that more will be received than required." These men had no prior connection to Mexico or its people, knowing only what they had read in their own local newspapers—that thousands of Americans like themselves were fighting a despotic regime.[77]

Efforts in the United States to suppress the recruitment and funding were half-hearted and ineffective. Henry Carleton, the New Orleans district attorney, briefly seized Christy's volunteer and donations books before determining, surprisingly, that he did not have enough evidence to prosecute him for filibustering. Carleton then informed US Secretary of State John Forsyth that, although "there can be no doubt that certain persons intend to proceed thither, to act in concert with the Texans," he had not observed any "regularly enlisting or entering" nor "any definite or tangible military expedition." Meanwhile, recruits inconspicuously referred to as "emigrants" in correspondence and enlistment rolls began to amass around the city, and "express wagons" traveled up and down its streets collecting donated arms, many of them from veterans of the Battle of New Orleans. None of these activities appeared to grab the attention of local authorities, perhaps because New Orleans was one of the largest centers of militia activity in the union, much of it geared toward suppressing potential slave revolts.[78]

Many of the recruits were motivated by self-interest as much as (if not more) by their attested desire to overthrow "despotism." As an incentive to join the fight, New Orleans financial supporters of the rebellion, many of them land and cotton speculators, had promised recruits remuneration in return for their service.[79] This was likely what motivated John Sowers Brooks, a recruit from Kentucky. Brooks employed the same accusation of self-interest and hypocrisy against Texas loyalists that the Mexican press had used to discredit them. In a letter home, he wrote, "The peace party seems to be actuated by a different motive than that which they profess." Whereas the Mexican press claimed that land speculation was responsible for Texans' betrayal of Mexico, Brooks argued that it was the basis of their loyalty to that country. "Their extensive speculations in land have acquired them an influence in the Mexican councils which, it is said, they have exerted to their own aggrandizement and to the detriment of the interest of the settlers." Their influence with prominent Mexican families, "enables them to govern the colony as they desire." Brooks supported "an open, bold, and fearless course, such as a declaration of independence," which would not only "ensure us the aid of every liberal in the United States," but secure Texas "for the general good of the bone and sinew of our country[,] the actual settlers."[80]

As more and more men like Brooks flooded into Texas, they quickly began to outnumber the more established Texans with much to lose from independence. In fact, Austin himself wondered if the independence movement had not been designed to overpower him and his allies. He accused Wharton and others of recruiting volunteers from the north for the specific purpose of adding to their pro-independence constituency and presenting their opinions "as the opinion of the people of Texas."[81] In December, Austin transmitted these sentiments to the provisional government of Texas, stating unequivocally that he was opposed to any measure that would give Mexico "any foundation to say that the Texan war is purely a national war against foreigners and foreign invaders." He confirmed his belief "that Texas should rigidly adhere to the leading principles of the declaration of the 7th Novr" in "strict conformity with the basis on which the federal party are acting." Austin conceded that although the "dissolution of the social compact" gave Texas "the *right* of declaring herself an independent community," it was not in her best interest to do so. Such a move would merely expose the "old settlers and men of property in this country to much risk." Furthermore, "it will turn all parties in Mexico against us" and "bring back the war to our own doors."82

Given that the prospect of a return to the 1824 constitution now seemed unlikely—following Santa Anna's brutal suppression of the Zacatecas rebels and with the rapidly changing social composition of Texas brought on by the flood of immigrants like Brooks—Austin risked losing his stature and influence if he remained opposed to independence. Yet, he continued to hold his ground. Although one correspondence written in December suggests he might have briefly wavered, a trip to the Brazos Valley during which he consulted with several of the older settlers evidently set him straight. Austin confirmed afterward that he was "more and more convinced every day and especially on calm reflection during a solitary ride down here, that the political position of Texas, should continue as established by the declaration of the 7th November last."83

Yet, throughout the winter of 1835 and 1836, most Texans remained largely indifferent to the General Council's appeal to join the rebel ranks, forcing its leaders to rely ever more heavily on men from the United States. "Out of more than four hundred men at or near this post, I doubt if twenty-five citizens of Texas can be mustered in the ranks," wrote one colonel. "Nay, I am informed, whilst writing the above, that there is not half that number." Thus, the fight for Texas was by and large conducted by US citizens who issued "just complaints and taunting remarks in regard to the absence of the old settlers and owners of the soil."84 Colonel James Fannin wrote that if the rebellion were to be crushed, "censure" would not fall "on the heads of those brave men who have left their homes in the United States," but on those who, "notwithstanding the repeated calls have remained at home without raising a finger to keep the enemy from their thresholds."85 As the rebellion became increasingly American in composition, so too did much of its rhetoric and aims. After the initial recruitment meetings in October, demands for the reinstatement of the 1824 constitution were rarely heard among the rebellion's Louisiana supporters. Instead, support for the Texas rebels was captured in declarations of national and racial solidarity between Texas and the United States. Wrote one northern sympathizer, "We know that you are bone of our bone! and flesh of our flesh! That none but a republican government can exist over you!" American supporters of the intervention declared republicanism to be a specifically Anglo-American characteristic and the rebellion itself a kind of extension of the US war for independence. As a Henry Meigs wrote to Austin, "You will conduct your affairs with the justice and courage which led our fathers in the revolution to establish the equal rights which we now enjoy."[86]

It would not take long before such rhetoric found expression among Texas rebels themselves. The earliest example of this was during the conflict at Gonzalez, when one speaker declared, "The same blood that animated the hearts of our ancestors still flows warm in our veins."[87] Similar declarations, of course, had been expressed in numerous rebellions in Mexico and the United States for decades. Austin had drawn on Anglo-American revolutionary heritage in his appeal to suppress the Fredonian rebels, but those appeals had been accompanied by assertions of loyalty to Mexico at a time when being American and being Mexican were not mutually exclusive. As the Texas rebellion became more complex in its composition, so too did its demands. While it was still officially a movement for the reinstatement of Mexican federalism, it was becoming increasingly clear by the end of 1835 that it contained conflicting and even contradictory aims.

Meanwhile, the Americanization of the rebellion supplied rhetorical ammunition to Mexican centralists eager to characterize its participants, regardless of their origin or intent, as foreign interlopers attempting to undermine Mexican sovereignty. On November 14, the *Telegraph and Texas Register* printed a translation of a letter from Gregorio Gómez, the Santa Anna–appointed colonel at Tres Villas. Gómez denounced the Texan colonists as "hypocritical and false" as well as ungrateful. In return for the "liberty and favors" that Mexico had granted them, they were attempting now to plunge a murderous poignard in her bosom." Gómez's letter insisted that the rebels' aim was "no less than dismember[ment]." The only appropriate response to the "gang of lawless foreigners," was "complete annihilation." Gómez cast the Texans as "foreigners" by "birth and principles," who, "by their treacherous conduct," had "forfeited all of the privileges and immunities granted to them by our too generous country." The letter concluded by cursing "the Mexican who should be dastardly enough to join in that murderous and anti-national plot."[88] The Gómez letter was so inflammatory that its authenticity should be questioned, but nonetheless, it reflected the well-formulated consensus among Mexico's centralist leaders about the rebellion at that time.

As Santa Anna began assembling his troops in San Luis Potosi in preparation for an invasion of Texas, the provisional government of Texas still felt the need to "correct the falsehoods circulated by the centralists." On 2 January 1836, they issued a statement reiterating, "The people of Texas have taken up arms in defence of their rights and liberties . . . and to sustain the republican principles of the Constitution of 1824." They insisted that Texans had been "living in peace, when the revolutionary flame reached their homes," making them victims of a "storm that originated elsewhere." It was only because they remained "faithful to their oaths" that the enemy "was trying to deceive the liberal Mexican with false reports."[89] As Texas leaders wrote those words, they were about to make a fateful decision that would have a profound impact on the course of the war.

Facing Santa Anna's imminent invasion, the provisional government determined to send Austin, Wharton, Mexía and Branch T. Archer on a fundraising mission to New Orleans. Neither Austin nor Mexía looked forward to the voyage. Austin believed that Wharton and Houston were attempting to undermine his authority, and Mexía, the only Mexican assigned to the mission, had developed doubts about the intent of the Anglo settlers.[90] It is difficult to know what might have happened had Mexía remained with the other ambassadors after their arrival in New Orleans instead of abandoning the mission almost immediately. The other Texans learned upon their own arrival in the Crescent City that further aid hinged on one condition—an unequivocal declaration of independence from the Texas General Council. Only this, Austin informed one of his associates back in Texas, would "give us the aid of men of capital and high standing and character who wish for a more extensive field, than a mere party war in Texas." Evidently, this was enough to convert the empresario, who had likely also been swayed by his travel companions. Regretting that he had earlier succumbed to the "warm and even violent feelings of some of my friends," he now made it clear that he was committed to independence since he had "no doubt" that it would secure aid for Texas. He thus determined that remaining loyal to the Constitution of 1824 not only "does us no good with the federalists," but it was also "doing us harm in this country, by keeping away the kind of men we most need."[91] In January 16, Austin informed his longtime friend, Thomas McKinney that he had negotiated a loan on the condition "that Texas would declare independence in March" and that "it could not have been had otherwise." As far as the federalists were concerned, "The accounts from Vera Cruz and Tampico are that the federal party have united with Santanna against Texas."[92]

Sensing his friend's opposition, Austin penned another letter the following week. "I know what reply you will make to this," but he assured him that it was in the best interest of "our country." After having once worked so feverishly to unite Texans against independence, Austin now scrambled to gain a consensus to the contrary. "The country ought to go *unanimously* for independence. Public opinion all over the U.S. expects and earnestly calls for it."[93] More than a month would pass before McKinney replied, but when he did, he made clear how he felt about his friend's recent change of heart and where their relationship stood as a result: "I have intended answering your letter to me from N. Orleans but have really been at a loss," he wrote. "You and I must sever totally in anything of a political character . . . My confidence in you is I think forever at an end." McKinney was not Austin's enemy, he assured him, "but at the same time, I am now fully convinced that you cannot be anything but an injury to your country." By embracing the appeal for independence, Austin had effectively confirmed the suspicions of Mexico City and thereby endangered Texas. McKinney could not find the words to describe his disappointment: "Your illusions and remarks in that letter to me from N. Orleans are - - -."[94]

Given Austin's enduring loyalty to his adopted republic and record of counseling calm and obedience, his embrace of independence may seem surprising. There were likely several reasons for his shift in position. As Austin knew all too well, the demographic composition of Texas had changed dramatically, even in the preceding six months. Due to Texas's reliance on US recruits, it was now dominated by men with little knowledge of Mexican politics and virtually no fealty to the country. Most such men likely desired, even expected, independence, and if Austin had any hope of remaining politically relevant, he would have to concede to their wishes. It is also possible that Austin envisioned a temporary secession in line with what Gómez Farías had proposed at the first meeting between Mexican federalists and New Orleans businessmen. It is important to remember that separatist attempts or threats were not unheard of in the late eighteen and early nineteenth centuries. Provincial supporters of federalism had threatened secession in 1823 and 1824, and before that, similar threats had plagued the United States in the wake of independence from Britain. For example, many of the defeated Regulators, seriously contemplated secession from either the state or the union following suppression.[95] In many respects, the Texas rebellion was merely another example, albeit a particularly pronounced and uniquely successful example, of a series of autonomist movements that rippled across North America during the age of independence. What most informed Austin's decision was that by January 1836, the survival of Texas depended upon independence. Santa Anna was preparing his assault to return Texas to Mexico

City's control. There appeared to be no viable federalist resistance left elsewhere in Mexico, and the sole source of financial assistance for those in Texas hinged on a declaration of independence.

Thus, Austin greeted each day hoping for news that the provisional government had offered up a declaration. Meanwhile, Texan leaders on both sides of the border found themselves in a near desperate situation as morale in Texas began to flag without aid from the north.[96] The longer Austin remained in New Orleans, however, the more he seemed to adopt rhetoric casting the rebellion as the cause of noble American liberators. In a letter to Nicholas Biddle, president of the Second Bank of the United States, Austin declared it "the cause of freedom and of mankind, but more emphatically of the people of the United States, than any other" and entreated Biddle to therefore "give to it the attention which its importance merits."[97]

In remarks to Senator L. F. Linn of Missouri, he referred to the conflict as a "war of extermination," "barbarism," and "despotic principles." It was the labor of Anglo colonists like him that had formed a "barrier of safety to the southwestern frontier" and served as a "beacon-light to the Mexicans in their search after liberty." The man who had once lauded the Mexican republic and proclaimed it the natural home of all freemen, now effectively turned his back on it. Without the help of brethren in the United States, the colonies would be destroyed and their place "supplied by a population of Indians, Mexicans, and renegades, all mixed together, and all the natural enemies of white men and of civilization." Calling Mexico a "usurper" and a "base, unprincipled, bloody monster" he insisted that its "war of extermination" would "crimson the waters of the Mississippi, and make *it* the eastern boundary of Mexico."[98]

In a letter to President Andrew Jackson, Austin asserted that in fighting Santa Anna's forces and demanding their rights, Texans were "obeying the dictates of an education received here: from you the American people, from our fathers, from the patriots of '76—the Republicans of 1836?"[99] It may be possible that Austin felt frustrated and betrayed by Mexico and now fostered a disillusionment with it like he had once felt toward the United States. Austin admitted that in the past, he had exhibited "more kind and charitable feelings for the Mexicans in general" but had "been much more faithful to them than they merited." Experience had taught him that it was "in vain to hope for any good from Mexican institutions, or Mexican justice."[100]

Meanwhile, back in Texas, independence was no longer the preferred path of a radical minority. In February 1836, a group of volunteers petitioned the Mexican government for the privilege to vote based on their being "citizen soldiers" sharing a "common interest" with the rest of Texas and "equally anxious for its prosperity." When their petitions were denied, the volunteers in some cases turned to physical intimidation. In Nacogdoches, a group of forty Kentucky volunteers drew their guns and advanced on election headquarters.[101] Such men seemed to share the view now prevalent in the New Orleans papers that Mexicans were simply unsuited to republicanism. When Governor Viesca and Brigadier General Mexía visited a camp of volunteers in mid-December, Austin observed that they "scarcely escaped insult."[102] By late February, even the *Telegraph and Texas Register* appeared to have abandoned Mexican federalism. "Shall We Declare for Independence?," its editors asked. They had clearly already made up their minds. How could they live as "*freemen*" under a government that changed "as often as the colors of the chameleon." Ultimately, it was of "little importance" whether the Mexican leadership called themselves "*republican* or *monarchists*, when we are withering under their misrule." Were the Texans "more strongly united by ties of kindred, blood, language and institutions to Mexico than the Americans had been to Great Britain"? The latter, after all, had "separated themselves from a people who were 'bone of their bone, and flesh of their flesh,'" an empire that had claimed "the endearing title of *parent*" and "a people whose institutions were knitted to them by the strongest ties of affinity." Meanwhile, the Texans were now separating from a people "one half of whom are the most depraved of the different races of Indians" and filled with so much "general ignorance and superstition" that it prevented the possibility of the two peoples ever "mingling in the same harmonious family." The only remaining consideration, the editorial insisted, should be the "prospect of success." While "all Mexico has quietly fallen into the arms of the tyrant," the "blood and treasure" pledged by citizens of the United States would "flow freely out, when offered in the cause of liberty and independence."[103]

"An inherent right of the sovereignty of nations"

As Santa Anna and his troops marched into San Antonio on 23 February 1836, the general observed, "Few of the colonists, properly speaking, ha[d] taken up arms in the struggle." Instead, most "were publicly known to have come from New Orleans and other points of the neighboring republic exclusively for the purpose of aiding the Texas rebellion."[104] His suspicion was likely informed by a letter the general received from his minister of war, José María Tornel, in late December as he was preparing to depart from San Luis Potosí after mustering his forces there. Tornel informed Santa Anna, "The supreme government has positive information that in the United States of the North public meetings are being held with the avowed purpose of arming expeditions against the Mexican nation, of helping those who have rebelled . . . and of bringing upon our territory all those evils attendant upon civil war." Based on such information, Tornel advised the president to "punish as pirates" any foreigners who entered the republic "armed and for the purpose of attacking our territory," reminding him that these men "are not subjects of any nation at war with the republic[,] nor do they militate under any recognized flag."[105] Santa Anna would echo these words when later explaining that Mexico had been attacked "not by Mexicans," but by foreigners "moved by the desire of conquest."[106] It was an accurate characterization, but it ignored that the rebellion had begun as an appendage of the Mexican federalist resistance. Furthermore, it was unclear exactly what Tornel meant by "foreigners." Did he mean immigrants, many of whom remained loyal to Mexico and had not even dared to pick up arms against it, or did he mean those who had arrived in recent months for the sole purpose of pursuing war against Mexico? It appears that Tornel, and likely most other Mexico City officials, understood the rebellion as little more than a filibustering attempt. While not receiving the official sanction of the Jackson administration, it was clear that the revolt represented some iteration of his plan to separate Texas from Mexico. Since most of those who had taken up arms by then were indeed not Mexican citizens and had expressed no desire or interest in the rebellion's original aims, Tornel's response seems reasonable, even if it failed to recognize the rebellion's original intent or the more conservative position of many Anglo-Texans.

Indeed, by March 2, just a week after Santa Anna arrived in San Antonio and commenced his siege at the Alamo, a new convention of Texas representatives in every sense of the word commenced in San Felipe. Only thirteen of the fifty-nine delegates had been present at the gathering months earlier, in November 1835. Only seven were veterans of the 1832 and 1833 disturbances at Anáhuac. Only eleven had held office during the period of Mexican rule. They tended to be younger, average age 37, and resident in Texas only recently, with almost a quarter having immigrated in only the previous year, and nearly half having lived there for two years or less. They had distinguished themselves through military rather than political experience. In a place plagued by a lack of military enthusiasm, 40 percent of these men had answered the call to take up arms against Mexico, and only a handful of them were ethnic Mexicans, including Zavala and José Antonio Navarro. All these factors contributed to the March convention yielding a very different outcome from the first.[107] Indeed, much had changed in the political landscape of both Texas and Mexico in the previous five months. The federalist resistance in the interior had been suppressed.

Austin, who had always counseled patience and obedience, was now pushing for independence. Those delegates who had sworn in November to support the Constitution of 1824 sensed that they were in the minority in March and mostly kept silent.

Ultimately, the fifty-nine delegates would vote unanimously for independence. In so doing, they would draw from the same transcendent principles many of their antecedents had cited to justify seceding from Britain. The Mexican government had "ceased to protect the lives, liberty and property of the people, from whom its legitimate powers are derived." When "anarchy" prevailed and civil society was "dissolved into its original elements," the "first law of nature" obligated the people "to abolish such government, and create another in its stead." The Mexican government had invited and "induced" them to colonize its territory "under the pledged faith of a written constitution" and "republican government." Since then, it had "sacrificed" their welfare to a "far distant seat of government" controlled by a "hostile majority."[108] The Texas declaration of independence resembled that of the United States in tone, rhetoric, and logic. In addition to a people's right "to alter or abolish" a government that had violated its obligation to them, they also drew from the principles of minority rights and local governance. What was different in Texas was that, unlike the numerous rebellions that had swept the western frontier of the United States during the 1780s and 1790s, Texans distinguished themselves in their decision to declare and follow through with independence. Regardless, their decision was as much a continuation of the political upheaval that characterized the United States after its founding as it represented the residue of a defeated Mexican resistance. Historians have long considered the Texas rebellion to be the inevitable outcome of two irreconcilable cultures, but what Anglo-Texans attempted in the winter of 1836 was not that different from what restive agrarian communities had long attempted in the United States. The Texas rebellion represented a culmination of separatist impulses that had characterized the United States and Mexico for decades. It began as a Mexican movement, but its conclusion was unmistakably Anglo-American.

While the rebellion was a justified act of democratic expression to the rebels and their supporters, it represented something else entirely to Mexican leaders. The generals responsible for the bloody battles of the Alamo and Goliad, including Santa Anna himself, would later insist that the men they killed were mostly foreigners who had waged an unsanctioned war against Mexico and a few treacherous Mexican citizens who had violated their contract with their adopted nation. In his message to the inhabitants of Texas issued just after reclaiming the Alamo, Santa Anna blamed the revolt on a "parcel" of "adventurers, maliciously protected by some inhabitants of a neighboring republic" who "dared to invade our territory, with an intention of dividing amongst themselves the fertile lands that are contained in the spacious department of Texas." For Santa Anna and his advisers, the rebellion was little more than an unsanctioned foreign invasion. Yet, he admitted that he was "pained" to find among the invaders "the names of some colonists, to whom had been granted repeated benefits" and thus had "no just motive" to complain.

Finally, and perhaps most significantly, while the Texas rebels had appealed to their transcendent right to rebellion, Santa Anna made it clear that the only authority he recognized was that of the "supreme authorities of the nation."[109] The rebels could whimper all they wanted about tyranny. Mexico had not only acted within its rights in violently suppressing the revolt, but "the nations of the world would never have forgiven Mexico had it accorded them rights, privileges, and considerations which the common law of peoples accords only to constituted nations."[110] Tornel agreed that the "use of force to restrain the restless, to punish the rebellious, and to maintain obedience" was "an inherent right of the sovereignty of nations" and that "what is right for one nation should be right for all."[111] Like Jackson during the nullification crisis and Webster in his debates with Hayne, Tornel advanced the notion of a permanent and indissoluble union. Invoking the same terms of mutuality to describe the relationship between citizen and nation that Jackson had, Tornel declared his astonishment "that those who have lived entirely without restraint should now clamor for their rights" and likewise found it "incomprehensible that they should sponsor a war without quarter against a country that gave them lands, good homes, generous laws, and the blessings of their own civilization."[112] The republic was only secure so long as it enjoyed the loyalty of its citizens who owed their own security and prosperity to the health and cohesion of the union. In the words of Santa Anna, the "protection and benefit" of Mexican laws were reserved for those who "fulfill always" their "duties as Mexican citizens."[113] The rebels betrayed this contract, just as the South Carolinians had threatened to betray theirs. To the rebels' claim that the fundamental compact had been dissolved when Mexico decided to overthrow its federalist constitution, Tornel insisted that the indissoluble ties of nation negated such a scenario. Mexico, after all, had been a monarchy "at the time when the first grants were made" and "no specific form of government was stipulated in the contract." Furthermore, the decision to discard the constitution was issued by a democratically elected Congress in response to widespread popular demand. "An insolent minority cannot arrogate to itself the right of determining the form of government of the republic in violation of the wishes of the great majority," asserted Tornel, and no minority had the right to violate national sovereignty by violating its institutions or alienating its land.[114]

When news of the siege of the Alamo and Texas's declaration of independence in March finally reached New Orleans a few weeks after the fact, publications across the country quickly filled with praise for the brave and courageous rebels carrying forth the banner of individual freedom and personal liberty against the "barbarian" Santa Anna and "his savage hordes."[115] Before long, newspapers all over the United States were praising them. The *New York Herald* published an article adding Texans to a republican lineage dating back to the ancient Greeks: "What Thermopalae was to ancient Greece—what Bunker Hill has been to the United States—so will Bexar be to Texas." The writer made no attempt to explain the complicated course of the rebellion: "It is idle—utterly so—futile—completely so, to enter into an examination of miserable technical points in the affairs between Mexico and Texas." Instead, he castigated Mexicans as a "race of miscreants," no match for the proud and just Anglo-American family.[116] The *Grand Gulf Advertiser* denied the Texans' earlier affirmation of their membership in a larger Mexican family: "They only left one confederacy of states for that of another—the protection of the parent for the protection of the friend. They were still, however, free, still citizens of a free country . . . emigrating to add light to the dawning of liberty in the new world." Americans had brought liberty and freedom to Mexico, not the other way around. Therefore, the fight in Texas was Americans' to claim. "They are our countrymen and brothers . . . inspired by the same heaven—born feeling which animated our fathers in '76," whose blood, "which crimsons the wall of the Alamo, cries aloud for retribution justice, and appeals to every American freeman for vengeance."[117]

As reports like these filled the pages of US newspapers, more and more men flooded into Texas. The *Richmond Enquirer* reported, "Meetings have been held, since the fall of the Alamo, at new Orleans and at Mobile," their attendees expressing a "most ardent spirit towards the people of Texas."[118] One newspaper reported that New Orleans had the "appearance of a great camp," another of a "military barrack" as it swelled with citizens "determined to aid their struggling friends."[119] The surge prompted a national debate over the diplomatic propriety and repercussions of thousands of US men flooding into a region whose status as an independent republic was questionable to fight in a conflict in which the United States had declared neutrality. "The policy of our government is doubtless not to interfere with foreign nations, or infringe the recognized law of nations," conceded the *Cincinnati Republican and Commercial Register*. "But it is not the policy of a government of free and independent people to stifle or suppress public sentiment, no matter how manifested or expressed."[120] Never mind that volunteers were promised land in exchange for their service.[121] As news of the atrocities at the Alamo and Goliad spread, Texas came to represent a humanitarian crisis whose respondents also stood to benefit economically.[122]

Yet, as late as May 1836, rumors of colonists rejecting Texas's declaration of independence continued to circulate.[123] As Santa Anna approached San Jacinto, he noticed widespread desertion and estimated that Houston could not have had more than 800 men at his disposal, a "very considerable number having perished." These observations were confirmed by the desperate pleas of David G. Burnet, interim Texas president and a late convert to the independence movement. As the citizens of eastern Texas began to evacuate ahead of Santa Anna's approach, Burnet implored them to "repair to the field forthwith."[124] Burnet's appeals seemed to be of limited impact. A group of Nacogdoches leaders wrote on April 11, "There is no organization of the physical force of this community, and we are without a head."[125] Other municipalities simply refused to comply. A few inhabitants were even seen still "daring to express sympathy with the cause of Mexico." Burnet's appeals grew increasingly desperate. "Texans, have you no pride? Will not the finger of scorn be pointed at you should you leave the country without an effort to retain it?"[126] As before, Texan leaders appealed to their common heritage: "Are you Americans? Are you freeman? If you are, prove your blood and birth by rallying at once to your country's standard!"[127] Santa Anna noted that the Texans losses at the Alamo and Goliad had resulted in "desperate" appeals by "the so-called government" for Americans to rescue their "defeated hosts." Meanwhile, the colonists "persisted in taking refuge beyond the scene of war." Consequently, the Mexican president had reason to suspect that his final expulsion of these "imposters" was not far off, since "it was not possible that those that remained could equal in number the army under my command."[128] His estimation was close. Houston had nine hundred men. Their median date of emigration was 1834, and a significant number had arrived so recently that the rebellion was their first Texas battle. Indeed, more than nine hundred men who responded to the initial call to arms in 1835 simply failed to enroll the following year. The most significant battle of the rebellion would be fought and won by men with little or no connection to Texas.[129]

These facts likely fueled Santa Anna's confidence as he set out in pursuit of Houston's army, knowing that he was only one more victory away from expelling the interlopers. On April 20, he finally caught up with the Texans, who had positioned themselves near a densely wooded riverbank near Galveston Bay and San Jacinto. The following day, General Cos arrived with several hundred recruits. The men were hungry and exhausted from their recent march. With Houston's forces trapped and little sign of activity from his camp, Santa Anna decided to allow his men a short respite. Having carefully surveyed the enemy's position and issued strict orders to his sentries to remain alert, the Mexican president settled into a brief nap while his men finished their lunch.[130] He was soon awakened by the sound of gunfire and shrieks of "Remember the Alamo! Remember La Bahia!" Detecting that the Mexican camp had let down its guard, Houston had decided to launch a surprise attack. The Mexican recruits scrambled to find their weapons and return fire. Others were too stunned to move. The battle lasted less than twenty minutes. Texan forces ultimately killed 650 of Santa Anna's men while losing no more than a dozen of their own. One witness described a scene of "such slaughter on the one side, and such almost miraculous preservation on the other," the likes of which had never been heard of "since the invention of gunpowder." The massacre continued even after Houston and his commanders pleaded with their men to stop and as the Mexicans pleaded for their lives. Some men fled into the water, where they continued to be shot.[131]

By the afternoon, Santa Anna's "choice and veteran troops lie in hundreds over the prairie."[132] Santa Anna himself, who had taken off past enemy lines in the hopes of reaching General Vicente Filisola's division and initiating a counterattack, was forced to hide in some brush after his horse collapsed. He stayed there until nightfall, hiding from his pursuers, before wading across the Brazos. He was fortunate enough to come across an abandoned farmhouse, where he changed out of his wet uniform, sparing him possible attack by a pair of Texan scouts he encountered the next day. The men, not recognizing him, decided to take the Mexican prisoner anyway. The Texans failed to realize who they had until he was reunited as a fellow prisoner of war with his men from the battle. They then immediately took him to meet a wounded General Houston, whom Santa Anna humbly congratulated for having beaten the "Napoleon of the West."[133]

American newspapers declared that Santa Anna should face extradition to the United States to answer for his crimes "against civilization and humanity."[134] Texan leaders, however, had other ideas. They believed that they were more likely to receive that country's recognition by returning Santa Anna to Mexico. In fact, they could use his release as leverage to extract it. While in captivity, Santa Anna would sign the controversial Treaty of Velasco (1836), in which he agreed to terminate hostilities, order Mexican troops to withdraw from Texas, and *attempt* to persuade the Mexican government to receive a Texas commission delegation, thereby introducing the possibility of Mexican recognition of an independent Republic of Texas. Despite later claims by Texan leaders, the treaty offered no such guarantee and, as a prisoner, Santa Anna had no authority to sign it. Santa Anna defended his actions against Mexican criticism of his handling of the situation, insisting that he had beguiled them into releasing him from captivity while promising them virtually nothing in return. "They wished the independence of Texas to be recognized from that very moment and the limits fixed."[135] In response, he had only pledged himself to acts which "our government could nullify."[136]

As far as the Mexican general was concerned, the Battle of San Jacinto had been lost by the failure of reinforcements. The result of that battle might have been different had Mexican authorities recruited even more manpower from Texas's sizable, enslaved population. Yet, when the opportunity presented itself, Mexican leaders stopped short. "Shall we permit those wretches to moan in chains any longer in a country whose kind laws protect the liberty of a man without distinction of cast or color?" Santa Anna queried his advisers back in Mexico City as he marched north from San Luis Potosí.[137] At least a few believed that he should not. One adviser denounced the contract labor system that had thrived in Texas since the earliest days of US immigration as a violation of Mexican antislavery law and advised recruiting Black men to the army, where they could become aware of their freed status. Tornel concurred, advising Santa Anna to grant them their "natural rights," including the freedom to live wherever they may choose, so long as it did not encourage "disorder or upheaval." Yet, a congressional decree published two months later made no mention of such a policy. Mexican forces did, however, manage to attract a fair number of enslaved Texans to their ranks as they retreated.[138]

Santa Anna and his cabinet made the reconquest of Texas the cornerstone of his administration and encountered little resistance. Nearly all Mexicans, regardless of political persuasion, agreed that the Texans had no right to independence. While centralists and federalists debated how best to reassert Mexican authority over the rebellious territory, nearly all concurred that the revolt constituted little more than a combination of treason and foreign interloping. Texas still belonged to Mexico. While the rebellion itself constituted a profound assault on Mexican sovereignty, it contributed mightily to still-nascent Mexican nationalism.

Although Mexico would continue to suffer from domestic conflict and civil war, and even as Texas came to serve as an ally and inspiration for rebellious peripheral states, the rebellion would also help to galvanize Mexican centralists, making the case for greater federal control, unity, and a national identity that distinguished itself from the republic to its north. Indeed, the North American continent was about to enter one of its most contentious periods as two competing visions of its geopolitical future began to take form—a period during which the United States would be far less prepared than Mexico.

PART TWO

CHAPTER FIVE

Toward a Single National Truth

By 1840 José María Gutiérrez Estrada believed that Mexico's experiment with republicanism was over. The conservative politician and former minister of interior and exterior affairs acknowledged that, although he would have preferred to see his country continue as a republic, reason could not deny that the previous twenty years had brought only "calamity and misery." Neither the Constitution of 1824 nor its 1836 successor had worked. The former brought "social dissolution," the latter rebellion. Mexico had experimented with republicanism in all its possible forms, but to no avail. Monarchy, he concluded, was the only system of governance appropriately suited to the "character, customs and traditions" of the Mexican people. Republicanism's time had simply not yet arrived for the Catholic world.[1] If Mexicans did not reject this "detached torrent from the north" then not twenty years would pass before "we witness the stars and stripes of the North Americans atop our National Palace."[2]

While such monarchist views would not gain popularity until some two decades later, by 1840 most members of the Mexican political class largely concurred that their country needed a government that could guarantee order, restore unity, and help define their national identity. In short, one that could accomplish, as Gutiérrez Estrada himself put it, a "single national truth." Others who shared many of Gutiérrez Estrada's anxieties about republicanism, though not necessarily his remedy, represented an important thread of political thought ascendant on the North American continent. These Mexican centralists, "*moderado* liberals," and northern Whigs tended to be nationalist, urban, educated, and generally hostile to slavery. They also tended to favor territorial containment and cultural uniformity and included among them conservative centralists Lucas Alamán, moderados like José Luis Mora, and disillusioned federalists like José María Tornel. In the United States, they included New England Whigs like John Quincy Adams and Daniel Webster.

For most of the 1840s, however, North American politics was dominated by a competing centrifugal, agrarian, and territorially incipient political vision that was also generally more tolerant of racial hierarchy or exclusion. This was the vision embraced by the peripheral Mexican states of Durango, Sonora, and in particular Yucatán; the US South, and of course the Republic of Texas, which served as an inspiration and ally to many such movements. But fear of association with the Lone Star rebels would prompt federalist movements in Mexico to moderate their declarations of independence, agreeing to rejoin the Mexican republic if federalism were restored or limiting their claims of political autonomy.

Indeed, competition for Texas would contribute to a more nationally minded and territorially assertive federalism in both Mexico and the United States that combined elements of both countries' dominant political visions, albeit in different ways and to very different ends. In Mexico, an ascendent group of federalists known as "puros" insisted that restoration of the 1824 constitution could coax Texans back into the national embrace, quell rebellion, and secure Mexico's territory. They embraced a multiracial, federalist, and sovereign political vision that was perhaps the first modern conception of nationalism to emerge on the continent. Yet, the federalism of 1824 would ultimately prove an inadequate guarantor of Mexican sovereignty in the face of renewed aggression from the United States, where expansionist Democrats attempted to wed a strengthened federal apparatus in pursuit of territorial expansion with their historic commitment to Anglo-American self-determination. The Democratic faction accomplished this by advancing a conception of citizenship that linked nation, race, and state in a way that departed sharply from that of the Mexican puros and the Texas settlers of the 1820s. This vision would facilitate the United States' dramatic expansion at mid-century, but it would also pave the way for its self-destruction.

"Union, union, and more union": The New Centralist Order

The events associated with the Texas rebellion transformed the course of Mexican politics for the next decade, leading to a new political consensus of conservatives, centralists, and moderado liberals who called for a reformed federalism capable of instilling order, individual liberty, and an end to clerical privilege.³ Many of these men would populate Santa Anna's second (1839) and third (1841–1842) administrations after the general managed to redeem himself by leading Mexican troops in the Pastry War (1839), in which French forces blockaded the Port of Veracruz to compel Mexico to pay for damages inflicted on French shops in a riot that swept through Mexico City during the electoral disputes between Vicente Guerrero and Manuel Gómez Pedraza.⁴ Determined to carry out the promise of the Plan of Cuernavaca (1834) by reversing many of the liberal reforms of the Gómez Farías regime, the santanistas did not go so far as to embrace Gutiérrez Estrada's remedy to the country's political crisis, but they did call for a new system that, in the words of the federalist Mariano Otero, was better suited "to the salvation of the homeland."⁵ Although this new political consensus included the support of conservatives, it was dominated by moderados, who believed that for self-rule to work in Mexico, it needed a "good government" capable of enforcing order, achieving stability, and establishing uniformity over the "vast extension of the republic."⁶

As it turns out, santanistas shared much in common with a coterminous ascendant political movement in the United States, the Whigs. Members of both groups tended to be educated, propertied, reform minded, and close to the centers of political and economic power in their respective republics. They also shared a skepticism of popular democracy, state sovereignty, and local rule, insisting instead that order, uniformity, and centralized authority overseen by an educated and enlightened middle class constituted the foundation of liberty and good governance.⁷ In Mexico, adherents of this philosophy were known as "hombres de bien," individuals whom Alamán defined as men "of faith, honor, property, education, and virtue."⁸ Ideological successors of the early Anglo-American federalists, Whigs placed their faith in a similar group of propertied and educated men.⁹ Such a political vision was undoubtedly elitist, but both groups pursued programs of individual and social improvement aimed at preparing the masses for political participation. The extension of public education and establishment of national institutions for the arts, sciences, and learning were favored policies and considered essential to instilling the kind of cultural and ideological uniformity that centralists craved.¹⁰

Indeed, one of the chief aims of both Mexican santanistas and their Whig counterparts was to redefine relations between citizens and the state. As Mora put it, "No one should be a citizen of any state without first being a citizen of the republic."[11] Whigs similarly insisted that supreme sovereignty rested in the people and not the states, and that the Union had been created by one common American identity, not thirteen separate and individual ones.[12] Both groups perceived radical federalism as a fundamental threat to the sovereignty, order, and cohesion of the nation. Perhaps no event played a more foundational role to Whigs' political philosophy than the 1832/33 nullification crisis, which was no less an inducement for the Whigs than Texas had been for the santanistas. Otero, for example, warned against the threat to individual liberties emanating from "interior powers" as well as "the general," and called for a set of institutions that could sustain disagreement and make the "mania of revolutions" disappear.[13] Whigs shared a similar suspicion of revolutionary impulses, believing that they represented a fundamental threat to both individual liberties and the Union itself. The US Constitution, Whigs believed, was "not a contract, but the result of a contract," and did not depend upon continuing consent to remain legitimate.[14]

Despite the many similarities between the Whigs' perspective and the new Mexican consensus, they generally disparaged Spanish American efforts at republican nation-building as part of their belief in Anglo-Saxon political exceptionalism and cultural superiority. In 1842, as santanistas began instituting their new political order, Massachusetts senator Daniel Webster, one of the most eloquent members of the Whig party, seemed to dismiss such efforts, drawing an unflattering comparison between the English American colonies and those of Spain. The former was established by a free people of the "middle, industrial, and prosperous class . . . among whom liberty first revived and respired." The Spanish colonies, on the other hand, were settled by "military commanders and common soldiers" who, motivated by greed and ambition, subjugated the Natives and colonized as much of the vast territory of the New World as they could. Spanish America, therefore, represented little more than an extension of European monarchy, whereas the English colonies represented the seeds of a new democratic order.[15]

As much as Whigs believed in the inherent superiority of their Anglo-American republic, they also envisioned a continent composed of multiple such republics, each embodying the institutions, practices, and ideologies that supposedly contributed to the United States' success. Thus, despite their general hostility to revolution and underlying commitment to social order, Whigs welcomed Texas's independence as a stage in the process of Anglo-American continental domination they desired, but they opposed its annexation on grounds that it would threaten the republican character of the United States. Functional republics, Whigs believed, should be contained and homogenous. Absorption of a foreign state, even one dominated by Anglo-Americans, would threaten the very uniformity, order, and cohesion that they craved. Thus, while Whigs envisioned Anglo-American institutions spreading across the continent, they did not support the expansion of a singular Anglo-American republic. That said, most did support Texans' decision to secede from Mexico. Many Whigs believed that a "military republic" like Mexico, founded on "mock elections," represented a "retrograde and disastrous" attempt at republicanism, justifying Texans' decision to separate.[16] The implication of such a position, of course, was that sovereignty was something that countries had to earn. Thus, Whigs encountered in Texas an important exception to their general hostility to revolution—a group of freedom-loving Anglo-Protestant men declaring their independence from despotism and tyranny.

As Webster spoke these very words, however, Mexican leaders were creating a new political order that he and other Whigs likely would have admired. After Santa Anna redeemed himself against the French and returned to power in 1839, he led Mexico in one of the most orderly periods of its history since independence. After establishing a temporary dictatorship and installing a handpicked Constituent Congress composed of federalists and conservatives, the general stepped aside to allow the new body to compose a new constitution, the Bases Orgánicas (1843). Without using the term *federalism*, the document contained many elements of the 1824 constitution, but it instituted a modern taxation system no longer dependent on the volition of the states. State governors were appointed by the national Congress, but their legislatures were granted virtual autonomy over their constitutions, judiciaries, and revenue collections operations. As such, the new system aimed to strike a balance between local and federal leadership. It limited the franchise to men who earned more than 200 pesos a year and restricted membership in the Senate to those with an even higher income. The new constitution preserved the spirit of press freedom while prohibiting material critical of the church. Roman Catholicism was again declared the established faith, and military and ecclesiastical *fueros*, that is, tribunals, were preserved.[17] The new constitution aimed at restoring political order and remedying Mexico's economic crisis, but it was hardly the most democratic charter of the age.

One of the masterminds behind the Bases Orgánicas was none other than José María Tornel, Santa Anna's secretary of war and one of his closest advisers.

A former liberal, by the 1840s Tornel shared many of Gutiérrez Estrada's concerns about the direction of Mexican politics, although he remained a committed republican.[18] A vociferous critic of the Texas rebels, Tornel directly challenged the early republican presumption that democracy was best served by a decentralized federal system, insisting instead that the "centralization of power is not just a tendency, but a need in any democratic country."[19] He was also the likely author of "On Democracy in France and Monarchy in the United States," an anonymous 1842 editorial published in *El Diario del Gobierno* in which the author, claiming to have traveled in both countries, concluded that the United States embraced democracy as a question of "political form" as opposed to reality since its society was based on relations of hierarchy and servitude.[20] Tornel departed from moderados like Otero and Mora, who tended to echo the Whigs critique of Mexico. Instead, he insisted that the violation of Mexican sovereignty, in the act of Texas seceding, was the result of US greed and hostility, not Mexican misrule. "For more than fifty years," Tornel wrote in an 1837 diatribe of Mexico's northern neighbor, "The prevailing thought in the United States of America has been the acquisition of the greater part of the territory that formerly belonged to Spain." US institutions, as Mexico's "mentor," had only produced anarchy and poverty, weakening Mexico's vigor and leaving it powerless against foreign encroachment. While many moderado admirers of the United States mentioned slavery only in the context of US prosperity or not at all, Tornel pointed to the institution as evidence of American hypocrisy and the chief cause of its aggression toward Mexico. "The old general [Andrew Jackson] has always felt a deep sympathy for the [US] South ... where he enjoys the greatest popularity," Tornel remarked. "It is in that section that the hateful traffic in slaves is still practiced, and it is that section that is interested in securing a new market where human beings may be sold." The Texas rebellion, Tornel believed, was merely the most recent phase in the United States' by now well-established practice of territorial dispossession that began with the continent's Native inhabitants and was intended to end with the Mexican republic.[21]

Tornel not only rejected the idea, shared by Whigs and expansionist Democrats alike, that the United States constituted a political and cultural model to the rest of the continents' inhabitants. Instead, he claimed that role for Mexico. The reconquest of Texas was not only essential to restoring Mexico's territorial integrity and redemption against the "Colossus of the North," it was also about the salvation of the Western Hemisphere from the "degradation and slavery" which threatened it. While "not proclaiming as pompously the rights of man," Mexico had proven itself their true defender.[22] In an October 1842 speech before Congress, Tornel explained that Mexicans had made a mistake in attempting to model themselves after the United States, a country "as fatal to Mexico for its power and greed, as for the seduction of its doctrines and examples," and dismissed US and Mexican critics of Mexico's evidently failed attempt at republicanism. The people of the United States had a unique heritage and colonial past that made them unsuitable as examples of democracy to the rest of the world. Many of the characteristics that Mexicans most admired about their northern neighbors—their ingenuity, their work ethic, their individualism—were in fact the most dangerous to Mexico. Rather than attempting to emulate the United States, Mexico should consider itself the "first line of defense" against this nation of "eminently enterprising men whose natural instinct is to improve their condition."

What, then, could Mexico do? "Union, union and more union" was Tornel's answer. Specifically, "union through a central government," for it was Mexico's "privileged duty" to prevent such a "foreign plant" from invading its territory, and allowing it to "alter our customs, mock our concerns, and destroy our beliefs."[23] In this regard, Tornel's views departed from the more aspirational aims of moderados, who rarely chastised the United States or compared it unfavorably to Mexico. Not so with Tornel, whose 1842 speech was likely as much directed at British leaders as it was at Mexico's. The war minister's hope of reasserting Mexico's geopolitical dominance on the continent and reclaiming its place as the true moral and political steward of Western democracy by forestalling the spread of US slavery complemented the aims of Great Britain.[24] Mexico had long attracted British economic interests. Now it promised to become an important political ally in British efforts to undermine US slavery, alienate the South from the rest of the Western world, and eventually break that region's monopoly on cotton production.

Mexican leaders found support in one particularly unlikely individual: John Quincy Adams. While secretary of state, Adams had attempted to purchase Texas from Spain as part of the 1819 Adams-Onís Treaty.[25] By 1837, however, the Massachusetts Whig was warning that the acquisition of Texas would not only permit slavery's extension into territory where the institution had been officially prohibited, but it would compromise American moral and political authority in the hemisphere and bring the country closer to a likely war with its southern neighbor in which the "banners of *freedom* will be the banners of Mexico." Following an inevitable defeat by the United States, Mexico would exact its revenge by recruiting the Seminoles, Creeks, and "Negro slaves" in a Mexican "march of desolation" across the southern states, proclaiming "emancipation to the slave and revenue to the native Indians."[26] The elder statesman's writings and those of Tornel shared several key elements: the Texas rebellion as a proslavery affront to Mexico, the hypocrisy of the United States as a self-proclaimed beacon of liberty, and the threat of violent redemption from enslaved Blacks and dispossessed Natives and Mexicans. It is therefore unsurprising that the Mexican secretary of war, in his lengthy indictment of the United States, found time to make an exception for "ex-president John Quincy Adams," noting his formal objection to Texan independence.[27] Yet Adams did not praise Mexico so much as he proffered a warning to the United States: Annex Texas and risk a continental race war.

Perhaps unsurprisingly, the strongest defenders of Mexican sovereignty came from the abolitionist ranks, among them William Channing, the Unitarian theologian whose public letter to Kentucky senator Henry Clay might as well have been written by Tornel himself. Channing directly disputed the claim that the Texans' "revolt" constituted a struggle "of the oppressed for freedom" and instead emphasized the "crime" of secession, reminding his readers that the Texan settlers had agreed to "submit" themselves to Spain and later Mexico. Dismissing accusations of Mexico's "civil and religious despotism," Channing pointed out that the settlers had sworn allegiance to its government "with full knowledge that the Catholic religion was . . . alone tolerated by the constitution." He also dismissed the Texans' opposition to Mexico's transition to centralism since it had been "ratified by the national Congress according to the rules prescribed by the constitution." Rather, Channing insisted, the rebellion represented an abuse of the right to revolution—which should only be used "in cases of fixed, pronounced and persevering oppression"—by a disgruntled minority who represented a "drop [in] the bucket compared with the Mexican population." Channing's indictment spoke the language of majoritarianism, constitutionalism, and sovereignty. Like most Whigs, Channing opposed unmitigated expansion, pointing out that the country was "already endangered" by its own "greatness" and could not extend further "without imminent peril to our institutions, union, prosperity, virtue, and peace."[28] He was also clear, however, about the origins of the impulse for such expansion. American slaveholders were feeling increasingly isolated in a world lurching toward emancipation,[29] and the annexation of Texas would not only help harness federal power to slaveholding interests, something that ran counter to "every principle of our government and religion," but would also compromise the United States' image and international standing by committing it to "a degrading policy" of spreading and perpetuating an institution in lands where it had been abolished. Slavery, not liberty, would be "branded on our front, as the great Idea, the prominent feature of the country," placing the United States at odds with most of the rest of the Western world and threatening to cut it off from the community of nations.[30]

Other abolitionists, namely Benjamin Lundy, had earlier sought to establish a colony of formerly enslaved people in Texas to show the profitability of freed Black labor.[31] The colony had been an ambitious but unsurprising goal for one of the first leaders of the US antislavery movement.[32] Before arriving in Mexico, Lundy had dedicated nearly twenty years of his life to the antislavery cause, contributing immeasurably by authoring *The Genius of Universal Emancipation*.[33] Mexico, Lundy believed, was the ideal location for such a project given its geographic proximity and climactic similarity to the southern United States, its laws prohibiting citizens of the United States from reclaiming fugitive slaves, and for its relatively liberal attitudes toward race. "There appears to be no distinction in this place as to freedom, or condition, by reason of colour," he noted, "One complexion is as much respected as another."[34] Like Channing and Tornel, Lundy believed that the Texas rebellion represented little more than a "pro-slavery plot" by the southern states to add "NINE" more slave states to the Union. The influence of American slaveholding interests "is now so completely in the ascendant, and so thoroughly sways the deliberations and proceedings of our federal government," wrote Lundy, "that it makes it the passive, if not the active instrument, in extending and permanently establishing that horrible system of oppression."[35]

Abolitionists and some antislavery Whigs like Adams dismissed the claim of Mexican despotism. Slavery's defenders called Mexicans a "semi-barbarous people" and spoke of "planting slavery where Mexico would not suffer it to live," and in turn, the abolitionists and their Whig allies cast aspersions on proslavery Southerners and their cherished institution, so adverse to "the principles of human nature, the destinies of race" that it was bound to come to an end. Where would the institution leave the United States as one of its last defenders? What would it mean for the republic's self-fashioned role as the ambassador of liberal institutions and moral steward to the rest of the Western Hemisphere? What would it mean for its relations with the nonslaveholding societies of the Caribbean, whose "whole history" as independent nations represented a reproach to slavery and "whose ardent sympathies will be enlisted in the cause of the slave." The best posture for the United States to take toward Texas was to support Mexico's efforts to reconquer it.[36] Such a position often echoed Tornel's claim that centralism could likely ensure the liberty, equality, and tranquility that had to that point evaded Mexico. Comparing the actions of the Texas rebels to those of the South Carolina nullifiers, they characterized them as both a threat to Mexico's "tranquility and prosperity" as well as to the "stability of its free institutions, and the permanency of the government." Having learned from experience, Mexico had decided to shed radical federalism for a more suitable system in a move that enjoyed the support of most of the Mexican people.[37]

Lundy, in a direct rebuke of southern slaveholders in his own country, noted that Mexico's people, unlike those of the United States, "never promulgated the doctrine, that a small minority in a community should exercise the right to prevent the *majority*" from carrying its principles forward.[38] Mexico's leaders, therefore, had no choice but to "resort to force" when Texas declared independence. As Mexican citizens partaking in the benefits attached to that status, the colonists had agreed to subject themselves to the rules and regulations of their adopted country. It was they who had violated the contract with Mexico, not the reverse.

"Pursuing the destiny indicated to us": Centrifugal Federalism and the Rise of the Lone Star Empire

While a vision for the future of the North American continent was emerging from the respective centers of national power in Mexico and the United States, a very different one was taking shape at the continent's core, and no one articulated it better than Mirabeau Buonaparte Lamar, the second president of Texas (1838–41). With the Republic of Texas having liberated itself from the "tyranny and oppression" of Mexican centralism in March 1836 Lamar touted it as the kind of agrarian utopia that Stephen Austin had once insisted was only possible if Texas remained a part of Mexico. In his inaugural address, he promised an administration that prioritized "agriculture, commerce, and the useful arts," pursued "free and unrestricted" trade, and observed "equality and impartiality" among "every class" of its white male inhabitants.[39] The Texas constitution promised much the same.

In a rushed convention two weeks after declaring independence, Texan framers produced a constitution that reflected the values and sensibilities that had attracted generations of Anglo migrants to the territory. It resembled the US Constitution with several key exceptions, including abolishing imprisonment for debt; guaranteeing universal male suffrage; prohibiting monopolies, primogeniture, and entailment; and shortening term limits for all branches of government. When it came to land policy, however, they borrowed heavily from Mexico. Each head of family was entitled to a league and one *labor* (177 acres) of land, and every male citizen was entitled to one-third of a league of land when he turned seventeen.[40] Yet, Texas framers made it abundantly clear that their land would be a racialized utopia. They showed none of the compunction that their US forbears had in securing slave property. Article 9 of the Texas document forbade congress from emancipating enslaved people or limiting their importation from the United States. It also banned free Blacks from residing in Texas, required slaveholders who liberated their human property to also provide for their transportation beyond the boundaries of the republic, and limited citizenship to "free white persons."[41]

The Texas constitution represented an amalgamation of early US, Jacksonian, and Mexican elements to produce a white man's populist republic on the Brazos that could not have come at a more fortuitous time. The same year as the annexation bill's defeat, the United States experienced its most devastating economic collapse since 1819. The Panic of 1837 was caused by many of the same factors that had contributed to the earlier depression—rampant land speculation, an unreliable banking system, and unchecked lending. It also produced the same disillusionment among thousands of agrarians, especially in the southwest, where immigration to Texas once again became the "order of the day." The exodus was made palpably visible by the acronym carved into debtors' homes when they left—"G.T.T." (Gone to Texas). The Anglo population of Texas more than tripled from 1836 to 1846,[42] but given the state of US politics and economy by the 1830s, it is perhaps not surprising that Lamar rejected annexation as the "grave of all Texas' hopes of happiness and greatness." Texans had overwhelmingly supported annexation in 1837, but according to the republic's second president, the kind of future that the Texan framers had envisioned—agrarian, prosperous, and proslavery—was only possible if Texas remained independent of both Mexico and the United States. Annexation, Lamar warned, would render Texas "divested of the most essential attributes of free government; reduced to the level of an unfelt fraction of a giant power." Even worse, Texas would be "divided into Territorial districts, with Governors and judges" from "abroad" tasked with administering "laws which [Texas] had no adequate voice in enacting" and thereby transforming it into a mere "vassal" to "remote and uncongenial communities." In other words, annexation would subject Texas to the same centralizing tendencies that Texans had always rejected. Furthermore, by remaining independent, Texas could avoid the division and conflict that plagued the antebellum United States and more aggressively pursue the supposedly shared interests of its own people. Instead of burdensome tariffs and fiscal policies, it could bring "equality of taxation, burthening none of the branches of industry for the benefits of the others."[43]

Instead of a national debate around Native sovereignty and displacement,

Texas would enjoy the "right of controlling the Indian tribes within her own borders," and instead of facing the "fanaticism" of a growing abolitionist movement that threatened the "very institution upon which her own hopes of happiness are based," an independent Lone Star Republic could guarantee its protection, having remedied what was quickly becoming the most divisive element of US constitutional law. In Texas, as Lamar noted, slavery was safe from those "known to be pernicious to her peculiar and essential interests." Lamar positioned an independent Texas as a kind of new and improved Anglo republic with the benefit of history and hindsight. Sharing none of the admiration for Mexico that an earlier generation of Texans had and deeming the US Constitution the "highest effort of political wisdom," Lamar also conceded that a "fair trial of fifty years" had revealed "many serious and alarming errors" that an independent Texas might "wisely avoid" while "adopting its favorable features and availing ourselves of all the lights of modern experience."[44]

Texas was only the first and most enduring of the Anglo-American republics to emerge on the North American continent during this period. A wave of similar political experiments cropped up from Oregon to Niagara, and while each differed in origin, character, and aim, they shared several key components, including a yearning for an idealized agrarianism past, a more attainable system of white male political and economic autonomy, and deep disillusionment with the United States. These "breakaway Americans" did not signify a rejection of American ideas so much as a belief that the United States had strayed from them. In other words, they resembled the early settlers of Mexican Texas, except they sought to establish their own republic instead of joining another one. Like the Republic of Texas, these polities, while often appealing to a white male egalitarianism, demonstrated a preference for other forms of hierarchy or exclusion. The Republic of Oregon, for example, was a "white yeoman's republic" that promised free land to all white settlers while explicitly prohibiting slavery and free Black residency. The Mormon refugees who established a theocratic society in the Salt Lake Valley of Utah practiced an extreme form of patriarchy that commanded that men take multiple wives. Yet, the Mormons also demonstrated an impulse toward the kind of cultural uniformity preferred by Whigs and, while they likely shared a suspicion of centralized governance, the desire to avoid it was rarely a stated aim. Indeed, the Mormon theocracies were highly centralized and antidemocratic.[45]

The other republics also differed from Texas in another way. Lamar had not just envisioned Texas becoming a prosperous republic, he envisioned it becoming a prosperous empire. Specifically, Lamar set his sights on the Mexican territory to the west. New Mexico's isolation, commercial orientation, and complicated relationship with Mexico City made it an ideal candidate for acquisition by Texas, or so Lamar and his allies believed. Annexation's failure had emboldened imperially minded Texans like Thomas J. Green and Memecum Hunt Jr., Texas's representative to the United States, who asserted that Texans would continue to push their western boundary all the way to the Pacific Ocean, thereby "pursuing the destiny indicated to us."[46]

On its surface, Lamar's aspirations seem wildly unattainable. During the ten years of Texas's independence, it never managed to develop a national currency, banking system, formal military, or infrastructure. Yet, as Lamar eagerly observed, Texas's strategic position, ample resources, fertile land, and rapidly growing population seemed to bode well for the republic. Furthermore, given Texans' historical hostility to national fiscal and military programs, many of them likely did not consider such accomplishments appropriate measures of their potential for greatness. Texas's future, Lamar and others had believed, rested with its land and its people. Thus, as an independent republic, Texas aimed to take the mantle of Anglo expansionism in the northwestern hemisphere, thereby placing it at odds with both the United States and Mexico.

The Federalist-Autonomist Movements of the Mexican Far North

In terms of origin and aim, Texas shared more in common with the rebellious states and territories of the Mexican far north, each of which was prompted by Mexico's sudden turn toward centralism, than it did with the Anglo-American polities of the continental west. Each of the Mexican movements leaned decidedly federalist, asserted some degree of political autonomy from Mexico City, and shared the specter of the Texas rebellion. Significantly, however, none ever declared independence from Mexico. Although often referred to as secessionist,[47] seceding was never really their aim. Instead, they sought to draw national attention to local grievances and occasionally redirect the course of Mexican politics. To this end, their assertions of autonomy were temporary, conditional, and limited. Yet, they also owed much of their ultimate success to the Texas rebellion. After 1836 Mexican leaders understood all too well the likely consequences of continued indifference to the demands of peripheral states. Consequently, centralists among them usually ended up conceding to rebel demands for better border security or reduced taxation. Although the example of Texas could be leveraged, it could also pose a liability. Threats to separate from Mexico often undermined northerners claims that they were committed defenders of Mexican sovereignty and fueled centralist accusations that they were little better than the treasonous Texans. Ultimately, these rebellions amounted to a renegotiation of relations between periphery and core in ways that strengthened Mexican sovereignty in the far north and redefined Mexican identity in the service of the centralist-nationalist vision advanced by Tornel and others.

Of all the far northern rebellions, none resembled Texas more than California, which by the 1840s was home to a much smaller but still significant Anglo immigrant population. Spain and later Mexico had struggled to lure Hispanics to settle the distant region and, for a time, relied on convicts from Mexico City to populate it. Then, in the 1840s, the territorial governor began opening public land to private development. About a third would fall into the hands of Anglo-American settlers, many of them escaping debt and other effects of the 1837 panic. There they encountered a patriarchal social order in which political and economic power rested in the hands of about fifty men, who owned most of the arable land and enjoyed almost exclusive control over Native laborers often bound to the ranchos where they worked.[48] Although not technically chattel slavery, the unfree labor system on California ranchos— in which workers were held in a permanent dependent status and paid in clothing, food, and sometimes cattle—led at least one observer to liken it to "absolute vassalage."[49] In late 1836, Alta California joined the wave of federalist rebellions under the leadership of a Juan Alvarado. The rebels aimed to overthrow the recently appointed centralist governor as well as centralism itself. With the assistance of a few US migrants to whom Alvarado promised land in exchange for their service, the Californio rebels managed to unseat their governor and, in phrasing nearly identical to those of the first Texas delegation, declared California a "free and independent state" until "she ceases to be oppressed by the present dominate faction called the central government."[50] The movement, however, was swiftly deflated when Mexico City sent a new commissioner, who with the support of loyalists from the southern part of the territory, allowed Alvarado to become governor and pledged to remove Mexican troops if he accepted the new constitution.[51]

As much as the events in California resembled the Texas rebellion, they were too remote to have much impact on Texas itself. This, however, was not the case for the departments on Texas's southern and western borders. By 1841 grievances with Mexico's centralist regime, specifically its Indian policy or lack thereof, had materialized in a wave of federalist revolts stretching from Tamaulipas, on the east coast, to Sinaloa, on the west coast, and as far north as New Mexico. With Mexico's transition to centralism, formerly sovereign states faced renewed vulnerability as the government redirected military and fiscal resources toward reconquering Texas and defending Mexico from foreign invasion. From the perspective of northwestern settlers, however, nothing threatened Mexican sovereignty more than the Apache, Navajo, and Comanche. Beginning in the 1830s, local and regional authorities documented their complaints in a series of published reports, all of which bemoaned the loss of economic potential wrought by years of Indian raids, accused Mexico City of neglect, and threatened separation if not remedied.

The settlers also raised a much larger question about Mexican citizenship and nationality. The 1824 constitution affirmed state sovereignty, but it made it clear that anyone born within the territorial confines of the republic was a Mexican citizen. This inclusive vision of the Mexican body politic was one that centralists aimed to preserve as they sought to position Mexico in opposition to the United States. For Mexican centralists, their country's true enemies were norteamericanos, who threatened to encroach on its land and sovereignty just as they had on that of its own Native population.[52] For northerners, however, marauding Indians were Mexico's enemies.[53] In other words, their racial attitudes more closely resembled those of Jacksonian Americans and Texans.

One of the first and most dramatic of the northern movements occurred in New Mexico, where, according to the local patriarch Albino Chacón, "great distances" from the rest of the republic had made the territory "subject to furious attacks from its barbaric neighbors" that "patriotic love and national honor" had compelled residents to resist.[54] After years of neglect by Mexico City, nuevomexicanos had optimistically greeted the arrival of a federally appointed governor, who shared Chacón's first name, hoping that it would finally draw national attention to their grievances. Albino Pérez managed to alienate local inhabitants, however, with a costly campaign against the Navajo that ultimately rendered few concessions. Relations worsened after he began restricting local governance in accordance with the 1836 constitution, and rumors circulated that New Mexico, now a department, would have to pay taxes from which as a territory it had previously been exempt. In August 1837, a group of Hispanic residents and local Pueblo Indians launched an armed rebellion from Santa Cruz de la Cañada. After capturing and beheading Governor Pérez, the rebels issued a pronunciamiento. Likely mindful of how their rebellion would be perceived a mere six months after Texas's declaration of independence, the Chimayó rebels pledged themselves "to sustain God and the nation and the faith of Jesus Christ," and expressed their opposition to the new constitution.[55]

However, lacking effective leadership, and even more alienated from Mexico City than before, a power vacuum quickly emerged that provided an opportunity for centralist-sympathizing elites like Manuel Armijo, a prominent landholder and former customs officer who skillfully presented the rebellion as a threat to order, property, and peace, as well as Mexican sovereignty. Pointing to the rebels' gruesome tactics and alliance with the "weak, credulous, and ignorant" Pueblo, Armijo accused the rebels of misrepresenting themselves, claiming instead that they aimed "to remain independent of the government of the Mexican nation; to put an end to every person who has an average education . . . and to live without subjection to any precept of authority, identifying themselves with the savage tribes and putting themselves in the same level."[56] He insisted that nuevomexicanos needed to "reestablish order at all costs" or else risk inviting further violence from both the Navajo and the Pueblo.

In a desperate attempt to hold on to power and avoid a return to centralism, the rebellion's hesitant and self-deprecating leader, José González, made a fateful proposition—that the territory withdraw from Mexico and annex itself to the United States. The rebels had now gone from patriotic Mexicans frustrated in their efforts to defend Mexico to outright traitors of the republic. González's suggestion merely confirmed Armijo's accusation that the rebels represented "anarchy, ruin, and desolation" and aimed at "shattering the national unity to which we are tied."[57] Centralists in New Mexico had turned the debate about Mexican identity against its rebel authors by equating them with the very anarchy, disorder, and insecurity of which nuevomexicanos complained and by presenting centralism, and Mexican authority generally, as the guarantor of safety, prosperity and order. By the end of 1839, centralism had been effectively restored in New Mexico, but only after the president exempted its residents from national taxes for seven years.[58]

Not only did the conclusion of what came to be known as the Chimayó rebellion kill any hope of a viable federalist resistance in New Mexico, it also killed Texan imperialists' dreams of acquiring the territory. Unfortunately for President Lamar, his term began after separatism had been effectively discredited in New Mexico. He was apparently unaware of this change in territorial politics because shortly after his inauguration he declared an interest in establishing a "correspondence and intercourse with the people of Santa Fe," asserting that they are "attached to the principles which gave rise to our revolution."[59] Lamar, of course, aimed for more than a mere federalist alliance with nuevomexicanos. He wanted to make them a part of Texas. Likely aware of González's proposal for New Mexico's secession, but not of the reassertion of centralist authority there, he would attempt three times to convince the people of Santa Fe to accept Texan authority, all to no avail.[60]

A similar scenario unfolded further south in Sonora, where federalists attempted to establish an independent government composed of Sonora and its surrounding states in 1837. As in New Mexico, Sonoran grievances were rooted in the inability to prosecute Indian raids under the new regime's fiscal structure, which taxed states so heavily that it rendered them unable to defend themselves without seeking aid from Mexico City. Although often characterized as an act of secession, Sonorans wished to claim only "as much independence as [was] necessary for the economy and interior government of the department,"[61] and, as their September pronunciamiento made clear, they wished only to remain politically independent from the rest of the republic. In all other respects, their state would continue to "belong to the national union."[62] President Anastasio Bustamante, however, denounced their actions as treasonous, refusing to acknowledge any distinction between what Sonorans were doing and what Texans had done. The impetuous response prompted General José Urrea, a Sonoran native, to his own federalist pronunciamiento that elevated earlier Sonoran demands by calling for a reinstatement of the 1824 constitution. Receiving near unanimous support from department officials and local leaders, Urrea decided to take his rebellion south to Sinaloa with the hope of organizing a coordinated campaign against the Apache and seizing customshouse revenues at Mazatlán.[63] Sonoran federalists continued to go to great lengths to clarify that they were not engaged in a secessionist revolt, declaring again in February 1841 that their department remained "free, sovereign, and independent" only in terms of its "internal government," and pledging to recognize the "union and integrity of the Mexican territory."[64] Fully aware of centralist efforts to disparage their movement, the federalists went to great lengths to distance themselves from the Texas affair. Urrea's forces would engage in a six-month civil war with their centralist rivals in Sonora that would only end when supporters in Chihuahua called for the conclusion of the conflict so that resources might be redirected to combating the French invasion at Veracruz.

Not yet ready to give up on the possibility of an autonomous northwestern republic, Urrea fled south to Durango, where federalist resistance experienced slightly more success. The inhabitants of that state shared the same grievances with the central republic as the Sonorans, and in October, they annulled the 1836 centralist constitution and declared Durango a "free and sovereign" state under the previous, 1824 federalist state constitution. Urrea managed to govern Durango as such for about a week, until Mexico City managed to reestablish its authority by appointing local leaders to departmental office. It did not hurt that Santa Anna managed to overthrow Bustamante in 1841. The new president rewarded his old friend Urrea by appointing him military commander of

Sonora, to which the general then returned and rejoined his home state's longstanding war against los bárbaros.⁶⁵

Nowhere did the specter of the Texas rebellion hang heavier than in the northeast, where Texans played an active role in sustaining and then ultimately dooming the Republic of the Rio Grande. After the centralist takeover in Mexico City, regional newspapers had accused the government of "cold indifference" to the suffering of inhabitants falling victim to Comanche raids, and in the fall of 1838 General Antonio Canales Rosillo led a coordinated movement among the settlements along the lower Rio Grande Valley for a return to the 1824 constitution. The cycle quickly spread to surrounding villages, and within months the rebels had gained control of both Monterrey and Saltillo.⁶⁶ A local lawyer and politician from Monterrey, Canales had been an early supporter of the Texas rebellion but withdrew once Texans declared independence. Canales insisted that his mobilizing the settlements had been in the honor and defense of Mexico, but this did not stop him from soliciting the support of his former allies, to whom his aims remained somewhat less clear.

In a letter to Lamar dated December 1838, Canales reported, "On the 3rd of last month these towns of the north declared for the federal states." The movement had "progressed very rapidly and uninterruptedly," and the general predicted that an independent republic would soon result, at which point, he assured Lamar, "those towns and yours will again . . . be united in bonds of former amity." After congratulating the president on such a prospect, Canales requested "protection in your republic, which interests (imperiously demand) that we . . . take up arms."⁶⁷ The Lamar administration received another appeal a few months later from a federalist ally of Canales then in New Orleans, suggesting that Texas and the northeastern states propose a "*political* intercourse" which would "cause the hordes of centralists, now advancing to the stroke of a whip, to fall back terrified."⁶⁸ The Lamar administration would ultimately decline Canales's invitation on the grounds that the ongoing wars with Texas Indians absorbed too much of the republic's meager resources. The president did, however, offer amnesty to the rebels and looked the other way as Canales and his allies appealed to private Texas citizens for support.

Ultimately, ambiguity about its aims divided and doomed the movement. Just days after a leading general from Laredo clarified that "the present fight against the central government was not for the purpose of dividing the Mexican republic,"⁶⁹ the *Telegraph and Texas Register* reported that the rebels were seeking support to establish a separate government.⁷⁰ By January 1839, Canales' men, with the aid of a small group of Texan recruits, established the independent Republic of the Rio Grande under a provisional government based on Mexico's 1824 constitution. The republic ambitiously, and perhaps presumptively, claimed the states of Chihuahua, Durango, New Mexico, Nuevo León, Tamaulipas, and Zacatecas. Yet its chief aim remained the overthrow of the Mexican central government, not permanent independence from Mexico. The day after soldiers hung the federal flag in the town center of Guerrero and swore "their oath of allegiance to the new govt," Canales sent a letter to Mariano Arista, the centralist general stationed in the Rio Grande, stating that it was of "little importance to the villages what kind of government the republic has," so long as they managed to end the "terrible" war with the central government. Arista evidently felt confident enough to dismiss Canales's overtures and press his position that the rebels had acted illegitimately in their efforts to overthrow a government "recognized and respected by all the nations." Arista had done better than his Mexico City counterparts in responding to the demands of northeastern residents for improved border security, and by January 1840 he and a combined force of 120 dragoons and local militia had defeated a group of Comanche at a bloody battle in Nuevo León.

Arista had heard the appeals of the northeasterners, but he did not appreciate the decision by Canales to court "those bloodthirsty enemies of our country"—the Texans. As in New Mexico, centralists in the northeast drew a direct connection between the rebels' behavior and those of Indian raiders. Arista responded to Canales' overtures by calling on local Mexicans "to rally to the standard of war, in order to save the country from the traitors, pirates, rebels, and savages."[71] Ultimately, the rebels were compelled to sign an armistice agreement confirming their loyalty to Mexico and denying that they had ever "thought to rebel against the nation, nor much less acknowledge the independence of Texas."[72]

Centralists in the north had effectively reframed the contest with federalism into one that united Mexicans against a set of common enemies, but they had also changed the terms of the national debate between centralism and federalism. If federalists ever wanted to return to national power, they would have to go to great lengths to distinguish themselves from the self-proclaimed independent republic to the north and to assert their commitment to preserving Mexican territoriality.

The "Quasi-independent" Republic of Yucatán

The most significant and enduring federalist rebellion to sweep across Mexico in the late 1830s and early 1840s took place more than 1,700 miles south of Texas, but was no less related to events in the far north. The movement that would culminate in the Republic of Yucatán began ostensibly as a response to the santanistas' imposing conscription policy enacted as part of the Texas reconquest project and their stringent property requirements for holding office. The first policy cut deeply into the region's agrarian workforce, and the second disqualified most regional elites from political participation.[73]

By 1842 centralists had effectively managed to reestablish authority across the far north, but their efforts would stall far longer in the southern department of Yucatán, where an autonomous federalist government remained active for nearly eight years. Indeed, if there was a region of Mexico equipped to secede, it was Yucatán. Its geographical isolation, delayed integration into the Spanish colonial system, and economic independence had long contributed to Yucatán's relative autonomy. Unlike the impoverished northern states, the peninsula enjoyed a lucrative economy in sugar and cattle, and it faced nothing comparable to the Native raids in the far north that made independence unfeasible.[74] Scholars, in fact, have compared nineteenth-century Yucatecan society to the antebellum South, with its landholding white minority steeped in gentility, patriarchy, and honorifics.[75] Its workforce was composed primarily of Mayan peasants, many of whom were bound to the estates where they labored after being dispossessed of their own land years earlier by a creole leadership intent on developing the region's sugar economy.[76] Unlike the more aspirational movements of the populations of central and northern Mexico, those in the Yucatán managed to sustain a fragile autonomy in the face of Mexico City's numerous efforts to reassert authority there.

Inspired by news of Santa Anna's capture in April 1836, Santiago Imán, a merchant and property owner, launched the first of several failed federalist revolts later that year. Government forces defeated each of them until 1838, when Imán managed to broaden his base of support by recruiting the peninsula's Mayan majority with promises of relief from hated church tithes. Within a year, the rebels had expelled the Mexican army, and on 12 February 1840, formally demanded reinstatement of the 1824 constitution. Several days later, Yucatán's urban gentry, emboldened by the rebellion's success, decided to take it a step further and declare Yucatán "free and independent" until Mexico City met the first demand. In May 1841, after a series of skirmishes with national troops stationed at Campeche that eventually resulted in the government forces' expulsion, Yucatecans declared their "absolute independence" from Mexico City. They celebrated with elaborate festivities that included music, gunfire, speeches, and the raising of a flag to symbolize the birth of their new republic. According to a local newspaper, Yucatán had "definitively and absolutely separated itself" from Mexico.[77]

Despite Yucatán's distance from the Lone Star Republic, Lamar enthusiastically welcomed news of the peninsula's independence. Unlike the secret envoy that Lamar had in Mexico who predicted that events in the south would only render the Mexican government "more timid" about recognizing Texan independence, he saw a golden opportunity.[78] Several months later upon receiving news that the peninsula had joined with Tobasco and Campeche to form an independent confederation, Lamar determined that Texas "should ascertain the position which they [the newly confederated Yucatec] intended to occupy towards us."[79] In July 1841, Lamar informed the Texas Senate of his intent "to establish with the States of Yucatan, Tobasco and such others as may throw off the yoke of central despotism in Mexico, [and establish] relations of amity and friendship." He then informed Imán that the ports of Texas were "open to the vessels and commerce of Yucatan upon the same terms as we extend to the most favoured nations."[80] Imán, now governor, welcomed Lamar's overtures and replied, "Yucatan desires to extend its relations with the people of [T]exas, and to unite with them to sustain the cause of liberty that they have proclaimed in contrast to the oppressive government of Mexico."[81] Relations between the two polities culminated in a treaty that obliged Texas to supply Yucatán with $8,000 to fund its ongoing fight against Mexico City.

Yucatán would remain functionally independent for the next seven years despite Mexico City's numerous attempts to negotiate its reentry. This in part stemmed from Imán's early decision to recruit the Mayan peasantry, who aimed to use the rebellion to reclaim appropriated lands once Mexico had been defeated. Unlike the other federalist-autonomist movements of the period, Yucatán's appeared permanent and unconditional. Yet, just one week after declaring itself "completely separate from the metropolis," an editorial in a regional paper pondered the "convenience" of independence. Noting the progress of federalist revolts farther north, the author wondered whether it might be preferable to rejoin the Mexican union if the 1824 constitution were reinstated, noting the uncertainty of Yucatán gaining foreign recognition beyond that of Texas or continuing "our march towards progress as an independent country."[82] As one US visitor noted, Yucatán society appeared divided for most of the rebellion between "two great parties"— one evidently favored the possibility of reconciliation, while the other demanded "immediate and absolute separation."[83] Such reluctance may have had to do with lessons learned from Texas. Although Yucatecan leaders invited Texan assistance, they ultimately demonstrated little desire to follow their example. Despite the promise of independence, Texas—with few natural resources, virtually no industry, and little agricultural diversity—had by 1841 yielded to the perils of pragmatics, and Yucatecans were taking note. Ultimately, they managed to extract a series of concessions from Mexico City, which agreed to recognize the peninsula as a politically autonomous governing partner with full exemption from national conscription and taxation.

The Republic of Yucatán would ultimately collapse from within, however, due to subregional rivalries, most significantly between Campeche and Mérida, the republic's de facto capital. Its worsening economic situation, increasing scarcity of land, and continued Hispanic monopolization of local politics frustrated and emboldened Mayans to launch their own internal revolt, eventually culminating in a prolonged ethnic uprising commonly known as the Caste War (1847–1915). Desperate for assistance in restoring order, the Yucatán leadership came crawling back to Mexico City in 1848.[84] Recollecting the moment when Santa Anna's ultimatum was read in the Yucatán Senate, B. A. Norman, a New Orleans book dealer on a tour of the peninsula, observed, "A smile of derision flitted over the faces of the senators[,] . . . yet no man rose to offer a declaration of independence." According to Norman, Yucatán's brief period of "quasi-independence" had produced an economic despair that stalled the push for full secession.[85] Mexico had succeeded in closing most of the regional ports, making trade virtually impossible, and the peninsula had never enjoyed a self-sustaining economy or tax base. News reports of the struggles faced by their Texan allies likely also played a part in their reluctance. Norman recalled a priest who often dismissed the Lone Star Republic's claims to sovereignty, stating, "Not a dollar in the treasury, and ten to fifteen millions of debt." The padre predicted the republic's collapse in short order and that the "conquering army in Texas would proclaim Santa Anna emperor."[86]

He was wrong about the second part, of course, but if the Mexican revolts of the late 1830s and 1840s demonstrate anything, it is that Mexico proved ultimately more durable than the United States would. Here again Mexico's weakness may have been its strength. Given the poverty and vulnerability of most of Mexico's federalist regions, it makes sense that local leaders would prefer to remain a part of the nation on terms more conducive to their local needs. It is also possible that they feared absorption by Texas or the United States if they separated. Whatever the case, despite the many grievances of peripheral states with Mexico City, they evidently preferred to remain a part of Mexico rather than separate from it.

Federalism Reformed

The political crises of the late 1830s and 1840s led not only to a more accommodating approach to centralism, but also to a reformed federalism. By 1841 Mexican federalists had begun to harness their demands for a reinstatement of the 1824 constitution to the struggle for territorial integrity. Acknowledging, like Tornel and others, that the Texans and "North Americans" were "one in the same" in their designs on Mexico, Urrea argued nonetheless that they also shared "relations and sympathies with the children of Alta California, New Mexico and the Rio Bravo," who would be tempted to follow the Texans' example if centralism were not rejected.[87] Three months later, the Sonoran general attempted to do just that. After a rebel battalion stationed nearby managed to free him from his prison cell in Mexico City's Old Inquisition building, Urrea stormed the National Palace and, with his liberators' assistance, took Bustamante prisoner and called for a return to federalism under the leadership of Valentín Gómez Farías, who had returned from his exile in New Orleans several years earlier.[88]

The *puro* (pure) federalist revolution, as it turns out, would be short-lived and ultimately pave the way for Santa Anna's return to power in the fall of 1841. Texans, however, welcomed the regime change, hoping that it might improve their chances of gaining Mexican recognition. They were sorely mistaken. By the 1840s, Gómez Farías and the federalist faction he led aimed to restore Mexican sovereignty, not compromise with Texas. Puros distinguished themselves from earlier generations of federalists by their awareness of Mexico's political and territorial challenges. They promoted the 1824 constitution for its ability to unite and secure the country. Federalism, not centralism, they insisted was essential to order, peace, and security. This more nationalist-minded federalism was a direct product of the political crisis of the previous decade and a strong signal that Texas represented only the first stage in the United States' effort to establish a transcontinental empire from the ravished territory of Mexico's far north. No one seemed better positioned to articulate this view than Gómez Farías, who while in New Orleans reported on the disparaging characterizations of Mexicans filling US newspapers. The former vice president of Mexico noted how some writers compared Mexicans to Blacks and Indians, groups hardly considered "part of the human race" in this "country of liberals."[89]

Any hope on the part of Texans that the new Mexican regime would somehow honor their claim to independence had been dashed years earlier, when

Lamar expressed hope that the Texans' former ally, Gómez Farías, might support the Lone Star Republic since "in you are to be found a concentration of all those liberal principles and enlightened views which tend to the promotion of civil and religious liberty." In turn, Gómez Farías had made it abundantly clear that he had no intention of placing ideological proclivity above Mexican sovereignty. As early as 1839, he had informed Texan leaders that, although he "loved men who are free," he nonetheless agreed with Santa Anna's position that Texas had no legitimate claim to independence.[90] If Mexico extended its recognition to the rebel province, then "Zacatecas, Sonora etc would soon be asking the same thing." Even more revealing, when Bernard E. Bee, Lamar's foreign secretary, pointed out that Texas's now overwhelming Anglo population made reunion with Mexico unrealistic if not impossible, Gómez Farías abruptly dismissed him, insisting, "Texas should at once propose to be *reunited* with Mexico," and after doing so would "be received with open arms." The president reminded Bee, "Mexico is the finest country in the world; avail yourself of its advantages [and] at a future day *your* son may be at its head."[91]

Indeed, Mexicans did not just disagree with Texans and their sympathizers in the United States when it came to territoriality. By the 1840s, race and nation were becoming far more closely linked in the minds of many norteamericanos, thanks in part to expansionist efforts to lure settlers back into the national embrace of the United States.[92] This contributed to a growing racialized nationalism that differed markedly from the multiethnic body politic that puros envisioned. There was little chance that the Lone Star Republic, now composed overwhelmingly of migrants from southern states, many of them slaveholders, would willingly rejoin Mexico. Neither centralism nor puro federalism had much to offer them, and, having never lived under the Mexican flag, their impressions of that country had been largely shaped by war and the anti-Mexican propaganda that accompanied it.

A sustained Texan independence appeared increasingly unlikely as well. For many, the dream of a "Lone Star Empire" was as brief as the republic's three-year presidential term limit. In 1841 Texans reelected Sam Houston, their first president and a strong supporter of annexation to the United States, who swiftly reopened talks with the Tyler administration. This time, however, annexation seemed less certain. Having declared a Mexican reconquest of Texas *"wholly improbable,"*[93] British diplomats were beginning to ponder if an independent Texas might hold the key to limiting US omnipotence on the continent. That spring, British prime minister Lord Palmerston received an exciting correspondence from the commissioner of the British and Foreign Courts for the Suppression of the Slave Trade in Sierra Leone. If Britain were to secure a reciprocal trade agreement with Texas, it might not only halt the spread of the "pestilential system of Negro slavery," but also undermine US dominance of the global cotton market. Moreover, Texas's lack of a manufacturing industry would allow Britain to exercise greater political influence within its borders, "and instead of a slave state, we should, by our aid, raise up a *free* and powerful republic between Mexico and the United States."[94]

Southerners, many of whom suspected British interest in acquiring Texas for precisely this reason, intensified their own demands for annexation. When expansionists, most of them Democrats, looked to Texas, they did not see the promising extension of the Anglo republican model as the Whigs did. Rather, they saw a polity composed of potential constituents and vulnerable to Britain's "emancipationist imperialism." Convinced that the British were attempting to undermine US dominance of the global cotton market, slavery's advocates in Washington—of which there were many by the 1840s—identified British meddling in the affairs of Texas and Mexico as evidence of a transatlantic abolitionist conspiracy to undermine US slavery.[95] As early as May 1836, Powhatan Ellis, the US envoy in Mexico City, had alluded to the possibility of a British-backed affront originating in Texas when he warned that Tornel, then Mexican secretary of state, entertained the "most bitter and rancorous feelings against the United States."[96] That same year, South Carolina senator John C. Calhoun cited the fear of Mexican "annoyance" should Texas fail to be annexed to the United States.[97]

As chimeral as Mexico's hope of reconquering Texas might have been, slaveholders in the United States took it seriously.[98] By the middle of 1842, the southern press was reporting anxiously on the prospect of an Anglo-Mexican assault on US slavery, in some cases citing directly from the manifestos of Mexican leaders.[99] Virginia representative Henry Wise warned his colleagues that the "tyrant" of Mexico "was now at war with Texas" and "would never stop till he had driven slavery beyond the Sabine."[100] Fears were heightened when Duff Green, the US envoy to London, alleged that he had discovered evidence that Britain may have offered Texas a loan in exchange for emancipation. Such an arrangement, Green warned, would transform Texas into "a depot for runaway slaves" who, after escaping to Texas, could cooperate with the "Indians on the western border" to threaten slavery in the United States.[101] British officials were more interested in undermining the South economically by securing a free labor alternative to southern cotton than in inciting slave revolt, but the threat of such a scenario loomed large over John Tyler's presidential administration.

Tyler was a Whig, but of a certain type. As a Virginian, he fostered a deep suspicion of centralized power that made him unwilling to pursue elements of his party's agenda, including its proposals for a national bank, protective tariff, and federal financing of internal improvements. As a slaveholding president, however, he was willing to use his executive authority in pursuit of related interests. Soon alienated from his party and eager for a policy initiative that could win him a second term, Tyler instructed Secretary of State Abel P. Upshur to reopen annexation talks with Texas in late 1843.[102] Tyler and Upshur were members of a new generation of southern statesmen willing to depart from their sections' traditional hostility to centralized power and interventionism to pursue an aggressive foreign policy committed to preserving and perpetuating slavery abroad. They saw Britain as meddling from Texas to Brazil and aimed to utilize the Monroe Doctrine's warning to the Europeans to shield emerging slave republics in the Western Hemisphere from the empire's influence or, even worse, its grasp.[103] To this end, the acquisition of Texas became the defining policy initiative of Tyler's presidency. Success would require clearing three major hurdles: obtaining northern support, given how Whig opposition defeated the initial attempt to annex Texas in 1837; convincing Texans, now largely accustomed to independence, to join the United States; and resolving ideological and constitutional issues, in particular how the United States might go about annexing what it considered to be a sovereign country.

The first was ably cleared by Mississippi senator Robert Walker, who outlined a compelling case for annexing Texas that transcended sectionalism. In a lengthy open letter published from Philadelphia in 1844, Walker began with a premise that nearly everyone agreed on: Texans had achieved independence through a legitimate revolution against a "central despotism" and therefore possessed all the "rights of sovereignty." The United States, as well as several European powers had by this point recognized Texas's independence, and Mexico's several failed attempts at reconquering it seemed to secure its status as such. Yet, several pages later, Walker seemed to contradict himself. Borrowing from Jackson's earlier assertion that Texas had been transferred to the United States as part of the Louisiana Purchase, and that Texans themselves had never assented to being transferred back to Spain, Walker concluded that the territory had effectively belonged to the United States all along. Of course, the inhabitants of the Louisiana territory had never consented to their transfer to the United States either, but this mattered little in Walker's assessment. What was at stake, he insisted, was "monarchy" versus "republicanism" and "which of the two forms of government shall preponderate throughout the world." Would the United

States allow a European monarchy to assert its foothold over the "fairest and most fertile portion of the American continent?"[104] The territorial boundaries of the union at the time, Walker warned, brought Great Britain "within a day's sail of the mouth of the Mississippi" and "to the banks of the Red River, in immediate contact with sixty thousand Indian warriors" and the "fiercest savage tribes in Texas." To refuse to accept "reannexation," Walker insisted, was "to lower the flag of the union before the cross of St. George" and surrender to Great Britain the entire region between the mouth of the Mississippi and the western Rio Grande.

Having ignited fears about what might happen to the Union if Texas were not annexed, Walker turned to allaying fears about what might happen if it were. Against Whigs' insistence that expansion was incompatible with republicanism and would compromise the union's durability, Walker countered that under the federal system, each state was responsible for "controlling its local concerns," which left the central government in charge of those that "appertain to commerce and our foreign relations." Echoing Madison, Walker insisted that expansion did not weaken the Union but strengthened it, since the "opposition of any one State is much less dangerous and formidable in a confederacy of thirty states, than of three." Furthermore, Walker asserted, inaccurately, that "no rebellion or insurrection" had ever taken place "within [the] limits of the United States," implying that the proliferation of such "traitorous or union-dissolving" movements in Mexico undermined that country's territorial sovereignty. Finally, and most disingenuously, Walker directly addressed the accusation of annexation opponents and tactfully capitalized on the racial anxieties of white northerners by explaining that Texas could function as a means of weakening slavery by supplying an escape valve for the South's Black population "through Texas and into Mexico."[105] Walker's manifesto capitalized on the era's burgeoning American exceptionalism as well as its racial anxieties. Annexation would facilitate and confirm the United States' position as both a beacon of liberty and a guarantor of peace and prosperity, while at the same time racially cleansing it. In short, annexation offered something for everyone, and Walker's letter quickly became a staple of pro-annexation propaganda.

Meanwhile, by 1844 the prospect of achieving a viable, independent Republic of Texas appeared far less likely than it had in 1838, at the start of Lamar's presidency. Not only had Lamar's planned conquest of Santa Fe culminated in disaster, with when Mexican forces captured all 321 Texan soldiers, but Texas also continued to struggle to defend its borders from Mexico's determined efforts toward it. In 1842 Mexican forces had managed to capture San Antonio de Béxar on two separate occasions. While neither occupation lasted more than a few days, it was clear that if Texans sought to avoid a reconquest, they would have to align themselves with a more powerful ally. Such an ally did not, however, need to be the United States. Initially, Houston entertained the possibility of an Anglo-Texan alliance but eventually reached a rough agreement with British diplomats that involved the latter negotiating a treaty with Mexico that would guarantee Texas's independence and, in return, Texans would agree not to join the United States. Of course, the prospect of such an arrangement was precisely what fueled the annexationist movement in the United States, but it is unlikely that by this point Texas's overwhelmingly Anglo population would have conceded to such an agreement either. Many had strong connections to the United States, and many were slaveholders, or aspiring slaveholders, who yearned for the kind of proslavery federal apparatus that now characterized the United States and preferred to attach themselves to it rather than a precarious alliance with an abolitionist Britain. And furthermore, economic conditions were improving after the 1837 panic, largely thanks to the United States' robust cotton empire, which also fueled northern manufacturing and trade. In short, there was much for Texans to gain by attaching themselves to the United States and even more to lose if they did not.[106] Furthermore, the United States was willing to coax Texas by promising to deploy a large armed force along its border with Mexico and position a naval squadron off its coast to secure the vulnerable republic while it engaged in annexation negotiations with Washington.[107]

Yet, annexationists encountered an unforeseen obstacle with Upshur's untimely death in February 1844 during a ceremony aboard the USS *Princeton*, when one of the ship's giant cannons misfired while docked on the Potomac. Upshur's replacement, John C. Calhoun, exposed the secretary's signature policy to a fate similar to that of its author.[108] Just before the Texas annexation treaty was set to be presented to the Senate, Calhoun penned a letter to the British minister in Washington in which he both defended American slavery as a "wise and humane" institution and tied its defense to the annexation of Texas. Calhoun's admission evidently unsettled northern Democrats enough that they joined their Whig allies in defeating the second attempt at annexation.[109]

Tyler's unconventional politics, especially regarding Texas, alienated him from the Whig Party, which instead nominated Henry Clay, a seasoned Whig politician and moderate. Neither of the two major party candidates for president in 1844 came out in support of annexation. The stance of the Democrat Martin Van Buren, making support for annexation contingent on Mexico's approval, enraged the expansionists in his party, who blocked his nomination.

After a series of ballots, James K. Polk emerged as the Democratic nominee, but his path to the presidency was unclear. Henry Clay seemed certain to beat the inexperienced and unseasoned Polk, but Clay's waffling on Texas compromised his standing with both northern Whigs, who opposed it, and southerners, who supported it. Even more costly to the Whigs was their failure to appeal to the rapidly growing population of overseas immigrants, who had instead swelled the ranks of the Democratic Party by 1844.[110] Whigs' elitism and Anglocentrism cost them support among a diversifying electorate, their party appearing to be anti-democratic and subsequently increasingly irrelevant along with their vision of a continent composed of multiple and competing Anglo republics and a contained nation-state led by an educated and prosperous class.

What made Polk's expansionism successful was that it extended beyond Texas. Prior expansionists, as it turned out, had been too timorous. By limiting themselves to the Lone Star Republic, they had never been able to fully shake accusations that they were motivated by proslavery interests. By embracing Oregon as well, Polk nationalized expansion even more effectively than Walker had, since his position did not require any disingenuous promise to weaken slavery. Rather, Polk and his supporters adeptly sidestepped slavery altogether, insisting instead that expansion was strictly about broadening the territory of liberty for Anglo-American men.[111] For most of the first part of the nineteenth century, the United States had enjoyed no such singularity. It had been just one of multiple republics scattered across the continent, and not necessarily the most promising from the perspective of many of Americans. Much had changed since the 1820s. Mexico's experiment with republicanism appeared to be faltering. Britain's hovering presence on the continent seemed to menace the continued existence of smaller, weaker republics. By comparison, the United States' economy was in recovery. Indian removal had been accomplished. Even the sectional dispute over slavery had subsided. Most important from a comparative perspective, the United States had managed to avoid the two chief threats to large, expansive republics—tyranny and disunion. It appeared the skeptics had been wrong. The United States could, in fact, extend its national domain without threat to its internal order and cohesion. How exactly it would continue to do so was another question.

Absorbing a sovereign territory like Texas necessitated the deployment of the very outsized federal power that Polk's party had long rejected and risked violating the very principle of self-determination that the United States now claimed to defend. Despite Texas's many challenges, it had managed to sustain itself as an independent republic for nearly a decade and might have continued to do so if US ambassadors had not sweetened their deal with the promise that the renegade republic could enter as a state, rather than a territory. Such an arrangement would permit Texas to enjoy much of its autonomy while also benefiting from the protection and patronage of the US government and its army. Its leaders would become senators and congressional representatives. Texans would retain control of most of the state's public lands and surrender responsibility for their sizable national debt. Such an arrangement afforded Texas leaders much of the autonomy and far less of the anxiety that they had experienced during independence. In another respect, it would allow Polk to extend the national domain while maintaining that such a "destiny" had been decided by the "people of this continent alone."[112]

Yet, accusations abounded, especially from Whig opponents, who continued to view annexation as a proslavery plot and saw flagrant hypocrisy in the questionable means by which it was being forged. Tyler and Calhoun, too impatient to wait for Polk to become president, had proposed legislating annexation through the constitutionally questionable method of a joint resolution, which required a simple majority of both houses, insisting that the Constitution granted the federal government broadened powers in the realm of foreign policy. When it came to the admission of new states, Congress could employ all means necessary and proper to accomplish the end. Many congressional members found the argument unconvincing. At least one opponent, from New York, remarked on the irony of "that man from South Carolina" who "could not hear of an appropriation for opening a harbor, improving a railroad, cutting a canal, or chartering a bank," now pushing a joint resolution through a lame-duck Congress to absorb a sovereign polity.[113] Even those who celebrated the accomplishment questioned its constitutionality. For congressional representative John Quincy Adams, the stakes were even higher. "Texas annexation," he warned, threatened to transform the confederation into a "conquering and warlike nation" of the very kind it hoped to never become. Texas, the senator bemoaned in his diary, was just the "first step to the conquest of all Mexico, of the West India islands, of a maritime, colonizing, slave-tainted monarchy, and of extinguished freedom."[114] Just three years earlier, Adams had complained that "the pursuit, the perpetuation, the propagation of slavery, was at the root of the whole system of the present administration."[115] Nothing had changed his mind.

Polk's expansionist supporters naturally viewed the situation differently. An editorial likely written by the journalist Mary Cazneau but published under John O'Sullivan's name in the *United States Magazine and Democratic Review*, laid out the case for the United States' ultimate absorption of the entire continent. The author tactfully positioned the United States as the singular defender of republican liberty and, in the process, effectively rewrote history. According to the editorial, Americans had settled Texas "on the express invitation of Mexico herself, accompanied with such guarantees of state independence, and the maintenance of a federal system analogous to our own." In fact, US immigrants had needed little coaxing by Mexican authorities to depart for Texas, and their allegiance to Mexico had never formally depended on the maintenance of federalism. The first immigrants to Texas, as Tornel aptly pointed out, had declared their loyalty to a monarchy, not a republic.[116] Yet, according to the editorial's author, Mexico's transition to centralism was enough to release Texas "from all Mexican allegiance, or duty of cohesion to the Mexican political body." Texan independence, therefore, was the "fault of Mexico herself."[117]

The editorial didn't just undermine Mexican claims to Texas, it also positioned US settlers themselves as the true ambassadors of US expansion. The distinction was crucial. The United States did not require an activist central state, much less military intervention, to expand. All the republic needed was its own people. Such a narrative, of course, ignored that many of those who had settled beyond the boundaries of the United States had done so to escape US dominion, not to perpetuate it. Supporters of this new credo of manifest destiny, however, viewed it very differently. Wherever US settlers went, the US state was destined to follow. Mexico, "imbecile and distracted," was no match for "the irresistible army of Anglo Saxon emigration" now making its way across the continent. Each of these Anglo communities would "necessarily become independent" and, most importantly, they would do so "without agency of [the US] government." Their subsequent attachment to the United States was almost as inevitable, however, because it was the only power on the continent that had proven itself capable of sustaining and defending liberty, of gaining territory as opposed to losing it. It was a profound mischaracterization of the factors and forces that contributed to mid-century expansion, but for its supporters, it adequately resolved the most pressing contradictions and inconsistencies of their movement.[118]

"Implacable enemies of our race": Annexation and the Rise of the Puro Federalists

In November 1844, General Mariano Paredes y Arrillaga, stationed in Guadalajara, issued a pronunciamiento accusing Santa Anna, whose presidency he had enabled, of corruption and mismanagement. The previous few years had, in fact, been a period of relative stability for Mexico under the santanista coalition. Yet, few of its promised reforms had come to fruition, and the regime's modern taxation policy, which Santa Anna had declared through emergency order, was particularly controversial. Most damning, however, was the regime's failure to retake Texas.[119] Unfortunately, José Joaquín Herrera, the man who replaced Santa Anna, brought Mexico no closer to this objective. Most members of the political class agreed on the need to reconquer Texas, but many moderados, including Herrera, viewed such a policy as more a liability than a necessity. By releasing Texas, Herrera believed, Mexico could refocus its energy and resources on restoring order and developing the national economy, things that Mexico sorely needed. Thus, not long after becoming president in 1844, Herrera made the inopportune decision to consider signing a British-backed treaty with Texas recognizing its independence.[120]

Herrera's actions prompted strident opposition from centralists and federalists alike, but few were more assertive than Gómez Farías, who issued a lengthy address to Congress in which he pressed an updated version of his earlier policy, calling for the restoration of federalism as well as the adoption of an aggressive stance toward the United States. In the aptly titled *Federación y Téjas* (Federation and Texas), Gómez Farías echoed many of the earlier claims of his centralist and santanista rivals: Texas was only the first of the United States' territorial aims, which included extending its reach all the way to the Pacific and as far south as Nicaragua. With this extension would come an expansion of slavery and the expulsion of the region's inhabitants—both Native and Mexican. Echoing Tornel, Gómez Farías reminded his audience that the Americans were a "people full of contradictions" who had declared many times "with their impure lips the sacred name of liberty." In a final effort to convince his skeptics, he stated that war with the United States was inevitable. Mexico could pursue it now or wait for the United States to initiate, but it would come either way. Where Gómez Farías departed from Tornel, Santa Anna, and others was his claim that such a policy required a return to the 1824 constitution. Centralists had struggled over the past decade to reconquer Texas under the Bases Orgánicas, but all that had done was embolden the Americans. A restoration of the original republican charter, the former vice president insisted, could rally the kind of popular support needed to fight a war with the United States and incentivize Texans to return.[121]

Gómez Farías began corresponding with federalist leaders throughout Mexico in the weeks following the publication of his pamphlet, gathering their views on Texas and the prospect of war with the United States. After the House and Senate passed the joint resolution for annexation in December 1845 at the end of Tyler's term, both federalist and centralist-leaning newspapers in Mexico published damning editorials accusing every administration of the previous ten years of having failed the republic by not prosecuting a more aggressive war with Texas. Numerous letters to the editor of *El Defensor de Las Leyes* (Mexico City) in April and May 1845, a centralist organ, echoed Gómez Farías's call and voiced their opposition to the pacifist stance of the Herrera regime. One such correspondence insisted that Mexico now faced a "true crisis" and warned officials against attempting to negotiate with hypocrites, Protestants, and "implacable enemies of our race."[122] The paper praised Francisco Alatorre, a congressman assigned to a special committee on Texas, for splitting with his colleagues and the administration by opposing recognition of Texas.[123] Alatorre explained his reasoning in a pamphlet of his own, in which he insisted it was constitutionally impossible for a nation to sign a treaty with one of its own provinces. As Alatorre insisted, Mexico's integrity, honor, reputation, and very existence depended on it not surrendering any of its territory. "Texas can only be and should only be Mexican," he asserted.[124]

Meanwhile, moderados like Herrera accepted annexation for many of the same reasons that Whigs opposed it. They believed Mexico's size and diversity had weakened it. A more contained and homogenous Mexico, they believed, would relieve political conflict, enable national development, foster unity, and hopefully appease the United States. What their opponents expressed, however, was more in line with a modern conception of the nation, in which its territory belonged not to its executive but to its people. They also believed that annexation would merely embolden US aggression toward Mexico. Furthermore, they viewed their simmering contest with the United States to be about more than merely land. Men as politically opposed as Tornel and Gómez Farías had characterized the contest between the United States and Mexico as one between slavery and freedom, oppression and liberty, theft and justice. In short, they believed Mexico, not the United States, to be the proper guardian of democracy on the North American continent. Because US leaders had such a low opinion of Mexicans' capacity for republican self-rule, they assumed that Mexicans would merely surrender their territory to them, but if the events of the past decade had demonstrated anything, it was that Mexicans remained mostly united around the need to preserve their national integrity.

The event that would ultimately seal the Herrera regime's fate was the arrival in early December 1845 of the American envoy, John Slidell. Herrera had agreed to receive Slidell in August on the condition that he function as an envoy and not minister plenipotentiary, reinforcing the fact that diplomatic relations between Mexico and the United States remained severed. This, evidently, meant little to the new US president, Polk, who had instructed Slidell to compel the Mexicans to recognize the Texas boundary. In exchange, the United States would forgive its citizens' claims against Mexican depredations. Polk viewed this as an advantageous arrangement for the bankrupt Mexicans. Operating on the same premise, he also instructed Slidell to offer to purchase California for $25 million. When Herrera learned of Slidell's objectives, he refused to accept him, insisting that he lacked proper credentials.[125] Nonetheless, it had taken Herrera too long to stand up to the Americans, and on December 14, General Paredes, the very man to whom Herrera owed his presidency, launched a rebellion from San Luis Potosí, where he had ostensibly been preparing for another attempted reconquest of Texas. Paredes had been receiving pleas from various centralist allies urging the general to act against Herrera. Slidell's arrival provided him with the excuse he felt he needed. He began his pronunciamiento by accusing the government of "trying to get rid of a necessary and glorious war" by "adjust[ing] the ignominious loss of our territory."[126]

Herrera, who had initially declined Paredes' invitation to resign, determined by the end of December that he lacked both the political and military support to counter him. Eventually replacing Herrera was none other than Gómez Farías, whose party enjoyed considerable gains in September 1845 elections. With assistance from puro allies and the recently exiled Santa Anna, who now pledged his allegiance to the 1824 constitution, conceding that it was the only means of securing Mexico's territory, the puro leader set about pursuing his dual policy of reinstating federalism and prosecuting a potential war with the United States.[127] Meanwhile, Polk ordered General Zachary Taylor to advance federal troops then stationed in Texas just south of the Nueces River, the border of the Texas republic. When the move prompted a small skirmish with Mexican troops on the other side, Polk used the event as an excuse to declare war in May 1846. In an address to Congress, the president insisted, inaccurately, that Mexico had "invaded our territory and shed the blood of our fellow-citizens on our own soil."[128]

As Mexican leaders from Tornel to Gómez Farías had long anticipated, Mexico and the United States were about to engage in much more than a competition over land. The war was, in fact, a conflict between two conceptions of nationalism, both informed by their struggle over Texas. The events of the preceding ten years had forced opponents of centralization in both countries to reconsider their positions on federal power, territoriality, democracy, and citizenship. Many Mexicans now advanced a nationalism defined, above all, by territorial inalienability. This objective had not only helped to unify much of Mexico's political class but forced both sides toward important concessions. Centralists understood that if they wished to restore order and salvage the union, they would have to concede to federalist demands for greater autonomy and political participation. Federalists, in turn, began to prioritize national sovereignty in ways they previously had not. Both sides advanced a racially inclusive idea of citizenship and national belonging that stood in stark contrast to the one taking hold in the United States. To be sure, agreement was not universal. As the federalist rebellions of the previous decade demonstrated, Mexicans remained divided around some of these questions, but what is perhaps most remarkable about these movements is that the republic held. The United States would enjoy no such luck. In many ways, the debate over the annexation of Texas highlighted the very questions that would ultimately divide that country. The next fifteen years would bring the United States' dramatic rise to continental dominance, but it would also prompt the emergence of two fundamentally opposed conceptions of US nationalism and a bloody civil conflict on a scale never before experienced on the continent.

CHAPTER SIX

Sovereignty, Secession, and the Decline of the Old Federalism

Few predictions were more prescient than that of Ralph Waldo Emerson when he compared the 1846 US invasion of Mexico to a "man [who] swallows arsenic": "Mexico will poison us."[1] The war itself would result in a staggering US victory and the eventual acquisition of nearly half of Mexico's territory, and it would also pave the way for one of the most devastating domestic conflicts of the age. In fact, the War of the Rebellion might never have occurred if not for the Mexican cession. Slavery's status in the western territories emerged as the central question of the decade, one that expansionist Democrats insisted the United States could resolve through self-determination. Yet, much of the legislation passed in the wake of the Treaty of Guadalupe Hidalgo, concluding the US-Mexican War (1846–1848), made a mockery of US federalism. When forced to choose between states' rights and slavery, southerners invariably picked the latter, yet they would return to federalism when it came to the very question that ultimately divided the Union.

By seizing on a particular interpretation of the Fifth Amendment's due process clause, slavery's defenders managed to wield congressional power in the interests of proslavery expansion without appearing to violate federalist precepts. Their efforts to do so, however, brought them into direct conflict with the principles of the Democratic Party and representatives of its northern constituency, who argued that the addition of a federal slave law undermined the party's historic commitment to unobtrusive central governance. In response, eleven southern states withdrew from the Democratic convention of 1860 and ultimately the Union itself, citing the very same compact theory that Texans had used to justify their earlier secession from Mexico.

Expansionists had credited the United States' recent defeat of Mexico to the supposed superiority and durability of Anglo republican institutions, yet the 1850s had been a showcase in US institutional failure. Slavery, of course, was at the center of every major political debate of the period, including sovereignty, territoriality, the Constitution, and the very intent and purpose of the republic itself. Ultimately, the US rupture would require no foreign invasion or forcible seizure of territory, as it did with Mexico. The United States would disintegrate from within. Over the course of a mere decade, the fragile ties that bound the Union, ties that expansionists insisted could be stretched indefinitely, would snap.

Meanwhile, the experience of war with the United States would strengthen a Mexican nationalism that had begun to take form in the years after Texas seceded. Although disagreements over the form of government continued as they always had, they were less intense than before because the conflict forced a reckoning among Mexican federalists. Returning to the Constitution of 1824 helped unite the country, but it failed to defeat the invaders or prevent a dishonorable peace. While US leaders remained largely blind to the limitations and inconsistencies of their institutions, Mexicans were keenly aware of their own. Mexicans emerged from the conflict more than ever committed to Mexico's territorial inalienability, federal supremacy, and democracy. The War for North America (1846–1848), as John Tutino has called the eighteen-month conflict between Mexico and the United States,[2] prepared its victor for self-destruction and propelled its vanquished toward modern nationhood.

"We are all Mexicans"

Contemporary observers and others since have credited the United States' staggering defeat of Mexico to the Mexicans' lack of unity and nationalism.[3] As historians of early Mexico have shown, however, Mexicans were divided over their country's political future—not whether it should exist. While some may have disputed the premise made by others, such as the editors of *El Tiempo*, that a return to centralism was necessary if Mexico wished to successfully defend itself militarily,[4] most agreed to the simpler proposition that the country essentially had no choice but to prosecute the war. The liberal editors of *El Siglo Diez y Nueve* declared that the ensuing "contest with the US is about defending the rights of man, it's about defending our homes and protecting our families; in short, it is about our very existence."⁵ The paper called on Mexicans to "march to the frontier to fight against the usurpers of our territory, and the enemies of our independence and prosperity."⁶ In March 1845, two months after Texas formally joined the United States, *El Voz del Pueblo,* followed suit, insisting that the "most iniquitous politics in modern times has been committed" and that "when it concerns nationality, or independence, there are no parties, we are all Mexicans."⁷

Some US historians have pondered Mexico's decision to engage in the conflict, implicitly faulting its leaders for not simply accepting annexation and complying with President James K. Polk's request to purchase California and New Mexico. Mexico's defeat was not a foregone conclusion, however, and the debates over Texas had contributed to a modern conception of sovereignty that considered unilateral cession of national territory to be antidemocratic. By 1846 nearly all leaders of the Mexican political class believed in a composite national people to whom the republic's territory ultimately belonged. Therefore, logically, no portion of that territory could be surrendered without the consent of the people's representatives. This was a theory that *puros* (pure) federalists drew on unsuccessfully when it came to Texas, but it was one they were no less firmly committed to on the eve of the foreign invasion. When Valentín Gómez Farías returned to the presidency in December 1846, he considered the Texas matter a question of "life and death" for Mexico.⁸

During the first half of 1845, President José Joaquín Herrera had entertained a British-backed recognition treaty that would have guaranteed Texas independence in exchange for its agreement not to join the United States. The James K. Polk administration desperately attempted to sabotage the negotiations in June, when it sent a 1,500-man force under the command General Zachary Taylor to a disputed strip of territory below the Nueces River in a show of force designed to send a clear message to Great Britain, Mexico, and Texas that it would not tolerate interference in any plans to absorb the Lone Star Republic. Taylor's forces remained on the border even after Texans rejected the treaty with Mexico and voted overwhelmingly to join the Union in July. When the administration sent John Mason Slidell to Mexico City to propose the purchase of California and New Mexico—rather than "settle the present dispute in a peaceful, reasonable, and honorable manner," as Herrera's regime had anticipated—relations between the two countries worsened.⁹

All the while, Gómez Farías received numerous letters from allies throughout Mexico expressing their dismay at the actions of the United States and unanimous support for what they believed to be an inevitable war to defend Mexican sovereignty.[10] Slidell's proposal merely confirmed their suspicions that Texas had been merely the first of the United States' territorial ambitions, which, according to the editors of *El Tiempo* even years before, were ultimately to "make Mexico disappear from the catalogue of nations."[11] General Mariano Arista claimed that the Americans aimed at nothing less than the creation of a new "Roman Empire." While the norteamericanos proclaimed freedom and universal liberty, Arista asserted, they despised all but members of their own race. They professed democracy while expanding slavery.[12] *El Tiempo* observed that in the United States there was "only public spirit in the material and pecuniary." It was a "decadent nation" with "no social links, no morality, no customs, [and] the laws are absurd and mocked." For many Mexicans, especially conservatives, the religious diversity of the United States represented a source of weakness, since it not only served to divide the populace, but relegated certain European immigrants to a pecuniary status that "mock[ed] the laws of citizenship."[13] Perhaps no one understood the impertinence of manifest destiny better than Gómez Farías, who declared, "What presumption! What pride!," when explaining the ideology that positioned the United States as the continent's sole purveyor of a "federal system" and aspired to a day "when the entire American continent w[ould] be represented by Washington City."[14]

Many Mexicans insisted that the significance of Mexico's conflict with the United States exceeded the country's own survival. Some newspapers depicted Mexico as at the vanguard of a hemispheric defense against the imperial aggression of the Anglo-Protestant republic. *El Mosquito Mexicano* likened the war to William III's conquest of the Irish in 1689.[15] Other papers reported on the disparaging attitude that Americans were said to foster toward Mexicans, largely due to their Catholicism, and suggested that if Mexico did not stop them, then all of the continent's Catholic and Spanish-speaking peoples would share the same fate as Natives and Blacks in the United States.[16] In evident contrast with other empire-building Europeans, the norteamericanos were a "race that forgives nothing, that does not take the trouble to conquer villages or civilize them or inculcate their customs among them or improve their condition; what they want is land and property and to realize their legitimate dreams without witnesses." For the editors of *El Siglo Diez y Nueve,* the stakes could not be clearer: "In this competition ours is the banner of liberty and the US's is that of slavery."[17]

Perhaps more than any single event since independence, the conflict with the United States contributed to the formation of a national purpose and identity.

Wartime Mexico was Catholic, free, and federalist. While preexisting divisions would continue to plague it during and after the conflict, the country remained united around a singular purpose and aim while at war. Furthermore, Mexicans sought to exploit the political and social divisions of the antebellum United States. Several weeks before the war began, Pedro Ampudia, conservative general and veteran of the Texas rebellion, printed a formal address to the "English and Irish [troops] under the order of the American General Taylor" in which he reminded them that the Protestant United States was guilty of "committing repeated acts of barbarous aggression" against Mexico and was therefore "unworthy" of the "designation of [a] Christian" country. He then called on Taylor's men to join the Mexican forces, where they would enjoy "good treatment."[18] A year later, while General Winfield Scott occupied Puebla, and Santa Anna was amassing men to secure the capital, Ampudia issued another, similar appeal. "Listen to the words of your brothers, hear the accents of the Catholic people," it read, encouraging them to "take refuge in this Catholic country," where they might meet "with a hearty welcome." Such religious solidarity could be viewed as Mexico's response to the racial solidarity that characterized US nationalism. In reference to the sectarian violence then plaguing the United States, the circular asked how the Irish soldiers of America could "fight by the side of those who put fires to your temples in Boston and Philadelphia?" If it was land and property that incentivized them to fight the United States' wars, then Mexico could promise the same if they deserted ranks and joined their "brother" Catholics: "May Mexicans and Irishmen, united by the sacred tie of religion and benevolence form only one people."[19] While Mexico may have technically lost the war, its strategy of encouraging desertion in US ranks was by all accounts a success. More than two hundred men would ultimately respond to Santa Anna's appeal and form the legendary San Patricio Battalion, or Saint Patrick's Battalion.[20]

In fact, the experiences of US troops themselves betrayed the hypocrisy of the very ideology that supposedly motivated them. Disease, poor pay, and abuse contributed to low morale, high desertion rates, and general doubt about the war's purpose. Major General George McClellan recorded in his diary, "I have seen more suffering since I came out here than I could have imagined to exist."[21] The high death toll compelled many to question their initial decision to enlist.[22] Unsanitary camp conditions and low or absent pay fueled frustration and prompted soldiers to question their mission. "Uncle Sam owes us near six months wages and why don't he pay up[?]"[23] In an entry dated 4 July 1846, Thomas Barclay, a twenty-year-old recruit, noted the troops' desire to "imbibe a pint of old Monongahela in drinking toasts to the men of '76 . . . But alas! humiliating as it is . . . we free and independent citizens had neither dinner to eat, toast to drink, orator to cheer or liquor to enliven the day."²⁴ Poor conditions caused theft and other forms of disobedience, for which the men faced harsh punishment, including floggings. One soldier recorded in his journal that "it chills my blood to see free born Americans tied up and whipped like dogs, in a market yard in a foreign land.²⁵ Barclay worried about the demoralizing impact that such punishment had on the troops as well as the impression it made on Mexican observers, noting in his journal that it was "unfitting for a republic like the United States."²⁶

Meanwhile, Mexico's return to federalism in 1846 helped galvanize popular support for the war. One author admitted that while in the past he had believed that democratic institutions constituted a "calamity" for a country whose people were ill-prepared for them, at present they were essential "to excite the people and nationalize the war."²⁷ Yet, the reinstatement of federalism produced mixed results. The decentralization of power undoubtedly hindered the national government's ability to coordinate defense. Regional elites, especially those in vulnerable coastal cities, jealously defended the human and fiscal resources that they had struggled tenaciously to reclaim just a few years earlier.²⁸ What Mexicans lacked in formal military victories, however, they made up for with devastating guerrilla tactics. In early 1847, a band of guerrillas from Tamaulipas and Nuevo León attacked a large government train of nearby wagons and pack mules, destroying 130 wagons and killing 110 teamsters. Monetary losses totaled more than a million dollars.²⁹ By late 1847, on the eve of the United States invading Mexico City, the guerrillas had succeeded in cutting off US communications between Mexico City and Veracruz. One US officer recorded in his journal, "During the skirmish with the internal guerrillas, we have suffered more frightfully than at the Battle of Cerro Gordo with the regular Mexican Army," and asserting that he suspected that the Americans "would rather face ten of the regular Mexican army than one of those outlawed guerrillas."³⁰

When Scott's forces finally managed to secure Mexico City, in late 1847, those Americans who had witnessed or experienced the hardships of the previous eighteen months understood the significance of the accomplishment. "The American army has enacted miracles," wrote one recruit, "performed deeds which will live forever upon the pages of history." He remarked that the second invaders of the ancient Aztec capital "had to contend with difficulties to which Cortes was a stranger." More than a quarter of the eleven thousand US troops who had set out from Puebla had been killed, wounded, or succumbed to disease, a "long peace" having "unprepared the United States for as vigorous a prosecution of the war as might have been desired." The poor infrastructure and the Polk administration's "erroneous idea as to the healthfulness of this country" had all contributed to a much longer, costlier, and more onerous war than most had anticipated.[31] Even after the stars and stripes appeared above the National Palace, the Mexican resistance continued, with American troops being fired on from rooftops and from behind buildings.[32] Contrary to the Polk administration's claim that the war against Mexico would be swift, cheap, and easy, it proved to be slow, expensive, and cumbersome. In fact, no US foreign war suffered from a higher desertion rate.[33] The Mexicans lodged a formidable resistance to the US invasion. All in all, it could be argued that the United States should have been able to claim more territory than the 521,000 square miles—including present-day New Mexico, Arizona, California, Nevada, Utah, and parts of western Colorado and Wyoming—that it did given its considerable economic advantage and considering the many financial, social, and political challenges that Mexico faced in the years leading up to and during the invasion.

The Mexican Cession and the Plea for Territorial Permanency
While the war against the United States unified Mexicans, it divided Americans and, for some, appeared to threaten the republic's very character and integrity. Having waffled on the Texas question as a presidential candidate in the 1844 election, Henry Clay, who lost his son and nephew in the war, left no question regarding his position on the conflict. In a rousing address delivered 13 November 1847 in his hometown of Lexington, the Kentucky statesmen proclaimed it to be an "offensive aggression," as well as "unnecessary" act, and reserved most of his aspersions for his fellow Whigs in Congress, whom he accused of capitulating to Polk's disingenuity. Asserting that he "I never, never, could have voted for that bill," Clay emphasized the senseless "sacrifice of human life" and "waste of human treasure" the conflict had so far caused. But most of the speech was dedicated to outlining the moral cost. The war had placed Mexico in a defensive posture, while the United States appeared to be motivated by a "spirit of rapacity" and "territorial aggrandizement." Annexing a country of eight million people without their consent would require the United States to abandon its republican institutions and function more like a military despotism. Republics, simply put, should not be imperial since it "extinguished" the "spirit of true liberty." Despite defending Mexican sovereignty, Clay drew on many of the same racist tropes that had long defined the Whigs and contributed to their anti-expansionist posture. How could anyone expect Anglo-Americans and

Mexicans to be "blended together in one harmonious mass," and happily governed by one common authority, as "rebellion, would inevitably ensue, until the incompatible parts would be broken asunder, and possibly, in the frightful struggle, our present glorious Union itself would be dissevered or dissolved." Mexicans, after all, had proven themselves ill-prepared for self-rule and the United States ill-prepared for the kind of "despotic sway" required to govern such a people. The United States would no longer be a republic of white self-governing men, but rather a "confused, distracted, and motley" government.[34]

Whig representative Thomas Corwin from Ohio similarly accused Polk of behaving more like a "king" and a "tyrant" than the leader of a republic. "Have you not room in your own country to bury your dead men?" he bellowed before Congress in February 1847. Corwin agreed that there was no honor in defeating a country so "anarchic and miserable" as Mexico and predicted, as Clay did, that doing so would threaten to "close our history as a free people," warning that the same military that was used to rule Mexico's people by force could just as easily be turned against its own. Yet, the senator's speech was perhaps most remarkable for its prescience. Like Clay, Corwin warned that if the United States insisted on behaving like a great empire, then it would meet the same fate as one. Corwin predicted, more accurately than Clay, that this rupture would come from the United States' own white population. "Should we prosecute this war another moment or expend one dollar in the purchase or conquest of a single acre of Mexican land, the North and the South are brought into collision on a point where neither will yield."[35]

No one more stridently criticized the war than the abolitionist Frederick Douglass, who made no mention of Mexican anarchy or ineptitude. Instead, he cast his aspersions upon defenders and Whig opponents of the war alike. The former he blamed for citing the "meanness and wickedness of the Mexican people" as a reason for declaring war upon them, and the latter for failing to defend them.[36] Douglass believed that Americans, in allowing themselves to be distracted by Mexico's supposed failures, had overlooked their own. The United States was engaged in a war to extend slavery into a sovereign country that had abolished it. Indeed, as the debate in the United States transitioned from the war itself to how much of Mexico's territory the United States should claim, most Whig opponents of expansion fixated on the supposed racial inferiority of Mexico's people as the chief reason to avoid annexing its territory. Even Senator John C. Calhoun conceded that extending slavery's domain was not worth such a cost. "Ours, sir, is the Government of the white race," he asserted, and the "greatest misfortune" of the Spanish American republics had been to place "these colored races on an equality." By absorbing Mexico, the United States would subject itself to being governed by "twenty-odd Mexican states" composed of "impure races" who were "unfit for liberty."[37] Most Whigs agreed with him on this point, terming Mexicans "an ignorant, a fanatic, a disorderly people" with "none of the elements of character in common with the people of this country." Some questioned their expansionist southern colleagues on whether such an acquisition would necessitate governing Mexicans "as you do your slaves in those states which now tolerate the institution of slavery" or perhaps serfs "belonging to the land which you acquire, attached to the soil." Would they be put on a "level with the people of this country" complete with "privileges" such as the ability "to regulate and control the destinies of your government?"[38] The last possibility seemed the least desirable scenario. Some expansionists responded that Mexico's population could in fact be trained to participate in an Anglo-dominated republic while others conceded that it would have to be governed indefinitely by American colonials.[39] Ultimately, however, leaders in Washington would have little say in determining the size of the Mexican cession. For all the talk about Mexico being too weak and miserable to defend itself, fear of a prolonged war would ultimately compel Polk's envoy, Nicholas Trist, to accept the terms offered by Manuel de la Peña y Peña, to whom Santa Anna had handed executive power.

Peña y Peña's moderado regime had shown signs of wanting to pursue a peace, even if it entailed the surrender of a significant portion of Mexico's territory. Gómez Farías and most of the puro faction pledged "an eternal war if necessary" to preserve Mexican sovereignty, indeed to preserve its very existence. As soon as puro leader Gómez Farías learned of the new president's intentions, he set out to organize a coalition of opposition states that included Aguascalientes, Jalisco, Querétaro, San Luis Potosí, and Zacatecas. In early November 1847, Mariano Otero, representing Jalisco, denounced any negotiations that might result in the loss of territory held by Mexico before the US invasion in spring 1846.[40]

On 8 September 1847, Scott's army advanced on Mexico City, where it engaged Mexican troops in the bloodiest confrontation of the entire war. On September 13, they captured Chapultepec Castle, the site of a boys' military academy, and Santa Anna surrendered the following day. In a lengthy letter, Trist explained that if the Polk administration did not pursue a treaty at this juncture, it likely risked an interminable war encouraged by the puros. Indeed, when news reached Mexico City in March 1847 that Veracruz had fallen to Scott, some puro congressional representatives refused to entertain even the possibility of peace until US forces had completely withdrawn from Mexican territory. On April 20, two days after Mexican forces lost the Battle of Cerro Gordo, the Mexican Congress passed a bill prohibiting the president from negotiating a peace with the United States or surrendering any part of Mexican territory. Two months later, however, it was effectively overturned by the Acta de Reformas, which confirmed the executive's constitutional authority to negotiate treaties, although it implied congressional approval for ratification and said nothing about surrendering territory.[41]

In April 1848, after the US Senate had voted to confirm the Treaty of Guadalupe Hidalgo, signed in February, the puro leader Manuel Crescencio Rejón attempted to stall its ratification and possibly prolong the war. In a sealed letter submitted to the new Mexican Congress, he argued that the treaty rendered Mexico completely economically dependent on the United States, violated the rights of Mexican citizens in the ceded territory, and would only invite future acts of US aggression. Rejón also argued that the alienation of "one half of our territory" to a foreign aggressor violated both "sacred right of nations" and the 1824 constitution since, according to that document, only the states possessed the right to alienate national territory.[42] In short, Rejón attempted to employ federalism in defense of Mexican sovereignty. It was not the first time, of course, but earlier efforts by puros had revolved around fostering popular support for the federal government and strengthening national unity. This time, Rejón made a constitutional appeal. Territory did not belong to the executive of a republic, but rather to the people of the sovereign states. Therefore, only they possessed the right to alienate the national territory. Unfortunately for Rejón and his puro allies, a Supreme Court ruling ultimately dismissed the appeal on the grounds that international relations fell under the purview of the executive, not the states.[43] Defenders of the treaty later insisted that it had saved Mexico from an even worse outcome by preventing even larger territorial losses. Ironically, many of them echoed the anti-expansionist claims of their Whig counterparts in defense of the treaty, suggesting, as Herrera had in defending his policy toward Texas, that a smaller, more contained territory would allow Mexico to better recover from the devastation of the past decade.[44]

In truth, the United States was in no position to push for more territory. On 6 January 1848, Scott reported that a measles epidemic had rendered more than two-thirds of his force incapacitated. In addition, the army continued to face isolated assaults and the possibility of losing communication with Taylor's forces in the north.[45] Given the United States' precarious position, Trist determined to violate Polk's order to halt negotiations and return to Washington in response to the puros' intransigence. Instead, he continued to work toward an agreement, a decision that proved to be the right one for the United States.[46] On February 2, Mexican ministers signed a treaty recognizing the Rio Grande as the international boundary, awarded Mexico thirty million dollars in exchange for the cession, which constituted nearly half of Mexico's territory, and obligated the United States to control Indian incursions from its side of the border. Despite falling far short of Polk's territorial ambitions, he accepted the treaty and passed it on to Congress for approval. Again, Scott's ominous warnings likely had something to do with this decision. The general had expressed in no uncertain terms that securing central Mexico would be difficult and insisted that annexation and military occupation would be "one and the same thing," since "any concessions of boundaries, satisfactory to the United States" would likely "create a revolt."[47] Also eager to end the conflict, the Mexican leadership agreed to the transfer.

For the US expansionists, the defeat of Mexico and acquisition of more than 1.2 million square miles represented a victory for republicanism, which was interesting, considering how it had been accomplished. Taylor, elected president in November 1848, spoke for many expansionists when he asserted that the United States now constituted an "empire of freemen," presenting to the rest of the world the "most stable and permanent government on earth."[48] For many, the Mexican cession represented confirmation of the superiority of US institutions, ignoring the warnings of overexpansion by Whig opponents. As long as the United States remained faithful to it precepts of decentralized governance and confederated self-rule, supporters of the cession insisted, it could expand indefinitely. For Polk, the United States' accomplishment disproved the "theories of those in other countries who maintain that the mass of mankind must be governed by force."[49] Yet, even as the president spoke those very words, his army was governing three million citizens of a neighboring republic by force. It had governed its own army regulars by force of corporal punishment for disobedience to make it happen. It was governing nearly four million enslaved people by force as well. These truths were lost on the president and his supporters. For him, the United States' dramatic defeat of Mexico and impending acquisition of nearly half its territory signaled that "an all-wise Creator directed and guarded us in our infant struggle for freedom and has constantly watched over our surprising progress until we have become one of the great nations of the earth."[50] Indeed, between 1846 and 1850, the republic grew by approximately 64 percent. Despite significant opposition, there had been no coups, no pronunciamientos, no civil wars. The exact form and nature of the republic, however, remained unresolved. While Mexicans would emerge from the war devasted, defeated, and in many ways still divided, the experience had nonetheless rendered a national identity and purpose that seemed to elude the United States. As Douglass predicted, in terms even more damning than Emerson's, "as sure as there is a God of justice," the United States "would not go unpunished."[51]

Divergent Paths: The United States' Federalist Appeal

For self-congratulatory expansionists, what propelled the United States' remarkable acquisition of Texas and Mexican territory was the same thing that would remedy the dangers that came with it. The expansionists insisted that slavery did not have to divide the country so long as the republic remained true to its precepts of local autonomy and federated self-government. The question of slavery's status in the territories arose even before the war began when in August 1845 David Wilmot, a first term Democratic representative from Pennsylvania, proposed an addendum to an appropriations bill, stating that "neither slavery nor involuntary servitude" be permitted to exist "in any part of" any territory acquired from Mexico. It passed the House but was defeated in the Senate in one of the first indications that slavery's status in the west would become a source of irreconcilable sectional disagreement. As the war with Mexico concluded, Americans were forced to confront the question of slavery in ways they never had previously. Both opponents and defenders of the institution understood that whoever ended up controlling the west would end up controlling the republic. Few southerners anticipated slavery taking hold in California or Nebraska, but they knew that if they failed to send proslavery legislators to Congress, they would lose the representative power they had come to rely on and, very likely, the institution itself would cease to exist in the United States. Northern Democrats joined their Whigs colleagues in crying foul, insisting that expanding slavery was not why they had supported the war and accusing the southerners of having concealed their true aims.

Democratic representative Stephen Douglas of Illinois believed that he had the solution: It was not the right of representatives from the northern states or the southern states to determine slavery's fate in the territories but the "right of American citizens inhabiting the territories to settle the question of slavery themselves."[52] Popular sovereignty to its proponents represented a return to the republic's founding precepts and means of resolving the sectionalism associated with westward expansion. It was the "glorious position" of the Anglo-American republic "to have grown not as monarchs do, with the top of the pyramid fixed as the foundation of it," declared one supporter, "but upon the broad basis of democratic liberty and republican principles."[53] According to the Michigan senator and ardent expansionist Lewis Cass, popular sovereignty confirmed "the right of man and the capacity of man to govern himself" that rested "at the very foundation of the glorious institutions of our country."[54] Less than two years after the signing of the Treaty of Guadalupe Hidalgo, Douglas castigated the war's Whig opponents for "taking the ground distinctly that our territory is already too large for any one system of government." Such a posture, he insisted, was "retrograding."[55]

Indeed, by 1852 Democrats, by refusing to take a position on slavery and insisting that it remain a local and state matter, attempted to tactfully position themselves as the true inheritors of the United States' revolutionary heritage. "[M]unicipal freedom," asserted Andrew Jackson Donelson, editor of the *Washington Union*, was the "foundation of the political building intended to be occupied by [the Anglo-American] people." Institutions built on any other basis produced only tyranny and despotism. The only safeguard for democracy was "local independence" and "states' rights" because they "first fix liberty in the individual."[56] This supposed truth, according to Douglas and his allies, was precisely what united the various peoples of the Union. Uniformity and consolidation only threatened to drive them from it.[57]

By 1854, Douglas, then chairman of the Committee on Territories, determined to see popular sovereignty applied to the unorganized territory of the Louisiana Purchase as well as the Mexican cession. His Nebraska bill, which proposed imposing popular sovereignty in the Nebraska Territory, was particularly controversial because it would overturn the Missouri Compromise of 1820, which had effectively prohibited slavery north of the 33rd parallel. Yet, the "effect" of the bill, as Douglas explained it, would be to shield Congress from having to legislate on slavery at all.[58] In addition, he claimed, it represented an extension of "Democratic principles, the Constitution, and the Union." Self-rule, after all, "was the principle upon which the colonies separated from the Crown of Great Britain; the principle upon which the battles of the revolution were fought, and the principle upon which our republican system was founded." Douglas called on his colleagues to "withdraw the slavery question from the political arena and remove it to the states and territories," leaving "the people thereof to the free enjoyment of all their rights under the Constitution."[59] A host of northern and midwestern Democrats joined him, echoing his claims that the proposal was "based upon the great principle which lays at the foundation of our government, to wit: the right and the ability of the people to govern themselves."[60]

Whig opponents of Douglas's bill were accused of "doubt[ing] the intelligence of the people" and whether "they are competent to decide what is best for their own interests." Accusations of infantilization and distrust of democracy filled the rhetoric of the bill's supporters. Senator Richard Broadhead of Pennsylvania remarked, "The truth is these gentlemen are afraid of the people, and so are the party to which they belong. They do not believe in their capacity for self-government, and, therefore, they will not place power in their hands."[61] If Democrats were the protectors of revolutionary heritage, then their opponents were the inheritors of colonial rule, for self-government was the "principle in defense of which the battles of the revolution were fought" and "to which all our free institutions owe their existence."[62] Their arguments evidently worked. The Nebraska bill passed the Senate with an overwhelming majority, eventually becoming the Kansas-Nebraska Act (1854). Although the vote was largely divided along sectional lines, its supporters' appeals to self-determination were ultimately too powerful to overcome.

Even more problematic, however, was the legislation that accompanied it as part of the Compromise of 1850, which dealt in part with slavery in the territories of the Mexican cession. The origins of the Fugitive Slave Act of 1850 date back to the Constitution's extraterritoriality doctrine, which obligated states to "deliver up" individuals whose labor or services were claimed by the citizens of another state. Not long after the Constitution's ratification, Congress passed a the Fugitive Slave Act of 1793, affirming slaveholders' right to cross state lines with the intent to seize their fugitive "property." In the following decades, northern states responded by passing personal liberty and due process protections for alleged fugitives. The strengthened 1850 Fugitive Slave Law intended to undermine these efforts by denying individuals the opportunity to prove that they were free. It made other elements of the compromise, including California's admission as a free state, more palatable to southerners, but it also aggravated the sectional debate over slavery that popular sovereignty had aimed to suppress and, even more significantly, revealed that southerners' commitment to slavery exceeded their commitment to states' rights.

No one pinpointed the hypocrisy of the 1850 slave act better than Massachusetts senator Charles Sumner, who in a speech to Congress in 1855 denounced it as a blatant violation of the right of northern states to determine their own set of obligations when it came to the capture of alleged fugitives. He went even further to claim that it also represented an abuse of congressional power in the service of slaveholding interests, and therefore a profound corruption of the republic itself. "Ours is a government of freedom," Sumner asserted, it should therefore "have nothing to do with slavery." It was one thing for the central government to be indifferent to slavery. It was another for it to take responsibility for enforcing it.[63]

In response to such accusations, southerners insisted that the Fifth Amendment's due process clause protected their right to own slaves just as it did all other forms of property. Many northerners, as it turns out, agreed with them. While they criticized the aggressiveness of the 1850 act, some northern opponents of slavery conceded that southerners had a constitutional right to reclaim fugitive property. Others insisted, however, that in northern states, where slavery had been abolished, fugitives should be treated, not as property, but as citizens with the same rights to life, liberty, property, and due process as anyone else. Indeed, the very constitutional ambiguity that had facilitated union at the republic's founding had led the country toward division and sectionalism by the middle of the nineteenth century. Southerners had the added advantage of being able to point to several constitutional clauses that "specifically recognized" the right to slavery. The three-fifths clause and extraterritoriality doctrine were understood by nearly all antebellum Americans to have been designed to protect the institution and privilege those who practiced it. So compelling was the proslavery interpretation of the Constitution that even radical abolitionists agreed with it, including William Lloyd Garrison, who publicly proclaimed the republic's framing document to be "dripping as it is with human blood" shortly before setting it ablaze before a shocked audience in Somerville, Massachusetts.[64] Most Americans expressed a reverence for their Constitution that exceeded what even most puros fostered for the Constitution of 1824. That was the problem. The ambiguity in the 1787 constitutional settlement had allowed its framers to mitigate division and form a union at the republic's founding, but it had also planted the seeds of future conflict. None of the Mexican constitutions evoked a similar uniformity of reverence or permanency, and they never solicited such a profound disagreement over their meaning.

Divergent Paths: Mexico's Centralist Rejoinder and the Rise of Territorial Inalienability

"My eyes are blind with so many tears," declared José María Tornel at an independence celebration in 1850. Terming Mexico's history to be "deplorable and desperate," Santa Anna's former war minister asserted that only a "miraculous concession from heaven" had prevented the country's complete destruction.[65] The editors of the santanista organ *La Palanca* concurred. They likened Mexico to a "sick man" in need "not just of a doctor but of a guardian who ensured the prescribed medicine."[66] It can be safely stated that Mexican leaders struck a very different tone from US expansionists in 1850. The events of the past several years had led many Mexican conservatives, and even some former federalists, to conclude that their country was simply not ready for republican government. *El Tiempo* began calling for "representative monarchy" as early as February 1846, declaring that since becoming a republic, Mexico's people had witnessed "nothing other than continuous revolts, bloody civil wars, the capital transformed numerous times into a battlefield, congresses dissolved, presidents precipitated from the seat of authority, the house destroyed, [and] interior order subverted."[67] The newspaper's editors went further than the prewar santanistas in denouncing republicanism as a foreign import and asserting that it had been the "great mistake" of Mexico's founders to adopt the institutions of its northern neighbor when the country's circumstances were "not only distinct, but diametrically contrary." The system worked in the United States because it was consistent with ideas and practices that had characterized British colonial society long before independence, and its "immortal" framers had the "prudence not to re-invent anything that was already established." In Mexico, however, "the opposite" existed.[68] The only remedy to the "misfortunes of today and tomorrow" was a representative monarchy in which an aristocracy "of merit, of wisdom, of service" would lead the Mexican people. This was the form of government, after all, which "governs the most civilized and liberal monarchies in Europe," and the only one that could guard against the "violent usurpations of the Anglo-American race."[69]

Even if most Mexicans did not go so far as the editors of *El Tiempo*, by 1850 members of nearly every political persuasion seemed to agree that in the three centuries since Mexico's birth, it had failed to achieve a durable system of representative government. If the outcome of the recent conflict had renewed US Democrats' faith in their republic, it did the opposite for most Mexican leaders. Conservatives were the most strident in their denunciations. Lucas Alamán, Santa Anna's close adviser and minister of internal and external affairs, declared himself unequivocally "against the election-based representative system . . . against elected town councils, against anything that may be termed a popular election."[70] The previous year, the santanista organ *La Palanca* acknowledged that Mexican federalism had weakened the country, contributing to its disorder and paving the way for the ultimate loss of "half our territory . . . *the wasted legacy of our elders.*"[71] By 1849 santanistas and conservatives were mostly united in their desire for a "concentrated" government composed of "only a handful of men" of "which the majority are not expected to participate," believing that only direct, centralized control could secure "local well-being." What Mexico needed, in short, was to be led by those most firmly committed to "union nationality."[72]

Following Mariano Arista's resignation in early 1853, the state governors elected Santa Anna as their temporary leader. The following month, the general arrived in Veracruz from exile in Colombia, where he had fled following the signing of the Treaty of Guadalupe Hidalgo and upon the return of the puro federalists. After three years of instability and collective national shame following the cession, however, conservative leaders orchestrated the aging general's return following José María Blancarte's centralist 1852 pronunciamiento from Jalisco that called on Santa Anna to return to the republic to "co-operate with . . . re-establishing order and peace" and to serve as Mexico's president one last time.[73] Shortly after his return, Santa Anna received a letter from Alamán in which the former pledged the support of Mexican conservatives and issued a program for the new government. It explained that the general's priority should be "to conserve the Catholic religion" because "we consider it the only common bond that links all Mexicans . . . and the only one capable of sustaining the Hispanic American race." He also called for the conversion of the states into departments with federally appointed governors. Alamán declared himself and his co-correspondents "decidedly against the federations, against the representative system by order of elections as they have been conducted up to this point; against elected town councils and against all popular elections."[74]

According to Alamán's biographer, he was, by this point, "antifederalist, antipopular, and arguably antirepublican."[75] But this was what he and his conservative allies believed Mexico needed, and Santa Anna seemed to agree. The Bases para la administración de la República hasta la promulgación de la Constitución, issued from the National Palace on 22 April 1854, established a centralized government with Santa Anna at its head. It also called for a five-member advisory council whose member secretaries would, in turn, receive advice from respective ministerial councils, as well as members of a twenty-one-person council of state. In short, it established a dictatorship with an elaborate system of institutional checks. At the same time, however, state legislators were ordered to recess, and their governors placed under the direct authority of the president "in order to exercise the broad power of the nation." Santa Anna believed wholeheartedly that the seeds of Mexico's mid-century humiliations "had their origins in the perverse doctrines and the anarchic system established in the 1824 charter."[76]

Mexican federalists had little with which to respond. The 1824 constitution that they hoped would reinvigorate and restore Mexico had failed to secure the national territory or prosecute the war to the extent necessary. It had been the moderado administration of Peña y Peña, after all, that surrendered to the United

States and negotiated the Treaty of Guadalupe Hidalgo. Puros, most of whom objected, lacked an adequate constitutional framework for overturning the treaty. Thus, most federalists were at a loss when centralists accused them of having primed the republic for absorption by the United States. The editors of the conservative *El Universal* asserted "[the federalists] will die a thousand times before admitting that the barbaric democracy of the Anglo-Saxons" represented the seed of destruction for the "Spanish race." How ridiculous were the claims of "liberty and democratic equality" anyway in a country where the institution of slavery existed "with all its horrors, with all its degradations, and with all its inhumanity."[77] Conservatives faulted the federalists for not only refusing to acknowledge the system's incompatibility with Mexico's political heritage, but for failing to recognize its inherent hypocrisy.

Mexico's political fate was not yet sealed, however. Federalists would have the opportunity to redeem themselves when the administration of President Franklin Pierce (1853–57) attempted to further enlarge the Mexican cession. Pierce's presidency, in fact, fused pro-expansion and proslavery interests more than any before it. Secretary of War Jefferson Davis's first act was to secure funding for a southern railway route to the Pacific, and he promptly assigned James Gadsden, his friend and former president of the South Carolina Railroad Company, to negotiate the purchase of the Gila Valley, in northern Sonora, just south of the present border, to that end. When Gadsden arrived in Mexico City in late 1853, he encountered a republic still reeling from its recent defeat by the United States and deeply disillusioned with the form of government that had once been its cornerstone. Unsurprisingly, relations between the two countries were at their worst ever. *El Orden* regularly criticized the United States for permitting unsanctioned invasions of Mexico by its citizens, typically in pursuit of marauding Indians or escaped slaves, and for its failure to fulfill its obligations under article 11 of the Treaty of Guadalupe Hidalgo to prevent Indian incursions. Terming the people of the United States "semi-savage," the paper insisted that the country's aggressions toward Mexico were in violation of the "idea" of its founders.[78] Thus, Mexican leaders were already on guard when they received Gadsden. Santa Anna, however, had reason to welcome him.

Upon returning to power earlier that year, Santa Anna had unleashed a series of political reforms that included restoring the power and centrality of the church, implementing a host of infrastructural projects—including a railroad—and initiating concessions to foreign companies willing to fund major projects. He was prepared to play both sides of the fence; not only did the United States' renewed interest in Mexican territory confirm Santa Anna's warnings to European leaders of impending US omnipotence, but they also offered his bankrupt republic an opportunity to profit from its neighbor's apparent unceasing desire for Mexican land.[79] US leaders, understanding the still delicate nature of relations with their southern neighbor, instructed Gadsden to declare a suitable route for a rail line as the sole motivation behind the request for more land. If Mexico agreed to such a purchase, Gadsden was instructed to push for a release from the obligations stipulated by article 11 of the Treaty of Guadalupe Hidalgo.[80] Yet in communications with Secretary of State William Marcy, Gadsden revealed more ambitious aims. He hoped to secure "all the states bordering the Rio Grande," to establish a natural boundary line along the Sierra Madre. Such a southern route would "embrace better ground for a road and greater inducements in the climate." He believed this would be supported by the leaders of those states, who had been "disappointed and discouraged in their repeated efforts to establish a constitutional republic of their own" and thus likely to welcome "ultimate annexation" to the United States.[81]

Gadsden's claims revealed a profound misreading of the national mood in Mexico City. Santa Anna swiftly rejected his proposal, insisting that his people simply would not tolerate the loss of more land to the United States.[82] Despite this, Gadsden felt confident that he could secure the territory he desired due to Santa Anna's vulnerable position. "He is on a volcano which may explode in a month," Gadsden wrote of the Mexican leader. "Money and an army . . . are the elements on which he must rely."[83] Mexican leaders instead pursued a policy that stressed Indian depredations, called for indemnifications, and avoided discussions that might lead to the transference of more territory.[84] For all of their disparaging of Mexicans' inability to secure and develop their land, Mexican officials insisted that Washington had proven no better. In October, the Pierce administration dispatched a secret messenger to Mexico City with a list of six possible boundary lines and the proposed sum that each should garner. The boundary preferred by Pierce would have included northern Coahuila, Sonora, and all of Lower California.[85] By mid-November, Gadsden had still made no headway in his negotiations. Mexican officials continued to insist that the United States owed them for its failure to enforce Article 11 and prevent its citizens from launching private assaults on Mexican sovereignty. A frustrated Gadsden penned a letter to Mexico's secretary of foreign relations, Manuel Díaz de Bonilla, reiterating his assertion that the United States had fulfilled its obligations to the "extent of its ability." He continued to insist that the incursions of which Mexico complained were the actions of its own Indians and therefore the fault of Mexican leaders, not of the US leadership. In the final lines of his correspondence, Gadsden revealed his diplomatic inexperience. In criticizing Mexican leaders for their "distrust and apprehension" of the United States, he bemoaned how a "country of vast capabilities, of illimitable resources, agricultural and mineral," had permitted itself to be "mystified" into interpreting the progress of the United States "as aggression to *overrun* and *occupy*." It was not aggression that propelled that republic's march westward, Gadsden insisted, but the "strength of the American union." Conceding that for three hundred years after Columbus's encounter with the Western Hemisphere, the "Castilian race was far in advance of . . . Anglo Saxon progress," now there was a "great spirit" which animated and drove the latter and "which no other country on the Globe" could resist.[86]

Ultimately, all Gadsden was able to convince Santa Anna to surrender was a small sliver of land that constitutes part of present-day southern Arizona. The Mesilla Treaty (1854), also known as the Gadsden Purchase, also released the US from article 11 while obligating it to assist Mexico in suppressing Indian incursions and any future filibustering attempts. The United States also gained the right to unimpeded navigation of the Gulf of California and Brazos Rivers, but had to honor Mexican land claims in the ceded territory.[87] Northerners, for their part, deemed the treaty yet another effort from the slaveholding south to secure its foothold in the west. The *Weekly Herald* bemoaned the millions of dollars for a "barren, uninhabited desert" in an "extraordinary project" that would only serve to "fill both the pockets of Santa Anna and a number of American railroad speculating politicians."[88] Knowing that too large a portion of territory would likely kill the bill in Congress, Sen. Thomas J. Rusk of Texas proposed acquiring even less territory than Gadsden had managed to negotiate, the complete abrogation of article 11, a reduction in the sum payable to Mexico, and the release from any obligation to cooperate with Mexico in the suppression of filibustering. On 25 April 1854, by a deeply sectional vote of 33–12, the Senate advised ratification of the treaty, by that time amended to a shadow of its original version. Its opponents were nearly all northern and antislavery. They were the same people who had opposed the Nebraska bill because it replaced an earlier prohibition on slavery in the territory with popular sovereignty.[89] Knowing that it was likely the best that he could hope for, President Pierce reluctantly ratified the treaty in June. Meanwhile, Gadsden was disgusted with the outcome.[90] Nonetheless, he pressed Mexico City to accept it, since any attempt to alter it "would most assuredly endanger the treaty."[91] Santa Anna was in no position to defy Gadsden's advice. A rebellion had just begun in the state of Guerrero, and he desperately needed funds to equip his army.[92]

The treaty did little to redeem Santa Anna's image among Mexicans. In a published circular, he justified the sale by characterizing it "as a political necessity to conserve the integrity and sovereignty of our territory." Without it, the United States would have likely continued its aggressions. Santa Anna insisted that Mexico had emerged from the deal in a better position than before. "I see the hand of Providence in all this," he insisted later. "Yesterday we did not even have the means of subsistence, and the government, affected by a lack of resources, did not know what to do; and today we resemble the man who wins the lottery, the beggar who becomes wealthy in a day." By surrendering a sparsely populated sliver of land that was of little use to Mexico, the Treaty of Mesilla awarded to the Mexican government "the only element it lacked to consolidate order and peace and to place in practice the material and moral improvements that will give the most beautiful results."[93] If Santa Anna believed he could convince his people that less territory was somehow better for their national security and well-being, he was sorely mistaken. If anything, their recent conflict with the United States had alerted Mexicans to the importance of their territorial inalienability. *El Rayo Federal* accused Santa Anna of surrendering a territory that was "no less important" than the original portion and accused the general of intending to use the funds from the sale for his coronation.[94] Santa Anna defended himself by insisting that he had few other options than to accommodate the United States. With that, the general had guaranteed his final demise and handed the mantle of Mexican sovereignty to his liberal critics.

While puros may have lost the political battle against the conservatives, their vociferous and persistent opposition to the terms of the Treaty of Mesilla had positioned them as defenders of the Mexican republic and of its people by highlighting the clear cost of such a concession to Mexican citizens themselves. They had also managed to launch a cogent defense of Mexico's territoriality in line with its republican constitution. They had also perhaps learned an important lesson about the vulnerability and ultimate inadequacy of their preferred form of government. While several state governors vowed to continue fighting, even after the Mesilla treaty's ratification, federalism had failed to seduce the Texans back into the national embrace, it had hindered Mexicans' ability to wage a coordinated military defense, and proven inadequate in preserving its territorial sovereignty. Simply put, the 1824 constitution had compromised Mexican sovereignty, not strengthened it, and many of its most ardent defenders now understood that if they wished to avoid a repetition of the tragedies of the last two decades and achieve national viability, they would have to come up with a new form of government.

Texas and the Rise of Southern Separatism

While Mexicans were uniting around the need to preserve the territorial integrity of their nation, a small but vociferous minority of southern leaders in the United States had already initiated a movement to dismember their own republic. At the Southern Commercial Convention of 1850 in Nashville, a group of radicals began calling for the South to separate from the rest of the country, insisting that it was the only way that the region could effectively pursue its proslavery ambitions. The ideological leader of the separatist bloc was none other than Nathaniel Beverly Tucker, law professor at the College of William and Mary, mastermind of the joint resolution enabling the annexation of Texas, and son of St. George Tucker, an early critic of the centralizing tendencies of the 1787 constitutional settlement. Nathaniel insisted bluntly that the Union represented nothing more than a "strict league of amity and alliance" from which any state could withdraw "whensoever she shall find the benefits of union exceeded by its evils."[95] What made Tucker's theory of secession so extreme is that it required no violation of the Constitution. A state could simply leave the Union whenever it felt that doing so exceeded the benefits of remaining a part of it.

Before Nashville, Tucker's theories had remained largely confined to the halls of academia, but at the Southern Commercial Convention, an annual meeting where southern leaders gathered to discuss how best to promote their region's economy, they gained a previously unattainable platform. "There is my misfortune," the professor bemoaned in a letter to a friend, "the want of a voice." At Nashville, Tucker found himself vaulted to near celebrity status. Delegates sought his advice, and reporters asked to sit next to him when he spoke. Remaining in the Union, Tucker insisted, would only result in the South suffering under an increasingly powerful federal government determined to serve the interests of a nonslaveholding national majority. A southern confederacy, however, promised a "magnificent future, and glorious destiny." Having discarded the northern states, the South could form a union "of congenial, not conflicting interests" and allow the "great school of domestic slavery" to continue to exist unhindered and unthreatened.[96]

Most of the convention's attendees, however, continued to believe that the South's prospects were better served from inside the Union than outside of it. In 1855, however, calls for secession erupted on the convention floor in response to the appeals of a different firebrand. "We are not yet what we ought to be, either in thought or act," declared Texas representative and former president of the Lone Star Republic, Mirabeau Buonaparte Lamar, who also accused the federal government of "neglecting" its southern states.[97] Northerners would have shaken their heads at such a claim, yet not been surprised that it had come from a Texan. Because of Texas's location, the Fugitive Slave Act largely did not benefit its slaveholders: Most of the state's fugitives escaped south, to Mexico. Proslavery "fire-eaters" had viewed Texas as an ally and inspiration, at least since 1839, when one admirer wrote to Lamar that if "infatuated fanaticks" ever drove the South "to separation," then it could "look to Texas as a country to fall back upon." Whether "a new confederation with the southern states shall be effected, or not," he had little doubt that "the southern country" would find "a powerful ally in that new, & I trust I may soon add powerful commonwealth."[98] Texas may have failed to become the powerful empire that Lamar and his southern admirers hoped for after independence, but it could still inspire southerners who deigned to entertain their own dreams of doing what Texas had done.

Indeed, Texas emerged as the centerpiece of the first major sectional dispute about slavery after the signing of the Treaty of Guadalupe Hidalgo in 1848. Even after being admitted as a slave state in 1845, Texas had claimed a significant portion of New Mexico's territory, including Santa Fe. Yet northerners and even some southern Whigs, including President Taylor, wished to see New Mexico admitted as a free state along with California. This seemed a reasonable aim since the presence of Anglo colonists and their slaves was small and many perceived the climate to be unconducive to slavery. Moreover, New Mexican statehood would help defray accusations that the war had been waged for purposes of conquest rather than spreading democracy. In November 1849, however, Texas governor Peter H. Bell denounced efforts to organize a state government in Santa Fe as a federal "usurpation" of Texas' rights and recommended that a militia force be dispatched to assert the state's authority.[99] By January, the *Austin Gazette* was reporting that many Texans "were for marching an armed force [into Santa Fe]" to put down the "rebels."[100] Back in Washington, Sam Houston, representing Texas in the Senate, submitted a resolution demanding that Taylor disclose all of his administration's correspondence concerning New Mexico and issue a formal statement about why he did not recognize Texas's claim to the territory. The Senate adopted the resolution on 7 January 1850.[101] That same week, Texas's fiery House representative Volney Howard published a letter in the *Daily Union* asserting that the United States had accepted Texas's territorial claims when it recognized its independence from Mexico and that Washington had functioned as a mere "trustee" of Texas's land during the recent negotiations related to the Treaty of Guadalupe Hidalgo. He further argued that the treaty of annexation prohibited the United States from reducing the territory of Texas and from barring slavery in any part of it.[102]

Meanwhile, the New Mexican leadership began taking steps to organize a government with assurances from the territorial governor, Lt. Col. George McCall, that the Taylor administration would support their efforts. Reports that an armed group led by Texas commissioner Robert Neighbors was already surveying land on the Rio Grande likely contributed to their urgency.[103] By the end of May, New Mexicans had a constitution ready to submit for congressional approval. To most southerners' chagrin, it prohibited the practice of slavery, declaring the institution a "moral, social, and political evil" that also happened to be "naturally impracticable" in New Mexico.[104] The *Houston Telegraph* declared it "but another of the *stealthy* and unprincipled acts of Gen Taylor to rob the southern states of their privileges" and added, "A more open, base act of government tyranny has perhaps never before been perpetrated."[105] Southerners accused the Taylor administration of violating Texas' sovereignty by prompting the people of Santa Fe to "rebel" against their state authority and even compared Taylor to Santa Anna. If the people of New Mexico could secede from their state and abolish slavery, then so too could those of western Virginia or a part of Missouri.[106]

In late June, President Taylor responded to Houston's request to present all correspondences concerning the administration's actions and orders involving New Mexico. While Taylor strongly denied accusations that he had interfered in Texas's sovereignty, he confirmed nonetheless that the territory Texas claimed had in fact been acquired by the United States from Mexico "and has since been held by the United States."[107] Texans nonetheless continued to insist that their state, and not Washington, enjoyed the only legitimate claim to the disputed territory and by early July news had reached Washington that Texas was preparing to send a force of twenty-five thousand to Santa Fe to confront the US military there.

The dispute merely fueled the sectional flames then smoldering in Washington that summer as Congress battled over the omnibus bill. On July 4 Georgia representative Alexander Stephens publicly stated that the first shot fired by a "*federal gun*" in the current dispute with Texas would prompt a swift and violent response from "the Delaware to the Rio Grande." Stephens warned that the "Rubicon" will have passed and the "days of the Republic will be numbered." The *Daily National Intelligencer* reported that Stephens's support served to boost Texan confidence.[108] Indeed, a few days later, news reached Washington that a series of similar meetings were being held throughout the state.[109] On July 19, the *Texian Advocate* reported that the citizens of Seguin had held a meeting and passed a series of resolutions similar to those of the Austin meeting.[110] On August 3, another meeting was held in Harris County. No resolutions were issued, but attendees elected a group of delegates to convene a few days later. Attendees at this meeting objected to any compromise with the federal government that violated Texas's territory and pledged to cooperate with their "fellow citizens" to defend the "honor[,] integrity[,] and interest of the State of Texas."[111]

Ultimately, confrontation was avoided when Sen. Henry Clay proposed that the US government pay Texas an unspecified sum in return for surrendering its territorial claims. This would permit Texas to repay its creditors and allow the New Mexicans to have their own government.[112] The government ultimately shifted the Texas border west and south, adding several hundred square miles to its territory and contributing to its distinctive western panhandle. Northerners, meanwhile, were reassured that the ceded land was completely inhospitable to slavery. Rusk and Houston reluctantly agreed to the compromise given reports that US military reinforcements were headed to New Mexico. Despite a lack of enthusiasm on all sides, the Senate ultimately passed the bill by a margin of ten votes.[113] It also foreshadowed the sectional debate ahead and revealed the precise question that would propel secession—slavery's status in the western territories.

The Failure of Popular Sovereignty and the Pronunciamiento of the Deep South

As with the Texas boundary dispute and the Fugitive Slave Act, the South's ultimate position on popular sovereignty revealed the limits of its commitment to local autonomy. Proslavery southerners won a small victory when popular sovereignty replaced the ban on slavery north of the Mason-Dixon line, but the system had little to offer them since nonslaveholding settlers outnumbered slaveholding ones in nearly every western territory. From the perspective of most opponents of slavery, popular sovereignty was prone to fraud and intimation. This was nowhere more evident than in its first test case in Kansas, where proslavery infiltrators from nearby Missouri, recognizing their numerical disadvantage, crossed the border and cast thousands of fraudulent ballots during the territorial election, resulting in two rival state governments and a bloody civil conflict between pro- and anti-slavery forces. Yet, popular sovereignty's defenders, many of them northern and midwestern Democrats, insisted that it was the only democratic means of determining slavery's status in the unincorporated territories and the only way to avoid a national sectional catastrophe.[114] Then the Supreme Court handed down its decision in *Dred Scott v. Sandford* (1857). The case considered whether Scott's residency in the free state of Illinois and later Wisconsin Territory, where he had been taken by his owner, rendered him free. Chief Justice Roger Taney's court ruled that it did not, a decision that undermined popular sovereignty, confirmed the Fugitive Slave Act, and denied Scott's right to even bring a case to federal court. The ruling marked a significant victory for southerners, but it also galvanized northern opposition, contributing to the growth of a new sectional political grouping, the Republican Party—founded in Wisconsin a few years earlier, in 1854, to oppose the expansion of slavery.[115]

Republicans asserted that slavery should not, under any circumstances, be permitted to extend into the territories and insisted that the three-fifths clause and extraterritoriality were not, as slavery's defenders claimed, evidence of the framers' proslavery inclinations, but rather concessions the north had made to the south to form the Union. The Constitution's authors, they insisted, had never intended to protect the institution indefinitely and certainly never intended to see it expand. Yet, at least since the annexation of Texas, the slaveholding states had attempted to corrupt and misdirect the federal apparatus by using it to extend and strengthen the institution in direct opposition to the republic's original purpose. Self-determination was an important component of republicanism, they conceded, but not as important as freedom and equality.[116]

A series of election debates over the summer of 1858 between incumbent Democratic senator Stephen Douglas of Illinois and his rival candidate, a young Republican named Abraham Lincoln cogently laid out the opposing particulars of the conflict. For Douglas, popular sovereignty presented the only sensible solution to the question of slavery's status in the west. Not only did it promise to remove the most divisive issue of the day from the realm of national debate, it also reflected what he and most other Democrats believed was the republic's founding aim as understood by the framers—that "in a country as wide and broad as this, with such a variety of climate, production, and interest, the people necessarily required different laws and institutions in different localities." If Americans would "only act conscientiously and rigidly upon this great principle of popular sovereignty which guarantees to each state and territory the right to do as it pleases on all things local and domestic," the senator promised, "[then] we will continue at peace with one another."[117]

Just a few months earlier, in an address at the Illinois state capitol, in Springfield, Lincoln had cited a well-known biblical adage in his rejection of Douglas's claim. He insisted that despite the framers' commitment to the precepts of self-governance and local rule in domestic matters like slavery, the Union could not continue to survive half slave and half free. It was a provocative assertion for the simple fact that the Union had, indeed, existed half slave and half free, virtually since its birth. Not only that, but it had thrived. For Douglas and other supporters of popular sovereignty, it was precisely this jurisdictional and ideological diversity that made the union strong and durable. For Lincoln, however, slavery was different. Unlike most other local matters, it stood in direct opposition to the founding principles as expressed in the Declaration of Independence. As such, it was necessarily a matter of national concern. While a system of localized self-rule might be relied upon to resolve most differences among the American people—indeed, nearly all of them—it could not resolve a division as fundamental as the meaning of freedom. The Union would "become *all* one thing, or *all* the other." Either slavery's opponents would "arrest" its spread and place it on a "course of ultimate extinction," or its proponents would "push it forward, till it shall become alike lawful in *all* the states." The events of the previous half century, and especially the past fifteen years, seemed to support Lincoln's hypothesis. The number of slave states had more than doubled since the republic's founding. Not only that, but recent legislation had ensured its perpetuity by protecting slaveholding rights in the territories and nonslaveholding states. Squatter sovereignty, Lincoln insisted, was all but an illusion considering the *Dred Scott* decision, which, he believed, revealed a conspiracy by slaveholders to "*fill up* the territories with slaves . . . and thus enhance the chances of *permanency* to the institution through all the future."[118]

For Douglas, Lincoln and the Republicans presented themselves as "wiser than these men who made this government," which had not only merely survived, but "flourished for seventy years under the principle of popular sovereignty." In his rebuttal, Douglas repeated the well-rehearsed party line: "Every people ought to possess the right to form and regulate their own domestic institutions in their own way." This, after all, was the "great principle . . . secured to us by the blood of our ancestors" and to which "no limitation ought to be applied." If the citizens of this republic were permitted to determine their own liquor ordinances, schools, banking systems, and marriage regulations, then why should they not be permitted to determine whether to own human property? Then, tipping his hat to federalism in terms akin to those of an earlier generation of Mexican liberals, Douglas asserted, "It is neither desirable nor possible that there should be uniformity in the local institutions and domestic regulations of the different states of this Union." In fact, the framers "never contemplated" it. Rather, they understood "that each locality, having separate and distinct interests, required separate and distinct laws, domestic institutions, and police regulations." Asserting that "the great fundamental principle which underlies our complex system of state and federal governments, contemplated diversity and dissimilarity," Douglas accused Lincoln of misapprehending the "great principles upon which our government rests." Localism was the basis of liberty, Douglas concluded, and uniformity the "parent of despotism the world over."[119]

Lincoln would get his chance to highlight the irreconcilability of Douglas's position with the aims of southern Democrats a few weeks later in Freeport, when he posed a question to Douglas that he would not be able to answer without compromising the party unity that he had worked so hard to sustain: Did popular sovereignty allow the residents of a territory to "exclude slavery from its limits prior to the formation of a state constitution?" If the answer was no, then popular sovereignty had little to offer nonslaveholding settlers or Democrats who wished to keep slavery out of the western territories. If the answer was yes, then Douglas risked enraging proslavery Democrats and contradicting the Supreme Court. Douglas tried to have it both ways. He answered that settlers could effectively prohibit slavery in a territory where it was technically legal by electing *local* representatives "who will, by unfriendly legislation, effectually prevent the introduction" of the institution.[120] The answer apparently satisfied the audience at Freeport, but whether he realized it at the time, Douglas had just sowed the seeds of his party's destruction.

The southern response to Stephens's so-called Freeport Doctrine was swift and unalloyed. In a manifesto addressed to the States Rights Party of South Carolina, petitioners accused the national Democratic Party of attempting to transform the so-called Confederacy into a "consolidated nation" and claimed that it was waging a war against the "great and glorious principles of states rights and state sovereignty."[121] To support their claims and buttress the *Dred Scott* decision, they relied on a theory first advanced by Calhoun in 1847, when the country was in the middle of the war with Mexico. It asserted that because the Union was a compact, the territories belonged not to Congress or the people, but to the states of the Union "as their joint and common property." Congress, therefore, was obligated to protect property in the territories *as the states defined it*. Settlers in a territory could choose to prohibit slavery at the point of statehood, but not before. The theory was consistent with compact theorists' long-standing assertion that sovereignty rested ultimately in the states, not local communities or "the people" of the United States. It also departed from the democratic precepts at the core of popular sovereignty.[122]

Southern Democrats demanded on the eve of the party's 1860 convention that it reject popular sovereignty and adopt instead a platform committed to the codification of *Dred Scott*. One of the most outspoken proponents of this idea was newly elected Texas senator Louis T. Wigfall who reminded his fellow senators that "neither Congress nor the territorial legislature" had the "right to exclude slavery from the territories of the United States." Only upon entering the Union as a state, Wigfall argued, could a people make that determination. "Any citizen of any state who owned property," whether it was "a watch, or a coat, or a hat, a horse, or a negro," had a right to go with his property "anywhere upon the broad face of the earth, until he reaches some country where the organic law declared he shall not hold property in that particular article."[123] Despite Douglas's best efforts to appease southern Democrats by insisting that no "unfriendly legislation" could actually go so far as to prevent slaveholders from reclaiming their escaped chattel,[124] secessionists cast the same set of aspersions at northern Democrats that Douglas had flung at Republicans. As former South Carolina senator Robert Barnwell Rhett warned a Grahamville audience on 4 July 1859, "squatter sovereignty" was in fact designed to accomplish a "consolidated democracy" with "limitless" power. "The North is to rule the South," Rhett warned, since the South, "being a minority," was "powerless to enforce its terms by legislation."[125]

At the party convention in April William Yancey, a delegate from Alabama, denounced popular sovereignty as inconsistent with the Fugitive Slave Law and the *Dred Scott* decision and directly disputed Douglas's claim that states and territories were juridically the same. The territories belonged to the "sovereign" and "co-equal" states with the federal government functioning as their trustee. This had been confirmed by the Supreme Court, which had already determined that "Congress cannot prohibit slavery in the territories." If not even Congress had the authority to prohibit slavery in the territories, how could the "most inferior form of our government" have the power to do so?[126] The northern Democrats rejected the southerners' demand for an amendment to the constitution that would have explicitly protected slavery in the territories, tenaciously insisting that such a resolution violated the party's commitment to unobtrusive federal authority, knowing well that such a platform would alienate their constituents.[127] In response, the delegates of Arkansas, Florida, Louisiana, Mississippi, South Carolina, and Texas walked out of the convention. At least one scholar has suggested that it was the southern delegates' aim to compel secession by dividing the Democratic Party, guaranteeing a Republican victory in the November 1860 presidential race, and thereby compelling southern moderates to finally embrace secession.[128] If true, it worked like a charm. In January 1861, before Lincoln took the presidential oath of office, which he would do that March, Mississippi senator Jefferson Davis lobbed a series of accusations at the new executive. He accused the Republican Party of failing to acknowledge that the Union constituted a "confederated republic" of diverse and often competing interests embodied in the sovereign states. Ignoring more than a decade of proslavery federal legislation designed to protect the institution, Davis charged Lincoln and his supporters with violating the republican precept "that the more power is given to the General Government the weaker it becomes."[129]

In the months leading up to and following Lincoln's election, southerners had rehearsed and refined their ideas to convince moderates that secession was little more than a continuation of the principles at the core of the American independence movement. In the spring of 1860, James DeBow, the proslavery editor of *DeBow's Review* and a former superintendent of the US census, queried whether the "general government" had the right to "coerce" a state to remain in the Union. If the people of a state believed that their constitutional rights had been violated, DeBow insisted, there was nothing to stop them from legitimately withdrawing their membership. Was this not, in fact, what the republic's founders themselves had done? "If secession was no offense in 1788 against the old confederation," DeBow asked, "then the right is reserved intact by the several states."[130] Wigfall agreed. In a speech on the Senate floor in December 1860, the Texan repeated the same theory that Calhoun had expressed during the nullification crisis and that states' rights southerners had referenced for more than a decade: "This union is a compact between the states," no different than "a treaty between Great Britain and France." The Constitution was a "treaty between states" formed "for their common defense and general welfare." Wigfall asserted that Lincoln and his allies had made a "fatal error" in assuming that "there is a national government" and that the "people who live between the two oceans, and between the Gulf and the lakes, are one people." If this were the case, he insisted, "there would have been no necessity for a union" or separate state governments. Lincoln and his party were attempting to destroy the republic the founders had conceived. "If we cannot save this union as it was originally formed by these states," Wigfall warned, "let it be dissolved rather than see a military despotism erected upon its ruins."[131]

Of course, it was the Constitution's very ambiguity regarding slavery that enabled secessionists to make such claims. Southerners cited the Fifth Amendment as the constitutional basis for their proslavery interpretations, insisting that protection of enslaved property represented a legitimate and necessary expression of congressional power. Therefore, they argued, what Lincoln and his party were attempting by prohibiting slavery in the territories constituted an illegitimate expression of executive power. Northerners responded the same way they always had, by accusing southerners of hypocrisy considering legislation how the Fugitive Slave Act had violated northern states' rights. That the US framing document rendered such radically opposing interpretations spoke to its inadequacy as it stood in 1860. Americans had pointed to the evident failure of Mexican republicanism for years, but the divisions that ultimately destroyed the Union in the winter of 1860 and 1861 revolved around issues that Mexicans had by then largely resolved. Despite Mexicans' numerous pronunciamientos and civil wars, they had never confronted an internal rupture as profound as what the United States experienced in 1860.

Indeed, as Wigfall was making his December 1861 speech from the Senate floor, state legislators throughout the South were convening to discuss declaring their independence from their republic, some of them, the Texans, for the second time. Given the Texans' recent experience with secession, one might have expected them to lead the lower South out of the Union. Instead, it was South Carolinians, which made sense given their historic role in the conceptualization of the compact theory. In December 1860, a group of Palmetto state delegates, nearly all of them drawn from its plantation ruling class, issued "An Ordinance: To Dissolve the Union between the State of South Carolina and Other States United with Her under the Compact Entitled, 'The Constitution of the United States of America.'" The document "repealed" the states' earlier ratification of the Constitution, thereby allowing South Carolina to resume "her separate and equal place among nations." The ordinance's authors cited earlier claims that the Declaration of Independence had made the colonies "free and independent states" with "full power to levy war, conclude peace, contract alliances, establish commerce, and to do all acts and things which independent states may of right do."[132] Despite the seceding states' insistence that their actions were in accordance with the "two great principles" proclaimed by the colonies at their independence—"the right of a state to govern itself; and the right of a people to abolish a government when it becomes destructive of the ends for which it was instituted"[133]—what the seceding states attempted to do was in fact unprecedented. Not only did they call for a complete and permanent separation from the Union, but their motivation for doing so went far beyond anything that had compelled Mexicans to pronounce against their central government up to that point. As several states' secession ordinances made explicitly clear, their reason for separating from the United States came from the singular desire to preserve, and in many cases, extend the institution of slavery.[134]

Federalism was how southerners seceded from the United States, but it was not why they did so. This was the most distinguishing factor between the political crises that characterized both republics at mid-century. For Mexicans, the primary disagreement had to do with the form of their government. Most federalists wanted to see a return to the political status quo, but what proslavery southerners attempted in the spring of 1861 was something unmatched in modern history—an explicitly proslavery republic premised on the idea that all men were not created equal.[135] In so doing, the Confederacy's framers sought to establish a government more firmly committed to "remed[ing]the errors of the past generation" than in returning to them. Proslavery southerners, as it turns out, had little interest in engaging in a debate about the original intent of the republic. The society they aspired to could never be achieved under a system that did not explicitly protect slavery and accept racial inequality as a universal truth. This was the republic they determined to establish in 1861.[136]

The victory over Mexico had seemingly blinded Americans to the flaws and inconsistencies in their own institutions. Many believed, naively, that decentralized governance and an overriding commitment to self-determination could serve to unite their Union and form the basis of a national identity. Their success in the war with Mexico seemed to confirm this, but it also distracted them from the enduring and irreconcilable divisions that far exceeded the form of government and that had characterized their Union since its founding. Mexicans, meanwhile, emerged from the conflict with a stronger sense of national purpose and a firmer commitment to their nation's preservation.

CHAPTER SEVEN

Ayutla, Antislavery, and the Rise of the New Liberalism

The crises of the 1850s that plagued Mexico and the United States not only exposed federalism's limitations and laid the groundwork for the social, political, and constitutional transformation of both countries, but also contributed to the birth of a new form of liberalism more firmly committed to equality, national sovereignty, and central state authority.[1] This period, referred to in Mexico as the Reforma, represented the most dramatic political transformation on the North American continent since US independence. It began in 1854, when a group of liberal opponents of Santa Anna under the leadership of retired militia colonel Ignacio Comonfort issued a pronunciamiento from the town of Ayutla, in southern Guerrero. They called for Santa Anna's removal and the establishment of a Constituent Congress composed of representatives from each state that would be tasked with drafting a new constitution. After failing to suppress the Revolution of Ayutla, Santa Anna, whose policies had by this point alienated nearly all of his allies, finally resigned in 1855 and stepped down from public office for the last time.

The government that emerged under Comonfort was one of the most transformative that any North American country had witnessed up to that point. Guided by a new generation of liberals, many of them from indigenous or mestizo backgrounds, the Comonfort administration sought to transform Mexican society by directly attacking church privilege and concentrated wealth, implementing social reform, and renewing Mexico's commitment to human equality. A new constitution crafted by the Reforma leadership was the product of nearly two years of intense debate, and although it did not go as far as some had hoped in liberalizing Mexican society, it went further than any North American document before it and provided a framework for Mexico's first modern republican president, Benito Juárez.[2]

A similar and contemporaneous movement emerged in the United States but would not find full expression until nearly a decade later, after the Union had defeated the South in the bloodiest civil conflict in North American history. As in the United States, the population in Mexico would confront forces fundamentally at odds with their vision of a modern democratic nation-state before they could witness such a state's manifestation. But by 1857 Reforma liberals had established a framework for what would come to define modern North American nationhood into the twentieth century.

In the United States, with the exception of radical abolitionists, few people were calling for the kind of structural change that Mexicans sought in 1857. Republicans wished neither to restructure their society nor discard its framing document. It was slavery's defenders, they insisted, who had corrupted the republic's institutions, objectives, and overall intent. Few believed that their republic needed a constitutional revolution, though it would get one anyway.[3] Southern secession triggered a civil war more sanguine than any singular conflict that had plagued Mexico up to that point, and the Lincoln administration would find itself hamstrung by institutions ill equipped for defeating the South and rebuilding the Union. Lincoln's initial response to secession ironically mirrored that of the Mexican federalists who opposed the surrender of Mexican territory following the US invasion of their country in 1846, and by the end of the War of the Rebellion, his administration would end up adopting many of the same precepts as those adopted by the Mexican framers of the 1850s, including universal suffrage, territorial inalienability, and the abolition of slavery.

Mexico's Constitutional Revolution of 1857

Santa Anna had returned to power in 1853 with the promise of restoring order, unity, and sovereignty to Mexico following the conservative military general José María Blancarte's issuance in September 1852 of the Plan de Guadalajara, which called on the exiled former president to return to Mexico and assist in "re-establishing order and peace."[4] Santa Anna struggled, however, to lead the deeply divided republic after the deaths of Lucás Alamán and José María Tornel, two of his closest advisers, and he soon reverted to his dictatorial tendencies. He alienated or exiled the few loyal and skilled advisers who remained, silenced his critics, and censored the press. He taxed heavily to fund the military, abolished state sovereignty, and by the end of his term, insisted on being addressed as His Royal Highness. Nothing, however, undermined Santa Anna's authority and doomed his political career more than his decision to sell more of Mexico's territory to the United States. The coalition that had helped bring him to power had done so because they believed that he would secure Mexico's territory. Instead, he compromised its territorial sovereignty even further.[5] The Plan de Ayutla, issued by Colonel Florencio Villareal in March 1854, called for an end to Santa Anna's regime and criticized the general for having "trampled upon those individual guarantees that even the least civilized countries respect" and "for sacrificing our brothers on the northern frontier." The plan itself was undeniably federalist. It asserted that "republican institutions" were the only ones suitable for Mexico and called on each state to elect a representative to a special congress to be convened for the "exclusive" purpose of establishing a "popular representative republican form." It also invited every state and territory that adopted the plan to draw up its own legal code. The only prerequisite was that each state's constitution had to declare unequivocally that "the nation is and will always be one, indivisible, and independent."[6]

Securing territorial integrity was foremost on the minds of the pronunciamientos' authors and would remain a paramount aim of their movement.[7] When *moderado* militia colonel Comonfort determined to alter the document and issue his own version from Acapulco on 11 March 1854, he did so fearing that the federalist inclinations of its authors were too transparent. Comonfort cited Santa Anna's decision to "unnecessarily" sell "a part of the territory of the Republic" at the top of the lengthy list of grievances in the preamble while clarifying that the authors of the original plan "had not the least intention" of reestablishing federalism "by force of arms." Instead, the form of Mexico's government would be left up to the Constituent Congress once it was formed. For good measure, the authors replaced all references to "states" with "departments and territories," so as not to appear preemptive.[8] The decision to include such clauses indicated both an admission of federalism's earlier limitations and offered something to conservatives. Villareal and Comonfort's plans inspired a series of pronunciamientos throughout the country, not all of which shared the liberal aspirations of the original insurrectionists. Some supporters of the movement vowed to defend "property, church, and army," while others, adhering vaguely to the original document, hoped to preserve the regional dominance and autonomy of local caciques, especially in the north.⁹ Indeed, the early stages of the movement appear to have been concerned primarily with ending the dictatorship and restoring local autonomy, but ultimately they paved the way for the ascendance of a group of men whose vision for Mexico's future far exceeded its aims.

The movement's most prominent leaders—among them Ponciano Arriaga, Benito Juárez, Miguel and Sebastián Lerdo de Tejada, Melchor Ocampo, Ignacio Ramírez, and other members of a new generation born after independence—had come of age during the political tumult of the 1830s and 1840s and commenced their political careers during or immediately after Mexico's war with the United States. These experiences would shape their worldview and the policies that reflected it. Unlike the liberals of the previous generation, many of these men were disillusioned with federalism and shared a desire for order, stability, and security, but unlike many conservatives, they had none of the nostalgia for the country's colonial past. Calls for monarchy or something akin to it struck them as anachronistic and even ridiculous. They craved more than just a new form of government. Rather, they aimed to transform their country's society and identity. For the first time in Mexico's history, mestizos and lower-class Creoles dominated its political leadership, its members proudly claiming to be the rightful inheritors of Mexico. They criticized the Mexican elite of all political persuasions for their backwardness, self-interest, and lack of nationalism; many of them had personally experienced racism and social discrimination at the hands of Mexican institutions. They were also students of some of the most progressive ideas of the age, having been educated at Mexico's few secular schools and universities, most of which served the country's marginalized populations. Thus, they fostered little sense of obligation or investment in Mexico's religious establishment and were in fact highly critical of it. Most had some legal training, even if law was not their chosen profession, and nearly all considered themselves to represent an unprecedented generation uniquely suited to modernize and democratize the country.¹⁰

Equality stood as the central principle of the Reforma generation. "Each age has its demands," and for their age it was a "firm and liberal" system that reflected the "new precept" of the "equality of men." Accordingly, that generation sought to create a political structure that could "help each one achieve all the good that is attainable." Social reorganization and expanded democracy, the new liberals insisted, were essential to securing the order and unity that had eluded Mexicans for so long. Only a government that could assure the "liberty, security, property, and equality" of all its citizens could guard against despotism, chaos, and fragmentation.¹¹ The Reforma generation sought unity and order as much as Mexican conservatives did, but they believed it had to be accomplished from below, not imposed from above. Given this, they aimed to create a political structure in which the executive remained answerable to the Mexican people—a profound repudiation of the conservatism of men like Alamán, but also of the liberals of the 1820s and 1830s, who had sought to consolidate power in the hands of regional elites. As José María Lafragua, one of the intellectual leaders of the Reforma generation, aptly put it, the "primary" duty of the new government was to elevate all men to equal status and make them "Mexicans above all else."[12]

Santa Anna would launch three failed expeditions against supporters of the Plan de Ayutla before ultimately abdicating on 9 August 1855. In his wake, the 1857 constitution, forged over two years under Comonfort's liberal presidency, asserted unequivocally that national sovereignty resided, not in the states nor in the local community or municipality, but in a still-vague conception of the people as a nation. This was not the early nineteenth-century liberalism of José Luis Mora, Lorenzo de Zavala, or Stephen Austin.[13] The men of the 1850s had little use for a system that had divided and weakened Mexico. Instead, they envisioned one that more explicitly embodied the idea that "all political power is based on the authority of the people" and "instituted to its benefit."[14] The chief representative of the Mexican people, therefore, would no longer be the states, as early liberals had insisted, or the executive, as centralists had, but the legislature.[15] Such an assertion revealed not only a shift in priorities between the initial pronuncios and the Comonfort government, but also a changing liberal conception of sovereignty. To declare human equality was one thing, to achieve it another, and doing so required the kind of activist central state that early nineteenth-century liberals had in fact sought to avoid. "We know that human rights are immutable and sacred," they declared, "but we cannot conceive of their full exercise without the social state."[16]

The Reforma liberals advanced a new understanding of the purpose and potential of central state authority. Rather than a threat to a free society, such authority was now understood to exist "for the good of society, for its improvement and perfection, morally as well as physically."[17] Thus, the very first lines of the constitutional project declared the "rights of man" to be the "base and objective of social institutions." Article 2 extended equal rights to "all inhabitants of the republic, without distinction of class or race," and while Mexico would remain a "federative republic, composed of sovereign states" that were "free in their internal regime," every law and authority of the country was bound to "respect and sustain the guarantees of the present constitution."[18] Mexico would no longer be a federation premised on state sovereignty and a weak center. Nor would it be a highly centralized regime with power imposed from above. It would be a nation unified by the singular purpose and aim of elevating "all the children of the same country to the moral dignity of citizen."[19]

A proliferation of critical assessments of Mexican politics and society followed Mexico's defeat by the United States. One of the most widely read was *Consideraciones de la situación política y social de la República Mexicana*, in which the puro federalist Mariano Otero wistfully asserted, "In Mexico there is nothing that might be called national spirit, because there is no nation." Patriotism, Otero insisted, could not exist among a people "lacerated by thirty-seven years of work and misery." He was referring to Mexico's "violated and mocked productive classes" who had come "to view their leaders as little more than enemies." Mexico had "all of the natural elements to make a great and happy nation," but it needed an "enlightened and energetic government" capable of transforming and advancing society. Only then could it secure the fealty of its citizens. "A nation is nothing other than a great family, and in order to be strong and powerful it is necessary that all its individual members be intimately united by ties of interest and affections of the heart."[20] Thus, for the liberals of the 1850s, territorial security and national sovereignty went hand-in-hand with democracy and equality. The challenge was to create a national government that had never existed in Mexico before, one that could secure the ultimate loyalty of its people.

Indeed, by extending rights and privileges to citizens, the authors of the constitution made clear that they expected something in return. The document's first section contained a lengthy list of rights guaranteed to the Mexico people, including free education, universal suffrage, and an end to imprisonment for debt, and article 36 obligated every Mexican citizen "to defend the independence, the territory, the honor, the rights and the just interests of their country" as well as contribute to both federal and state "expenses." Section 6 specifically prohibited the states from regulating foreign trade, maintaining permanent troops or warships without the consent of Congress, or forming any "alliance, treaty, or coalition" with any other state or foreign power. The specter of Mexico's dismemberment was nowhere more evident than in section 7, which prohibited the president from alienating any part of the national territory and ensured that all "federal powers" should have as their primary object "sustaining the national independence and providing for the preservation and security of the union."[21]

From the perspective of this new generation of liberals, no Mexican institution posed a greater challenge to their conception of national sovereignty than the church or more embodied the residue of Spanish colonialism that they long wished to shed. Not only did the church remain the largest single landholder in the country nearly three decades after the first liberal efforts at wealth redistribution, but it also oversaw the registration of births and deaths, contracted marriages, and controlled access to civil rights through baptism. It accrued wealth through rent, interest, and fees. Nothing seemed to pose a threat to secular state authority more than the ecclesiastical *fueros*, independent clerical tribunals. Originating under colonial rule and preserved in the Constitution of 1824, these bodies constituted a rival judiciary that occasionally directly collided with the secular justice system. Thus, by 1855, most liberals agreed that Mexico would never become a fully realized nation-state until it was secularized. Thus unsurprisingly, one of the first Reforma measures approved by Comonfort's provisional government, authored by Oaxacan representative Benito Juárez, aimed to establish judicial equality and uniformity by abolishing nearly all special tribunals and ecclesiastical courts that handled civil matters. The most radical element of the measure permitted defendants to circumvent their fuero and have their cases heard before a secular criminal court.[22] It prompted an immediate protest by the clerics, who insisted that the church's authority transcended that of any secular state. Consequently, the most controversial part of the constitutional project was article 15, which aimed to establish the religious tolerance that Mexican liberals had longed for since the republic's founding.

Yet, some moderates feared that article 15, which merely legalized the practice of faiths other than Roman Catholicism, went too far. They insisted that nearly four decades after Mexico's founding, its people still lacked the capacity for self-government and that church dominance in the intellectual and spiritual lives of most Mexicans was therefore essential to preventing the country from dissolving into chaos. Radicals retorted that it was this very control that had kept Mexico's people in a state of "semi-savagery."[23] If the country's leaders ever wished to see their citizens become fully competent republicans capable of participating in the political process, then they had to liberate them from the church's intellectual and spiritual control. The compromise was article 123, which did not guarantee religious freedom but permitted the state to interfere in religious activity to enforce federal laws. Its supporters, including secular radicals like Arriaga, summed up the dominant view by insisting that if the new constitution did not contain some clause asserting national sovereignty in ecclesiastical matters, then the Mexican nation might as well "disappear."[24]

The final constitution contained nearly all the elements of the earlier draft, including the first article, which declared that "the rights of man are the base and objective of social institutions" and that "all rights and authorities of the country should respect and defend those guarantees granted by the constitution." It also confirmed Mexico's position on abolitionism in article 2: "In the republic all are born free" and "any enslaved person who sets foot on national territory would recover their freedom by that fact alone."[25] The document also guaranteed free education to all citizens, universal suffrage, abolishment of debt peonage, and freedom of speech and the press. It outlawed imprisonment for debt, corporal punishment, monopolies, and all special laws and tribunals, including the fueros. It also legalized the confiscation and redistribution of corporate property, including that of the church.[26] It was a remarkable document by any measure and went further than any other contemporaneous constitution—including the 1787 settlement—in extending equal rights, asserting national sovereignty, and democratizing society. While some have faulted its authors for their caution and ambivalence toward the church, insisting that it hindered their movement and contributed to the political chaos that followed,[27] such criticism ignores the overall radicalism of the document and that it made Mexico a vanguard in modern nation-building. It also well equipped the subsequent administration, headed by Juárez, for the ensuing conflict with the forces of antidemocracy simmering in Mexico and in the United States—more so, as it turned out, than their counterparts in the United States.

The Republican Party and the New Mexican Liberalism

As far as anyone knows, William H. Seward, Salmon P. Chase, and Abraham Lincoln never read the writings of the new Mexican liberals, but they might as well have. As Mexicans were redrafting their constitution, a similar movement was emerging in the United States consisting of former Whigs, abolitionists, and Democrats disillusioned by their cohorts' concessions on slavery. The Republican Party was a heterogenous movement united by a belief that the framers had aspired, above all, to establish a republic committed to human equality but that the so-called Slave Power had corrupted this intent through its outsized control of the federal apparatus. Republicans, like their Mexican counterparts, attacked hierarchical systems of power—of which slavery was the most profound—as retrograde, exploitative, antidemocratic, and anti-national. No one articulated the Republicans' ideology more astutely than Senator William H. Seward, also a lawyer and former governor of New York. An outspoken opponent of slavery, Seward insisted that his party had been founded on the singular and "noble" idea of the "equality of all men before human tribunals and human laws," which was itself the only idea consistent with both "divine law" and modern morality. Slavery, meanwhile, assumed the inherent inequality of man and, as such, represented the residue of a bygone age in which propertied classes ruled in absolution.[28] Arriaga expressed a similar view when he reminded his fellow representatives in the constitutional congress, "The great principle of equality is incontrovertible because divine right, privileged castes, classes born exclusively to direct and govern are discredited theories."[29] What Republicans recognized in slavery, Mexicans identified in the caudillo system, debt peonage, and the church. Each institution was functionally distinct, but they all concentrated wealth, exploited labor, and preserved social inequality.

Furthermore, Mexico's Reforma liberals and the opponents of slavery in the United States frequently blamed such institutions for corrupting or undermining the administrative capacities of the central state. Seward accused the "slaveholding class" of "systematically and successfully perverting the administration of the government" and of endangering the "stability, welfare and liberty of the union."[30] Another cogent Republican spokesperson, Salmon P. Chase—a former governor of Ohio and future Supreme Court justice—advocated the theories of majoritarianism expressed by Tornel when he asserted that "it is wrong, it is unjust, it is absurd" that a slaveholding minority enjoyed "influence in all the departments of government so entirely disproportionate to our own."[31] To many, the 1857 *Dred Scott* decision, which effectively legalized slavery in the territories, exemplified the Slave Power's corruption of democracy. Republicans considered the Taney Court's ruling the most glaring example of the "prostituting" of republican institutions to slaveholding interests and clear evidence that those interests wished to see slavery expand throughout the union.[32]

Similarly, Mexican liberals routinely criticized the church for functioning as a state within a state. "The bishops are not sovereign," as Ocampo, former governor of Michoacán, firmly asserted. Thus, they did not have the "right to govern a single society." He and others also challenged the claims of conservatives and moderates that the church could continue to function as a moral and spiritual guide to Mexico's people.[33] José Antonio Gamboa, a Oaxacan deputy to the 1857 constitutional convention, argued that the church was to blame for virtually all of Mexico ills, including its lack of community and national fealty, lack of agrarian productivity, extreme poverty, and national weakness that invited foreign aggression. Like Ocampo, Gamboa disputed that the clergy fostered any regard for Mexico's rural provinces or the people who inhabited them.[34] Otero criticized both the hacienda system and the church for hindering the nation-state's ability to establish a direct relationship with its citizens. As a result, Otero explained that Mexico's indigenous population formed a "family apart from the white and mixed races," kept in a state of "semi-savagery" that impaired their identity with and loyalty to the nation.[35]

Liberals in both the United States and Mexico envisioned an economic system devoid of forced labor. Illinois congressional representative Richard Yates called "free labor" the "great idea and basis" of the Republican Party. "To elevate, to dignify, to advance, to reward, to ennoble labor—to make labor honorable is the object, is the end and aim of the Republican Party," he asserted.[36] Meanwhile, slavery, according to Seward, functioned on the basic principle "that labor in every society, by whomsoever performed, is necessarily unintellectual, groveling and base; and that the laborer, equally for his own good and for the welfare of the state, ought to be enslaved." Thus slavery not only contradicted the "divine law" of human equality, but also hindered national prosperity and security.[37] Mexican liberals were no different in their criticism of debt peonage. In a country where three-fourths of the population were bound under the system, they were keenly aware of the importance of securing the fealty of Mexico's "violated and mocked productive classes." National honor, Otero explained, was virtually impossible "in a country where the working man has to live in isolation from the rest of the country, unable to enjoy the fruits of his labor." Reflecting on the political state of his country in 1848, Otero advanced perhaps the most cogent criticism of the hacienda system to date, blaming Mexico's Spanish antecedents for failing to impart a love for labor among their "children."[38]

For the authors of the 1857 constitution, however, economic reform extended well beyond abolishing the prevailing labor system. Mexican liberals had long identified wealth concentration as an underlying source of Mexico's poverty and underdevelopment and had sought to remedy it through modest redistribution programs. The debate resurfaced with unprecedented vigor in 1855. "The constitution should be the law of the land," Arriaga conceded, but Mexicans had not "constituted or examined" the land itself. For Arriaga, free labor and wealth redistribution were one in the same. His appeal struck at the heart of modern conceptions of private property, which, he argued, had been constituted "on the principle of appropriation by certain individuals of the labor of others . . . on the principle of the exploitation of the majority by the privileged minority." It was a profound indictment of the modern liberal economic system. Arriaga insisted that he was not calling for the abolition of property—that would be "absurd"—but rather for ending the ancient privileges associated with property ownership. To that end, he called for a constitutional amendment that would limit property rights to "occupation or possession." The idea drew on decades of Mexican criticism of the concentration of landed wealth and agrarian radicalism more generally, and for Arriaga and his supporters, it was essential to a functional democracy. "The accumulation of power in one or a few people, of large territorial possessions, without work, cultivation, or production," he stated, "is contrary to the nature of the republican and democratic government."[39]

Republicans also criticized wealth concentration, but they stopped short of calling for the kind of redistributive program sought by their Mexican counterparts. Their primary aim, much like that of their Jacksonian and Whig antecedents, was not to redistribute wealth, but to enable redistribution by broadening the path for social advancement. "Let not him who is houseless, pull down the house of another;" Lincoln declared before a delegation of workers, "but let him labor diligently and build one for himself, thus by example assuring that his own shall be safe from violence when built."[40] Many Mexican liberals called for greater structural change and a more thorough transformation of society than the Republicans, believing it necessary in creating the free, equal, and democratic national community that they envisioned. Arriaga, for example, challenged his colleagues to do more than simply "proclaim abstract rights" and "beautiful theories" that were ultimately "impracticable" in light of Mexico's "absurd" economic system. "Ideas are proclaimed, and things are forgotten," the congressman asserted. "We ramble on about the discussion of rights, and we ignore the positive facts."[41] Indeed, articles 4 and 5 struck at the heart of Mexico's prevailing debt peonage system. Article 4 stated that every individual had the right to choose their profession, industry, or labor, and article 5 proclaimed that no individual could be "forced to provide personal work, without fair compensation" or "full consent." It also prohibited "any contract that has as its object the loss or the irrevocable sacrifice of the freedom of man." The most radical of the new provisions, however, was article 27, which prohibited corporate ownership of property except that designated "immediately and directly for the service or purpose of the institution." While it did not go as far as Arriaga's initial proposal to immediately nationalize all church property, break up and redistribute sizeable haciendas, and formally recognize the legal rights of rural workers, the law did allow for the compensated appropriation of most corporate property.[42]

Republicans, meanwhile, believed that their society's problems would be remedied if US institutions were simply freed from the corruption of proslavery and monopolistic forces. They called for neither an immediate end to slavery nor any significant alteration to the framing document. To the contrary, they believed that the 1787 Constitution already possessed the mechanisms necessary to bring the institution of slavery to an inevitable if gradual end. As they would learn, however, slavery's abolition would in fact require significant structural transformations, and US leaders would need to adopt some of the very same legislation as their Mexican counterparts to defeat the South and bring its social order more in line with the one they envisioned. In truth, liberals in both countries found themselves constrained by institutional limitations and tradition. If Republicans conceded that the Constitution did not grant the federal government the right to abolish slavery in states where it existed, Mexican liberals conceded to federalist governors who had made their revolution possible. Article 111 of the 1857 constitution, for example, exempted border states from the prohibition against forming coalitions among themselves or alliances with foreign powers if the end goal was "offensive or defensive war against" Native raiders.[43]

Despite everything that the opponents of slavery in the United States shared with Mexican reformers, they expressed little admiration for or even awareness of what was happening in Mexico in the 1850s. Rather, they tended to engage in the same disparaging discourse that had characterized US perceptions of Mexican politics for years, even while rejecting the ethnocentrism and elitism of their Whig predecessors. Seward called the United States a refuge for "every nation, kindred, and tongue under heaven," crediting Germans for providing free labor to the United States, while blaming the Spaniards for introducing slavery to the Western Hemisphere, ignoring the fact that Spanish American republics had led the way in outlawing the institution years ahead of the United States.[44] Most Republicans also continued to insist, as noted above, that slavery was a local institution constitutionally protected in states that had opted to make it legal and even tactfully side-stepped the issue of racial equality. Their attitude was notably ironic not only because the United States would soon find itself engulfed in chaos and violence rivaling that in Mexico, but also because Republicans would end up adopting many of the very same policies as Mexican liberals, including birth-right citizenship, universal suffrage, wealth redistribution (for a time), and the abolition of slavery.[45]

As Otero asserted in the wake of Mexico's devastating military defeat by the United States, "A nation is nothing if not a great family," and Mexico's failure had been its inability to secure the loyalty of its sizeable indigenous population, which constituted a "family apart from the white and mixed races."[46] By 1857 Mexicans had laid the groundwork for a new national family. They had not only declared all men equal but had also adopted the framework necessary to turn this ideal into a reality. In the United States, however, liberating its four million enslaved inhabitants remained a legal and constitutional impossibility, and the steps necessary for doing so would not become fully evident until the war against the Confederacy was nearly over. The only national family that Lincoln could imagine in 1858 was one that maintained some element of the very divisions that he himself acknowledged were unsustainable. Unlike their Mexican counterparts, liberals in the United States had yet to confront the institutional barriers to their national vision. They would have to make them up as they went along.

"Lineal descendants of the deceased": The Texan Secessionist Tradition

If any group saw similarities between the emerging political trends in the northern United States and Mexico, it was the Texans. As slavery expanded in Texas, Mexico served as an enticement for fugitive slaves, straining relations between Washington and the newest state in the Union. Texans had requested that an extradition agreement between the United States and Mexico be included in the Treaty of Guadalupe Hidalgo, but US leaders were hesitant to do so, wanting to prioritize the land transfer instead. They did, however, commence talks for such a provision in 1849, but the agreement signed the following year did nothing to benefit Texas slaveholders since it only concerned the mutual surrender of fugitives from justice, not individuals fleeing slavery.[47] Frustrated, Texas congressional representatives responded with a resolution requesting an agreement requiring the surrender by Mexico of "all persons held in bondage."[48] Their effort was unsuccessful, and Mexico remained a destination for hundreds of fugitives from US slavery, especially after the passage of the Fugitive Slave Act of 1850. The lack of an extradition agreement meant that once enslaved people crossed the Rio Grande, they were far less likely to be returned to their owner than if they had fled to a northern state, where federal law required the slave's capture and return. In 1857, passage of a new constitution in Mexico extended freedom to any enslaved person from the moment they set foot on Mexican soil and explicitly prohibited the extradition of such individuals, making Mexico an even more appealing alternative to fugitives and effectively dooming any future concession to Texas slaveholders.[49]

During a trip through Texas in late 1853 and early 1854, Frederick Law Olmsted observed that the "poor yellow-faced, priest-ridden" Mexicans apparently seemed to take seriously the ideas expressed in "that good old joke of our fathers—the Declaration of American Independence." He had heard numerous reports of Texas slaves escaping to Mexico, despite the evident dangers involved, and spoke with one formerly enslaved man who had arrived there several years earlier and at the time worked as a mechanic. Olmsted reported that the man "could speak Spanish fluently and had traveled extensively in Mexico, sometimes on his own business, and sometimes as a servant or a muleteer." He even claimed to have "joined the Catholic True Church" with which "he was very well satisfied." Olmsted wrote, "The Mexican Government was very just to [the formerly enslaved]; they could always have their rights as fully protected as if they were Mexican born." Some of them had even "connected themselves by marriage" to local families.[50]

Frustrated, Texas slaveholders launched their own cross-border raids into Mexico, prompting anger among Mexican authorities and repeated requests by Mexican officials that Washington take action against its rogue citizens.[51] Washington was hardly in a position to oblige. The US Army emerged from the war with Mexico exhausted and depleted, a situation that would worsen as the decade progressed. It numbered fewer than 14,000 enlisted men, only a fraction of whom were mounted cavalry. Furthermore, most of the troops had no training or experience in defending desert terrain. Poor diet, minimalist living conditions, and isolation made service in the far west undesirable, and usually the least skilled and experienced soldiers wound up there. Yet, in light of the sectional controversy, Washington proved reluctant to commit more funds and soldiers to guarding a border that many Americans believed would not exist but for the interests of southern slaveholders.[52] Furthermore, an explosion of westward migration after 1849, years of drought, and a series of epidemics prompted the Comanche to renew raids on Texas settlements and ranches, thereby necessitating an increased military presence.

Texas remained a stronghold of unionism in the 1850s despite declining confidence in Washington. Part of this had to do with its large Mexican and immigrant populations, and its continued hope that once the war in Kansas between pro-slavery and antislavery settlers had been suppressed, federal troops might return to the border to assist them in their war against the Comanche. Texas senator and later governor, Sam Houston, remained a steadfast unionist throughout his career, making every effort to keep Texas out of the sectional debates of the 1850s and reminding Texans that they had "entered not into the North nor into the South, but into the Union." Whereas men like Mirabeau Lamar, Texas's second president and a diehard secessionist, highlighted differences between Texas and the United States, Houston emphasized Texans' uniquely vulnerable position as a distant western state bordered by hostile neighbors and ultimately dependent on federal protection.[53] Yet, this became an increasingly untenable position as conditions in the west began to deteriorate. In the absence of a sufficient federal military presence, Texans turned to their own ranger units to secure their lives and property.

By 1858, however, a new generation of leaders in Texas was aligning state politics with the rest of the South's. Guy M. Bryan, nephew of the then-late Stephen Austin, had been born on the Missouri frontier in 1821, the same year that his grandfather Moses obtained his first colonization contract from Spain. His family moved to Texas ten years later, after his mother, Emily Margaret Brown Austin, Stephen's sister, married Stephen Perry following the death of her first husband, James Bryan, Guy's father. He was a teenager during the Texas rebellion and attended Kenyon College, in Ohio, before returning to Texas. In 1846 Bryan, on behalf of his family, complained in a letter to David G. Burnet, provisional president of Texas during the rebellion, that the "'old settlers'—those who founded and they who labored with the founders of our country to bring it into existence and build it up" were "being forgot." Meanwhile, the "eleventh hour men"— those who had arrived with the "heat and burden of the day"— were receiving "all credit and all reward." Despite Bryan's youth, he made his allegiance clear: "[T]o me and to every 'old settler' this must be cause of deep regret." The entire breadth of his family's grievances was not made evident, but Bryan feared that his uncle's generation was being misrepresented in the public memory, and he appealed to Burnet to rectify the wrong. "It is due to the dead and to the living that a fair and honest statement of the past should be made," he wrote. "You knew [my uncle], his nature, his character his deeds, and devotion to his country." In order to correct such misperception, Bryan requested that Burnet author a biography of Austin "without which no *correct* history of Texas can ever be written."[54] Bryan was not specific about what aspects he found objectionable about the memorializing of his uncle, but considering that the letter to Burnet came soon after the annexation of Texas, an event that Bryan opposed, it likely had something to do with how Texans of the 1850s imagined Austin's hopes for them. Bryan would someday have his own chance to redirect the course of Texas politics.

In 1847 residents of the Brazoria district elected Bryan to the State House of Representatives, where he served for the next six years. After that, he served four years in the Texas Senate before being elected to the US House of Representatives. Reporting on the national congressional election in spring of 1857, the *Texas State Gazette* noted that Bryan "is well known to the people," is an "old Texian" with "considerable brilliancy of mind and great industry, and will doubtless faithlessly attend to the interests of his constituents."[55] Bryan soon became associated with a young and aspiring group of politicians who by the end of the 1850s were beginning to vocalize a distinctly pro-southern platform. This position made him popular among his constituency, which had by then grown tired of a federal government that more than a decade after annexation had still failed to deliver on frontier defense, internal improvements, and protection for slaveholders' human property.

In 1857 Bryan was elected by Texas's 2nd District to the US House of Representatives and within two years had joined the increasingly vociferous calls for disunion in terms that emphasized the similarities between the secession of Texas from Mexico and its ensuing separation from the United States. The centralization of power in Mexico, Bryan wrote, had "caused Texas to appeal in 1835 to the state of the Mexican union, on behalf of the violated constitution of 1824." When the appeal was "disregarded" by other states, he explained, Texas declared independence "in the same spirit as that which influenced the declaration made on the 4th of July 1776." Bryan drew a straight line from the founding of Texas to what would soon be the founding of the Confederacy, which, he insisted, was motivated by the underlying principle of "state sovereignty." According to the *Southern Intelligencer*, "indications of public sentiment, not so plainly seen as sensibly felt," would ensure Bryan's political ascendance. The ghosts of "the uncles . . . must have been gratified" with the rapid ascendance of these "lineal descendants of the deceased."[56] Bryan would serve only one term in the US House, however, and Texas would end up electing the Unionist Sam Houston to the governorship in 1859. Indeed, at that time, secession by Texas seemed unlikely.

The outlook on secession changed in the summer of 1860, when, on a particularly hot day in early July, a series of fires erupted in the commercial districts of several northern towns, including Dallas, sometimes hours, and even minutes, apart. In Denton, the flames reached a barrel of keg powder, causing an explosion that set fire to buildings on the opposite side of the town square before some fast-acting citizens suppressed it. The people of Dallas were less fortunate. The fire there consumed the entire town center. No deaths were reported, but the destruction was estimated at close to $700,000.[57] The offices of at least two newspapers, including the pro-southern *Dallas Herald News*, suffered damage or destruction.[58] The fires seemed more than coincidental, and before long, reports of an abolitionist conspiracy began sweeping the South. The *San Antonio Ledger* reported that there was "no doubt" the fires were "all the work of abolitionists" and indicated that a plot had been uncovered of a grand "insurrection by the negroes."[59] As paranoia swept the state, citizens organized Committees of Safety tasked with identifying and punishing those suspected of inciting or participating in the plot. In the town of Chappell Hill, three men were arrested and expelled after being convicted of taking part in a "grand" abolitionist plot to take over the state.[60] In Fort Worth, a man was hanged after being accused of arming the town's Black residents. The *New Orleans Picayune* expressed concern about reports of "summary justice" and cautioned that such prosecutions, regardless of their urgency, still merited "thorough and impartial justice."[61] Regardless of who or what was to blame for the "Texas terrors," they fueled sectionalism across the state. "The disunion element was beginning to sleep," reported the *San Antonio Ledger*, but these transactions have aroused it and ten times stronger than before."[62]

The lack of an extradition agreement with Mexico that enabled Texans to reclaim the enslaved, the seeming absence of federal assistance in helping to fight the Comanche, and suspicions of an abolitionist plot convinced many Texans that their well-being and security were perhaps no better under the United States than it had been under Mexico. In December 1860, the *Dallas Weekly Herald* staked out its position: "Let Texas declare her independence, and let her never consent to pass homage to an administration, the chief of which, in days past, laughed over the destruction of the lives and property of her citizens."[63] Unlike other southern states, which relied exclusively on the US independence struggle as a precedent, Texans accompanied references to 1776 with references to 1836. *Texas State Gazette* editors invited their readers "to perpetuate the glory of the Texas Revolution, by maintaining their rights at all hazards and to the last extremity." They drew a direct parallel comparing Lincoln and the "Black Republicans" of 1861 to Santa Anna and the "tyranny of Mexico," from which Texans had liberated themselves in 1836, calling once again for Texas to declare itself free of those who "would rob us of our rights and institutions." By equating the current movement with their "past history, in which courage, wisdom, and patriotism united to found a republic and a state," Texas secessionists drew on a reservoir of Texas exceptionalism that had existed at least since Lamar's presidency twenty years earlier.[64]

Sensing a division between the people and their Unionist governor, the Confederate commissioners—representatives dispatched to fellow southern states—were eager to know who, in fact, spoke for the people of Texas. Houston himself answered the question by declaring that the people themselves did and that a "fair and legitimate expression of their will" could only be determined "through the ballot-box." On 8 January 1861, Texans held state-wide elections for delegates to a secession convention in Austin. Most candidates were nominated and elected at public meetings organized by secessionists, ensuring that the elected would likely be secessionists too. In addition, on January 21, the state Texas legislature passed a nonbinding resolution in support of a secession convention.

Of the 180 secessionist delegates who gathered in the chamber of the Texas House of Representatives the following week on January 31, more than 90 percent had been born in the South, and the majority were slaveholders. The following day, John Wharton, a convention delegate and the son of William H. Wharton, who had helped lead Texas out of Mexico twenty-five years earlier, was symbolically chosen to ask the convention to declare Texan independence once again. His motion was seconded and, without further debate, passed. The next day, the Committee on Federal Relations issued an ordinance eerily similar to the complaints lodged against Santa Anna's government. Claiming that the federal government had "failed to accomplish the purposes of the compact of union between the states in giving protection either to the persons of our people upon an exposed frontier or to the property of our citizens," the ordinance declared annexation "hereby repealed and annulled," and Texas "absolved for all restraints and obligations incurred by said compact." The ordinance also attacked the federal government for excluding slaveholding citizens from "all the immense territory owned in common by all the states on the Pacific Ocean," for failing "to protect the lives and liberty of the people of Texas against Indian savages," and finally for proclaiming the "debasing doctrine of the equality of all men, irrespective of race or color." Texans confirmed their conviction that the "government of the various states, and of the confederacy itself, were established exclusively by the white race, for themselves and their posterity" and "that the African race had no agency in their establishment" and were "rightfully held and regarded as an inferior race."[65]

After 24,000 copies of the document were printed—2,000 each in Spanish and German and 20,000 in English—it was submitted for a popular vote on February 23. By that point, a force of more than one thousand volunteers, led by Texas Ranger and US Marshal Ben McCulloch, had already seized and forced the surrender of US troops stationed at San Antonio under General David E. Twiggs, who offered little resistance. They also arrested US Army Colonel Robert E. Lee, stationed at Fort Mason, after failing to convince him to join the Confederacy. The evacuation of federal troops made it possible for the secession convention's Public Safety Commission to take over the remaining outposts along the frontier and launch a vigorous display of force and intimidation in the days leading up to the referendum. In the end, Texans overwhelmingly voted for secession on February 23.

By the time of the secession convention, most unionists had already been muffled. The pro-unionist editor of the *Harrison Flag* had ceased publication of the paper. The violent reaction to the Texas fires had already silenced anyone whose remarks might have been perceived as friendly to abolitionism or critical of slavery. Texan secessionists had managed to extract an uneasy consensus in terms of secession, but there were other reasons for Texans to support disunion. Texas's still significant Mexican population had little reason to demonstrate much loyalty to a country that had conquered and dispossessed them. Finally, as the rest of the lower South seceded in December 1860 and January 1861, Texans likely assessed what life would be like if a barrier of seceded states cut them off from the already meager federal protection Washington struggled to provide. In March 1861, the *San Antonio Ledger and Texan* reported, "The Confederate Congress already stands pledged to give protection to our exposed frontier." Furthermore, it reported, the confederate body would facilitate rather than hinder local efforts to police the border: "If the state will call out a permanent force, it will be recognized by the southern Congress, and liberal appropriations made for its support, as soon as Texas joins the Confederacy."[66]

Another factor likely informing Texans' decision was their tradition of secession, which hung like a shroud over the 1861 secession convention. The vocabulary and symbolism of 1836 were everywhere, especially on January 30, when it was resolved that veterans of the conflict with Mexico be invited into the Texas House to observe the proceedings "provided they are in favor of another revolution."[67] On the day of the secession referendum, one secessionist delegate confidently predicted that the "possibility of settling our difficulties by a reconstruction of the Union" would receive "about the same encouragement as a proposition to re-annex Texas to the State of Mexico."[68] The convention waited until March 2, the date Texas declared independence from Mexico, to formally declare the same from the United States. Eleven days later, O. M. Roberts, associate justice of the Texas Supreme Court and a Confederate general, reported on a recent procurement of arms, including two pieces of ordnance that had been used in the Battle of San Jacinto, informing a friend in New Orleans that he "expected that the guns will soon be again upon the soil they so nobly assisted in rescuing from Mexican tyranny." Observing the swiftness with which the Texas convention had acted, the South Carolina commissioner, John McQueen, reported on the "remarkable courage and fortitude" of a people then facing "three distinct" classes of enemies, "Indians, Mexicans, and Abolitionists," and predicted that Texas "would never again be united, in any union whatever, with a non-slaveholding or fanatical people."[69]

"A mighty obstacle in the way of universal freedom"

One person who would have likely admired Mexico's constitution of 1857 was the radical abolitionist William Lloyd Garrison. By the 1850s, Garrison had made his disdain for the United States' founding document well-known in private letters, in the pages of his newspaper, *The Liberator* (Boston), and in public speeches. For Garrison and his allies, the various concessions to slavery enshrined in it irreparably sullied the document. During the nullification crisis of 1832—in which leaders in South Carolina insisted that states had the right to ignore federal laws and that the Union was little more than a compact among the states—Garrison distinguished himself from both sides of the controversy in his denunciations extending beyond Calhoun and the nullifiers. Garrison conceded that the two men's interpretation of the Constitution as a compact among the states was flawed, but, he argued, the document nonetheless represented a "sacrifice of the bodies and souls of millions . . . an unblushing coalition to do evil that good might come."[70] The 1840s controversy over Texas annexation had confirmed Garrison's conviction that slavery could never be abolished within the existing framework. He echoed Tornel in calling the American union a "subtle and atrocious compromise" for its extermination of Native Americans, embrace of the "despotism" of slavery, and "immolation of the individual." Standing as "a mighty obstacle in the way of universal freedom and equality," Garrison called for a new framing document, insisting that abolition could never be accomplished with the original one.[71]

Such rebukes had only intensified by the 1850s as the question of slavery's expansion became the central national debate,[72] but Garrisonian irreverence for the settlement represented a minority view. Most opponents of slavery, and nearly all Republicans, insisted, as Seward did, that the document was a "constitution of freedom" that was "being converted into a constitution of slavery."[73] Charles Sumner, Republican senator from Massachusetts and opponent of slavery, concurred, writing, "It is plain that our constitution was framed by lovers of freedom."[74] Although both men proclaimed that the Republican Party represented a "revolution,"[75] the party's positions and rhetoric were more restorative. Republicans aimed "to recover back again" the republic's virtues and "to confound and overthrow, by one decisive blow, the betrayers of the constitution and freedom forever."[76] In short, they believed that the document contained the necessary mechanisms for slavery's eventual end. The charter's true purpose, they insisted, was not to form a confederation of sovereign states, as southerners had long insisted, but rested upon the preamble's promise to ensure life, liberty, and the pursuit of happiness. Well expressing the views of the mainstream antislavery movement, the jurist William Jay in *A View of the Action of the Federal Government, in Behalf of Slavery* (1839) called the constitution a "guilty compromise" when it came to slavery. Rather than attacking the document generally, he directed his criticism more specifically at the parts that favored the interests of the slaveholding minority. The three-fifths clause—which inflated Southern representative power at the federal level by allowing southern states to count every three enslaved persons as one white citizen— gave "slaveholders an undue weight in the national councils" in a way that violated both the founding precept of human equality and representative democracy, thereby transforming the Union into a "remorseless despotism—a despotism sooner or later to be engulfed in blood."[77] A few years earlier, the American Anti-Slavery Society (AASS) had codified these views in its Declaration of Sentiments (1833), the society's founding document, which insisted, "The cornerstone upon which [the republic's framers] founded the TEMPLE OF FREEDOM was broadly this— 'that all men are created equal; that they are empowered by their Creator with certain inalienable rights; that among these are life, LIBERTY, and the pursuit of happiness." The authors asserted, as Garrison had, that slavery contradicted the Declaration of Independence, but they also insisted that there were marginal exceptions to the document's fundamental purpose of preserving and protecting the "principles of natural rights."

Yet, as much as opponents of slavery pointed to slavery's immorality and inconsistency with republican precepts, most of them acknowledged what they regarded as the real constitutional limits to abolition. Indeed, article 2 of the society's declaration explicitly stated that each state enjoyed an "exclusive right to *legislate* in regard to its abolition."[78] This was something that Jay himself had insisted that his colleagues in the AASS concede. Radical abolitionists who called for an immediate end to slavery, failed to "acknowledge the existence of slavery under state authority" in "strict accordance to the Constitution."[79] This, of course, begged the question of how exactly slavery could be abolished in the United States. Unable to interfere with the institution in states where it already existed, opponents turned their attention to one of the only parts of the Union that did fall directly under Congress's jurisdictional authority—the territories.

By the middle of the decade, prohibiting slavery's expansion had become the lynchpin of the "antislavery project," as historians have designated the mainstream movement, and the central platform of the new Republican Party. As one of the movement's most eloquent advocates and the Republican Party's first presidential nominee, Abraham Lincoln remains the most reliable source for understanding the theory of non-extension and its potential role in rendering slavery's ultimate extinction. In his oft-cited address at Peoria in October 1854, the former Whig pointed to the precedent set by the Northwest Ordinances of the 1790s, laying out a system for surveying and settling the unincorporated northwestern territories, in that the framers, while permitting slavery to continue in the states and in various facets under federal jurisdiction, never intended it to expand. Rather, Jefferson envisioned the west becoming the "happy home of teeming millions of free, white, prosperous people and no slave amongst them." Echoing the views of antislavery antecedents, Lincoln pointed to the Declaration of Independence as the best indicator of the framers' true intent. He attacked popular sovereignty as a "*declared* indifference" that concealed the "covert *real* zeal for the spread of slavery." Furthermore, Lincoln insisted, it undermined the very principle of self-rule that its proponents claimed it embodied by enabling one man to govern the other "*without that other's consent.*" If the republic was premised on the idea of consent of the governed, was slavery not a direct violation of that precept? "The master not only governs the slave without his consent; but he governs him by a set of rules altogether different from those which he prescribes to himself," Lincoln said. Self-government should guarantee "all the governed an equal voice in the government." Yet even Lincoln conceded that the framers, while they had aimed to limit slavery's expansion, intended that each state be allowed to "regulate its domestic concerns in its own way" and that this stipulation likely "had some reference to the existence of slavery amongst them."[80]

The abolitionist and jurist William Goodell, meanwhile, insisted that the Constitution empowered the national government to abolish slavery outright, with little regard to the desires of the states or to the Constitution's various concessions to slaveholding interests. Rather than finding any fault in the document, Goodell criticized federal leadership for failing to exercise its full authority when it came to abolition. "*Be it so* that all this decisive and even fatal action *against general liberty* is the action of our own national government in which we have confided, to secure the blessings of liberty."[81] That Goodell's position remained marginal testifies to the enduring power of federalism in the United States. In his time, most people in the United States understood slavery to be one of those "local" institutions that rested beyond the purview of federal interference even though the Constitution remained silent on the matter. Lincoln himself acknowledged that he could not point to the precise clause in the constitution that shielded slavery from federal intervention. Yet, he went to great lengths to ensure that his party's platform represented no threat to the sovereignty of the southern states.[82] Still, Republicans and other members of the antislavery project might have been more willing to push for a more immediate end to the institution barring the belief that there was another, perhaps less confrontational path to abolition. Most Republicans believed the end could be accomplished by simply halting slavery's extension. If free labor was permitted to expand into the west instead of slavery, then its proponents would not only be able to reclaim federal power and purify the republic, but the preexisting slave states would eventually feel compelled to abandon the institution.[83]

The debates of the 1850s and the various competing interpretations of constitutional law that they rendered exposed the profound ambiguity of the 1787 constitutional settlement, especially compared to its 1857 Mexican counterpart. The United States simply hadn't resolved the pressing questions regarding slavery, citizenship, and federalism that Mexico had by the middle of the nineteenth century. Having never been the victims of the kind of territorial aggressions that they had subjected Mexico to, having never experienced the kinds of threats to their national security and territorial sovereignty, norteamericanos simply ignored the inherent flaws and inconsistencies in their own republican framework. Thus by the end of the 1850s, the United States was about to confront a crisis of sovereignty not dissimilar from what Mexico had been forced to confront only a few years earlier and had, by the time the sectional crisis was in full swing in the United States, largely resolved. Time had run out to perhaps learn from the Mexican experience.

"The Union is unbroken"

The first constitutional conundrum to confront Lincoln after taking office in March 1861 had little to do with slavery. The US Constitution was mostly silent on the question of territorial inalienability. Thus, despite the claims of Massachusetts representative George S. Boutwell that the "Constitution, if it secures anything, secures the integrity of the territory over which and to which ... [it] applies,"[84] the document itself gave the new administration few specific tools with which to dispute the legitimacy of what the Confederate states had done. By the time Lincoln took office in March 1861, nearly all the lower southern states had seceded from the Union and formed the Confederate States of America; they had established a provisional government on February 8. Each of the states had issued ordinances like Texas's—though Texas remained alone in putting the question of secession to a popular vote—all of them drawing on the theory that the Union was essentially a compact of sovereign states who could legitimately withdraw from the Union whenever they found their "rights" threatened within it. Lincoln's position from the outset was that the people of the nation were sovereign and that unilateral secession, as the southern states were attempting, was illegitimate. Thus, the best Lincoln could muster in his inaugural address to Congress was that the Union's perpetuity was "implied, if not expressed, in the fundamental law of all national governments."[85]

In fact, the president conceded that secession was possible under certain circumstances, though not those in which the South had attempted it. Legitimate secession could be accomplished through a two-fold democratic process in which a majority of the people of said state demonstrated their desire to secede and a majority of the other states of the Union demonstrated their consent.[86] Without these prerequisites, the Union remained "unbroken."[87] Thus, secession as the eleven southern states had attempted it represented a "sophism" derived from the mistaken assumption "that there is some omnipotent, and sacred supremacy, pertaining to a *state*." As scholars have noted, Lincoln regarded statehood as dependent upon membership within the Union, asserting that the "Union is older than the states, and, in fact, created them as states."[88] It was an interesting theory, but not exactly accurate. This might have been the case for his own state or any that had entered the Union following the ratification of the Constitution, but it could not be said for those that had existed as states under the Articles of Confederation, whose very approval had been essential to the ratification of the document that Lincoln claimed granted them their statehood status.[89]

More compelling was Lincoln's assertion that sovereignty ultimately rested with the people of the United States, not with the states themselves as southern thinkers had long insisted. Here, again, Lincoln had to rely on abstract theories about sovereignty and majoritarianism since there was nothing in the 1789 document that asserted, at least as explicitly as Mexico's 1857 constitution did, that the nation's sovereignty ultimately rested in the "people of the nation." To support their theory, Lincoln and his allies pointed to the opening lines of the preamble, which claimed to speak on behalf of "we the people"; references to "a more perfect union" implied permanency.[90] These were essentially the same theories that Mexican critics of the Texas rebellion had espoused. Lincoln's claim that a "majority, held in restraint by constitutional checks, and limitations . . .

is the only true sovereign of a free people" resembled Tornel's reasoning that opposition to the 1836 constitution, which had been legally instituted and received the support of a majority of Mexico's people at the time of its adoption, did not constitute a legitimate justification for secession. If the southern states could not lawfully secede without the consent of the majority of the nation's people in 1861, then certainly the Texans, who had not even managed to form a state government before declaring their independence from Mexico, could not have done so in 1836.

Early on in Lincoln's administration, he and his advisers would sharpen their theory of territorial inalienability, bringing it even more unintentionally in line with that of their Mexican counterparts. Lincoln's ideas on secession, sovereignty, and federal power were not informed by Mexican thinkers. Instead, Francis Lieber, a Prussian American jurist and academic and one of the president's most influential advisers, was likely the one responsible for helping the president develop his theory of territorial inalienability. Having already witnessed the destructive potential of centrifugalism in his native Prussia, Lieber was appalled by the secessionism of his colleagues at South Carolina College, where he taught history and political philosophy. In 1851, only a few years before he would relocate to Columbia College, Lieber delivered a July 4 address in which he warned his audience of the dangers of disunion. Sovereignty, according to Lieber, meant that there was "but one absolute ruler—one true sovereign." States, therefore, could not take actions that were destructive to the other members of the union. What would South Carolina have said only a few years ago, Lieber queried, "if a state of the interior, say Ohio, were to vindicate the presumed right of secession?" In forming the Union, each of the states had surrendered certain rights to receive the "advantages" of being part of the whole. Consequently, the Union had "shaped and balanced all our systems that no member can withdraw without deranging and embarrassing all and ultimately destroying the whole." Just as Lincoln would later do, Lieber dismissed the idea that the constitution somehow contained the "tacit acknowledgement of the right of secession" since this amounted to the ludicrous "assumption that a principle of self-destruction had been infused by its own makers." The framers had not addressed secession in their founding document for the same reason that the Roman penal laws failed to mention patricide—"no one thought of such a deed." Like Mexican nationals of a generation earlier, Lieber pointed to the inherent anarchy entailed and engendered in secession, calling it the "secret of all civil and religious wars" and "of divided families." The history of his own native land—"the battlefield of Europe for these three centuries"—proved this.[91]

Lieber had elaborated on his theories of sovereignty and liberty in *On Civil Liberty and Self-Government* (1853) in which he stated that government "must derive its rights from the people," as opposed to any other entity like the states, and that civil liberty only existed "in a state of union with equals" in which self-determination was limited and circumscribed, so that no individual or collection of individuals could impede the rights of any other. The government's primary obligation, therefore, was to protect each citizen "in his most important rights." Here Lieber expressed a theory of the relationship between state power and liberty considerably at odds with the earlier federalist presumption that government, especially central government, necessarily represented a threat to individual liberty. Such threats, as Lieber pointed out, could come from any source, even other individuals. Liberty was the "protection of checks against undue interference" whether from individuals, the states, or the central government. Like contemporaneous Mexican liberals, Lieber rejected the Gallican liberty of an earlier generation, insisting that it led to mob rule in favor of a system that emphasized a strong nationalist state committed to the enforcement of juridical equality and individual rights. Regardless of form of government, the "supremacy of the law" was an "elementary requisite" to all free and functional governments.[92]

By Lincoln's second annual address, he rejected secession even more assertively than he had a year earlier. "A nation," he declared, "may be said to consist of its territory, its people, and its laws," and then he clarified, "the territory being the only part that is of certain durability." It was a powerful assertion that pointed to a shift in the conceptualization of nationhood that Lincoln and his party represented. The idea of a changing or evolving national people suggested the potential for a more inclusive or diverse body politic. That its laws could change left space for the evolving set of legislation that would emerge from the current conflict, including dramatic changes to the country's framing document. That its territory remained "durable," however, suggested that it was the one component of the nation that could not be ruptured or compromised. This assertion, while essential to Lincoln's position toward the seceding states, was ironic for two reasons: First, it was the nation's territory—or more specifically questions relating to it—that had propelled it toward war in the first place. Now, territoriality would constitute the key to its reunification. As Lincoln pointed out, the nation's territory was not the property of any single or sovereign state, but rather of the people of the nation. Second, Mexican liberals could use, in fact had used, the very same logic to protest the United States' acquisition of their national territory. In Mexico's case, of course, it had been to no avail in preventing dismemberment by a foreign power. Lincoln used the same logic in the hopes of accomplishing a different outcome in the face of "domestic foes." Yet, lacking a clear constitutional prohibition to secession or a prohibition of the right of states to "celebrate alliance," as existed in the 1857 constitution in Mexico, he had to rely on implied principles of national sovereignty and majoritarian democracy. Here, even his terminology could not have been more like that of his Mexican counterparts. Lincoln asserted that any "portion of the earth's surface which is owned and inhabited by the people of the United States" is constituted no less than the "home of one national family." By the late 1850s, both Republicans in the United States and Mexicans of nearly every political stripe were describing their respective nations in the same terms—as singular "families," undivided by region, race, generation, or other distinctions.[93]

Yet, Lincoln, unlike his Mexican counterparts, did not have a powerful foreign aggressor with which to contend. He could assert that in declaring their independence, the rebel states had done nothing of any consequence, and he could rely on an extensive and preexisting federal presence in the southern states through which to assert federal power. Thus, the US president need do little more than promise "that the laws of the Union [would] be faithfully executed in all the states" just as they had been before secession. This entailed "holding and occupying" and possessing the "property, and places belonging to the government" and collecting its "duties and imposts." Beyond this, however, Lincoln promised that there would be no invasion. "In *your* hands my dissatisfied countrymen," he concluded, "and not in *mine*, is the momentous issue of civil war."[94] When Kentucky senator John J. Crittenden, in a last-ditch effort to prevent secession, proposed an amendment to the Constitution that would effectively extend the line of the Missouri Compromise all the way to the Pacific, Lincoln declined, insisting that he had run and been elected on a platform prohibiting the extension of slavery.

The US Constitution would fail to prevent secession. It would fail ultimately to prevent a civil conflict of unrivaled proportion. US institutions were just strong enough, however, to guide the president through the most pressing domestic challenge that the country had confronted to date. In April 1861, as US forces attempted to resupply Fort Sumter, South Carolina, secessionists fired on them. The nation that Lincoln envisioned in December 1861 had not yet been born and, as with Mexico, the United States would need to confront a trauma of unrivaled proportion before it could be.

CHAPTER EIGHT

The Birth of Two Nations

By the middle of the nineteenth century, Mexico and the United States were convulsed in parallel political and societal conflicts. Both the Second Mexican Empire (1864–1867) and the Confederate States of America (1861–1865) were part of a trans-Atlantic reaction ascendant in many parts of Europe and the Americas that blamed democracy and liberalism for the perceived chaos, poverty, and instability plaguing modern societies. Adherents of this view pointed to European revolutions like those in France (1848) and Germany (1848/49) as evidence of the failure of liberal republicanism and instead called for a return to traditional forms of social relations and governance.[1] To be clear, these movements were not themselves anti-modern. As scholars have shown, slavery's form of racialized and coerced labor was in fact highly compatible with the profit-driven market economy of the nineteenth-century Atlantic world and particularly crucial to the economic development of the United States.[2] Likewise, many Mexican imperialists—those who supported the French intervention and subsequent reign of Emperor Maximilian I as Napoleon III's appointee—were products of the same long-standing Mexican debate on governance that had occupied the country for generations. Their support for the return of a European-style monarchy came from the same desire that many Mexican Reforma liberals were also expressing by the 1850s—to consolidate and secure the Mexican nation-state.³ What imperialists feared about modernity was not capitalism or centralized governance, but democracy and the growing discourse of individual rights, equality, and social transformation. They doubted most people's capacity for self-governance and their ability to function productively or successfully in a modern capitalist society and thus called for a resurrection of hierarchical social relations as a means of mitigating the chaos and disorder of modernity, not rejecting it all together. They envisioned a society in which the family, the parish, or the community, not the nation-state, constituted the primary form of social organization. They rarely spoke of a sovereign "people" or a nation, and their actions suggest that they largely did not believe in one. As such, the particular political vision they embraced fundamentally opposed that of Reforma liberals as well as their Republican Party counterparts in the United States. Consequently, the administrations of President Benito Juárez and President Abraham Lincoln came to understand the domestic conflicts they faced as part of a larger continental struggle between the forces of democracy, equality, and individual rights against those of aristocracy, privilege, and inequality.⁴

The Juárez administration's efforts to defeat their respective foes would transform relations between the United States and Mexico and, ultimately, bring the former more in line with the policies and disposition of the latter. Yet, neither Juárez nor Lincoln would be able to fully defeat their respective foes until they had, ironically, exercised a degree of federal, and especially executive, power characteristic of Mexican centralism, thereby defeating the residue of traditional federalism. Before that process was complete, the Lincoln administration would take a stance toward the rebel South akin to that which Santa Anna adopted in 1836 against the federalist states of Mexico—suspending statehood status and exercising direct military rule while the legislature effectively rewrote the constitution. Meanwhile Juárez would exercise a degree of federal power unmatched by any liberal president before him and implement a series of draconian wartime measures akin to those of Maximilian I, who would rule from 1864 to 1867 amid a civil war pitting his supporters against those of Juárez's republican government.

By the time both countries emerged from their respective civil conflicts in 1867, they would share more in common than they ever had. The United States would amend its Constitution in a way that not only brought it more in line with Mexico's 1857 charter but also transform the powers and purpose of the federal government and the very character of the nation. Ultimately, the leaders of both countries would emerge from their respective conflicts having abandoned many of their earlier assumptions about liberty and governance and move forward as sovereign, indivisible nation-states committed to the ideas of human equality that had first found expression on the continent nearly a century earlier.

Las familias enfermas—The Sick Families

The Mexican conflict between supporters of the Juárez government and those of Maximilian I began, much as its US counterpart had, as an ostensible dispute over sovereignty. Despite a compromise measure in the 1857 constitution that allowed the state to interfere in ecclesiastical matters, but stopped short of declaring religious freedom, church leaders and their conservative allies denounced the new constitution as atheistic and refused to accept it.[5] Particularly controversial was an oath of loyalty to the central government required of all public officials. Insisting that the oath violated the church's transcendent authority, by 1859 church officials were threatening to excommunicate anyone who swore allegiance to the secular state.[6] The Reforma government responded by seizing church property in noncompliant states, justifying its actions with strident appeals to national sovereignty and strong denunciations of an institution that even some moderates began referring to as an "enemy of the nation."[7] The simmering conflict radicalized moderate liberals and hardened radicals against the church, complaining that the church's actions undermined the government's legitimacy and hindered its administration. By December 1857, the Reforma administration's overwhelmed and exhausted interim president, Ignacio Comonfort, abrogated the constitution, issuing a pronunciamiento from the National Palace against his own administration. Comonfort had criticized the constitution for placing too much power in the hands of Congress rather than the executive. His actions alienated nearly all of his liberal supporters, and on 21 January 1858 he surrendered the presidency and fled to the United States. In accordance with the constitution, the Supreme Court president, Benito Juárez, took over as acting president.[8]

Over the next few years, the Juárez administration would pass a series of laws considered progressive in any Catholic country, but especially in Mexico, where religion and nation had historically been closely linked. Bankrupt and preempted by state governors, the Juárez administration issued a series of laws in July 1859 designed to assert its authority and check the actions of belligerent church officials. The first of these called for the complete separation of church and state, nationalization of all church property, and religious tolerance.[9] In an accompanying manifesto, the administration explained its new position. Issued by Juárez and three of his closest advisers—Melchor Ocampo, Manuel

Ruiz, and Sebastián Lerdo de Tejada—the manifesto declared that the current conflict represented a "solemn moment" for the nation, in which "principles of freedom and social progress" found themselves obstructed by the "diverse elements of despotism, hypocrisy, immorality, and disorder." They accused the clergy and their supporters of waging a "bloody and fratricidal war" for the sole purpose of preserving their "interests and privileges inherited from the colonial system." As such, the Juárez administration positioned itself as the legitimate protector of Mexican nationalism and defender of "equality, justice, and progress," as Juárez later described it. Such principles were not only consistent with the age, the authors asserted, but also essential to the "liberty and peace" of the republic. The church, meanwhile, represented a danger to Mexico through its unrelenting efforts to undermine the patriotism of its people, monopolize its lands, and control its political and civil institutions.[10]

For Conservatives, however, the Reforma government represented an assault on Mexican identity and doomed the Catholic republican experiment. The church, they argued, had helped to unite and secure Mexico in its most vulnerable moments. Its control over the country's landed wealth and its command of the people's allegiance was essential to its ongoing security and unification. Conservatives viewed the constitution and laws of the Liberal regime as an extension of the rupture and revolution that plagued much of the modern world, posing a profound threat to the Catholic order and ultimately to Mexico itself. Many of them believed that the only a return to monarchy could secure Mexico's territory from further outside aggression and its society from the political instability that had plagued it over the previous three decades.[11] After temporarily forcing the Juárez administration from Mexico City and into refuge in Veracruz, from where it continued to govern, the leaders of the conservative movement issued a manifesto that same month, January 1858, declaring their desire to "promote union among all Mexicans," disparaging attacks on the church (to them the only institution capable of uniting the divided and "disgraced country"), and promising a new era of "legality and concord."[12]

By the time the Conservative leadership issued a resolution from Mexico City in July 1863, they had been at war with the Juárez regime for more than three years and had just managed to expel their rivals from the capital for a second time. Exhausted from the conflict between what was effectively two dueling governments, and resigned to the outcome that monarchists like José María Gutiérrez Estrada had long believed was Mexico's fate, the Assembly of Notables, a self-appointed group of conservative leaders, attempted to lay out their case for why Mexico should invite the rule of a foreign prince.[13] Calling Mexico "la familia inferma"—the sick family—Ignacio Aguilar y Marocho, a conservative lawyer and political leader, seemed to suggest that the republic's failure was part of a global reckoning. "In politics and in morality . . . nothing occurs which is not related to the marvelous whole," he wrote in a resolution issued July 10. It was clear that Mexico's fate had been "intimately linked" to the collapse of the French republic and the "division of the United States, who now devour themselves without mercy," referring to the internecine civil wars between the forces of democratic liberalism and social conservatism plaguing those countries. What could this series of events, unfolding over the previous two decades, signify other than that the "republican system" was the "fecund fountainhead of all the evils afflicting the Fatherland"? Republicanism in Mexico had created a "false liberty" in which disorder and anarchy reigned and traditional mechanisms of social organization, such as the church, family, and religious communities, were undermined. The only alternative, according to the assembly, was for Mexico to return to a form of government that Gutiérrez Estrada had called for in 1841. Only a handful of people were willing to publicly advocate for monarchy in 1841, but nearly four decades of political instability, foreign invasion, and territorial rupture had proven, Conservatives said, that Mexico needed a "dike" that could place limits on "natural liberty," protect Mexicans from natural liberty's "poisonous influences," and introduce Mexicans to the "efficacy of law."[14]

According to the Conservatives, Mexico needed to be saved, not transformed. The Reforma laws represented perhaps the most egregious assault on Mexican identity and nationalism since the US invasion and threatened to undermine the only institution that had managed to sustain the country. The Mexican imperialists wanted order, stability, and security. In this respect they differed little from their liberal rivals. Yet most imperialists, while diverse in the particulars of their national vision, distrusted democracy and believed, as generations of Conservatives had before them, that most Mexicans lacked the ability to self-govern. They had little desire to redistribute landed wealth or significantly alter the economic order, and, as noted, they rejected the idea of a sovereign national state or people. They had a few things in common with proslavery ideologues in the United States.

Responding to the same global phenomena as the Mexican imperialists, southern thinkers had managed by the late 1850s to advance a set of ideas that not only criticized the "free" societies of the North and Great Britain, but also offered what they believed to be a near perfect alternative.[15] Many of slavery's defenders would have found the Conservative critique of modern liberalism and its call for a return to traditional hierarchy compelling, but they also insisted that their form racialized slavery constituted the most perfect version of such a hierarchy, rooted as it was in what Alexander Stephens called "the great truth that the negro is not equal to the white man."[16] In pamphlets and articles published in the lead-up to secession, proslavery ideologues praised traditional forms of social hierarchy as the most "natural" form of human organization and celebrated their own form of racialized coercive labor as the most perfect manifestation of it. The secessionist Leonidas Spratt of South Carolina insisted that slavery was "perhaps the purest form of aristocracy, the world has ever seen." Unlike the "forced and artificial" aristocracies in Europe and elsewhere, the South's was "natural and necessary" because it was based on the supposedly natural inequality of the races. Spratt, however, conceded, "The principle that equality is the right of man is true to an extent," but only insofar as "men of the same race are equal. It is not true that men of all races are equal."[17]

Also like the Mexican Conservatives, many proslavery southerners denounced what Spratt called the "democratic plane" as a source of chaos, disorder, and misery. "Let the inquirer look at the fearful vibrations from anarchy to despotism in Rome. Let him look at the rivers of blood that flowed from free and equal France along the streets of Paris. Let him look at the brigandage that rules in Mexico. Let him look at the fearful portents of the North." These "social revolutions" were disastrous because they were based on "unnatural relations" that inevitably led "to collisions of conflicting interest." In the South, however, "there can be no march of slaves upon the ranks of masters" because "there is no contest of classes for the same position."[18] George Fitzhugh, one of the most prolific proslavery writers of the 1850s, flatly denounced the principles expressed in the Declaration of Independence as "dangerous" and celebrated instead the "feudal nobility" and "Catholic rule" of an earlier age, in which "every man had his house and his home" and "the baron and priest vied with each other in their care of the vassal." Under the modern social order, "the poor have been turned over from the parental and protective rule of kings, barons, and churchmen, to the unfeeling despotism of capitalists, employers, usurers, and extortionists." For Fitzhugh, slavery represented the endpoint on a continuum of hierarchical social relations that had characterized civilization since the beginning of human history.[19]

Significant differences, of course, existed between slavery's defenders in the United States and the Mexican Conservatives of the 1860s. For one, the former never called for a return to monarchy. Instead, what they envisioned, as Stephanie McCurry has described it, was "an explicitly proslavery and antidemocratic nation-state" capable of resolving the problems of "labor, capital, and democracy." Their aim was not to reject the United States, but rather reconstitute it to conform with what they believed its original conception of "the people" had entailed. As president of the Confederacy, Jefferson Davis, put it in his inaugural address, theirs was a republic of "brethren, not in name merely but in fact, men of one flesh, one bone, one interest, one purpose."[20] That purpose, of course, was the perpetual preservation, and even expansion, of Black enslavement. Meanwhile, most imperialists not only rejected slavery as their liberal compatriots had decades earlier and recognized it as the force behind the United States' egregious assaults on Mexico as Conservatives long had, but many of them hoped that the empire would be temporary. Many therefore embraced cooperation with a European monarchy defensively and cautiously. This perspective stemmed from a desire to defend and protect their nation's territorial sovereignty, not to rupture it. Even more importantly, most envisioned a society in which all Mexicans could eventually enjoy equal rights, even if such a society was not possible at that moment.[21] In short, the political vision of the imperialists, especially those who were once liberals, was more edifying and temporary than that of the Confederates, whose rigid racial hierarchy relegating a large segment of the population to the status of property made it exceptional among modern states.

Despite these significant differences, both regimes shared a general anxiety and remedy, and both presented formidable obstacles to the liberal order envisioned by their rivals against whom they would form an alliance. For decades, southern advocates had fervently, if disingenuously, denounced the possibility of the return of European monarchy to North American. Many had cited the danger of such a possibility in their efforts to justify the US acquisition of Texas and Oregon. Nonetheless, the Confederates recognized an important foreign policy opportunity with the French invasion of Mexico in 1861. For the Confederacy—facing a Union blockade and having failed to receive recognition from any foreign power—Mexico became essential to its foreign policy. Its initial efforts to gain recognition from the Juárez regime ended disastrously in 1861, when intercepted correspondence between Richmond's envoy, John Pickett, and its secretary of state, Robert Toombs, revealed that the former had made disparaging remarks about Mexico and its people and raised the possibility of Confederate designs on its territory even after Toombs had explicitly directed him to dissuade Mexican officials of any such thoughts. Their efforts with Mexican Conservatives fared little better, so by 1863 an intervention by France represented a welcomed third chance for Confederate leaders to gain recognition from a major European power, and a buyer for Southern cotton, as well as to form a workable alliance with its southern neighbor.

James Williams, the former US ambassador to the Ottoman Empire, articulated the South's foreign policy about-face in his lengthy 1863 treatise, *The Rise and Fall of the Modern Republic*, in which he rejected the notion that republicanism constituted a universally appealing form of government, especially for non-European or mixed-race peoples. The United States had thrived under "democratical institutions," but in "almost every other part of the American continent," Williams asserted, the experiment in self-rule had "ended in complete and hopeless failure." This was especially true of Mexico, which, since its adoption of a republican system, had suffered from "intrinsically bad government." Williams predicted, "Mexicans may well hail the establishment of different political institutions, founded upon a properly organized monarchy as . . . the full stop in their downward career, the harbinger of a great future for the nation." Indeed, if there was one thing that remained consistent about southerners' evolving doctrine, it was its enduring racism. What had doomed the Spanish American republics, according to Williams, was their racial amalgamation. What made republicanism successful in the United States was that the "European races" had "always maintained a social and political superiority." Such an explanation, of course, implied an even more favorable outcome for the Confederacy. Williams and other Confederates did not interpret secession and the collapse of the North American republic as an indication of Anglo Americans' inability to self-govern, but merely as an attempt "to amend or correct errors of mere detail." Meanwhile, in racially amalgamated Mexico, "the only hope of regeneration consists of wiping out the past" and "laying the foundations of future prosperity by the adoption of a monarchical government." In addition to bringing order, stability, and "happiness" to the Mexican people, a French intervention would attract an "influx of European immigrants," who would develop and enrich the country. Under French rule, a "great and prosperous empire" would emerge ready to "take her position as one of the first-class powers, not only of the American continent, but of the civilized world."[22]

The French welcomed the birth of the Confederacy as a hedge against US omnipotence, their primary aim in accepting conservative overtures in 1863, two years after they had invaded Mexico, ostensibly in response to Juárez's decision to suspend repayment of the country's foreign debt to European creditors. In fact, Napoleon III had been looking for an opportunity to extend his imperial reach into the Americas in accordance with his Grand Design, which involved strengthening and unifying the Catholic world under a French empire capable of counterbalancing the Anglo-Protestant realm. When the emperor and the rest of Europe's Catholic aristocrats looked at the North American continent, they saw a region profoundly vulnerable to an aggressive and hostile Anglo-dominated republic. The combined events of Mexico's default and a compromised United States appeared to supply the perfect opportunity. According to "France, Mexico, and the Confederate States," a pamphlet published 1863 by the French statesman and intellectual, Michel Chevalier, the aim of the French intervention was neither conquest nor enrichment, but "to aid the Mexicans in establishing—according to their own free will and choice—a government which shall have some chances of stability" through the imposition of "order," "cohesion," and "industry." While France did not object to "seeing the republic of the United States prosperous and powerful," it opposed the "absorption of South America by Northern America" and the "diminution of the Latin races on the other side of the ocean."[23] Napoleon III's ambitions, thus, neatly complemented the longstanding aims of Mexican Conservatives—the establishment of order through highly centralized governance, the creation of a powerful state capable of preventing further US encroachment, and the defense of the Catholic faith and the "Latin race." [24]

Freedom International

Yet, as far as supporters of Juárez were concerned, Lincoln's election in 1860 negated the primary motivation behind the French intervention, since his party did not share the territorial aggressions of its slaveholding rivals and, to many Mexican liberals, signaled a new era of US foreign policy. The Juárez administration enthusiastically welcomed the Republican victory, not only because the party was ideologically similar to its own, but for what it likely represented for future relations between Mexico and the United States.[25] In the days following the election, Matías Romero, the Juárez administration's representative in Washington, reported to his superiors, "The coming administration has new ideas and its politics are distinct from those followed by the government that proceeded it." He anticipated a "radical change" in relations between the two countries.[26] Knowing that US expansionism had been largely propelled by southern Democrats, Romero optimistically noted that the Republicans were "at heart abolitionists," a position that, he concluded, made them natural allies of Mexico's republican administration. He, therefore, wasted little time in establishing relations with Lincoln himself, in short order going to visit the president-elect at his home in Springfield in November 1860. Instructed to gain the incoming administration's recognition and, if possible secure a loan to aid the fight against the Conservatives, Romero took his job seriously and proved himself not above the use of flattery. He informed Lincoln that Mexico wished "to adopt the same principles of liberty and progress which are followed [in the United States]" and travel "the same path to arrive at the grandeur and unequaled prosperity currently enjoyed" in that country. He also noted that the Republican platform was "in harmony with the principles rooted very deeply in the hearts of Mexicans." Therefore, he expected that Republican policy toward Mexico would be "truly fraternal" as opposed to the "egotistical and antihumanitarian principles which the Democratic administrations had pursued," identifying slavery as the force responsible for "pillaging the Mexican Republic."[27] Yet, Lincoln demonstrated little interest in either abolishing slavery or assisting Mexico for the first two years of his presidency.

Lincoln's aim was to coax southerners back into the Union. Insisting, as he always had, that the constitutional status of the rebel states remained unchanged, he and his advisers initially dismissed abolitionist appeals to intervene against the Confederacy's cornerstone institution, insisting that the federal government remained obligated to protect the rights of the seceding states.[28] In the months following the outbreak of the war in April 1861, officers of the US Army, or Union Army, were initially instructed to assist Confederates in reclaiming enslaved people, some of whom were fleeing to Union lines in the few occupied parts of the Confederacy like Virginia. In May 1861, Major Benjamin H. Butler, stationed at Fort Monroe, informed the commanding general of the US Army, Winfield Scott, that Confederate forces were firing on his men from Sewall's Point with batteries that had been constructed by enslaved men, several of whom had sought refuge with the army. Butler had written an earlier letter to Scott defending his decision not to return fugitives to the Confederates and asking why rebels should be allowed to use this "property" against the United States "and we not allowed its use in aid of the United States?" Without waiting for Scott's reply, Butler ordered one of his officers to see to it that "all able-bodied negroes within your lines"—including women and children—be "taken" and put to work digging trenches and constructing "works."[29] The administration swiftly approved Butler's policy, its first modest step in undermining slavery. United States soldiers were not to interfere with the institution directly, but if enslaved people managed to escape to Union lines, they were to be put to work in service of the United States. The First Confiscation Act of 1861 cited international law in its refusal to return such "contraband." Yet, the term *contraband* itself implied that such individuals were still considered property, likely to be returned upon Confederate surrender.[30]

However modest, the Confiscation Act set in motion a long, gradual process of dismantling slavery, a goal that would reveal itself to be essential to the rebellion's suppression. As Butler and his troops continued south, they confronted so many enslaved people eager to join their forces that the general deemed it "a physical impossibility to take them all." Successful occupation of the Lower Mississippi Alluvial Valley, the heart of the South's cotton economy, brought 150,000 enslaved individuals under the federal government's jurisdiction. Furthermore, it was becoming increasingly difficult to determine which individuals belonged to loyalists and which to rebels. Meanwhile, back in Washington, radical Republicans were pointing to such reports as evidence of the need for a more aggressive law that would allow the federal government to extend freedom to more people. Congress passed and the president signed the Second Confiscation Act of 1862, which officially declared secession to be "treasonous," promised swift punishment of rebel leaders (including their execution), and declared "forever free of their servitude" any individuals belonging to them who came into US-occupied territory. It also authorized Lincoln to "employ as many persons of African descent as he may deem necessary . . . for the suppression of the rebellion."[31] Finally, it enabled passage of the Militia Act of 1862, which Lincoln signed into law on the same day, reversing legislation that had existed since US independence barring African Americans from military service. Military leaders had argued for such a policy since the war's commencement and fugitives fleeing to so-called contraband camps, located behind Union lines. With the Militia Act, Congress officially authorized the army to receive "persons of African descent" into service "for the purpose of labor, or any other military . . . service."[32] In doing so, it paved the way for a transformation of African Americans' status by granting them the means to claim citizenship in the reconstructed nation. It was the same republican idea that Mexico had reflexively extended to Anglo American settlers in Texas and later to Irish immigrants serving in the invading US Army. Now it was being used for the specific purpose of emancipation.

Yet, by the end of 1862, Lincoln had yet to issue a presidential emancipation decree, something that Romero, and likely most of the Mexicans he corresponded with, found both bewildering and frustrating. Even before the war's start, abolitionists had identified slavery as the rebel lifeblood. "The very stomach of the rebellion is a negro in the form of a slave," declared Frederick Douglass, who insisted that if the administration could "arrest that hoe in the hands of the

Negro," it would "smite the rebellion in the very seat of its life."[33] As the war progressed, radical Republicans in Congress and their abolitionist allies continued to insist that a US victory would require not just the confiscation of some of the enslaved, but the destruction of slavery altogether, and called on the president to use his executive wartime authority to do so. Finding his mission somewhat forestalled by the protracted debate over whether slavery should be abolished and whether the president had the power to do so unilaterally, Romero noted that such division so distracted northerners that they had "forgotten to make war on the common enemy." Two months later, he reported vexingly that abolition was "still subservient to maintaining the Union" and that the administration had "neither debated nor evaluated the measure" in terms of its "intrinsic justice."[34] Just as problematic was the fact that the only relations that the administration did seem interested in pursuing with Mexico was the purchase of a portion of Mexico's territory for the purpose of establishing a colony of freed Blacks beyond the borders of the United States. In the annual message to Congress in 1862, Lincoln had gone so far as to ask for an amendment authorizing that funding be allocated for such a project.[35] Romero dutifully dismissed the possibility of an additional acquisition of Mexican territory, insisting that the United States "would receive more benefit from Mexico as an independent nation with its actual boundaries than if it were inside the Union."[36]

The administration's long, stilted, and technical path toward emancipation certainly differed from the swift, unilateral character of Mexican policymaking in that regard. Ultimately, however, the president would employ the same tactic that Mexican leaders had almost every time they sought to bypass federalism in pursuit of urgent national policy. On 22 September 1862, after months of agonized debate between moderate and radical Republicans within his own administration and concurrence that a direct attack on slavery was essential to undermining the South, Lincoln issued the Preliminary Emancipation Proclamation. It did little more than confirm earlier actions by Congress and express his intention to prosecute the war so long as it took to restore the "constitutional relations" between the Union and the rebel states. It also offered remuneration and assistance in colonizing the freed Blacks of states that surrendered to the United States and adopted gradual emancipation, while those states that continued the rebellion would have their human property declared "forever free" by the president. It was the most sweeping legislation that Congress had passed up to that point and demonstrated a profound acceptance of executive power, yet it did not come close to ending slavery throughout the Union.

When, at year's end, not a single southern state had heeded Lincoln's warning, he issued the Emancipation Proclamation on 1 January 1863. This time he made no mention of colonization or remuneration.[37] It was neither as sweeping nor as unilateral as Guerrero's 1828 decree, which emancipated all enslaved persons throughout the republic, but it nonetheless represented a significant step in the United States' long process of eventually abolishing slavery altogether, which, considering the scope and significance of slavery by the midpoint of the nineteenth century, was a remarkable feat. Like the Reforma amortization laws, it was a profound expression of national sovereignty and executive authority in compliance with legal and constitutional boundaries and revealed a determination to destroy earlier systems of privilege and remake society in accordance with the equalizing principles to which liberals throughout the Western world were committing themselves.[38]

Scholars have deservedly credited the efforts of Black abolitionists in pushing the Lincoln administration to abandon colonization as part of its emancipation process. Indeed, several months before issuing the Emancipation Proclamation, Lincoln had met with a group of prominent Black leaders to discuss a colonization project. During that meeting, he reportedly claimed that Blacks and whites were separated by a broader difference "than exists between almost any other two races."[39] The delegation expressed their disapproval of the plan in no uncertain terms, and it was ultimately omitted from the president's final draft. Yet, it is likely that Romero's refusal to negotiate a US acquisition of more Mexican territory for such a purpose also contributed to Lincoln's decision-making. Regardless, the Emancipation Proclamation did not simply transform the administration's posture toward the rebel states and slavery itself, it also altered relations between the United States and Mexico. Indeed, mere weeks after Lincoln issued the proclamation, Congress passed a resolution denouncing the French invasion of Mexico and pledged to support the Mexicans country in their war against France.[40] Two months later, Romero reported to his superiors that the "US has recognized that it cannot look with indifference" upon European intervention in North America, having recognized "that the interests of all the nations of the continent are aligned."[41]

As the ranks of the Union Army began to swell with the formerly enslaved in response to news of Lincoln's proclamation, the tide of the war began to shift decisively in the Union's favor. That July, as the Assembly of Notables issued their resolution from Mexico's capital, and the Juárez administration fled north into the desert, several thousand miles away in Gettysburg, Pennsylvania, Confederate and US forces confronted each other in what would become the most decisive battle of the US civil war and one that carried implications for the

Mexican conflict as well. Four months after the Union victory at Gettysburg, Lincoln would take a rare train voyage to the site of the battle to deliver a speech honoring the deceased and their sacrifice.

In November 1863, in an address noted for its brevity and brilliance, Lincoln articulated the precise stakes of the conflict in terms notably different than he had before. It was no longer a war about restoring the Union as it had existed when he assumed the presidency. Rather, it was a war about the birth of, as he put it, "a new nation"—a sovereign, uniform, and indivisible political body dedicated to the "proposition that all men are created equal." For scholars, the Gettysburg Address represents a pivotal transition in Lincoln's thinking. The United States, if it managed to defeat the Confederacy, would not emerge from the War of the Rebellion as the loose confederation of sovereign states and territories that it had been previously. It would emerge as something else entirely: a sovereign nation "of the people, by the people, and for the people." It was also clear, however, that Lincoln was not only talking about the United States. He described the conflict as a "great civil war, testing whether that nation, or any nation so conceived and so dedicated, can long endure." Lincoln did not mention Mexico or any other country by name, and it's impossible to know if he was thinking of it, but considering the lengths that Romero had gone to convince his administration of the similarities between the two countries and their respective conflicts, it is likely he was.

In April 1862, about eighteen months before Lincoln spoke these words, Juárez had delivered a similar address in which he declared that "salvaging the independence of Mexico" from the throes of European imperialism would represent "a triumph not only for our own country, but also for the principles of respect and inviolability of the sovereignty of the nations."[42] In March 1863, more than six months before the speech at Gettysburg, yet in terms striking similar to it, he declared, "The continent of America and free men of all nations are depending on us [Mexicans], because we defend their cause, the cause of liberty, humanity, and civilization."[43] It is hard to imagine that Juárez did not have the United States in mind when he spoke those words, especially given his administration's evident awareness of the similarities between their two conflicts. Indeed, Mexican leaders had since the 1840s acknowledged a continental struggle pitting the forces of equality, democracy, and republicanism against those of hierarchy, aristocracy, and empire. It had taken the US leaders about two decades to do the same. Regardless, after years of territorial competition and antagonism, the presidents of the two countries seemed to identify a shared condition and that they both were now engaged in a similar struggle. Both identified their own nation as setting a precedent for others similarly situated, but if any republic had set the example of abolition and national sovereignty, it was Mexico. If there was one individual more responsible for the conceptualization of a continental struggle between the forces of liberty, equality, and freedom and the forces of slavery, aristocracy, and empire, it was Romero.

Approximately seven months before Lincoln's speech at Gettysburg, a legation of Mexican leaders arrived in the United States. In an address to a group of Republican sympathizers, Romero would make his most precise observation of the two struggles then engulfing the continent:

> It appears to me gentlemen that there exists a striking similarity between the church party of Mexico and the pro-slavery party in the United States. The church was there a power stronger than the state; so was slavery in this country. The church has there been the only cause of our civil wars; so now is slavery here. The church party in Mexico, after being conquered by the people, solicited foreign intervention in order to be reestablished in power; so slavery in this country, as I understand, has sought foreign aid even before being conquered by the government of the United States.[44]

By that point, conservative forces were only a few months away from dislodging Juárez and his government from Mexico City and issuing their dictamen. What Romero conveyed more explicitly than either Lincoln or Juárez was that despite the functional differences between the church and slavery, both institutions threatened the liberal nation-building effort. Both represented critical hindrances to precisely the kind of modern democratic nation that the two regimes envisioned.

Meanwhile, the Emancipation Proclamation transformed what had once been the South's greatest asset into its main vulnerability. Unable to gain formal recognition abroad by the end of 1863, the Confederacy now faced chaos from within. With the issuance of the proclamation, the South's slave regime began to collapse as scores of formerly enslaved people fled their farms and plantations for US lines. Those who remained often refused to work, damaged machinery, or began demanding wages. Meanwhile, the South's numerical disadvantage became an increasingly insurmountable obstacle as the war dragged on. Most wealthy slaveholders showed little interest in contributing to the war effort, sending substitutes in their place and refusing to release their slaves to the Confederacy for fear that they might be injured, killed, or escape. When the Confederate Congress assembled in December 1863, the president of the Confederacy, Davis, urged its members to remedy the South's manpower crisis and in that regard proposed passage of a law that would employ free and enslaved Blacks as noncombatant laborers. The legislators responded by authorizing the use of 20,000 unpaid Black laborers to perform such duties as digging ditches and constructing railroads. They also expanded the age bracket for conscription to include all white men between 18 and 45. By this point, however, the South's manpower reserve was already near depletion, desertion high, and the Confederacy with little luck recruiting additional men.[45]

The situation was even worse to the west. Texans simply refused to comply with requisitions from Confederate authorities, insisting that the threat of Indian and Mexican incursions was too great, so the state had to maintain a well-organized force there. Confederate authorities found it necessary to impose martial law over the entire state as early as May 1862. Every white male over the age of sixteen was ordered to report their age, name, and address to the provost marshal under threat of summary punishment if they failed.[46] In late 1863, the Texas governor, Pendleton Murrah, refused to comply with Confederate Colonel Kirby Smith's request to renew the term of Texas troops then serving in the Confederate army. The Texas legislature supported the governor, passing a law in February 1864 requiring every conscript not already in Confederate service to remain in Texas.[47] With Richmond apparently unmoved by Texas's particular security needs as a frontier state, some of the most outspoken proponents for joining the Confederacy quickly became its loudest critics. Louis Wigfall, former Texas representative to the House of Representatives and an ardent secessionist, attacked nearly every nationalizing effort by Davis, from establishing a supreme court to a national railroad. Murrah accused Davis of "dictatorial power" and "national encroachment," insisting that Richmond could not enforce a draft law that threatened the security of the state.[48]

As the liberal nation-state that Juárez and Lincoln envisioned came into being, the decentralized slave republic that the Confederacy claimed to stand for became ever more diminished. Pronounced disagreement gripped state authorities and slaveholders as well as Confederate leaders, who recognized the severe limitations of such a system in a war against the United States. The Confederate constitution had awarded the central government considerable power with which to enact its wartime legislation, but state governments seemed unwilling to concede it. Then, in January 1864 Patrick Cleburne, a major general in the Confederate army, made the radical proposition that the Confederacy follow the North's example and emancipate and arm its enslaved population. This, he insisted, was the only remedy to the South's crushing manpower problem and the only way to secure independence.[49] Cleburne's proposal was too extreme for most Confederate leaders, who instead proposed arming slaves without the promise of freedom.[50] The Confederates somehow believed that they could wage a successful war in defense of slavery with an enslaved military force against an emancipationist state. By October, even Davis had conceded that enslaved individuals could no longer be regarded "merely as property." Without their "loyalty," enslaved persons were simply useless to the Confederacy. Yet, such a policy was a direct affront to the very basis on which the Confederacy had been established. The Confederacy, the most exceptional political experiment the continent had witnessed, had failed.[51]

From Wolves to Neighbors

On 4 April 1864, Rep. Henry Winter Davis, a Republican from Maryland and chairman of the House Foreign Affairs Committee, stood to propose a measure unrelated to the issues of the ongoing war. Instead he rose to address the United States' relationship with Mexico—in particular what he perceived as the Lincoln administration's failure to pursue a more aggressive posture toward the French regime. As the chairman spoke, Mexican forces were engaged in an intense effort to repel the French military and their allies' attempt to install Maximilian, archduke of Austria and Napoleon III's chosen emperor for Mexico. Six days after Davis's address, Maximilian formally accepted the crown, landing in Veracruz aboard the SMS *Novara* on the May 26. Despite Romero's years-long effort to highlight the similarities between the two wars, Republicans had been hesitant to involve themselves in the Mexican conflict until now, resisting appeals from the Juárez administration for aid. Davis insisted that that had to change. Not only was the North now winning the war, but France had installed a European emperor on American soil. He criticized his colleagues for "willing by silence to leave the nations of the world under the impression that [we] are indifferent spectators of the deplorable events now transpiring in the Republic of Mexico." Most of the senator's statement, however, was dedicated to drawing a distinction between his proposed resolution and the past policies of Democratic administrations toward Mexico. While the Democrats' approach had been like that "of a wolf to a lamb," the Republican party wished "to cultivate friendship with our republican brethren of Mexico and South America, to aid in consolidating republican principles, to retain popular government in all this continent from the fangs of monarchical and aristocratic power, and to lead the sisterhood of American republics in the path of peace, prosperity, and power."[52] For the first time in four decades, North Americans were speaking of their southern neighbor in familial terms. Davis was hardly alone. In the coming months, other leading voices of his party would echo his views. With Maximilian's departure for Mexico, Republicans could no longer dismiss the threat of European encroachment on North American soil.

Plans for a US intervention had in fact been circulating since August 1863, when the military governor of Texas, Andrew Jackson Hamilton, urged Lincoln to send a regiment of Black soldiers to aid the Juárez government in its fight against Napoleon III in response to rumors that France had secured the cooperation of the Confederacy in arranging a "new government under the imperial sanction and favor of Louis Napoleon."[53] Indeed, Lincoln did not foresee the thousands of Confederates who would flee, first to Texas, and then to Mexico during the final months of the war.[54] The United States might have emerged from the conflict with a renewed sense of purpose and strength, but it could not fully defeat the Confederacy until it had helped Juárez expel the French from North America.

The Confederate exodus to Mexico was largely the doing of men like scientist and Confederate naval officer Matthew Fontaine Maury who, in June 1865, presented Maximilian with a plan for southern colonization. The relocation and settlement of thousands of white and Black southerners, Maury explained, would bring long-awaited prosperity and order to Mexico in accordance with the French Grand Design. "Mexico may gather and transfer to her own borders the very intelligence, skill, and labor which made the South what she was in her palmy days," Maury wrote. It would also secure the northern states of Mexico from an aggressive United States and ongoing Indian raids. In return, white southerners would get the chance to reestablish themselves in a country whose rich fertile lands and strategic location could become an agricultural promised land in the right hands, all while advancing the "humane system of African emancipation" by allowing their formerly enslaved to work under the Mexican indenture system. Interestingly, Maury and other promoters did not present their project as a scheme to reinstate slavery, perhaps sensing that the French would oppose it if they did. Instead, like their predecessors of nearly forty years earlier, they promised to conform to the Mexican labor system.[55] Maximilian was prepared to meet Maury and like-minded Confederates halfway. Having "strong[ly] and heartily" embraced Maury's proposition, in September the emperor revised Mexico's laws regarding debt peonage, easing the way for landholders to apprentice the children of their workers. The aim was to encourage the last Confederate holdouts to settle in Mexico. At the same time, his administrators approved land grants north of Veracuz.

Unsurprisingly, news of Maximilian's decision and the plan to establish a colony of Confederate exiles enraged the Lincoln administration when it reached Washington. The scheme not only undermined the effort to abolish slavery on the continent, but also put US security at risk by paving the way for a future Confederate invasion from Mexico. In fact, Maximilian had even more ambitious plans. In the fall of 1865, he began promoting the idea of establishing Mexican settlements in Texas, Louisiana, and Tennessee and chose Maury as his "imperial colonization commissioner." US officials privately expressed the concern that the scheme would drain the country of the "best and most industrious negroes," thereby saddling it with only the "idle and vicious" who refused their owners' order to relocate with them to Mexico. Black colonization had gone from a primary aim of the administration in its dealings with Mexico to something that Republicans wanted to prevent.[56] In addition to spreading the notion among southern Blacks that they faced re-enslavement in Mexico, Washington began to assert its presence in Texas to a then-unprecedented extent, reassigning nearly fifty thousand federal troops, half of them African American, to the north bank of the Rio Grande.[57]

As devastating as these developments were for Republicans, they were rather fortuitous for the *juaristas*, Juárez supporters, who finally seemed to be making headway after years of trying to convince the Lincoln administration to assist them against the French. Although Secretary of State William H. Seward was hesitant to intervene on behalf of the liberals, most military officials were not. In late April 1865, Romero informed his superiors about a conversation he had had with General Ulysses S. Grant in which the American informed him that "although he is tired of war, his major desire is to fight in Mexico against the French."[58] Earlier that month, the Confederate general Robert E. Lee had surrendered his army to Grant at Appomattox, bringing the war to its conclusion, and four days later, Lincoln had been assassinated by the Confederate sympathizer John Wilkes Booth. Grant, perhaps more than any other US official, concurred with the juaristas' view that the conflict then unfolding in Mexico was an extension of the one that had plagued his own and quickly became Romero's chief ally in lobbying President Andrew Johnson's administration to take a more aggressive posture toward the French than Lincoln had, urging Johnson to supply arms and ammunition to Juárez and asserting that more republican victories would likely prompt a French withdrawal. Meanwhile, the general encouraged General Phillip H. Sheridan, commander of US forces along the Rio Grande, to gather intelligence on the movement and plans of imperialist forces at the border. When Johnson chose to follow Seward's advice and resist the temptation to directly involve the United States in Mexico, Grant ordered Sheridan to leave arms and ammunition "at convenient places on our side of the river to fall into [the liberals'] hands" and thereby place the affairs of the republic "on a substantial basis." Sheridan complied. Meanwhile, Romero managed to secure a private meeting with Johnson, during which Grant proposed funneling US arms to the juaristas with the aid of private merchants.

Although willing to engage in clandestine support of the republicans, the Johnson administration preferred instead to compel the French to leave through diplomatic means. Criticizing the administration's methods as "slow and pokey," Sheridan and Grant proceeded to encourage their own discharged men to join the Mexican republican army.[59] The Juárez government complemented this effort by publishing its own decree inviting "all foreigners who may present themselves armed with the weapons requisite for military or cavalry" to serve "in the defense of the independence of Mexico and its republican institutions." In addition to the monetary compensation "required by law," volunteers would receive a "bounty in land" that had been seized from "all those guilty of treason . . . or any other lands considered as national property." In an effort "to promote the division of property," plots awarded would not exceed the "fourth part of a Mexican square league." Finally, in accordance with Mexican law, all foreign individuals who served in the republican army would "immediately become Mexican citizens, with all the rights and obligations of such citizens."[60] Romero reported, "confidentially and quite reliably," that he knew that the government's purpose in sending the 25th Army Corps, "composed only of colored soldiers" was "to offer them the opportunity to cross over to us" and concluded that "supposedly, large numbers will do this because of the advantages they will enjoy in Mexico, where the Negro race is not the victim of prejudice."[61] When the governor of Tennessee, Parson Brownlow, expressed his desire to relocate the African American regiment then stationed there, Union Army general R. Delevan Mussey informed Romero that he would remove them to Arizona ostensibly to protect residents there against the threat of Indian raids, something the general himself did not take seriously. Once Mussey informed his superiors that "all is quiet" and there was "nothing to fear from the Indians," the troops could be mustered out and "follow their inclination to cross into Mexico and enter our service in Sonora."[62]

Concern about the French presence in Mexico and fears of the country becoming the site of renewed Confederate aggression was not confined to the military. Special interest groups, like the Monroe League of San Francisco and the Defenders of the Monroe Doctrine in New Orleans and Brownsville, applied much of the pressure to intervene. These organizations, mostly composed of wealthy businessmen motivated at least as much by opportunities for investment as they were by political sympathy, eagerly cast their new interest in Mexico as part of a noble effort to preserve republican democracy on the continent. In July 1865, members of the Mexican Patriot Club met at the Cooper Institute, in New York City, where organizers dining on a meal of roasted duck and nougat parisien claimed to represent the avant-garde on the US posture toward Mexico. "Never before," the preface of the published proceedings proclaimed, had the "true representatives" of a Spanish American republic appeared before such an assemblage "to receive a fraternal welcome as acknowledged members of the general American brotherhood." The club, consisting of prominent liberal exiles, including Romero, had been struggling for decades, the meeting's organizers claimed, to secure the freedoms enjoyed by citizens of the United States, but the conservative opposition had undermined their efforts with "misrepresentations, slanders, and calumnies." It was the purpose of the gathering to rectify this wrong by "overcoming the obstacles which had been placed between Anglo-Saxon republicans and those of the Spanish race." Not since Mexican independence had Americans employed terms so saturated with fraternal affection when describing leaders of a Spanish American republic, and not since that time had Americans identified events unfolding in Mexico as part of the same set of conflicts facing their own country. The members of the Mexican Patriot Club themselves echoed these sentiments, insisting that their compatriots were fighting "not only in defense of their own independence and institutions, but also in defense of all American nationalities which are threatened by European intervention." The war's outcome, they insisted, would determine the fate of the competition "between despotism and liberty, between monarchy and republicanism." What the organization and its guests did not discuss was the opportunities for economic investment that US businesses expected as their reward. After years of struggling to secure financial assistance from the Lincoln administration, Romero and his allies were willing to oblige them.[63]

Toward "one national family"

The defeat of the Confederacy and the interventionist forces ultimately required a tremendous assertion of federal power by the juaristas and the Republicans that rivaled that of the staunchest Mexican centralist regimes. By the end of 1865, Lincoln had managed to extract a surrender from the Confederate commander, Lee, but the challenge of reconstructing the new nation that he described in his speech at Gettysburg posed an even greater challenge in many ways as former rebels and their supporters attempted to reassert power at the state level.

Likewise, in Mexico, Juárez's greatest obstacles to reestablishing his regime were autonomous state governors, specifically Santiago Vidaurri of Nuevo León, intent on reclaiming their sovereignty. For Lincoln and Juárez to defeat their rivals and restore their respective nations in accordance with the new liberal order they envisioned, it became necessary to exercise a degree of federal authority unprecedented for both countries. In certain respects, this was more difficult in the United States, which lacked precedence for the kind of unilateral federal control that Reconstruction demanded and a constitution that was ill-equipped for the kind of political, legal, and social transformation about to take place. By the end of the decade, however, Congress had added three crucial amendments to the document that not only redefined its original purpose, but also brought it more in line with the Mexican document's commitment to equality, antislavery, and birth right citizenship.

In the days following the address at Gettysburg, Lincoln turned his attention to the question of how best to reintegrate the rebel states into the Union. This issue had been a question since the beginning of the war, but the answer had become more complicated as the depth and scope of the rebellion grew more evident and as both the administration and congress became increasingly committed to emancipation. By 1863 everyone understood that the rebel states could not be readmitted under the same leadership and legislation as before. Lincoln and Congress agreed that abolition and the disenfranchisement of at least the highest-ranking Confederate officials should constitute basic prerequisites to admission, but how could the administration guarantee this? Both slavery and voting had long been considered the purview of state sovereignty, and Lincoln had long insisted that the rebel states retained their statehood status even as they engaged in open rebellion against the United States. Lincoln's answer would resemble a tactic that Mexican centralists had employed to exercise unilateral federal control over rebellious states and regions.

Massachusetts senator Charles Sumner and Rep. John Bingham of Ohio had introduced the theory of "territorialization" in early 1862. They argued that the southern states had effectively forfeited their status by rebelling against the Union and declaring their independence. Thus, they were no longer states, but territories and therefore "subject to federal jurisdiction."[64] The theory resembled the santanista government's decision to convert the states to "departments" under the 1836 Mexican constitution. Both systems brought former states under the direct authority of the president and Congress. In the case of the United States, territorialization supplied a legal framework for Lincoln to do what he had once insisted he could not—dictate the terms of readmission.

Indeed, just a few weeks after Gettysburg, Lincoln issued the Proclamation of Amnesty and Reconciliation to provide a mode by which individual southerners could be granted amnesty and loyal state governments reorganized and readmitted. Except for top cadre of Confederate military and political leaders, the plan offered full pardons and the restoration "of all rights and property, except as to slaves" to anyone who had participated in the rebellion. All former rebels needed to do was take an oath "to support, protect, and defend the Constitution of the United States, and the Union of the States thereunder" and to "abide by and faithfully support all acts of Congress . . . and proclamations of the president made during the existing rebellion." After 10 percent or more of the population of a state had taken the oath, that state could be readmitted to the Union and permitted to establish its own government and constitution formally abolishing slavery. All other components of the new government—"the name of the state, the boundary, the subdivisions, the constitution, and the general code of laws"—could remain the same as before the war.[65]

Considering the "criminal and treasonous" acts that Lincoln asserted the rebels had committed, the terms of his proclamation were relatively generous. It was too generous by the estimation of some members of Congress, who—pointing to conditions in Louisiana, where moderates authored a state constitution that did nothing to improve or assist recently freed people while compensating former slaveholders who had remained loyal to the Union—called for a more meaningful reform along the lines of what Mexican liberals like Ponciano Arriaga had envisioned. "The nation," asserted the abolitionist Wendell Phillips, "owes the negro, not merely freedom, but land and education."[66] They responded with a stringent bill in 1864, authored by Sen. Benjamin Wade of Ohio and Representative Davis, that required new state governments to declare all enslaved or formerly enslaved persons "forever free," disenfranchise former Confederate leaders, and guarantee legal justice "to all persons." Most notably, however, it required a "majority" of a state's white male citizens to take an oath of loyalty to the United States before the process of reorganization could take place.[67] To the chagrin of congressional republicans, Lincoln refused to sign the bill, allowing it to idle on his desk until the end of his first term. After his re-election on the heels of Sherman's remarkable triumph in Georgia, he pursued a series of policies designed to guarantee the complete capitulation of the former Confederacy and the reentry of rebel territories under terms agreeable to the administration and Congress. He demanded the dissolution of all rebel forces, the restoration of "national authority" across the rebel territory, and the complete "capitulation" of the Confederate state.[68] Most significantly, Lincoln pushed for passage of a constitutional amendment to explicitly prohibit slavery and involuntary servitude, "except as a punishment for crime," in any part of the present United States or its future territories and to authorize congressional action to guarantee such freedom wherever in the United States it might be necessary to do so.

The Thirteenth Amendment was the first amendment added to the Constitution in more than sixty years and the first of several that would bring the document more in line with its Mexican counterpart, contributing to what Eric Foner calls the United States' "second founding."[69] Its passage and adoption in 1865 initiated a process whereby federal power no longer centered only around fiscal and military matters, but also extended to those related to human liberty. A momentous shift had taken place in the United States, one that not only promised to redefine the country's very identity, but also the purpose, aim and scope of its federal government. Lincoln and Congress may have disagreed over which branch of government had ultimate authority over reconstruction, but they both agreed that individual liberty now fell under the ultimate authority and protection of the federal government, not the states. The United States was no longer a loose confederation of autonomous states and territories, as southern leaders had so long insisted,[70] but a sovereign and indivisible nation forming, as Lincoln himself had initially proclaimed in 1862—"one national family."[71]

Back in the summer of 1863, Juárez had found himself in a position very different from Lincoln's after Conservative forces invited French emperor Napoleon III to extend his authority over Mexico. By 1864 the constitutional government had been evicted from the nation's capital, lacked control over the country's most populous regions, and struggled to secure foreign aid. One thing in Juárez's favor, however, were the emergency powers granted him by the Constituent Congress and a series of laws, passed as early as 1856, that sanctioned severe penalties for crimes against "nation, public peace, and order." After Congress conceded extraordinary powers to him 11 December 1861 following the French invasion, Juárez passed the law of 25 January 1862 which targeted collaborators by establishing the death penalty for those found guilty of committing crimes "against the nation."[72] On 20 October 1862, he elevated collaboration with a foreign entity to treason.[73] The following year, on 16 August 1863, Juárez expanded the category of collaborator to include all public administrators associated with the intervention or anyone who had participated in the organization of a "mock government" in occupied territory, and he established a graded penalty system for offenders. Anything that facilitated or legitimated the interventionists, including behavior as seemingly innocuous as attending a meeting, signing a petition, or voting, became a punishable crime. For local authorities, simply remaining in occupied territory was deemed treasonous. After 1863, the republican government was not in a position to enforce such laws, but that was not the point. This was a war of legitimacy above all else in which, according to the republican government, anyone who opposed or undermined the Constitution of 1857 was an enemy of the Mexican state. The related laws were instituted at an individual level, with no concern about the reintegration of secessionist states or territories. Military tribunals were established and tasked with identifying and judging suspects. Convictions had to be delivered within twenty-four hours, and all decisions were final, without resort to appeal or executive pardon.[74]

Although in Mexico there had been no secession, no rupture of the national territory, as there had been in the United States, federalism haunted the Juárez administration's efforts to reconstruct the nation, albeit to a lesser degree than Lincoln's experienced. Juárez, unlike his US counterpart, had relied on the assertiveness of state governors in the borderlands who had denounced the conservative regime and declared, as they had done before, their own sovereignty in the face of what they deemed an illegitimate government. When forced to choose between the nation and their own regional or personal interests, however, state leaders inevitably chose the latter.[75] The most formidable was Santiago Vidaurri of Nuevo León, who in 1855 had joined the Revolution of Ayutla, which overthrew Santa Anna and ushered in the Reforma. After seizing Monterrey that same year, Vidaurri issued the Plan de Restaurador de la Libertad, which called for the return of full state sovereignty (including locally controlled militias) throughout Mexico.[76] He declared Nuevo León to be coordinating with Coahuila and Tamalulipas "to restore the power to live . . . under rules defined and derived from the will of the nation." He rejected Santa Anna and declared federalism to be the only "truly Mexican" system of government. Then, in a particularly bold move reminiscent of the Texas rebellion, he declared that "the State of Nuevo León resumes its sovereignty, liberty and independence," until Congress had established "the system and form of Government that should rule the republic."[77] Vidaurri's decision to resist encouragement from Texans to declare his state completely and permanently independent from Mexico and his militia's success at repelling cross-border raids earned him favor in the eyes of Mexico City liberals, who in 1856 allowed his state to absorb Coahuila. In August of the following year, Vidaurri issued a revised constitution for Nuevo León y Coahuila which, among other things, outlawed slavery in accordance with the forthcoming federal constitution. Vidaurri had initially declared in favor of Juárez and was in fact the first state governor to legislate the complete nationalization of church property.[78] He ultimately proved an unreliable ally. When Juárez refused to appoint Vidaurri supreme commander of the Mexican army in August 1859, instead awarding the post to Manuel Doblado, Vidaurri responded by repudiating the president and declaring Nuevo León–Coahuila a sovereign state.[79]

Vidaurri eventually retreated into Texas, where he realized that he shared more in common with the southerners' position on local autonomy, states' rights, and economic development than he did with Mexican liberals' vision of a sovereign, egalitarian, and inalienable nation.[80] This was good news for southerners, especially after secession, when Confederate leaders thought Mexico crucial to their recognition and survival. When Pickett, the Confederate envoy to Mexico, accidentally sabotaged efforts to gain Mexican recognition, Vidaurri's falling out with Juárez presented a unique opportunity. Vidaurri, it turned out, was just as eager as the Confederates to craft some kind of arrangement. Increasingly concerned about Juárez's centralization of power from the government's temporary headquarters in neighboring Chihuahua, the caudillo viewed the Confederacy's offer to establish trade relations with Vidaurri's government, as the best way to comfortably maintain his autonomy and perhaps obtain some leverage. He agreed to police and secure the border from US invasion and to allow the Confederates desperately needed access to weapons, ammunition, and other necessities. By 1864, he was enjoying a profitable trade with the Confederacy, purchasing raw cotton from southern suppliers, and using to fuel his state's burgeoning manufacturing sector, and facilitating the shipment of consumable goods like coffee, wheat, corn, and flour to the blockaded South, all in defiance of Juárez's demands that he stop.[81]

When Vidaurri, bolstered by a lucrative commerce with the Confederacy, declared his intention to permit the people of Nuevo León y Coahuila to determine which Mexican authority to support by putting the matter to a popular vote, Juárez accused him of treason. The nation's sovereignty, Juárez reminded him, was not subject to democratic deliberation.[82] In February 1864, Juárez issued a decree separating Nuevo León and Coahuila and soon followed up with another formally deposing Vidaurri as governor and declaring Nuevo León to be in an open state of rebellion. Upon news that Juárez was planning an invasion, Vidaurri fled. When his forces were overtaken by Juárez's troops at Villa Aldama in the spring, they surrendered and offered their services to the juaristas.

In mid-1865 Juárez controversially dissolved Congress and extended his presidential term indefinitely. When Maximilian's government dismissed his regime as illegitimate, Juárez confidently asserted otherwise, insisting that his actions were entirely consistent with executive war powers granted in the constitution.[83] By the end of the year, the Confederacy, whose survival Napoleon III had hoped to rely on to weaken the United States, had all but collapsed. Furthermore, Maximilian alienated his conservative base in his efforts to broaden his base of support by attracting moderates. Specifically, his refusal to rescind the Reform Laws and his insistence that church sovereignty should be subservient to that of the nation irreversibly soured his relations with ecclesiastical hierarchy and eventually also alienated him from Napoleon III, who by 1866 had begun to question the wisdom of the intervention in general. When he formally withdrew support from Maximilian, the emperor found himself with few resources and little hope of ever securing his hold over Mexico.[84]

With the Second Mexican Empire's imminent collapse in 1866, and the republican regime's outlook considerably improved, the draconian laws that Juárez had imposed years earlier now became a means for discrediting his enemies and controlling the narrative of the war. Juárez and his supporters presented the conflict not as a civil war, but as a "rebellion" of a few self-interested and treasonous malcontents, who received the punishment of death after their conviction. While Juárez targeted the intervention's top officials for punishment, the regime extended a conciliatory hand to those Mexicans who had committed lesser offenses, such as remaining in occupied territory or serving in municipal governments controlled or aligned with the empire. The 1867 codification of the Juárez treason laws stripped the citizenship of anyone who had recognized the empire and required such individuals to apply for "rehabilitation." The policy, of course, had its critics, who criticized its harshness and insisted that the republic needed to be healed. By pardoning most cases, however, Juárez was able to foster a sense of loyalty and forge a relationship between citizens and the central state that had not previously existed in Mexico.[85] Ironically, aside from the US invasion, the French intervention did more to instill Mexican national identity and strengthen sovereignty than any other episode in the country's history.

Meanwhile, the United States' rehabilitation experienced a severe setback with Lincoln's assassination on 14 April 1865 at Ford's Theatre in Washington. Booth had purportedly been enraged after hearing of the president's expressed support for Black enfranchisement a few days earlier and had hoped to create chaos in the government and give the Confederate army a chance to rally. For a time, it looked like it might work. Lincoln's successor, Andrew Johnson, a Tennessee Democrat, despised the slaveholding elite who had authored the rebellion, and his initial speeches resonated with the language of punishment and retribution for the leaders of the movement, but the terms of his ultimate proclamation, issued 25 December 1868, were even more lenient than Lincoln's had been. Johnson promised to pardon all but the most elite cadre of Confederate leaders. Upon receiving their pardons and taking the oath of loyalty to the United States, they would receive full restoration of their civil and political rights, including the return of confiscated property. Former rebels who received a pardon could also participate in authoring their new state constitutions by either voting for delegates or serving as delegates themselves. While Johnson hinted at the potential for Black enfranchisement in the future, he did not require the new state constitutions to include it, insisting only that they abolish slavery and renounce secession. Critics of the administration's policy warned that it would render a postwar society little different from the one that proceeded it and even invite a second rebellion.[86] Unlike Juárez, Johnson was more interested in restoring the Union than in punishing its offenders or ensuring against another assault on its sovereignty.

The fears of Johnson's critics were soon confirmed by elections and conventions that took place across the South that summer and fall. The Mississippi and Alabama conventions only acknowledged the abolition of slavery, and several states simply repealed their secession ordinances in terms that suggested that they could later resurrect them. Many of the legislatures created under the new constitutions were populated or even dominated by rebels, some of whom refused to accept that the war was in fact over. These men were determined to construct a world that resembled the prewar South as much as possible. They enacted laws designed to restrict the civil and political realms of the recently freed and compel them to live and work under conditions as close to slavery as legally possible. Many of the constitutions prohibited Blacks from purchasing land or laboring for anyone other than their former masters.[87]

These events convinced both radical and moderate Republicans that if they were going to defeat the slave South and realize the post-emancipation world they had long envisioned, then they would have to discard the language of accommodation, employ federal power in ways that only a few years earlier many had thought impossible, and, as in the case of Mexico, ultimately transform their constitution. Unlike in Mexico, however, such a federal initiative would come from Congress, not the president. Indeed, it started in 1865 with a bill designed to extend the life of the Freedmen's Bureau, a civil agency responsible for extending federal authority into the southern countryside by distributing food and clothing, registering voters, and enforcing contracts.[88] Congress also passed the Civil Rights Act of 1866, which, for the first time in US history, defined who is a citizen and the rights and responsibilities of citizenship.[89] Despite Republican insistence that such laws were necessary to ensure that the rebel states rejoined the United States on terms that guaranteed the future security of the Union and the South's compliance with federal law, Johnson vetoed both of them, dismissing them as "strides towards centralization and the concentration of all legislative powers in the national government."[90] In so doing, he echoed generations of traditional federalist thinking. It was the same debate over the scope and purpose of federal power that had long characterized North American politics. This time, however, the outcome would be different.

Johnson's actions only unified Republicans and emboldened Congress, eventually leading to the Fourteenth Amendment, which in 1868 effectively enshrined the civil rights bill in the Constitution by instituting citizenship for all individuals born in the nation's territory. In so doing, the United States joined Mexico as one of the only industrialized countries to guarantee birthright citizenship. It also took significant steps, as the Mexicans' 1857 constitution had a decade earlier, in offering the same "privileges and immunities" to all citizens across the nation's states and territories. Its assertion that all persons born in the US were entitled to "equal protection of laws" echoed the first article of the Mexican document. Section 3 of the amendment, banning public officeholding by former Confederates officials mirrored article 31 of that Mexican document, which asserted the obligation of every Mexican citizen "to defend the independence, the territory, the honor, the rights and the just interests of their country."[91] It had taken another decade and a bloody civil conflict, but the United States was falling in line with its southern neighbor.

Passing such legislation, however, did not guarantee enforcement. To ensure compliance, Congress also passed the Military Reconstruction Acts of 1867, which divided the South into five military districts, each controlled by a general of the US military responsible for overseeing the readmission of rebel states under constitutions and governments put in place with the participation of Black male voters.[92] Constitutional conventions composed of Black men and their white sympathizers helped bring the southern states more in line with those of the North and ensure the election of representatives to Congress who were determined to protect, rather than undermine, the war's accomplishments. This change in the political composition of the country would eventually lead to the Fifteenth Amendment, guaranteeing voting rights to all male citizens "regardless of race, color, or previous condition of servitude." Although it failed to meet a longstanding demand of women's rights activists by not including gender among the criteria and left the door open to state-imposed restrictions on Black voting, it effectively consummated the intent of the Fourteenth Amendment. As Charles Schultz put it, "Out of a republic of arbitrary local organizations, it made a republic of equal citizens."[93]

The Fifteenth Amendment's passage in 1869 and its ratification in 1870 in many ways marked the completion of the United States' transformation into a nation now able to deliver on its founding promise. It also marked the start of a northern retrenchment that in many ways would enable the reversal of many of Reconstruction's most significant accomplishments. By the 1870s, northerners and white southerners alike had grown wary of military reconstruction and the unending efforts of Confederate supporters to reassert their control over the South. Furthermore, many of the political and economic transformations that had taken place had in some ways hindered the aims of profit-minded Republicans eager to invest in a southern economy. Their vision of the economic world in the wake of slavery differed profoundly from that of the formerly enslaved. Instead of small individually owned plots, they wanted something akin to wage labor with land concentrated in the lands of white owners. By the 1870s, white terrorist organizations like the Ku Klux Klan were attempting to reassert the old order through violence and intimidation. The decision to withdraw federal troops from the South in 1877 was a fateful one. Just as southern Black leaders and their allies had warned, former Confederates and their sympathizers resumed control of state and local governments through a combination of violence, chaos, and corruption. Southern states passed laws that although ostensibly complying with the Fifteenth Amendment effectively prohibited voting on such grounds. Through force and intimidation, former slaveholders reclaimed their land and imposed a series of economic arrangements designed to keep the formerly enslaved in positions of financial dependency.[94]

Much of this tragic reversal of Reconstruction's accomplishments stemmed from the federal government—despite its remarkable expression of power and demonstrated ability to transform southern society following the war—never vigorously prosecuting most of the former Confederate leaders. Both Confederate president Davis and his vice president, Alexander Stephens, had been arrested, but Johnson failed to prosecute either of them for treason. Instead, as noted, he extended pardons to nearly every individual who asked for them.[95] His decision both guaranteed the return of former rebels and their supporters to social and political dominance and that such individuals would exercise considerable control over the war's narrative. Instead of a conflict to extend freedom and realize the founding intent of the Republic, these men cast it as an unfortunate and unnecessary act of northern aggression against southerners' legitimate expression of states' rights.[96] Juárez made no such mistake. He swiftly executed Maximilian and his staunchest supporters while simultaneously creating a space for others to return to the nation's embrace.

Although it would take several more decades and another revolution before Mexico realized the agrarian reform that many Mexican liberals had envisioned and that reconstruction had initiated, Juárez and his supporters claimed the memory of the conflict and used it to reshape Mexican identity more effectively than US leaders managed to do after the South's rebellion. Unlike the Confederates, the imperial regimes' defenders did not seek to defend their political vision, and the lower-level administrators who had supported them insisted that they had done so out of fear or necessity. Ultimately, however, Mexico's own clerical leadership defeated the conservative vision. Archbishop Munguía, who had long denounced liberal policies, ultimately conceded that the security and interests of the church were best preserved by remaining independent of the state.[97] As for Vidaurri, after his defeat by Juárez's forces, he escaped into Texas, where he was briefly welcomed by Confederate leaders, until their own defeat. In a dramatic political about-face, he then joined Maximilian's regime in the hopes of one day resecuring control over his original dominion. He would ultimately become one of the emperor's most trusted advisers, but his long-term scheme of restoring himself as a politically autonomous regional leader would meet a bitter end in July 1867. As republican forces descended on Mexico City, they captured Vidaurri as he attempted to escape the city walls. He became one of the few imperial collaborators that Juárez determined to punish to the full legal extent. Weeks after being arrested, Vidaurri was summarily executed, without a trial, his back to the firing squad.[98]

Epilogue

The United States was a loosely connected collection of states and regions united by a weak center for the better part of a century after its founding. The same was true of Mexico. By 1870, both states had emerged as coherent, unified nation-states with strong centers capable of exercising direct control over their respective peoples, implementing and imposing legislation, and besting earlier systems of power and authority. Indeed, in 1864 just two years after President Abraham Lincoln declared in his Second Annual Address that US territory "is well adapted to be the home of one national family,"[1] formerly enslaved Black men from Maine to Texas were asserting their rights as citizens of the renewed United States, reminding their fellow white countrymen that they had fought and sacrificed to defend the nation. It now owed them in rights, in land, and with wages. They employed the same notion of a reciprocal relationship between citizen and state that the first cohort of US citizens to settle in Mexican Texas had, and in the formerly rebellious South they expressed the same desire as those settlers for agricultural independence, landed proprietorship, and communal governance; while the power, authority, and responsibilities of the nation-state had changed, the aspirations of many of its residents had not.[2] Reconstruction represented the most assertive expression of federal power in US history. The Union Army in the South did not just liberate slaves and redistribute land, it also occupied towns and municipalities, in some cases for years, dismissing and arresting local leaders and creating the conditions under which freed people could claim their rights. The government's mission was to politically, economically, and socially remake the South to better reflect the democratic and universalist principles that Republicans insisted had been the original and sustaining elements of the Union all along. Yet, Reconstruction rendered mixed results.

Lincoln's reference to "one national family" left little room for groups or individuals who challenged the nation's new vision for a coherent, unified, and prosperous nation. Native Americans in the West, especially those who had dared to take advantage of the southern rebellion to attempt to reassert their sovereignty or reclaim lost lands, or who simply dared to entertain an alliance with the Confederacy in the hopes that they might benefit from a divided and weakened Union—much as Mexican conservatives hoped that they might—were some of the earliest victims of a strengthened and reconstituted federal government that quickly dismissed recalcitrant tribes, among them the Sioux and the Cheyenne, as enemies of the state.[3] Many Republicans, including members of Lincoln's own administration, had wanted, like proslavery southerners before them, to harness the newly empowered federal government to an emergent capitalist order, and their economic vision for the nation's future left little room for either autonomous tribes or a landed Black yeomanry. Ironically, their vision more resembled the old slave South, with large concentrations of landed wealth worked by the poor, only now as low-wage earners. In many parts of the South, this meant that the plantation system and slavery continued to exist in all but name. In parts of the trans-Mississippi and interior West, it meant the growth of railroad, mining, and other extractive industries backed by the federal government and eastern finance capital.[4]

In Mexico, a similar and simultaneous transformation occurred after President Benito Juárez and his supporters managed to defeat Emperor Maximilian and reassert power in 1867. With the conservative opposition finally suppressed, Mexican liberals were able to pursue the policy of land redistribution and privatization that they had sought for decades. Yet, it was not a policy embraced by those who had lived and worked the land. Once they seized power, liberals swiftly moved to privatize communal lands, undermining community autonomy in the process. The Lerdo Law of 1856, passed by Comonfort's radical provisional congress, had promised to prioritize current renters when it came to land sales, but it gave tenants only three months to claim land, and subsequent rulings indicated that the intent had been to end community control of land all along and thereby facilitate commercial expansion and entrepreneurial control. Mexican liberals' desire for commercial progress, like that of their Republican Party counterparts in the United States, overwhelmed their democratic impulses and left little room for semiautonomous indigenous communities.[5] Federal leaders in both the United States and Mexico pursued policies designed to stimulate economic progress and facilitate economic and cultural integration by seizing indigenous communal property rights. The Dawes Act of 1887, for example, empowered the president to seize and privatize tribal land under the auspices of promoting private land proprietorship within the tribes.[6] In both countries, such policies were viewed as the only means to promote progress, self-sufficiency, and integration into the new nation.

For Mexico, seizure and privatization of communal land and more amicable relations with the United States ironically paved the way for a new form of commercial imperialism. By the late 1800s, Americans were no longer interested in acquiring territory from Mexico or anywhere else. Their imperial vision was commercial. With the defeat of Mexican conservatism and with the church's iron grip finally broken, northern Mexico became a metaphorical and literal gold mine for American investors. Indeed, Matías Romero, the Juárez government's wartime ambassador to Washington, had offered the promise of investing in Mexico in his attempts to convince prominent Americans to contribute to the juarista cause in the Juárez government's struggle against the conservatives and their French allies. Millions of dollars in Mexican bonds were purchased by US investors and financiers beginning in 1865, and their investments in Mexico continued long after the French withdrawal, which concluded in November 1867. Sharing the modernizing view of the Republican Party, many Mexican leaders were eager to invite US companies to build their railroads and mine their precious metals. Initially, they did so only cautiously. Leery that such investment might ultimately compromise Mexican sovereignty, the Juárez government and that of his successor, Sebastián Lerdo de Tejada, pursued a haphazard policy when it came to authorizing US investment. Then, in 1876, aggrieved American financiers and industrialists joined forces with General Porfirio Díaz, Lerdo's one-time ally and defeated rival in the recent Mexican presidential election, to overthrow the government and install Díaz. A member of provincial Oaxacan elite and juarista war hero, Díaz was a strong advocate of privatization, modernization, and infrastructural development, all of which, he insisted, had to be accomplished at breakneck speed if Mexico was going to achieve its fullest potential. During his thirty-one-year dictatorship, 1876–1911, Díaz not only removed barriers to US investment in Mexico, but subsidized US railroad companies while vigorously and violently suppressing agrarian unrest and labor union activity. His actions mirrored those of the alliance between powerful US companies and the state that had emerged by the 1890s and which utilized paramilitary organizations to suppress resistance to its national capitalist projects.[7]

Indeed, the new corporate states emerging in both Mexico and the United States did not go unchallenged. By the end of the nineteenth century, both countries would witness the rise of formidable labor and agrarian resistance movements. In the United States, the former Confederate states and the US-Mexico borderlands became hotbeds of unrest and insurrection. In language strikingly like that of Stephen Austin and his generation of disillusioned agrarians, these groups—which ranged from the Greenback Labor Party to the Populists to the Knights of Labor—pointed to the inherent hypocrisy of a Republican Party that claimed to serve the interests of the poor, while facilitating the concentration of wealth in the hands of eastern elites. Unsurprisingly, this new agrarian radicalism took off in places like Texas and other parts of the trans-Mississippi West, where the postwar economic and social transformations were most striking, and where suspicion of concentrated wealth was nothing new. In Texas, the Farmers' Alliance, briefly affiliated with the Greenback Labor Party, was established in 1877 "for the purpose of bettering the conditions of the agricultural classes," and in Arkansas the similarly aimed Agricultural Wheel emerged five years later, largely thanks to the grassroots organizing efforts of the Knights of Labor. Although short-lived, often troubled by racism, and ultimately co-opted by the postwar Democratic Party, these movements offered cogent critiques of the overconcentration of wealth and power developing on both sides of the border. Shortly after the suppression of the 1886 Great Southwest strike, in which thousands of railroad workers demanded an eight-hour workday, the Farmers' Alliance hammered out a platform that included recognition for trade unions, taxation of railroads and corporations, an end to alien landownership, and taxation of land held for speculation.[8] The failure of the strike to draw the support of locomotive engineers along with the railways company's use of strikebreakers contributed to the action's ultimate defeat, and by the end of the century the broad-based workers alliance envisioned by the Knights of Labor was in decline.

These movements shared much in common with a similar series of agrarian insurrections that erupted in Mexico in the early twentieth century and were ultimately more widespread and more transformative. They began modestly in 1910, organized by middle-class reformers hoping to restore democracy and reclaim some of Mexico's wealth from American interests. The movement's initial leader, Francisco Madero, challenged Díaz in his 1910 reelection bid before being briefly detained in jail by his rival. Madero, the scion of a prominent

Coahuila family who enjoyed the support of US interests, soon found his presidency challenged by more radical elements of the very factions that had helped him defeat Díaz. In late 1911, from the southern Mexican state of Morelos, Emiliano Zapata, the son of a middling mestizo family from Anenecuilco, and his peasant followers issued the Plan de Ayala, which demanded a new administration committed to widespread agrarian reform. Zapata's men wanted a return to the kind of communal autonomy and patriarchy that had existed before the liberal reforms. With "Tierra y Libertad" (Land and Freedom) as a rallying cry, zapatistas linked landownership to masculine freedom, much as Austin and other American and Mexican agrarians of the 1820s had. Their plan launched the Mexican Revolution (1910–1917) and caused near panic within President Woodrow Wilson's administration, which employed by now familiar language of Mexican political instability to justify an intervention.[9] It also inspired and reinvigorated similar movements in the American Southwest, where many of the 1910 revolution's leaders had lived and worked.

The brothers Ricardo and Enrique Flores Magón were among those who had lived in the United States before the revolution. Like many anti-Díaz activists during the early 1900s, they had sought refuge in the United States, where they joined anarchist and socialist circles. Their publication *Regeneración* brought these ideas and their Mexican counterparts to Spanish-reading communities in the United States and Mexico. In 1906, the brothers established the Partido Liberal Mexicano (PLM; Mexican Liberal Party), which called for broadened political participation, taxation of church property, an eight-hour workday, and an end to child labor. Although some of their ideas drew on classic liberalism, they rejected private property and called for a massive redistribution of wealth in Mexico. Yet, their views of the United States sounded eerily like those of Mexican conservatives of the early nineteenth century too. The United States, they insisted, was a hostile land, more enemy than friend to Mexico and its people. In less than a decade, the PLM had become a transnational organization whose members claimed ancestral rights to lands along the United States–Mexico border. Its primary aim was to "improve the social conditions of the Mexican proletariat on both sides of the border," but it also sought solidarity with "American, Italian, Polish, and Negro compañeros," recognizing the shared plight of rural people in both countries.[10]

As the Mexican Revolution spread to the northern Mexican borderlands, where it found stewardship under Francisco Villa, property-owning interests in Texas—mostly Anglo farmers from the Midwest who had been lured to the region by the promise of its agrarian potential and had taken advantage of the morass of land titles dating back to the Mexican period—took note. Prior to the revolution, thousands of acres of Texas land had been transferred from Tejano to Anglo ownership, and previous political and social systems had been upended, replaced by a racial hierarchy akin to that of the South, with landownership concentrated in the hands of white owners. Anglos, to secure their status, adopted many of the same Jim Crow strategies as the rest of the South, including poll taxes, white primaries, and, in the case of Texas, secret ballots and the elimination of interpreters at polling stations.[11] Members of the PLM and the readers of *Regeneración* well understood the economic and racial oppression that they faced from the successor of the system that had oppressed and exploited African Americans in the South for centuries. Thus, they often combined their calls for economic equality with appeals for racial solidarity and an end to the Jim Crow racism imposed on Mexicans and Blacks alike. They shared with Mexican revolutionaries and US labor leaders, socialists, and tenant farmers a vision for a new transnational order—one that shared as much in common with Thomas Jefferson as with Karl Marx.[12] They sought to harness the power of the central state to the interests of urban workers and the rural poor in ways that guaranteed greater autonomy and self-sufficiency for these people.

The Plan de San Diego of 1914 eloquently expressed this vision. Bearing the name of the tiny south Texas town where it was authored, the plan called for the "liberty of the individuals of the black race," condemned the United States for its "lynching of an entire people, an entire race, and entire continent," and cited the oppression of all "proletarians" in the United States. It called for "social revolution" and the return of all arable land to the hands of "proletarians" and combatants for the revolution, who would have the option of later "communizing" it. Most striking was the plan's call for the "independence and segregation of the states" of "Texas, New Mexico, Arizona, Colorado, and California" and their reattachment to Mexico, from which they had been "robbed in a most perfidious manner by North American imperialism." The plan also called for aiding African Americans in "obtaining six [other] states of the American Union" so that they may form their own independent republic. Finally, it proposed the return of the ancestral lands to the Apache in return for their support. It was an extraordinary document, not only for the way it identified the need for a transnational proletarian movement, but also in the way it sought to redeem Mexico and return North American geopolitics to an earlier period, when the United States was smaller and weaker. Just as notable was its vision for a redeemed Mexico.[13] The authors, a group of anonymous Mexican and Tejano rebels who had clearly drawn inspiration from socialist, anarchist, and labor movements in the United States, also obviously believed that Mexico held the greatest potential for the realization of the agrarian utopia they envisioned. The interception and discovery of the Plan de San Diego would unleash a period of brutal repression and racial violence in south Texas, where virtually all Tejanos were suspected of being "sedicios." The revolution that inspired it would go down in history as the "first great peasant revolution" of the modern age.[14]

Out of the Mexican Revolution came a new nationalist order embodied in the country's Constitution of 1917. That document, which moderate Mexicans had hoped would echo many of the nationalist elements of the 1857 constitution, actually ended up going much further in harnessing the state to egalitarian and majoritarian aims. It guaranteed universal education, an eight-hour workday, a minimum wage, and a right to collective bargaining and strikes. It also placed Mexican land and resources under the control of a national state empowered to limit private ownership and restrict it to Mexicans and Mexican companies. Foreign ownership of Mexican property was permitted only with the direct permission of the federal state. The revolution's promise came to fruition under the presidency of Lázaro Cárdenas (1934–1940), who, while the United States was distracted with its own economic crisis in the 1930s, would redistribute land and nationalize all foreign-owned companies.[15]

Meanwhile, back in the United States, similar demands were adopted by the Democratic Party, but the results would be much slower in coming and ultimately less extensive. By the end of the twentieth century, both the United States and Mexico had managed to secure many of the basic rights established in the 1917 Mexican constitution. In the United States, this would be accomplished largely through the transformative federal legislation of the New Deal and the Great Society. The United States did not, however, experience the kind of large-scale political, economic, and social transformation that Mexico did at the start of the twentieth century. As the US corporate state now stands arguably more powerful than ever under the political stewardship of a Republican Party that in the 1860s briefly attempted to redistribute landed wealth on a scale never seen before or since, it is perhaps fitting that leaders of it have chosen to disparage and ridicule Mexico as a land of dysfunction, violence, and crime.

Yet, as of early 2024, events have shown that US democracy has not fully redeemed itself. The United States has found itself confronted by such persistent structural and institutional problems as wealth disparity, political polarization, geographic alienation, deepening stratification, a general disillusionment with its institutions, and an inability to deliver on its founding promises. Meanwhile, federalism remains a powerfully appealing rhetorical and legal tool to limit democracy as much as it promises to extend it. In earlier times, southern states had returned to it in their efforts to impose a new racial order in the twentieth century by mitigating the Reconstruction amendments and "redeeming" the former Confederacy. In the twenty-first century, federalism has returned to the forefront of political discourse, as some states, including Texas, have used it to attack voting and reproductive rights. At the same time, however, the United States is witnessing a renewed interest in challenging that order.

Infused with the rhetoric and imagery of the Mexican Revolution, as well as socialist and communitarian movements in other parts of Latin American and the developing world, US progressives are calling as loudly as ever for the kind of egalitarianism expressed by an earlier generation of visionaries who attempted to harness the national state to the demands of its most marginalized groups. Perhaps, in time, norteamericanos will experience another reckoning like the one at the midpoint of the nineteenth century, possibly taking applicable lessons from their southern neighbor, and revealing themselves, yet again, to be children of the great Mexican family.

NOTES

Introduction

1. Luís de Onís, *Memoria sobre las negociaciones entre España y los Estados Unidos de América* (Madrid: Imprenta de D. M. Burgos, 1820).

2. Reginald Horsman, *Race and American Manifest Destiny: The Origins of American Racial Anglo-Saxonism* (Cambridge, MA: Harvard University Press, 1981), 86; John Quincy Adams, *Memoirs of John Quincy Adams* (Philadelphia: J. B. Lippincott & Co., 1874–1877), 4:439; D. W. Meinig, *The Shaping of America: A Geographical Perspective on 500 Years of History* (New Haven, CT: Yale University Press, 1993), 2:211.

3. Timothy E. Anna, *Forging Mexico, 1821–1835* (Lincoln: University of Nebraska Press, 1998), 266, holds that the "disorder thesis" has exercised "a compelling influence on the historiography" of nineteenth-century Mexico. For an example, see Josefina Zoraida Vázquez, *El establecimiento del federalismo en México* (Mexico City: Colegio de México, 2003), 19–38.

4. Thomas Richards, Jr., *Breakaway Americas: The Unmanifest Future of the Jacksonian United States* (Baltimore: John Hopkins University Press, 2020), 19; Peter Onuf, *Jefferson's Empire: The Language of American Nationhood* (Charlottesville: University of Virginia Press, 2000), 53; Cathy D. Matson and Peter Onuf, *A Union of Interests: Political and Economic Thought in Revolutionary America* (Lawrence: University Press of Kansas, 1990), 3.

5. Max M. Edling, *A Revolution in Favor of Government: Origins of the US Constitution and the Making of the American State* (New York: Oxford University Press, 2002), 4; Woody Holton, *Unruly Americans and the Origins of the Constitution* (New York: Hill and Wang, 2007), 9–10; Terry Bouton, *Taming Democracy: "The People," the Founders, and the Troubled Ending of the American Revolution* (New York: Oxford University Press, 2007), 61, 105.

6. Anna, *Forging Mexico*, 127–29.

7. Anna, *Forging Mexico*, 260–62; Michael P. Costeloe, *The Central Republic in Mexico, 1835–1846* (New York: Cambridge University Press, 1996), 47–52.

8. Matthew J. Karp, *The Vast Southern Empire: Slaveholders at the Helm of American Foreign Policy* (Cambridge, MA: Harvard University Press, 2016), 5.

9. Andrew J. Torget, *Seeds of Empire: Cotton, Slavery, and the Transformation of Texas Borderlands, 1800–1850* (Chapel Hill: University of North Carolina Press, 2015), chap. 6.

10. Brian DeLay, *War of a Thousand Deserts: Indian Raids and the US-Mexican War* (New Haven, CT: Yale University Press, 2008), 245, 195.

11. David M. Potter, *The Impending Crisis: American before the Civil War* (New York: Harper Perennial, 2011), 17.

12. Douglas R. Egerton, *Year of Meteors: Stephen Douglas, Abraham Lincoln, and the Election That Brought on the Civil War* (New York: Bloomsbury Press, 2010), 152; Michael A. Morris, *Slavery and the American West: The Eclipse of Manifest Destiny and the Coming of Civil War* (Chapel Hill: University of North Carolina Press, 1997), 220.

13. Erika Pani, *Una Serie de admirables acontecimientos: México y el mundo en la época de la reforma, 1848–1867* (Mexico City: Educación y Cultura, Asesoría y Promoción; Puebla, México: Benemérita Universidad Autónoma de Puebla, 2013), 112. Also see Erika Pani, "Law, Allegiance, and Sovereignty in Civil War Mexico, 1857–1867," *Journal of the Civil War Era* 7, no. 4 (December 2017): 570–96.

14. For a critical discussion of this scholarship, see Laura Lyons McLemore, *Inventing Texas: Early Historians of the Lone Star State* (College Station: Texas A&M University Press, 2004), chaps. 2 and 3.

15. Sam W. Haynes, *Unsettled Land: From Revolution to Republic, the Struggle for Texas* (New York: Basic Books, 2022); David Montejano, *Anglos and Mexicans in the Making of Texas, 1836–1986* (Austin: University of Texas Press, 1987).

16. Torget, *Seeds of Empire*, 5; Kevin Waite, *West of Slavery: The Southern Dream of a Transcontinental Empire* (Chapel Hill: University of North Carolina Press, 2021).

17. Eric Schlereth, "Privileges of Locomotion: Expatriation and the Politics of Southwestern Border Crossing," *Journal of American History* 11, no. 4 (March 2014): 995–1020.

18. Brian DeLay, *War of a Thousand Deserts: Indian Raids in the US-Mexican War* (New Haven, CT: Yale University Press, 2008); Pekka Hämäläinen, *Comanche Empire* (New Haven, CT: Yale University Press, 2008).

19. John Tutino, "The Americas and the Rise of Industrial Capitalism," in *New Countries: Capitalism, Revolutions, and Nations in the Americas, 1750–1870*, ed. John Tutino (Durham, NC: Duke University Press, 2016), 25–70; Michael P. Costeloe, *Bubbles and Bonanzas: British Investors and Investments in Mexico, 1821–1860* (New York: Rowman & Littlefield, 2011); Richard J. Salvucci, *Politics, Markets, and Mexico's "London Debt," 1823–1887* (New York: Cambridge University Press, 2009); Barbara Tenenbaum, *The Politics of Penury: Debts and Taxes in Mexico, 1821–1856* (Albuquerque: University of New Mexico Press, 1986); Jaime E. Rodríguez O., *The Independence of Mexico and the Creation of the New Nation* (Los Angeles: UCLA Latin American Center Publications, University of California; Irvine: Mexico/Chicano Program, University of California, 1989).

20. Will Fowler, *Independent Mexico: The Pronunciamiento in the Age of Santa Anna, 1821–1858* (Lincoln: University of Nebraska Press, 2016); Anna, *Forging Mexico*; Stanley C. Green, *The Mexican Republic: The First Decade, 1823–1832* (Pittsburgh: University of Pittsburgh Press, 1987); Jan Bazant, "From Independence to the Liberal Republic, 1821–1867," in *Mexico since Independence*, ed. Leslie Bethell (New York: Cambridge University Press, 1991).

21. For a critical discussion of the thesis, see Anna, *Forging Mexico*, 266.

22. Examples are numerous and diverse. For the frailty of early American identity, see Kathleen DuVal, *Independence Lost: Lives on the Edge of the American Revolution* (New York: Random House, 2016). For political and social fissures mostly brought on by the economic crisis of the 1780s and 1790s, see Cathy D. Matson and Peter S. Onuf, *A Union*

of Interests: Political and Economic Thought in Revolutionary America (Lawrence: University Press of Kansas, 1990), and Woody Holton, *Unruly Americans and the Origins of the Constitution* (New York: Hill and Wang, 2007). For more on opposition to the Constitution, see Saul Cornell, *The Other Founders: Anti-Federalism and the Dissenting Tradition in America, 1788–1828* (Chapel Hill: Published for the Omohundro Institute of Early American History and Culture, Williamsburg, Virginia, by the University of North Carolina Press, 1999). For constitutional ambiguity and how it contributed to the War of the Rebellion, see Michael F. Conlin, *The Constitutional Origins of the American Civil War* (New York: Cambridge University Press, 2019).

23. Eric Van Young, *A Life Together: Lucas Alamán and Mexico, 1792–1853* (New Haven, CT: Yale University Press, 2021); Will Fowler, *Santa Anna of Mexico* (Lincoln: University of Nebraska Press, 2007); Erika Pani, *El Segundo Imperio: pasados de usos múltiples* (Mexico City: Centro de Investigación y Docencia Económicas, Fondo de Cultura Económica, 2004); Erika Pani, "Dreaming of a Mexican Empire: The Political Projects of the Imperialistas," *Hispanic American Review* 82, no. 1 (February 2002): 1–31.

24. For a comprehensive discussion of the scholarship and popular understanding of Santa Anna, see the introduction in Fowler, *Santa Anna of Mexico*.

25. Eric Foner, *Free Soil, Free Labor, Free Men: The Ideology of the Republican Party before the Civil War* (New York: Oxford University Press, 1995); Daniel Walker Howe, *The Political Culture of the American Whigs* (Chicago: University of Chicago Press, 1979).

26. Eric Foner, *The Second Founding: How the Civil War and Reconstruction Remade the Constitution* (New York: W. W. Norton & Co., 2019); Graham A. Peck, *Making an Antislavery Nation: Lincoln, Douglas, and the Battle over Freedom* (Urbana: University of Illinois Press, 2017); James Oakes, *Freedom National: The Destruction of Slavery in the United States, 1861–1865* (W. W. Norton & Co., 2013); Allen C. Guelzo, *Lincoln and Douglas: The Debates That Defined America* (New York: Simon and Schuster, 2008); Eric Foner, ed. *Our Lincoln: New Perspectives on Lincoln and His World* (New York: W. W. Norton & Co., 2008).

27. Haynes, *Unsettled Land*, 102–3.

28. Benjamin E. Park, *American Nationalisms: Imagining Union in the Age of Revolutions, 1783–1833* (New York: Cambridge University Press, 2018), 6.

29. For a summary of this debate, see Torget, *Seeds of Empire*, 140.

30. Manisha Sinha, *The Counterrevolution of Slavery: Politics and Ideology in Antebellum South Carolina* (Chapel Hill: University of North Carolina Press, 2000), chap. 2.

31. Most work comparing early Mexico and the United States has been by scholars from Mexico and Spanish America. See specifically, Pani, *Una serie de admirables acontecimientos*; John Tutino, "The Americas and the Rise of Industrial Capitalism," in *New Countries: Capitalism, Revolutions, and Nations in the Americas, 1750–1870*, ed. John Tutino (Durham, NC: Duke University Press, 2016), 1–24; Peter Guardino, *The Dead March: A History of the Mexican-American War* (Cambridge, MA: Harvard University Press, 2017); Alice L. Baumgardner, *South to Freedom: Runaway Slaves to Mexico and the Road to Civil War* (New York: Basic Books, 2020).

32. Don H. Doyle, ed., *American Civil Wars: The United States, Latin America, Europe and the Crisis of the 1860s* (Chapel Hill: University of North Carolina Press, 2017); Don H. Doyle, *The Cause of All Nations: An International History of the American Civil War* (New York: Basic Books, 2015); Don H. Doyle, ed., *Secession as an International*

Phenomenon: From America's Civil War to Contemporary Separatist Movements (Athens: University of Georgia Press, 2010); Adam Arensen and Andrew R. Graybill, eds., *Civil War Wests: Testing the Limits of the United States* (Oakland: University of California Press, 2015).

Chapter 1 · The Greatest Nation on Earth

1. William Walker to his father, 27 August 1822, folder 168, Mississippi Documents, Samuel E. Asbury Papers, Daughters of the Republic of Texas Library, San Antonio.

2. D. W. Meinig, *The Shaping of America: A Geographical Perspective on 500 Years of History* (New Haven, CT: Yale University Press, 1993), 129–32; for more comments on Mexico's territorial scope, see Nettie Lee Benson, "Territorial Integrity in Mexican Politics, 1821–1833," in *The Independence of Mexico and the Creation of the New Nation*, ed. Jaime E. Rodríguez O. (Los Angeles: UCLA Latin American Center Publications, University of California Press; Irvine: Mexico/Chicano Program, University of California, 1989), 276.

3. Josefina Zoraida Vásquez, "Comentario," in *Nación, constitución, y reforma, 1821–1908*, ed. Erika Pani (Mexico City: Fondo de Cultura Economica; CIDE; INEHRM; CONACULTA, 2010), and Timothy E. Anna, *Forging Mexico, 1821–1835* (Lincoln: University of Nebraska Press, 1998).

4. The scholarship on early American localism and the anti-federalist tradition is extensive. See Saul Cornell, *The Other Founders: Anti-Federalism and the Dissenting Tradition, 1788–1828* (Chapel Hill: University of North Carolina Press, 1999); Jack P. Greene, *Peripheries and Center: Constitutional Development in the Extended Polities of the British Empire and the United States, 1607–1788* (Athens: University of Georgia Press, 1986); Bernard Bailyn, *The Ideological Origins of the American Revolution* (Cambridge, MA: Belknap Press of Harvard University Press, 1967); Bernard Bailyn, *The Origins of American Politics* (New York: Knopf, 1968).

5. Andrés Reséndez, *Changing National Identities at the Frontier: Texas and New Mexico, 1800–1850* (New York: Cambridge University Press, 2005).

6. Max M. Edling, *Perfecting the Union: National and State Authority in the US Constitution* (New York: Oxford University Press, 2021); Max M. Edling, *A Revolution in Favor of Government: Origins of the U.S. Constitution and the Making of the American State* (New York: Oxford University Press, 2003); Andrew Shankman, *Original Intents: Hamilton, Jefferson, Madison, and the American Founding* (New York: Oxford University Press, 2018); Woody Holton, *Unruly Americans and the Origins of the Constitution* (New York: Hill and Wang, 2007).

7. Jaime E. Rodríguez O., *We Are Now the True Spaniards: Sovereignty, Revolution, Independence, and the Emergence of the Federal Republic of Mexico, 1808–1824* (Stanford, CA: Stanford University Press, 2012); Anna, *Forging Mexico*; Stanley C. Green, *The Mexican Republic: The First Decade, 1823–1832* (Pittsburgh: University of Pittsburgh Press, 1987).

8. Greene, *Peripheries and Center*, chap. 1

9. Green, *The Mexican Republic*, 10.

10. Green, *The Mexican Republic*; Bernard Bailyn, "Liberty and Power: A Theory of Politics," in *The Ideological Origins of the American Revolution* (Cambridge, MA: Harvard University Press, 1992).

11. Green, *The Mexican Republic*, 10.

12. Thomas Slaughter, *The Whiskey Rebellion: Frontier Epilogue to the American Revolution* (New York: Oxford University Press, 1986).

13. Slaughter, *The Whiskey Rebellion*, 28–31.

14. John R. Van Atta, *Securing the West: Politics, Public Lands, and the Fate of the Old Republic, 1785–1850* (Baltimore: Johns Hopkins University Press, 2014), 17.

15. Van Atta, *Securing the West*, 15; Thomas Richards, Jr., *Breakaway Americas: The Unmanifest Future of the Jacksonian United States* (Baltimore: Johns Hopkins University Press, 2020), 19.

16. Slaughter, *The Whiskey Rebellion*, 31–32.

17. Van Atta, *Securing the West*, 42.

18. Peter S. Onuf, *Jefferson's Empire: The Language of American Nationhood* (Charlottesville: University of Virginia Press, 2000), 4.

19. Slaughter, *The Whiskey Rebellion*, 31–32.

20. Shankman, *Original Intents*, 9–16.

21. Cathy D. Matson and Peter Onuf, *A Union of Interests: Political and Economic Thought in Revolutionary America* (Lawrence: University Press of Kansas, 1990), 51–54.

22. Matson and Onuf, *A Union of Interests*, chap. 5.

23. Ramsey quoted in Madson and Onuf, *A Union of Interests*, 87.

24. Hamilton quoted in Madson and Onuf, *A Union of Interests*, 88.

25. Brutus I, 18 October 1787, in Robert J. Allison and Bernard Bailyn, eds., *The Essential Debate on the Constitution: Federalist and Antifederalist Speeches and Writings. The Brilliant Battle of Ideas That Still Shapes the Nation* (New York: Library of America, 2018), 23.

26. Edling, *Perfecting the Union*, 9.

27. David Waldstreicher, *Slavery's Constitution: From Revolution to Ratification* (New York: Hill and Wang, 2009), 8.

28. Holton, *Unruly Americans and the Origins of the Constitution*, 9–10.

29. "Letters from the Federal Farmer," 8 November 1778, in Allison and Bailyn, *The Essential Debate on the Constitution*, 69, 78.

30. George Mason, "Objections to the Constitution," 22 November 1787, in Allison and Bailyn, *The Essential Debate on the Constitution*, 115.

31. Patrick Henry in Allison and Bailyn, *The Essential Debate on the Constitution*, 350–68, quotes on 351, 367.

32. James Madison, *Federalist*, no. 51, in Allison and Bailyn, *The Essential Debate on the Constitution*, 214–15.

33. Terry Bouton, *Taming Democracy: "The People," The Framers, and the Troubled Ending of the American Revolution* (New York: Oxford University Press, 2007). For the regulation as an extension of the American Revolution, see chapter 5. For the framers' reaction, see chapter 8.

34. For opposition to the constitution that extended well into the nineteenth century, see Cornell, *The Other Founders*.

35. Holton, *Unruly Americans and the Origins of the Constitution*, x.

36. Van Atta, *Securing the West*, 34–39.

37. George Washington, Farewell Address, in James D. Richardson, ed., *A Compilation of the Messages and Papers of the Presidents, 1789–1897*, 10 vols. (Washington, DC: Government Printing Office, 1896–1899), 1:223–24.

38. See John Taylor, "Examination of the Late Proceedings in Congress, Respecting the Official Conduct of the Secretary of the Treasury," 8 March 1793, Richmond, 7, 11, 12, 27.

39. Steven Aron, *American Confluence: The Missouri Frontier from Borderland to Border State* (Bloomington: Indiana University Press, 2006), x, xviii.

40. Kathleen DuVal, "Independence for Whom? Expansion and Conflict in the South and Southwest," in Andrew Shankman, ed. *The World of the Revolutionary American Republic: Land, Labor, and the Conflict for a Continent* (New York: Routledge, 2014), 97–115.

41. Andrew McMichael, *Americans in Spanish West Florida, 1785–1810* (Athens: University of Georgia Press, 2008), 10–34.

42. DuVal, "Independence for Whom?," 105.

43. McMichael, *Americans in Spanish West Florida*, 36–37.

44. DuVal, "Independence for Whom?," 104–5, James White on 104.

45. Greg Cantrell, *Stephen F. Austin, Empresario of Texas* (New Haven, CT: Yale University Press, 2001), 15–59.

46. Cantrell, *Stephen F. Austin*, 56–61.

47. Cantrell, *Stephen F. Austin*, 63–65.

48. Charles Sellers, *The Market Revolution: Jacksonian America, 1815–1846* (New York: Oxford University Press, 1991), 133–38, Benton on 138; Edward S. Kaplan, *The Bank of the United States and the American Economy* (Westport, CT: Greenwood Press, 1999), chaps. 4 and 5; Stephen Aron, *How the West Was Lost: The Transformation of Kentucky from Daniel Boone to Henry Clay* (Baltimore: Johns Hopkins University Press, 192).

49. Gregg Cantrell, *Stephen F. Austin: Empresario of Texas*, 69.

50. Cornell, *The Other Founders*, 172–79.

51. Moses Austin to the Citizens of Jefferson County, 10 January 1820, *The Austin Papers*, ed. Eugene C. Barker, vol. 1, pt. 1 (Washington, DC: Government Printing Office, 1924), 352–53 (errors retained from original) (hereafter *AP*).

52. Moses Austin to J. E. B. Austin, 8 April 1821, *AP*, vol. 1, pt. 1, 385.

53. Cantrell, *Stephen F. Austin*, 73–74.

54. Cantrell, *Stephen F. Austin*, 77.

55. Jaime E. Rodríguez O., "Introduction," *The Evolution of the Mexican Political System* (Wilmington, DE: SR Books, 1993), quote on 1. For more on the changing historiography of early Mexico, see Anna, *Forging Mexico*, chap. 1.

56. Anna, *Forging Mexico*, 379.

57. Anna, *Forging Mexico*, 34–38.

58. Jaime E. Rodríguez O., *The Independence of Spanish America* (New York: Cambridge University Press, 1998), 75–82; Rodríguez, *We Are Now the True Spaniards*, 68–69.

59. Miguel Ramos Arizpe, *Report to the August Congress on the Natural, Political, and Civil Condition of the Provinces of Coahuila, Nuevo León, Nuevo Santander, and Texas of the Four Eastern Interior Provinces of the Kingdom of Mexico*, trans. Nettie Lee Benson (New York: Greenwood Press, 1969), 28, 30, 37–38.

60. Rodríguez, *Independence of Spanish America*, 84–94.

61. Anna, *Forging Mexico*, 34.

62. Rodríguez, *We Are the True Spaniards*, 228–29.

63. Rodríguez, *We Are the True Spaniards*, 240.
64. Anna, *Forging Mexico*, 67–72.
65. Anna, *Forging Mexico*, 78; Rodríguez, *We Are the True Spaniards*, 263–65.
66. Alexander von Humboldt, *Political Essay on the Kingdom of New Spain*, ed. Mary Maples Dunn, trans. John Black (Norman: University of Oklahoma Press, 1988), 29, 117–19, 148, 235.
67. *Arkansas Gazette*, 9 October 1822.
68. *St. Louis Enquirer*, 19 August 1822.
69. *St. Louis Enquirer*, 26 February 1822.
70. *St. Louis Enquirer*, 9 October 1822.
71. *St. Louis Enquirer*, 13 April 1822.
72. Anna, *Forging Mexico*, 94.
73. "Revolution in Mexico," *Le Courrier de la Louisiane*, 28 May 1821.
74. Caitlyn Fitz, *Our Sister Republics: The United States in an Age of American Revolutions* (New York: Liveright Publishing Corporation, 2016), 43–44. Fitz argues that enthusiasm for Mexican independence was not as great as it was for republics further South, suggesting that one reason for this "geographic predilection" was the trade with Mexico lagged behind trade with the Caribbean and South America. While this may have been the case for those living further from the border, Fitz is primarily referring to celebratory toasts and not newspaper reports, although she does conclude that enthusiasm for Mexican independence was generally less notable than it was for other Spanish American republics.
75. The Plan of Iguala appeared in *Le Courriere de la Louisiane*, 18 June 1821; *Nashville Gazette*, 24 February 1824; and *Richmond Enquirer*, 8 June 1821.
76. "Revolution in Mexico," *Le Courrier de la Louisiane*, 28 May 1821.
77. *Frankfort Argus*, 28 March 1822.
78. Reséndez, *Changing National Identities at the Frontier*, 56–57.
79. Nemesio Salcedo, 26 June 1812, folder 227, Nacogdoches Archives Transcripts, Samuel E. Asbury Papers, Daughters of the Republic of Texas Library, San Antonio.
80. Manuel Sambrano to the commanding general, 4 September 1813, folder 228, Nacogdoches Archives Transcripts, Samuel E, Asbury Papers, Daughters of the Republic of Texas Library, San Antonio.
81. Cantrell, *Stephen F. Austin*, 174.
82. Martínez quoted in Cantrell, *Stephen F. Austin*, 86.
83. Moses Austin to J. E. B. Austin, 8 April 1821, *AP*, 385.
84. Cantrell, *Stephen F. Austin*, 77–79, 88–91, 98–100.
85. SFA to prospective settlers, 1 July 1821, *AP*, 399.
86. SFA to J. E. B. Austin, 1 January 1823, *AP*, 566.
87. SFA to J. E. B. Austin, 20 May 1823, *AP*, 644.
88. Joseph H. Hawkins to SFA, 6 February 1822, *AP*, 476–78.
89. Daniel Dunklin to SFA, 25 December 1821, *AP*, 455.
90. James Bryan to SFA, 4 March 1822, *AP*, 481.
91. William Walker to a relative, 27 August 1822, folder 168, Mississippi Documents, Samuel E. Asbury Papers, Daughters of the Republic of Texas Library, San Antonio.
92. SFA to Joseph H. Hawkins, 1 May 1822, *AP*, 505.
93. SFA to Joseph H. Hawkins, July 1822, *AP*, 536.

94. For more on the debate, see Timothy E. Anna, "Augustín de Iturbide and the Process of Consensus," in *The Birth of Modern Mexico, 1780–1824*, ed. Christon I. Archer (Wilmington, DE: Scholarly Resources Inc., 2003); and Jaime E. Rodríguez O., "The Struggle for Dominance: The Legislature vs. the Executive in Early Mexico," in Archer, *The Birth of Modern Mexico*; Rodríguez, *We Are Now the True Spaniards*, 268–304.

95. Will Fowler, *Independent Mexico: The Pronunciamiento in the Age of Santa Anna, 1821–1858* (Lincoln: University of Nebraska Press, 2006), 6–11: "The pronunciamientos of Independent Mexico, with some notable exceptions in the 1840s, were *not* coups d'état; or if they were, they were precisely that; soft coups d'état. They were meant to be bloodless, and they were meant to negotiate political change forcefully, by use of threats and intimidation but without necessarily overthrowing the entire government" (p. 6).

96. Fowler, *Independent Mexico*, 96–102; Anna, *Forging Mexico*, 89–94, 109.

97. *New York Spectator*, 25 October 1822, folder 168, Mississippi Documents, Samuel E. Asbury Papers, Daughters of the Republic of Texas Library, San Antonio.

98. William Walker to his father, 27 August 1822, folder 168, Mississippi Documents, Samuel E. Asbury Papers, Daughters of the Republic of Texas Library, San Antonio.

99. Anna, *Forging Mexico*, 110; J. Lloyd Mecham, "The Origins of Federalism in Mexico," *Hispanic American Historical Review* 18, no. 2 (May 1938): 167–68.

100. According to one historian, "federalism had become the national creed," as it became "almost un-Mexican" to advance the notion that states should be subordinate to the central government." Green, *The Mexican Republic*, 7, 32.

101. Manifiesto de Luis Quintanar, 3 July 1822, box 48, file 8, Archivo General de Nación, Gobernación, Sin Sección, Mexico City.

102. Proclama del Sr. Quintanar a los habitantes de Nueva Galicia sobre la separación del congreso mexicano, (Mexico City: Reimp. En la Of. liberal del C. Juan Cabrera, 1823), Miscellaneous: Various authors, no. 9, doc. 13, Centro de Estudios de Histora de México, Mexico City. Also cited in Jaime E. Rodríguez O., "The Formation of the Federal Republic," in *Five Centuries of Mexican History*, ed. Virginia Guedea and Jaime E. Rodríguez O. (Mexico City: Instituto Mora; Irvine: University of California, 1992), 318; José María Bocanegra, *Memorias para la historia de México independiente, 1822–1846* (Mexico: Imprenta del gobierno federal en el ex-Arzobispado, 1892), 1:260–61.

103. Anna, *Forging Mexico*, 120–21.

104. Anna, *Forging Mexico*, 117–22, provides a helpful timeline of events from March to October 1823.

105. *Kentucky Gazette*, 1 January 1824.

106. Rodríguez, *We Are Now the True Spaniards*, 308–14; Anna, *Forging Mexico*, 131.

107. See Rodríguez, *We Are Now the True Spaniards*, 326–27, for precise text of all three key articles of the Acta Constitutiva.

108. *El Aguila Mexicana*, 23 November 1823.

109. *Profesia política: del sabio de Dr. Teresa de Mier, y disputado de Nueva León con respecto a la federación mexicana, ó sea, discurso que el dia 13 de diciembre de 1823 pronunció sobre el artículo 5 de la acta constitutive* (Oaxaca: Reimpreso por el C. Antonio Valdés y Moya, 1835), 3; for complete published copy, vol. 219, file 1, Archivo General de Nación, Gobernación, Mexico City; also cited at length in *El Aguila Mexicana*, 14 and 15 December 1823. See also *El pensamiento del Padre Mier* (Mexico City: Biblioteca Enciclopédia Popular, 1944), 77.

110. *Profesia política: del sabio de Dr. Teresa de Mier, y diputado de Nueva León con respecto a la federación mexicana, ó sea, discurso que el dia 13 de diciembre de 1823 pronunció sobre el artículo 5 de la acta constitutive*, 8.

111. Shankman, *Original Intents*, 10–11.

112. Printed circular, 17 June 1823, vol. 21, file 37, Archivo General de Nación, Gobernación, Mexico City.

113. Printed circular, 3 June 1823, quoted at length in Eric Van Young, *A Life Together: Lucas Alamán and Mexico, 1792–1853* (New Haven, CT: Yale University Press, 2021), 160.

114. Lucas Alamán to Luis Quintanar, 19 July 1823, vol. 47, file 24, Archivo General de Nación, Gobernación, Sin Sección, Mexico City; also cited in Van Young, *A Life Together*, 179.

115. Valentín Gómez Farías cited in Jesús Reyes Heroles, *El liberalism mexicano*, 3 vols. (Mexico City: UNAM, 1957–1961), 1:412; also quoted in Anna, *Forging Mexico*, 144–47.

116. Reyes Heroles, *El liberalism mexicano*, 3:400.

117. Anna, *Forging Mexico*,128; Rodríguez, *We Are the True Spaniards*, 328.

118. Anna, *Forging Mexico*, 156.

119. Rodríguez, *We Are the True Spaniards*, 331–32.

120. Anna, *Forging Mexico*, 127–28, has argued that the Mexican constitution exceeded that of the United States in its privileging of regional sovereignty. In fact, the only other constitution to come close to Mexico's in this regard is that of the Confederate States of America, established nearly four decades later.

121. SFA, "Proclamation," 1 May 1824, *AP*, 781–82.

122. *St. Louis Enquirer*, 7 June 1823.

123. *Arkansas Gazette*, 15 August 1825.

124. *Louisiana State Gazette*, 16 December 1825.

125. *Manifiesto sobre la necesidad de preservar el Pacto Federal para evitar la anarquía*, expedido por el presidente Guadalupe Victoria con motive de su toma de posesión, 10 October 1824, in *Documentos para le historia del México independiente: Insurgencia y la república federal, 1808–1824*, ed. Ernesto Lemoine (Mexico City: Junta de Coordinación Política, 2010), 255–69.

Chapter 2 · Land, Loyalty, and Identity in the Trans-Mississippi Corridor

1. Stephen F. Austin (hereafter SFA) to Emperor Augustín Iturbide, 25 May 1822, in *The Austin Papers*, ed. Eugene C. Barker, 3 vols. (Washington, DC: Government Printing Office, 1924, 1928), vol. 2, pt. 1, 519.

2. For a thorough explanation of the principles at the core of Jeffersonian republicanism and white male citizenship in the early republic, see Thomas Richards, Jr., *Breakaway Americas: The Unmanifest Future of the Jacksonian United States* (Baltimore: Johns Hopkins University Press, 2020), chap. 1. Richards makes a similar argument about the decoupling of identity and nation, yet he misidentifies these Anglo-American men as inheritors of the "plebian populist" strain of anti-federalism. I argue that they were far too invested in the security of Mexico to be considered as such and are better understood as inheritors of "middling" anti-federalists. See Drew R. McCoy, *The Elusive Republic: Political Economy in Jeffersonian America* (Chapel Hill: University of North Carolina

Press, 1980); Peter Onuf, *Jefferson's Empire: The Language of American Nationhood* (Chapel Hill: University of North Carolina Press, 2000); Stephanie McCurry, *Masters of Small Worlds: Yeoman Households, Gender Relations, and the Political Culture of the South Carolina Low Country* (New York: Oxford University Press, 1995).

3. Historians have long greeted Stephen's words with skepticism. Randolph B. Campbell, *Gone to Texas: A History of the Lone Star State* (New York: Oxford University Press, 2003), 104, argues, "Anglo-Americans poured into Austin's colony for one simple reason—cheap land." David J. Weber, *The Mexican Frontier, 1821–1846: The American Southwest under Mexico* (Albuquerque: University of New Mexico Press, 1982), 166, asserts that immigration was primarily a result of the economic depression in the United States following the Panic of 1819: "The 'push' of the bill collector and the sheriff seems to have been more important in causing immigration to Texas than was the 'pull' of cheap land."

4. Sam W. Haynes, *Unsettled Land: From Revolution to Republic, the Struggle for Texas* (New York: Basic Books, 2022), 4.

5. Benjamin E. Park, *American Nationalisms: Imagining Union in the Age of Revolutions, 1783–1833* (Cambridge: Cambridge University Press, 2018), 5–7.

6. Saul Cornell, *The Other Founders: Anti-Federalism and the Dissenting Tradition, 1788–1828* (Chapel Hill: Published for the Omohundro Institute of Early American History and Culture, Williamsburg, Virginia, by the University of North Carolina Press, 1999), 85–96.

7. Donald E. Chipman and Harriet Denise Joseph, eds., *Spanish Texas, 1519–1821* (Austin: University of Texas Press, 1821), 12–19.

8. David J. Weber, *The Spanish Frontier in North America* (New Haven, CT: Yale University Press, 1992), 147–71.

9. Weber, *Spanish Frontier*, 148–52.

10. "Communication Touching the Conversion of the Indians, 1730," box 2Q457, P. L. Buquor Papers, Dolph Briscoe Center of American History, University of Texas at Austin.

11. Weber, *Spanish Frontier*, 190–91.

12. Weber, *Spanish Frontier*, 186–95; Pekka Hämäläinen, *Comanche Empire* (New Haven, CT: Yale University Press, 2008), chap. 1.

13. Chipman and Joseph, *Spanish Texas*, chap. 9.

14. Hämäläinen, *Comanche Empire*, 112.

15. Hämäläinen, *Comanche Empire*, 145–46; Chipman and Joseph, *Spanish Texas*, 226–27.

16. Juan Bautisa Elguézabal, general commanding the Eastern Interior Provinces, to the Manuel Muñoz, governor of Texas, 30 July 1795, box 2Q457, P. L. Buquor Papers, Dolph Briscoe Center for American History, University of Texas at Austin.

17. Miguel Ramos Arizpe, *Report to the August Congress of the Natural, Political, and Civil Condition of the Province of Coahuila, Nuevo León, Nuevo Santander, and Texas of the Four Eastern Interior Provinces of the Kingdom of Mexico*, trans. Nettie Lee Benson (New York: Greenwood Press, 1969), 5–7.

18. Arizpe, *Report to the August Congress*, 34.

19. Arizpe, *Report to the August Congress*, 39–40.

20. Weber, *The Mexican Frontier*, 160–61, Martínez on 161.

21. Gregg Cantrell, *Stephen F. Austin, Empresario of Texas* (New Haven, CT: Yale University Press, 2001), 85–86, Martínez on 86.

22. Anastasio Bustamante to Captain General of the Eastern Internal Provinces, 5 January 1822, box 2Q166, vol. 303, Fomento-Colonización: 1821–1834, Archivo General de México, Dolph Briscoe Center for American History, University of Texas at Austin.

23. SFA to Emperor Augustín Iturbide, 13 May 1822, box 2Q166, vol. 303, Fomento-Colonización: 1821–1834, Archivo General de México, Dolph Briscoe Center for American History, University of Texas at Austin.

24. Anastasio Bustamante, general of the Internal Provinces to the secretary of internal and external relations, José Manuel de Herrera, 12 September 1822, box 2Q166, vol. 303, Fomento-Colonización: 1821–1834, Archivo General de México, Dolph Briscoe Center for American History, University of Texas at Austin.

25. Tadeo Ortíz, *Resumen de la estadística del imperio mexicano* (Mexico: Imprenta de doña Herculena del Villar y Socios, 1822), 53; also cited in Nettie Lee Benson, "Territorial Integrity in Mexican Politics," in *The Independence of Mexico and the Creation of the New Nation*, ed. Jaime E. Rodríguez (Los Angeles: UCLA Latin American Center Publications, University of California; Irvine: Mexico/Chicano Program, University of California, 1989), 275–76.

26. Ortíz, *Resumen de la estadística del imperio mexicano*, 56.

27. Ortíz, *Resumen de la estadística del imperio mexicano*, 55–60, 85.

28. Charles A. Hale, *Mexican Liberalism in the Age of Mora, 1821–1853* (New Haven, CT: Yale University Press, 1968), 188–214.

29. Arizpe, *Report to the August Congress*, viii.

30. Reséndez, *Changing National Identities on the Frontier*, 93–123.

31. Committee on Foreign Affairs, Recommendations, 22 February 1822, Fomento-Colonización: 1821–1834, box 2Q166, vol. 303, Archivo General de México, Dolph Briscoe Center for American History, University of Texas at Austin. For a summary of the report by the Committee on Foreign Affairs, see Benson, "Territorial Integrity in Mexican Politics," 277.

32. "The Imperial Colonization Law," 4 January 1823, in *Documents of Texas History*, ed. Ernest Wallace, David B. Vigness, and George B. Ward (Austin: Texas State Historical Association, 2002), 47–48.

33. Ricki S. Jacineck, "The Development of Early Mexican Land Policy: Coahuila and Texas, 1810–1825" (PhD diss., Tulane University, 1985), 112.

34. Jacineck, "The Development of Early Mexican Land Policy," 132–34.

35. Jacineck, "The Development of Early Mexican Land Policy," 134–35.

36. Jacineck, "The Development of Early Texas Land Policy," 148–56; Arizpe quoted in Reséndez, *Changing National Identities*, 63.

37. Jacineck, "The Development of Early Texas Land Policy," 200.

38. Jacineck, "The Development of Texas Land Policy," 200, 211; "The National Colonization Law," 18 August 1824, in Wallace, Vigness, and Ward, *Documents of Texas History*, 48.

39. "The National Colonization Law," 18 August 1824, in Wallace, Vigness, and Ward, *Documents of Texas History*, 48; also cited in Weber, *The Mexican Frontier*, 163, 166.

40. "Petition of the Americans Residing in Nacogdoches," 16 February 1824, folder 242, Nacogdoches Archives, Samuel E. Asbury Papers, Daughters of the Republic of Texas Library, San Antonio.

41. S. Charles Bolton, "Jeffersonian Indian Removal and the Emergence of Arkansas Territory," in *A Whole Country in Commotion: The Louisiana Purchase and the American Southwest*, ed. Patrick C. Williams, S. Charles Bolton, and Jeannie M. Whayne (Fayetteville: University of Arkansas Press, 2004), 77–90, quotes on 83.

42. "William Rabb," "Thomas J. Rabb," and "Joseph Newman," in *Austin's Old Three Hundred: The First Anglo Colony in Texas, by Their Descendants* (Austin: Eakin Press, 1999), 60–61, 70, 71.

43. Wilkinson cited in Bolton, "Jeffersonian Indian Removal and the Emergence of Arkansas Territory," 83.

44. Honor Sachs, *Home Rule: Households, Manhood, and National Expansion on the Eighteenth-Century Kentucky Frontier* (New Haven, CT: Yale University Press, 2015) 104.

45. SFA to Mateo Ahumada, Mexican military commander, 8 September 1825, *AP*, vol. 1, pt. 2, pp. 1196–97.

46. SFA, "Referendum on Indian Relations," 28 September 1825, *AP*, vol. 1, pt. 2, 1208–11.

47. SFA to Governor Rafael González, 4 April 1825, *AP*, vol. 1, pt. 2, 1065–67.

48. Cantrell, *Stephen F. Austin*, 174–75; T. R. Fehrenbach, *Lone Star: A History of Texas and the Texans* (Boston: Da Capo Press, 2000), 146–47.

49. Fehrenbach, *Lone Star*, 142–44.

50. SFA, "Organization of Militia Battalion," 22 June 1824, *AP*, vol. 1, pt. 1, 838–39.

51. Edmund Morgan has written that the notion of popular sovereignty rested on the "righteousness, independence, and military might of the yeoman farmer, the man who owned his own land, made his living from it and stood ready to defend it and his country by force of arms." Edmund Morgan, *Inventing the People: The Rise of Popular Sovereignty in England and America* (New York: W. W. Norton & Company, 1988), 153–73, quote on 154.

52. John Dwiggins, "The Military Establishment and Democratic Politics in the United States, 1783–1848" (PhD diss., University of Pennsylvania, 2012).

53. Mary Ellen Rowe, *Bulwark of the Republic: The American Militia in Antebellum West* (Westport, CT: Praeger Publishers, 2003), vii–xiii.

54. Historians have long assumed that only in the Anglo world did the militia carry such a close association with republican values. "Though the citizen soldier was never a uniquely American figure," wrote Rowe, "in the British North American colonies he came to represent a powerful set of ideas, drawn from the British tradition but enhanced and elaborated in America." The militia constituted "the supreme expression of civic values in a traditional, communal and agrarian civil society." Rowe, *Bulwark of the Republic*, ix–x.

55. Hilda Sabato, *Republics of the New World: The Revolutionary Political Experience in Nineteenth-Century Latin America* (Princeton, NJ: Princeton University Press, 2018), 89–102. Manuel Chust observed, "With the establishment of the federal republic, the civic militia would be configured as an armed civic battalion of the states against the centralist or conservative tendencies of the executive branch and some of its officers." Manuel Chust, "Armed Citizens: The Civic Militia in the Origins of the Mexican

National State, 1812–1827," in *The Divine Charter: Constitutionalism and Liberalism in Nineteenth-Century Mexico*, ed. Jaime E. Rodríguez O. (New York: Rowman & Littlefield Publishers, 2005), 235–52, quote on 239.

56. Andrés Tijerina, *Tejanos and Texas under the Mexican Flag, 1821–1836* (College Station: Texas A&M University Press, 1994), 79.

57. Tijerina, *Tejanos and Texas under the Mexican Flag*, 81.

58. Arizpe, *Report to the August Congress*, 16–17.

59. Tijerina, *Tejanos and Texas under the Mexican Flag*, 83.

60. Baron de Bastrop to Colonists, 4 August 1823, *AP*, vol. 1, pt. 1, 677–78.

61. Petition of the Americans Residing at Nacogdoches, 16 February 1824, folder 242, Nacogdoches Archives, Samuel E. Asbury Papers, Daughter of the Republic of Texas Library, San Antonio.

62. José Antonio Saucedo to Colonists, 18 March 1824, *AP*, vol. 1, pt. 1, 753–54.

63. José Antonio Saucedo to Juan Seguín, 21 July 1826, folder 229, Samuel E. Asbury Papers, Daughters of the Republic of Texas Library, San Antonio.

64. Military Commander of Texas Col. Mateo Ahumada to Saucedo, 13 November 1826, box 3G297, file 11, Spanish Archives Transcripts, Robert Bruce Blake Papers, Dolph Briscoe Center for American History, University of Texas at Austin.

65. B. W. Edwards to SFA, 21 July 1826, *AP*, vol. 1, pt. 2, 1380–86.

66. Military commander of Texas, Col. Mateo Ahumada to the commander of Coahuila, date unknown, folder 299, Samuel E. Asbury Papers, Daughters of the Republic of Texas Archives, San Antonio.

67. B. W. Edwards, H. B. Mayo, Richard Fields, and John D. Hunter, 21 December 1826, folder 243, Samuel E. Asbury Papers, Daughters of the Republic of Texas Archives, San Antonio.

68. B. W. Edwards to James Ross, 25 December 1826, *AP*, vol. 1, pt. 2, 1545–56.

69. Peter Ellis Bean to SFA, 31 December 1826, *AP*, vol. 1, pt. 2, 1554.

70. Buttil J. Thompson to SFA, 17 February 1827, *AP*, vol. 1, pt. 2, 1602–4.

71. SFA to Buttil J. Thompson, 24 December 1826, *AP*, vol. 1, pt. 2, 1538–41.

72. SFA to citizens of Victoria, 1 January 1827, *AP*, vol. 1, pt. 2, 1558–59.

73. SFA to John Sproul, 1 January 1827, *AP*, vol. 1, pt. 2, 1555–56.

74. SFA to citizens of Victoria, 1 January 1827, *AP*, vol. 1, pt. 2, 1558–59.

75. SFA to Buttil J. Thompson, 1 January 1827, *AP*, vol. 1, pt. 2, 1556–57.

76. SFA to José Antonio Saucedo, 4 December 1826, *AP*, vol. 1, pt. 2, 1528.

77. Resolution of Loyalty, district of San Felipe, 6 January 1827, *AP*, vol. 1, pt. 2, 1575.

78. Resolution of Loyalty, district of Bravo, 9 January 1827, *AP*, vol. 1, pt. 2, 1573–74.

79. Resolution of Loyalty, Dewitt's colony, 27 January 1827, *AP*, vol. 1, pt. 2, 1594–95.

80. José Antonio Navarro to inhabitants of Nacogdoches, 28 December 1826, box 3G297, file 11, Spanish Archives Transcripts, Robert Bruce Blake Papers, Dolph Briscoe Center for American History University of Texas at Austin.

81. John A. Williams to Mateo Ahumada, military commander in Texas, 5 February–14 May 1827, folder 237, Nacogdoches Archives, Samuel E. Asbury Papers, Daughters of the Republic of Texas Archives, San Antonio.

82. J. E. B. Austin to Mrs. E. M. Perry, 23 February 1827, *AP*, vol. 1, pt. 2, 1605–6.

83. Samuel Richard Kinney to Mateo Ahumada, military commander in Texas, 9 February 1827, box 3G297, file 11, Spanish Archives Transcripts, Robert Bruce Blake Papers, Dolph Briscoe Center for American History, University of Texas at Austin.

84. Anastasio Bustamante to José Antonio Saucedo, 7 April 1827, box 3G297, file 11, Spanish Archives Transcripts, Robert Bruce Blake Papers, Dolph Briscoe Center for American History, University of Texas at Austin.

85. SFA to B. W. Edwards, 15 September 1825, *AP*, vol. 1, pt. 2, 2101–5.

86. Unknown immigrant quoted in "Marriage Customs in Early Texas," box 2B111, Transcriptions and Notes, Early Texas Colonies, Social Conditions, Eugene Barker Papers, Dolph Briscoe Center for American History, University of Texas at Austin.

87. Roberto Breña, "The Cádiz Liberal Revolution and Spanish American Independence," in *New Countries: Capitalism, Revolutions, and Nations in the Americas, 1750–1870*, ed. John Tutino (Durham, NC: Duke University Press, 2016), 71–104.

88. Brian Connaughton, "Conjuring the Body Politic from the *Corpus Mysticum*: The Post-Independent Pursuit of Public Opinion in Mexico, 1821–1853," *The Americas* 55, no. 3 (January 1999): 459–79.

89. Ira Ingram to Roswell Ingram, 29 May 1830, folder 86, Ira Ingram Papers, Daughters of the Republic of Texas, San Antonio.

90. Ira Ingram to Roswell Ingram, 29 May 1830, folder 86, Ira Ingram Papers, Daughters of the Republic of Texas Archives, San Antonio.

91. Ira Ingram to Roswell Ingram, 15 February 1832, folder 86, Ira Ingram Papers, Dolph Briscoe Center for American History, University of Texas at Austin.

92. Ira Ingram to Roswell Ingram, 29 May 1830, folder 86, Ira Ingram Papers, Daughters of the Republic of Texas Archives, San Antonio.

93. James D. Bratt, "Religious Anti-Revivalism in Antebellum America," *Journal of the Early Republic* 24, no. 1 (Spring 2004): 56–106.

94. SFA to Mary Austin Holly, 19 July 1831, *AP*, vol. 1, pt. 2, 674–77. Austin had been educated at Lexington's Transylvania University, one of the nation's most liberal institutions. On antebellum religious society, see Jon Butler, *Awash in a Sea of Faith: Christianizing the American People* (Cambridge, MA: Harvard University Press, 1990).

95. SFA to Mrs. James F. Perry, 17 December 1824, *AP*, vol. 1, pt. 1, 991–92.

96. James T. Dunbar and others to SFA, 12 December 1821, *AP*, vol. 1, pt. 2, 447: "No feature in any government could be more abhorrent to men born in the land of liberty and matured in the arms of universal toleration than religious restraint." An immigrant from Kentucky asked if the settlers would "be allowed to worship their god agreeable to the dictates of their minds" or "be compelled to acknowledge the Catholic religion as the supreme religion of the land." Elijah Noble to Stephen F. Austin, 29 June 1822, *AP*, vol. 1, pt. 1, 528.

97. Howard Miller, one of the few scholars who has written on this topic, explains that Anglo-American immigrants to Texas, unlike their forefathers—who had "fled religious persecution for a land in which they hoped to find religious freedom"—left "the 'land of liberty' for one dominated by the church most closely associated in the nineteenth-century American mind with religious intolerance." This, however, overemphasizes the difference between the two nations. See Howard Miller, "Stephen F. Austin and the Anglo-Texas Response to the Religious Establishment in Texas, 1821–1836," *Southwestern Historical Quarterly* 91 (January 1988): 283–316.

98. Padre Mariano Sosa, curate of Nacogdoches, to Gov. Antonio Martínez, 26 May 1810, box 2Q457, P. L. Buquor Papers, Dolph Briscoe Center for American History, University of Texas at Austin.

99. Timothy M. Matovina, *Tejano Religion and Ethnicity, San Antonio, 1821–1860* (Austin: University of Texas Press, 1995), chap. 2.

100. Thomas Barnett to SFA, 15 June 1831, *AP*, vol. 1, pt. 2, 666–67. Barnett wrote that he would not be able to attend the mass ceremony "owing to the extreme indisposition of myself and the helpless situation of my family." He therefore requested that Father Muldoon "call at my home on the way down."

101. Hugh B. Johnson to SFA, 29 November 1829, *AP*, vol. 1, pt. 2, 283–84.

102. Miller, "Stephen F. Austin and the Anglo-Texas Response to the Religious Establishment in Texas," 286–88.

103. SFA to the colonists, 6 August 1823, *AP*, vol. 1, pt. 1, 679–81.

104. Lorenzo de Zavala, *Ensayo histórico de las revoluciones de México desde 1808 hasta 1830*, 3rd ed. (Mexico City: SRA, CEHAM, 1981), 189.

105. Lorenzo de Zavala, *Journey to the United States of North America*, ed. John-Michael Rivera (Houston: Arte Público Press, 2005), 31–37, 72–77.

106. Vicente Rocafuerte, *Ensayo sobre tolerancia religiosa* (Mexico City: Imprenta de M. Rivera a Cargo de Tomás Urobe, 1831), 14.

107. Rocafuerte, *Ensayo sobre tolerancia religiosa*, 62–63.

108. Rocafuerte, *Ensayo sobre tolerancia religiosa*, 69.

109. Rocafuerte, *Ensayo sobre tolerancia religiosa*, 15, 19.

110. SFA to J. E. B. Austin, 20 May 1823, *AP*, vol. 1, pt. 2, 644–45.

111. Ira Ingram to Roswell Ingram, 28 May 1830, folder 86, Ira Ingram Papers, Dolph Briscoe Center for American History, University of Texas at Austin.

112. Ira Ingram to Roswell Ingram, 28 May 1830, folder 86, Ira Ingram Papers, Dolph Briscoe Center for American History, University of Texas at Austin.

113. Cornell, *The Other Founders*, 107–9.

Chapter 3 · Slavery, Federalism, and Mexico's First Civil War

1. Juan Francisco de Azcarate to J. M. Duran, 21 September 1827, box 2Q170, vol. 326, Guerra: Colonización, 1827–1831, Archivo General de Mexico, Dolph Briscoe Center for American History, University of Texas at Austin.

2. Edith Louise Kelly and Mattie Kelly, eds., "Tadeo Ortiz de Ayala and the Colonization of Texas, 1822–1833, I," *Southwestern Historical Quarterly* 32, no. 1 (July 1928): 74–86, 237, 334.

3. Vicente Guerrero, *Manifiesto del ciudadano Vicente Guerrero, segunda presidente de los Estados Unidos Mexicanos, a sus compatriatos* (Mexico City: Imprenta del Aguila, dirigida por José Ximeno, 1829), 20.

4. Harry Watson, *Liberty and Power: The Politics of Jacksonian America* (New York: Hill and Wang, 2006), 117–18.

5. Watson, *Liberty and Power*, 34; Marvin Meyers, *The Jacksonian Persuasion: Politics and Belief* (Stanford, CA: Stanford University Press, 1960), 22; Arthur Schlesinger, Jr., *The Age of Jackson* (New York: Little, Brown and Co., 1945), 30–32.

6. Andrew Jackson, "Speech on the Bank Veto," 10 July 1832, in *A Compilation of the Messages and Papers of the Presidents, 1789–1897*, comp. James D. Richardson, 10 vols

(Washington, DC: Government Printing Office, 1896–1899), 2:576–99, quotes on pages 576, 580, 590,

7. Watson, *Liberty and Power*, 13.

8. Andrew Jackson, "Second Annual Message to Congress," 6 December 1830, Richardson, *Messages and Papers of the Presidents*, 2:500–29.

9. Timothy E. Anna, *Forging Mexico, 1821–1835* (Lincoln: University of Nebraska Press, 1998), 211–12; Peter F. Guardino, *Peasants, Politics, and the Formation of Mexico's National State, Guerrero, 1800–1857* (Stanford, CA: Stanford University Press, 1996), 91.

10. Copy of the emancipation decree, 16 September 1829, file 27, folder 19, Archivo General de Nación, Gobernación, Legajo, Mexico City.

11. Anna, *Forging Mexico*, 217.

12. Lorenzo de Zavala, *Ensayo histórico de las revoluciones de México desde 1808 hasta 1830*, vol. 2 (New York: Imprenta en cargo de Manuel N. de la Vega, 1832), 413.

13. Anna, *Forging Mexico*, 216–18.

14. Watson, *Liberty and Power*, 140, 111.

15. Zavala quoted in Anna, *Forging Mexico*, 211.

16. Charles A. Hale, *Mexican Liberalism in the Age of Mora, 1821–1853* (New Haven, CT: Yale University Press, 1968), 246–47.

17. Ortíz quoted in John Tutino, *The Mexican Heartland: How Communities Shaped Capitalism, a Nation, and Mexican History* (Princeton, NJ: Princeton University Press, 2018), 184.

18. Kelly and Hatcher, "Tadeo Ortiz de Ayala and the Colonization of Texas, 1822–1833, I," 1, 79, 84.

19. Tadeo Ortíz de Ayala, *México considerado como una nación independiente y libre* (Mexico City: Imprenta de Carlos Lawalle Sobrino, 1832), 280.

20. José María Tornel quoted in Will Fowler, *Tornel and Santa Anna: The Writer and the Caudillo Mexico 1795–1853* (London: Greenwood Press, 2002), 115–16.

21. Tornel quoted in Fowler, *Tornel and Santa Anna*, 115–16.

22. Lorenzo de Zavala, *Journey to the United States of North America*, trans. Wallace Woolsey, ed. John-Michael Rivera (Houston: Arte Público Press, 2005), 8, 153–54.

23. Daniel Walker Howe, *What Hath God Wrought: The Transformation of America, 1815–1848* (New York: Oxford University Press, 2007), 131–32.

24. Sven Beckert, *Empire of Cotton: A Global History* (New York: Vintage Books, 2015), 103–5.

25. Zavala, *Journey to the United States of North America*, 16–17.

26. Edith Louise Kelly and Mattie Kelly and Austin, trans., "Tadeo Ortiz de Ayala and the Colonization of Texas, 1822–1833, III," *Southwestern Historical Quarterly* 32, no. 3 (January 1929): 237.

27. Hale, *Mexican Liberalism in the Age of Mora*, 247.

28. Hale, *Mexican Liberalism in the Age of Mora*, 139.

29. Guerrero, *Manifiesto de ciudadano Vicente Guerrero*, 20.

30. Jackson quoted in Watson, *Liberty and Power*, 48–49.

31. For Jackson's interest in Texas, see Robert Remini, *Andrew Jackson and the Course of American Empire* (New York: Harper & Row, 1977), 305–7, 378–98.

32. Stephen F. Austin (hereafter SFA) to W. C. Carr, 4 March 1829, in *The Austin*

Papers, ed. Eugene C. Barker (Washington, DC: Government Printing Office, 1924), vol. 1, pt. 2, 177–79 (hereafter *AP*).

33. David G. Burnet to SFA, 10 March 1829, *AP*, vol. 1, pt. 2, 180.
34. SFA to W. C. Carr, 4 March 1829, in *AP*, vol. 1, pt. 2, 177–79.
35. SFA to W. C. Carr, 4 March 1829, *AP*, vol. 1, pt. 2, 177–79.
36. SFA to W. C. Carr, 4 March 1829, *AP*, vol. 1, pt. 2, 177–79.
37. Andrés Reséndez, *The Other Slavery: The Uncovered Story of Indian Enslavement in America* (New York: Houghton Mifflin Harcourt, 2016), 218.
38. Andrew J. Torget, *Seeds of Empire: Cotton, Slavery, and the Transformation of the Texas Borderlands, 1800–1850* (Chapel Hill: University of North Carolina Press, 2015), 60, 74–75.
39. Jared E. Groce, diary, Groce Family Papers, Dolph Briscoe Center for American History, University of Texas at Austin.
40. Torget, *Seeds of Empire*, 84.
41. Adam Rothman, *Slave Country: American Expansion and the Origins of the Deep South* (Cambridge, MA: Harvard University Press, 2005).
42. SFA to Federal Congress, "Petition Concerning Slavery," 10 June 1824, *AP* vol. 2, pt. 1, 827–28.
43. Juan Nepomuceno Seguin, *A Revolution Remembered: Memoirs and Selected Correspondence of Juan N. Seguín*, ed. Jesús F. de la Teja (Austin: Texas State Historical Society, 2002).
44. Torget, *Seeds of Empire*, 79.
45. Torget, *Seeds of Empire*, 100–101, Elizondo on 101.
46. James A. Phelps to SFA, 16 January 1825, *AP*, vol. 1, pt. 2, 1020–21.
47. "Governor's Opinion Concerning Slavery," 30 November 1826, *AP*, vol. 1, pt. 2, 1523–26; also cited in Torget, *Seeds of Empire*, 110.
48. Torget, *Seeds of Empire*, 111.
49. Torget, *Seeds of Empire*, 116–17.
50. Torget, *Seeds of Empire*, 116–17. According to Torget, Bean made this recommendation in July 1826 after hearing that the state legislators were unlikely to pass a constitution that would outlaw chattel slavery (pp. 57, 130); Reséndez, *The Other Slavery*, 104–16.
51. Torget, *Seeds of Empire*, 127–24; Randolph B. Campbell, *Gone to Texas: A History of the Lone Star State* (New York: Oxford University Press, 2003), 23.
52. Frost Thorn to SFA, 22 July 1828, *AP*, vol. 1, pt. 2, 74–75.
53. Ramón Músquiz to José María Viesca, 25 October 1829, *AP*, vol. 2, pt. 2, 273–75.
54. José Antonio Padilla to SFA, 26 November 1829, *AP*, vol. 2, pt. 2 293–94.
55. José María Viesca to the minister of foreign relations, José María Bocanegra, 14 November 1829, *AP*, vol. 2, pt. 2, 286–88.
56. SFA to John Durst, 17 November 1829, *AP*, vol. 1, pt. 2, 288–89.
57. Theodore G. Vincent, *The Legacy of Guerrero, Mexico's First Black President* (Gainesville, University of Florida, 2001), 197; Terán to SFA, 20 November 1829, *AP*, vol. 1, pt. 2, 290.
58. Músquiz to SFA, 24 December 1829, *AP*, vol. 1, pt. 2, 303–4.
59. Maque et al. petition, 25 May 1830, box 2S13, and "Thomas Maque," 15

December 1832, box 2S15, Bexar Archives, Dolph Briscoe Center for American History, University of Texas at Austin.

60. "Peter," 23 May 1832, box 2S15, Béxar Archives, Dolph Briscoe Center for American History, University of Texas at Austin

61. Ramon Músquiz, 3 June 1832, folder 312, Government Records, John W. Smith Papers, Daughters of the Republic of Texas Library, San Antonio.

62. For more on Músquiz, his view of Texas slaveholders, and Peter's case, see Andrés Reséndez, "Ramón Músquiz: The Ultimate Insider," in *Tejano Leadership in Mexican and Revolutionary Texas*, ed. Jesús F. de la Teja (College Station: Texas A&M Press, 2010), 129–45, Músquiz on 136.

63. J. Child to SFA, 24 January 1830, *AP*, vol. 2, pt. 2, 323–325. This falls in line with Reséndez's observation that in contrast to national leaders, state and local leaders wanted a "harmonious community composed of different races but united in a common cause for prosperity," Andrés Reséndez, *Changing National Identities at the Frontier: Texas and New Mexico, 1800–1850* (New York: Cambridge University Press, 2004), 29.

64. Reséndez, *Changing National Identities*, chap. 3.

65. J. Child to SFA, 26 January 1830, *AP*, vol. 2, 323–25.

66. SFA to Emily Perry, 24, July 1828, *AP*, vol. 2, pt. 2, 76–77.

67. SFA to Henry Austin, 27 August 1829, *AP*, vol. 2, pt. 2, 250–53.

68. SFA to Commodore David Porter, 16 February 1828, *AP*, vol. 2, pt. 2, 166–68.

69. Anna, *Forging Mexico*, 224; Eric Van Young, *A Life Together: Lucas Alamán and Mexico, 1792–1853* (New Haven, CT: Yale University Press, 2021), 446.

70. SFA to Manuel Mier y Teràn, 24 May 1828, *AP*, vol. 1, pt. 2, 42–45. In a petition to Terán, dated 30 June 1828, Austin requested a formal exemption from the import tariff until 1835, permission to raise tobacco for export, and regulation of the coasting trade to permit Texas products into Mexican ports. SFA to Manuel Mier y Terán, 23 June 1828, *AP*, vol. 1, pt. 2, 59–66.

71. Austin made a series of appeals to various Mexican officials for exemption from the tariff. SFA to Manuel Mier y Terán, 30 June 1828; SFA to Ramón Músquiz, 28 July 1828; SFA to Manuel Mier y Terán, 20 September 1828, *AP*, vol. 1, pt. 2, 59–66, 78–80, 116–18.

72. SFA to Guerrero, 8 September 1828, *AP*, vol. 1, pt. 2, 99–102.

73. SFA to Guerrero, 8 September 1828, *AP*, vol. 1, pt. 2, 99–102.

74. SFA to Ramón Músquiz and Lorenzo de Zavala, 23 July 1829, *AP*, vol. 1, pt. 2, 235–40.

75. SFA to J. Bell, 17 March 1829, *AP*, vol. 1, pt. 2, 183–92.

76. SFA to Thomas White, 31 March 1829, *AP*, vol. 1, pt. 2, 197–99.

77. Will Fowler, *The Pronunciamiento in the Age of Santa Anna, 1821–1855*, 115–19. Guardino, *Peasants, Politics, and the Formation of Mexico's National State*, Guerrero, 127–28.

78. Unsigned note to Guerrero, Jalapa, 6 December 1829, vol. 72, file 1, Archivo General de Nación, Gobernación, Mexico City.

79. For a full transcript of the Plan de Jalapa, see *El pensamiento de la reacción Mexicana*, vol. 1, *Historia documental, 1810–1859*, ed. Gastón García Cantú (Mexico City: Universidad Nacional Autónoma de México, 1986), 135–38.

80. *Representación que el supremo gobierno de San Luis Potosí hace al general de le Unión*

para se derogue el decreto del 16 se[p]tiembre, 29 September 1829, vol. 27, file 16, Archivo General de Nación, Legajo, Mexico City.

81. Van Young, *A Life Together*, 204.
82. Alamán cited in Van Young, *A Life Together*, 163.
83. Simón Bolívar, *An Address of Bolívar at the Congress of Angostura (February 15, 1819)* (repr., Washington, DC: Press of B. S. Adams, 1919).
84. Alamán quoted in Van Young, *A Life Together*, 442–44.
85. Alexander Hamilton, "Final Version of the Report on the Subject of Manufactures, 5 December 1791," in *The Papers of Alexander Hamilton*, vol. 10, *December 1791–January 1792*, ed. Harold C. Syrett (New York: Columbia University Press, 1966), 230–340.
86. Van Young, *A Life Together*, 357.
87. Jean Luis Berlandier, *Journey to Mexico during the Years, 1826–1834*, ed. C. H. Muller and Katherine Muller, trans. Sheila Ohlendorf, Josette M. Bigelow, and Mary Standifer, 2 vols. (Austin: Texas State Historical Association, 1980), 1:290–91.
88. José María Sánchez, "A Trip to Texas in 1828," ed. and trans. Carlos E. Castañeda, *Southwestern Historical Quarterly* 29 (April 1826): 249–88, quote on 283.
89. Berlandier, *Journey to Mexico*, 283, 290–91.
90. Sánchez, "Trip to Texas," 260.
91. Terán to the president of Mexico (Guerrero), 30 June 1828, *Texas by Terán: The Diary Kept by General Manuel de Mier y Terán on His 1828 Inspection of Texas*, ed. Jack Jackson and trans. John Wheat (Austin: University of Texas, 2000), 98.
92. Terán, *Diary*, 96.
93. Terán, *Diary*, 53.
94. Berlandier, *Journey to Mexico*, 318.
95. Sánchez, "Trip to Texas," 260–61, 271, 274, 278.
96. Berlandier, *Journey to Mexico*, 298.
97. Terán, *Diary*, 100.
98. Terán, *Diary*, 178–79.
99. As cited in Van Young, *A Life Together*, 417.
100. Lucas Alamán, 25 October 1830, box 2Q170, vol. 326, Guerra 1827–1831, Archivo General de Mexico , Dolph Briscoe Center for American History, University of Texas at Austin.
101. Decreto del congreso general, 6 April 1830, vol. 110, file 6, Archivo General de Nación, Legajo, Mexico City.
102. Decreto del congreso general, 16 October 1830, vol. 110, file 5, Archivo General de Nación, Legajo, Mexico City.
103. Decreto del congreso general, 30 September 1831, vol. 112, file 8, and 21 November 1831, vol. 112, file 10, Archivo General de Nación, Legajo, Mexico City.
104. Edith Louise Kelly and Mattie Kelly, eds., "Tadeo Ortiz de Ayala and the Colonization of Texas, 1822–1833, II," *Southwestern Historical Quarterly* 32, no. 2 (October 1928): 153–55, 162.
105. Van Young, *A Life Together*, 357.
106. SFA to President Bustamante, 17 May 1830, *AP*, vol. 2, 377–79.
107. SFA to Alamán, 18 May 1830, *AP*, vol. 2, 383–85.
108. S.F.A. to Piedras, 12 July 1830, *AP*, vol. 1, pt. 2, 447–48.

109. Editorial by Austin, *Texas Gazette*, 3 July 1830, *AP*, vol. 1, pt. 2, 437–40.
110. SFA to Samuel May Williams, 18 February 1831, *AP*, vol. 1, pt. 2, 599–604.
111. For statistical information on the changing pattern of migration before and after 1830, see Campbell, *Gone to Texas*, 111; Reséndez, *Changing National Identities*, 21–22.
112. Edna Rowe, "The Disturbances at Anahuac in 1832," *Southwestern Historical Quarterly* 6 (April 1903): 265–99, 270.
113. Anna, *Forging Mexico*, 231.
114. Anna, *Forging Mexico*, 233.
115. Acta y plan de Veracruz sobre remoción del Ministerio, 2 January 1832.
116. Reséndez, *Changing National Identities*, 121.
117. Reséndez, *Changing National Identities*, 271; J. Francisco Madero to Samuel May Williams, 15 March 1831, unit id. 23-0598, Samuel May Williams Papers, Rosenberg Library, Galveston, Texas.
118. Sam W. Haynes, *Unsettled Land: From Revolution to Republic: The Struggle for Texas* (New York: Basic Books, 2022), 98.
119. SFA to Bradburn, 30 December 1831, *AP*, vol. 2, 731–32; Bradburn to Terán quoted in Rowe, "The Disturbances at Anahuac in 1832," 275.
120. Haynes, *Unsettled Land*, 98–99.
121. Rowe, "The Disturbances at Anahuac in 1832," 277; Manuel Mier y Terán to SFA, 25 June 1832, *AP*, vol. 1, pt. 2, 799–800.
122. SFA to Manuel Mier y Terán, 5 February 1832, *AP*, vol. 1, pt. 2, 747–53; Ayuntamiento of San Felipe to supreme government, 18 February 1832, *AP*, vol. 1, pt. 2, 749–53.
123. For examples, see the contents of box 339, file 35, Archivo General de Nación, Gobernación, Mexico City.
124. "Citizens Meeting," 20 June 1832, *The Papers of Mirabeau Buonaparte Lamar*, ed. Charles Adam Gulick, Jr., and K. Elliott, 6 vols. (New York: AMS Press, 1973), 1:128–29.
125. D. Ugartechea to F. Duclor, 23 June 1832, *LP*, vol. 1, 119–20.
126. Horatio Christman and Samuel May Williams, "Address to the Inhabitants of Austin's Colony," 30 June 1832, Unit id. 23-0964, Samuel May Williams papers, Rosenberg Library, Galveston.
127. "Citizens' Meeting," 28 June 1832, *LP*, vol. 2, 125–27.
128. Report of Ugartechea, 1 July 1832, *LP*, vol. 2, 132–36.
129. James Perry to John Perry, 7 May 1832, box 2J30, James F. and Stephen S. Perry Papers, Dolph Briscoe Center for American History, University of Texas at Austin.
130. Ira Ingram to Samuel May Williams, March 1830, box 2E264, Ira Ingram Papers, Dolph Briscoe Center for American History, University of Texas at Austin.
131. "Account of a Public Dinner," 22 August 1832, *LP*, vol. 2, 146–47.
132. Juan Francisco de Azcarate to J. M. Duran, 21 September 1827, box 2Q170, vol. 326, Guerra, 1827–1831, Archivo General de Mexico, Dolph Briscoe Center for American History, University of Texas at Austin.

Chapter 4 · *Anti-national and Contemptible Intrigues*

1. Ramón Músquiz cited in C. A. Hutchinson, "Valentín Gómez Farías and the 'Secret Pact of New Orleans,'" *Hispanic American Historical Review* 36, no. 4 (1956): 471–89.

2. Edith Louise Kelly and Mattie Austin Hatter, eds., "Tadeo Ortíz de Ayala and the Colonization of Texas, 1822–1833, IV," *Southwestern Historical Quarterly* 32, no. 4 (April 1929): 319.

3. Richard E. Ellis, *The Union at Risk: Jacksonian Democracy, States' Rights and the Nullification Crisis* (New York: Oxford University Press, 1987), chap. 2. For more on Jacksonian ideas of democracy and federal power, see Harry L. Watson, *Liberty and Power: The Politics of Jacksonian America* (New York: Hill and Wang, 2006), chaps. 1 and 2; Marvin Meyers, introduction to *The Jacksonian Persuasion: Politics and Belief* (Stanford, CA: Stanford University Press, 1957); Arthur M. Schlesinger, Jr., *The Age of Jackson* (New York: Little, Brown and Co., 1947), chap. 31.

4. Ellis, *The Union at Risk*, 8, wrote, "Most nullifiers never subscribed to the localist and anti-government Old Republican values at the heart of the 'Spirit of 1798.'" For a similar conclusion, see Manisha Sinha, *The Counterrevolution of Slavery: Politics and Ideology in Antebellum South Carolina* (Chapel Hill: University of North Carolina Press, 2000), 25: "The ideological roots of Calhoun's concept of nullification lay more in the archfederalism of a later period than in Madisonian theory. It was profoundly conservative, designed to check what Carolinian slaveholders saw as the excesses of democracy and majoritarianism."

5. For more on this threat of elite anti-federalism, see Saul Cornell, *The Other Founders: Anti-Federalism and the Dissenting Tradition in America, 1788–1828* (Chapel Hill: Published for the Omohundro Institute of Early American History and Culture, Williamsburg, Virginia, by the University of North Carolina Press, 1999), chap. 2.

6. For scholarship on the nullification crisis and the nullifiers' theory of states' rights, see Frank Towers, "The Threat of Consolidation: States' Rights and American Discourses of Nation and Empire in the Nineteenth Century," *Journal of the American Civil War* 9, no. 4 (December 2019): 612–42, and Sinha, *The Counterrevolution of Slavery*, 9–32; Ellis, *The Union at Risk*, chap. 1. All of these scholars agree that the 1830s nullifiers represented a departure from the country's republican heritage by rejecting majority rule at both the state and national levels. Yet, it could be characterized as embodying the kind of "middling" anti-federalist tradition of men like Stephen Austin by making power in Texas only accessible to men of means. John C. Calhoun insisted that the "naked question" was whether the US government rested "on the solid basis of the sovereignty of the states, or on the unrestrained will of the majority." See John C. Calhoun, "The Fort Hill Address: On the Relations of the States and the Federal Government [July 26, 1831]," in *Union and Liberty: The Political Philosophy of John C. Calhoun*, ed. Ross M. Lence (Indianapolis: Liberty Fund, 1992), 383.

7. Cornell, *The Other Founders*, 296.

8. John C. Calhoun, "Exposition and Protest," in *Union and Liberty*, 313, 338, 344, and 350.

9. John C. Calhoun, "Fort Hill Address." This view was also shared by John Quitman, future Mississippi senator and Calhoun protégé, in *Address to the People of Mississippi by the Committee Appointed by the States' Rights Convention Assembled at Jackson, May 21, 1834* (Natchez, MS: Printed at the Courier and Journal Office, 1834), 6.

10. Joseph Story summarized and quoted in Sinha, *The Counterrevolution of Slavery*, 201.

11. Abel P. Upshur summarized and quoted in Sinha, *The Counterrevolution of Slavery*, 202.

12. "Speech of Mr. Hayne, of South Carolina, January 25, 1830," in Daniel Webster, *The Webster Hayne Debate on the Nature of the Union, Selected Documents*, ed. Herman Belz (Indianapolis: Liberty Fund, 2000), 35–80, quote on 75; "Speech of Mr. Webster, of Massachusetts, January 26 and 27, 1830," 80–154, in Webster, *The Webster Hayne Debate on the Nature of the Union*, 125–26.

13. José María Tornel, close adviser to Santa Anna and former governor of Veracruz, predicted secession as early as 1830 in a letter to Lucás Alamán, 18 December 1830, box 2Q223, vol. 564, 32–38, Relaciones Exteriores, Internacional, Estados Unidos, 1806–1840, Archivo General de Mexico, Dolph Briscoe Center for American History, University of Texas at Austin. Also cited in Gene M. Brack, *Mexico Views Manifest Destiny, 1821–1846: An Essay on the Mexican War* (Albuquerque: University of New Mexico Press, 1975), 58.

14. *El Fénix de la Libertad* (Mexico City), 15 February 1833.

15. *El Fénix de Libertad* (Mexico City), 16 February 1833.

16. *El Telégrafo* (Mexico City), 22 February 1833.

17. Timothy E. Anna, *Forging Mexico, 1821–1835* (Lincoln: University of Nebraska Press, 1998), 258.

18. Will Fowler, "Valentín Gómez Farías: Perceptions of Radicalism in Independent Mexico, 1821–1847," in "Mexican Politics in the Nineteenth Century," special issue, *Bulletin of Latin American Research* 15, no. 1 (1996): 39–62.

19. Kelly and Hatter, "Tadeo Ortíz de Ayala and the Colonization of Texas," 311–43.

20. Fowler, "Valentín Gómez Farías," 39–62, 40–41.

21. Andrew W. Torget, *Seeds of Empire: Cotton, Slavery, and Transformation of the Texas Borderlands, 1800–1850* (Chapel Hill: University of North Carolina Press, 2015), 152; Andrés Reséndez, *Changing National Identities at the Frontier: Texas and New Mexico, 1800–1850* (New York: Cambridge University Press, 2005), 22–23.

22. Anna, *Forging Mexico*, 254–58; Greg Cantrell, *Stephen F. Austin, Empresario of Texas* (New Haven, CT: Yale University Press, 1999), 283.

23. Sam W. Haynes, *Unsettled Land: From Revolution to Republic, the Struggle for Texas* (New York: Basic Books, 2022), 110.

24. Haynes, *Unsettled Land*, 73–75.

25. Jonas Harrison, colonist, to Stephen F. Austin (hereafter SFA), 30 November 1832, in *The Austin Papers*, ed. Eugene C. Barker, 3 vols. (Washington, DC: Government Printing Office, 1924), vol. 1, pt. 2, 895–96 (hereafter *AP*).

26. Haynes, *Unsettled Land*, 112–16.

27. SFA to Mary Austin Holley, 20 April 1833, *AP*, vol. 1, pt. 2, 954–56.

28. SFA to Central Committee, 24 July 1833, *AP*, vol. 1, pt. 2, 988–91.

29. SFA to Central Committee, 24 July 1833, *AP*, vol. 1, pt. 2, 988–91.

30. He purportedly died while on the way to New Orleans, where he was supposed to meet a group of European immigrants in accordance with his government-sponsored colonization project. See Wilbert H. Timmons, *Tadeo Ortiz: Mexican Colonizer and Reformer* (El Paso: Texas Western Press, 1974).

31. "Public Instructions to General Almonte," in *Almonte's Texas: Juan N. Almonte's 1834 Inspection, Secret Report, and Role in the 1836 Campaign*, ed. Jack Jackson, trans. John Wheat (Austin: Texas State Historical Association, 2003), 31–33.

32. Jackson, *Almonte's Texas*, 38–45.

33. "Almonte's Letter no. 11," 13 April 1834, in Jackson, *Almonte's Texas*, 91–93.
34. Juan Nepomuceno Almonte, "Secret Report on the Present Situation in Texas," in Jackson, *Almonte's Texas*, 210–83, quotes on 224.
35. Juan Nepomuceno Almonte to Juan José Elguezábal, 23 September 1834, in Jackson, *Almonte's Texas*, 183–86.
36. Jackson, *Almonte's Texas*, "Secret Report," 221 and 223.
37. Juan Nepomuceno Almonte to Samuel May Williams, 20 December 1834, unit id. 23-1381, Samuel May Williams Papers, Rosenberg Library, Galveston; SFA to Thomas McKinney, 2 December 1834, *AP*, vol. 3, 30–31; SFA to Samuel May Williams, 31 December 1834, *AP*, vol. 3, 36–37.
38. SFA to James F. Perry, 4 March 1835; SFA to James F. Perry, 10 March 1835; SFA to Samuel May Williams, 4 April 1835, *AP*, vol. 3, 45–48, 60.
39. *El Mosquito Mexicano* (Mexico City), 1 April 1834. On the alliance of military officers and clergy, see Anna, *Forging Mexico*, 258.
40. Michael P. Costeloe, *The Central Republic in Mexico, 1835–1846: Hombres de bien in the Age of Santa Anna* (Cambridge: Cambridge University Press, 1993), 33–39, 35; Anna, *Forging Mexico*, 259–60.
41. Anna, *Forging Mexico*, 153–55, 259–60.
42. Plan de Toluca (1834), box 410, folder 1, Archivo General de Nación, Gobernación Sin Sección, Mexico City; also cited in Will Fowler, *Independent Mexico: The Pronunciamiento in the Age of Santa Anna, 1821–1858* (Lincoln: University of Nebraska Press, 2016), 170.
43. Many of these can be found in file 158, Archivo General de Nación, Gobernación, Mexico City. The Plan de Orizaba (1835) called for replacing the federalist constitution with one "more analogous to [the Mexican] people's needs, exigencies and customs" and thereby better suited to guarantee their "independence, internal peace, and Catholic religion." See Will Fowler, *Santa Anna of Mexico* (Lincoln: University of Nebraska Press, 2007), 161. Likewise, the Plan of Toluca called for a "popular representative central republic" in conformity with the "desires of the nation." Many Mexican leaders became convinced that their nation needed a new constitution more in line with the "habits, customs, and even preoccupations" of its people.
44. Will Fowler, *Tornel and Santa Anna: The Writer and the Caudillo, Mexico, 1795–1853* (Westport, CT: Greenwood Press, 2000), 143–45, Bocanegra and the pronunciamiento of Orizaba on 143.
45. Santa Anna to José Fernando Ramírez, in Fowler, *Tornel and Santa Anna*, 155–56.
46. C. A. Hutchinson, "Mexican Federalists in New Orleans and the Texas Revolution," *Louisiana Historical Quarterly* 39, no. 1 (1956): 3. A similar account is also found in Edward L. Miller, *New Orleans and the Texas Revolution* (College Station: Texas A&M University Press, 2004), 19.
47. C. A. Hutchinson, "General José Antonio Mexía and His Texas Interests," *Southwestern Historical Quarterly* 82, no. 2 (October 1978): 117–28.
48. *El Tiempo* (Mexico City), 3 July 1834.
49. *El Tiempo* (Mexico City), 5 July 1834.
50. *El Mosquito Mexicano* (Mexico City), 30 June 1835.
51. Anna, *Forging Mexico*, 261.
52. Cited in Fowler, *Independent Mexico*, 171–72.

53. Tornel cited in Anna, *Forging Mexico*, 260.
54. Viesca cited in Reséndez, *Changing National Identities at the Frontier*, 150.
55. Lorenzo de Zavala, address to Colonists, 8 August 1835, *The Papers of Mirabeau Buonaparte Lamar*, ed. Charles Adam Gulick, Jr., and K. Elliott, 6 vols. (New York: AMS Press, 1973), 1:221–22.
56. SFA to the people of Texas, 29 September 1835, *AP*, vol. 3, 139.
57. "San Felipe Meeting," clipping from the *Texas Republican*, *AP*, vol. 3, 121–23.
58. *Telegraph and Texas Register*, 10 October 1835.
59. *Telegraph and Texas Register*, 17 October 1835.
60. D. C. Barrett, to the Consultation, 4 November 1835, *Papers of the Texas Revolution, 1835–1836*, 10 vols. (Austin: Presidial Press, 1973), 2:312–13.
61. SFA to the Texas Militia, 23 October 1835; Philip Dimmit to SFA, 25 October 1835, *AP*, vol. 3, 204, 207–9.
62. *Telegraph and Texas Register*, 2 January 1836.
63. *El Regenado* (Mexico City), December 1835, folder 219, file 2, Archivo General de Nación, Gobernación, Legajo, Mexico City.
64. Miller, *New Orleans and the Texas Revolution*, 6–15.
65. *El Mosquito Mexicano* (Mexico City), 11 December 1835; also cited at length in Miller, *New Orleans and the Texas Revolution*, 30–31.
66. For a comprehensive summary of *El Mosquito Mexicano*'s coverage of the meetings, see Hutchinson "Mexican Federalists in New Orleans and the Texas Revolution," 9–16; also see Miller, *New Orleans and the Texas Revolution*, 29–33.
67. *El Mosquito Mexicano* (Mexico City), 11 December 1835.
68. *El Mosquito Mexicano* (Mexico City), 11 December 1835.
69. For US slaveholders' fear of British abolition, see Matthew J. Karp, *The Vast Southern Empire: Slaveholders at the Helm of American Foreign Policy* (Cambridge, MA: Harvard University Press, 2016), chap. 1; Miller, *New Orleans and the Texas Revolution*, 29–33.
70. Ambrose Cowperthwaite Fulton, *A Life's Voyage: A Diary of a Sailor and Land, Jotted Down during a Seventy-Years' Voyage* (New York: Ambrose Cowperthwaite Fulton, 1898), 95; Miller, *New Orleans and the Texas Revolution*, 58–59.
71. Fisher's speech is summarized in Mary F. Parmenter, *The Life of George Fisher, (1795–1873), and the History of the Fisher Family in Mississippi* (Jacksonville, FL: H. W. & W. B. Drew Company, 1959), 52–53.
72. Miller, *New Orleans and the Texas Revolution*, 59–60.
73. Miller, *New Orleans and the Texas Revolution*, 60–68.
74. *El Anteojo* (Mexico City), 4 November 1835.
75. Thomas McKinney to SFA, 17 December 1835, *AP*, vol. 3, pp. 286.
76. *Telegraph and Texas Register*, 14 November 1835.
77. James Ramage to SFA, 21 October 1835, *AP*, vol. 3, 197–99.
78. Miller, *New Orleans and the Texas Revolution*, 77.
79. Miller, *New Orleans and the Texas Revolution*, 77.
80. John S. Brooks to Miss Mary Ann Brooks, 8 January 1836, box 3H90, John Sowers Brooks Papers, Daughters of the Republic of Texas Library, San Antonio.
81. SFA to Richard R. Royall, 25 December 1836, *AP*, vol. 3, 292–94.
82. SFA to the provisional government of Texas, 22 December 1835, *AP*, vol. 3, 290–92.

83. SFA to the provisional government of Texas, 14 December 1835, *AP*, vol. 3 282–84.

84. James Fannin to Provisional Government and General Council, 7 February 1836; Fannin to the Acting Governor and General Council of the Provisional Government of Texas, 28 February 1836, *PTR*, 4:455–56.

85. James Fannin to Joseph Mims, 28 February 1836; James Fannin to the Honorable Governor and General Council of Texas, 1 March 1836, *PTR*, 4:455. Lack notes that whereas at least 1,100 of the 1,300 men who rushed to arms in October and November 1835 were Texan, about three-quarters of the more than 900 soldiers who defended Texas between January and March 1836 had emigrated after October, and only about one-fourth as many Texans fought. Paul D. Lack, *The Texas Revolutionary Experience: A Political and Social History, 1835–1836* (College Station: Texas A&M University Press, 1992), 122.

86. Henry Meigs to SFA, 15 November 1835, *AP*, vol. 3, 254–55; Reséndez, *Changing National Identities*, 166.

87. Haynes, *Unsettled Land*, 144.

88. *Telegraph and Texas Register*, 14 November 1835.

89. *Telegraph and Texas Register*, 2 January 1836.

90. Haynes, *Unsettled Land*, 161.

91. SFA to Henry Austin, 7 January 1836, *AP*, vol. 3, 297–98. On slaveholding interests in New Orleans contributing significant funds to the rebellion, see Torget, *Seeds of Empire*, 167–68.

92. SFA to Thomas McKinney, 16 January 1836, *AP*, vol. 3, 304–5.

93. SFA to Thomas McKinney, 21 January 1836, *AP*, vol. 3, 308–9.

94. Thomas McKinney to SFA, 22 February 1836, *AP*, vol. 3, 316–17.

95. Bouton, 235.

96. SFA, Branch T. Archer and William H. Wharton to Guy M. Bryan, 31 March 1836, *AP*, vol. 3, 319–20.

97. SFA to Nicholas Biddle, 9 April 1836; SFA to David G. Burnet, 3 April 1836, *AP*, vol. 3, 328–29, 341–44.

98. SFA to Senator L. F. Linn, 4 May 1835, *AP*, vol. 3, 344–45.

99. SFA to Andrew Jackson, 15 April 1836, *AP*, vol. 3, 332–33.

100. SFA to Senator L. F. Linn, 4 May 1835, *AP*, vol. 3, 344–45.

101. "A Memorial of the Volunteers in the Actual Service of Texas to the Convention to be Assembled at Washington on the First Day of March 1836, February 1836," *PTR*, 4:473–74; and Sam Houston to soldiers, 15 January 1836, *PTR*, 4:29–30.

102. SFA to Thomas McKinney, 16 December 1835, *AP*, vol. 3, 285.

103. "Shall We Declare for Independence," *Telegraph and Texas Register*, 27 February 1836.

104. Antonio López de Santa Anna, "Manifesto Relative to His Operations in the Texas Campaign and His Capture," *The Mexican Side of the Texas Revolution*, ed. and trans. Carlos E. Castañeda (Washington, DC: Documentary Publications, 1971), 5–49, 16–17.

105. José María Tornel to Antonio López de Santa Anna, 30 December 1835, in Castañeda, *The Mexican Side of the Texas Revolution*, 55–56.

106. Santa Anna, "Manifesto," 17, wrote, "The nations of the world would never have

forgiven Mexico had it accorded them rights, privileges, and considerations which the common law of peoples accords only to constituted nations."

107. Lack, *Texas Revolutionary Experience*, 83–85.

108. "The Texas Declaration of Independence," 2 March 1836, in *Documents of Texas History*, ed. Ernest Wallace, David M. Vigness, and George B. Ward (Austin: Texas State Historical Association, 2002), 98–99.

109. Antonio López de Santa Anna, "Message to the Inhabitants of Texas," in *The Papers of the Texas Revolution, 1835–1836*, ed. John H. Jenkins, 10 vols. (Austin: Presidial Press, 1973), 4:20–21 (hereafter *PTR*).

110. Santa Anna, "Manifesto," 17; also on the rebels, see Vicente Filisola, "Representación dirigida al supremo gobierno por el General Vicente Filisla, en defense de su honor y aclaración de sus operaciones como general de gefe del ejército sobre Téjas," in Castañeda, *The Mexican Side of the Texas Revolution*, 171; and José Urrea, "Diario de las operaciones militares de la division que al mando del General José Urrea hizo la compana de Téjas," in Castañeda, *The Mexican Side of the Texas Revolution*, 242.

111. José María Tornel, "Relations between Texas, the United States of America and Mexico," in Castañeda, *The Mexican Side of the Texas Revolution*, 287–379, quote on 348.

112. Tornel, "Relations between Texas, the United States of America and Mexico," 343.

113. Santa Anna, "Message to the Inhabitants of Texas," 7 March 1836, in *The U.S. War with Mexico: A Brief History with Documents*, ed. Ernesto Chávez (New York: Bedford/St. Martin's Press, 2008), 60.

114. Tornel, "Relations between Texas, the United States of America and Mexico," 346.

115. *Cincinnati Daily Whigs and Commercial Intelligencer*, 19 April 1836, box 146, Samuel E. Asbury Papers, Daughters of the Republic of Texas Library, San Antonio.

116. *New York Herald*, 14 April 1836, box 2A136, Juan Nepomuceno Almonte Papers, Dolph Briscoe Center for American History, University of Texas at Austin.

117. *Grand Gulf (MS) Advertiser*, 28 April 1836.

118. *Richmond Enquirer*, 22 April 1836.

119. *New York Evening Post*, 4 April 1836, reprinted from the *New York Courier*; *Richmond Enquirer*, 26 April 1836.

120. *Cincinnati Republican and Commercial Register*, 11 May 1836, folder 147, Samuel Asbury Papers, Daughters of the Republic of Texas Library, San Antonio.

121. *Cincinnati Daily Gazette*, 8 September 1836, folder 149, Samuel E. Asbury Papers, Daughters of the Republic of Texas Library, San Antonio.

122. *Cincinnati Daily Gazette*, 8 September 1836, folder 149, Samuel E. Asbury Papers, Daughters of the Republic of Texas Library, San Antonio.

123. E. P. Gaines to David G. Burnet, 28 May 1836, box 2B159, David G. Burnet Papers, Dolph Briscoe Center for American History, University of Texas at Austin, attributing such behavior to a "John Durst and many of his disciples."

124. David G. Burnet, address to the people in eastern Texas, 18 May 1836, box 2B159, David G. Burnet Papers, Dolph Briscoe Center for American History, University of Texas at Austin.

125. Lack, *Texas Revolutionary Experience*, 100.

126. David G. Burnet, address to the citizens of Texas, 6 April 1836, box 2B159,

David G. Burnet Papers, Dolph Briscoe Center for American History, University of Texas at Austin.

127. Sam Houston and Thomas J. Rusk, address to the public, 19 April 1836, *PTR*, 4:504–5.

128. Santa Anna, "Manifesto," 21, 25.

129. E. P. Gaines to David G. Burnet, 28 May 1836, box 2B159, David G. Burnet Papers, Dolph Briscoe Center for American History, University of Texas at Austin; Lack, *Texas Revolutionary Experience*, 125–32.

130. Fowler, *Santa Anna of Mexico*, 171–72.

131. *The New-York Spectator*, 13 June 1836.

132. *Baltimore Gazette and Daily Advertiser*, 11 June 1836.

133. Fowler, *Santa Anna of Mexico*, 172–73; *New-York Spectator*, 13 June 1836.

134. *Hampshire Gazette* (Northampton, MA), 29 June 1836, reprinted from the *New York Journal*.

135. Santa Anna, "Manifesto," 30; also in Fowler, *Santa Anna of Mexico*, 176–77.

136. Santa Anna, "Manifesto," 40, 46.

137. Santa Anna, "Manifesto," 65.

138. Paul D. Lack, "Slavery in the Texas Revolution," *Southwestern Historical Quarterly* 89, no. 2 (October 1985): 181–202.

Chapter 5 · Toward a Single National Truth

1. For Mexican perceptions of the French Revolution, see Erika Pani, *Una serie de admirables acontecimientos: México y el mundo en la época de la Reforma, 1848–1867* (México City: Educación y Cultura, Asesoría y Promoción; Puebla: Benemérita Universidad Autónoma de Puebla, 2013), chap. 1.

2. José María Gutiérrez Estrada, *Carta dirigida al Escmo. Sr. Presidente de La República, sobre la necesidad de buscar en una convención el posible remedio de los males que aquejan á la República,* (Mexico City: Impreso por I. Cumplido, 1840), 36, 57–59.

3. Michael P. Costeloe, *The Central Republic in Mexico, 1835–1846: Hombres de Bien in the Age of Santa Anna* (New York: Cambridge University Press, 1993), 29–30, 66. Charles A. Hale, *Mexican Liberalism in the Age of Mora* (New Haven, CT: Yale University Press, 1968), 8.

4. Will Fowler, *Santa Anna of Mexico* (Lincoln: University of Nebraska Press, 2007), 186; Timothy E. Anna, *Forging Mexico, 1821–1835* (Lincoln: University of Nebraska Press, 1998), 218–19.

5. Mariano Otero, *Ensayo sobre el verdadero estado de la cuestion social y política que se agita en la República Mexicana* (Mexico City: Impreso por I. Cumplido, 1842), 9.

6. Otero, *Ensayo sobre el verdadero estado de la cuestion social y política que se agita en la República Mexicana*, 93.

7. Daniel Walker Howe, *The Political Culture of the American Whigs* (Chicago: University of Chicago Press, 1979), 29–34; Costeloe, *The Central Republic in Mexico*, 59. José María Luis Mora, "Discurso sobre la necesidad e importancia e la observador de las leyes," in *Obras suelta*, vol. 2 (Paris, 1837), 46, 90.

8. Costeloe, *The Central Republic in Mexico*, 212, Alamán on 17.

9. Howe, *The Political Culture of the American Whigs*, 30.

10. Howe, *The Political Culture of the American Whigs*, 20–21, 36; John Quincy

Adams in James D. Richardson, ed., *A Compilation of the Messages and Papers of the Presidents, 1789–1897*, 10 vols. (Washington, DC: Government Printing Office, 1896–1899), 2:878–82; Will Fowler, *Tornel and Santa Anna: The Writer and the Caudillo, Mexico 1795–1853* (Westport, CT: Greenwood Press, 2000), 218–30.

11. Mora, "Discurso sobre la necesidad e importancia e la observador de las leyes," 290–92.

12. Costeloe, *The Central Republic in Mexico*, 83.

13. Costeloe, *The Central Republic in Mexico*, 123–24.

14. Costeloe, *The Central Republic in Mexico*, 83–84, Webster on 84.

15. Daniel Webster, "The Completion of the Bunker Hill Monument," in *The Writings and Speeches of Daniel Webster*, vol. 1 (Boston: Little, Brown, 1903), 259–83, quotes on 273

16. Webster, "The Completion of the Bunker Hill Monument," 272–77.

17. Costeloe, *The Central Republic*, chap. 8; Fowler, *Tornel and Santa Anna*, 197–99.

18. Fowler, *Tornel and Santa Anna*, 195–96.

19. José María Tornel y Mendívil, *Discurso pronunciado por el exmo. sr. general ministro de guerra y marina don José Maria Tornel en la sesión del 12 de octubre de 1842 del Congreso constituyente* (Mexico City: Impr. de J. M. Lara, 1842), 7–8, 27; also cited in Fowler, *Tornel and Santa Anna*, 141.

20. *El Diario del Gobierno* (Mexico City), 26 April 1842; also cited in Gene M. Brack, *Mexico Views Manifest Destiny, 1821–1846: An Essay on the Mexican War* (Albuquerque: University of New Mexico Press, 1975), 104–5.

21. José María Tornel, "Relations between Texas, the United States of America, and Mexico," in *The Mexican Side of the Texas Revolution*, ed. and trans. Carlos E. Castañeda (Washington, DC: Documentary Publications, 1971), 287, 364.

22. Tornel, "Relations between Texas, the United States of America, and Mexico," 328, 369–70.

23. Tornel, *Discurso pronunciado por el exmo. sr. general ministro de guerra y marina*, 13–14, 24, 26–27; also discussed in Brack, *Mexico Views Manifest Destiny*, 105–6.

24. Richard Huzzey, *Freedom Burning: Anti-slavery and Empire in Victorian Britain* (Ithaca, NY: Cornell University Press, 2012); Matthew Karp, *This Vast Southern Empire: Slaveholders at the Helm of American Foreign Policy* (Cambridge, MA: Harvard University Press, 2016), chap. 1.

25. For Adams's role in the attempted purchase, see Robert V. Remini, *Andrew Jackson and the Course of American Empire, 1767–1821* (New York: Harper & Row, 1977), 382–86.

26. John Quincy Adams, speech before the U.S. House of Representatives, 25 May 1835, in Benjamin Lundy, *The War in Texas: A Review of Facts and Circumstances, Showing That This Contest Is a Crusade against Mexico, Set on Foot and Supported by Slaveholders, Land Speculators, &c. in order to Re-establish, Extend, and Perpetuate the System of Slavery and the Slave Trade*, 2nd ed. (Philadelphia: Printed for the publishers by Merrihew and Gunn, 1837), 34–37.

27. Tornel, "Relations between Texas, the United States of America, and Mexico," 372.

28. William E. Channing, *Letter to the Hon. Henry Clay on the Annexation of Texas to the United States* (Boston: James Munroe and Co.,1837), 1–30.

29. Channing, *Letter to the Hon. Henry Clay*, 46.
30. Channing, *Letter to the Hon. Henry Clay*, 33–45.
31. Merton L. Dillon, *Benjamin Lundy and the Struggle for Negro Freedom* (Urbana: University of Illinois Press, 1966), chaps. 2 and 6, for Lundy's view on colonization. Also see Benjamin Lundy, *Life, Travels, and Opinions of Benjamin Lundy, including His Journeys to Texas and Mexico, with a Sketch of Contemporary Events, and a Notice of the Revolution in Hayti* (Philadelphia: W. D. Parrish, 1847), chap. 22.
32. Lundy, *Life, Travels, and Opinions*, chap. 2; Dillon, *Benjamin Lundy*, chap. 1.
33. Lundy, *Life, Travels, and Opinions*, chaps. 3–5; Dillon, *Benjamin Lundy*, chap. 3.
34. Lundy, *Life, Travels, and Opinions*, 63, and for Lundy's experiences in Mexico, chaps. 9–11. Also see Dillon, *Benjamin Lundy*, chap. 10.
35. Lundy, *Life, Travels, and Opinions*, 63; Benjamin Lundy, *The Origin and True Causes of the Texas Insurrection, Commenced in the Year 1835* (Philadelphia, 1836). For more on the Slave Power thesis and Lundy's role in developing it, see Leonard L. Richards, *The Slave Power: The Free North and Southern Domination, 1780–1860* (Baton Rouge: Louisiana State University Press, 2009), 1–27.
36. Lundy, *The Origin and True Cause of the Texas Revolution*.
37. Channing, *Letter to the Hon. Henry Clay*, 13.
38. Lundy, *The War in Texas*, 10–14, quote on 14.
39. Mirabeau B. Lamar, "The Inaugural Address of Mirabeau Lamar," in *The Papers of Mirabeau Buonaparte Lamar*, ed. Charles Adam Gulick, Jr., and K. Elliott, 6 vols. (New York: AMS Press, 1973), 2:316–27. This speech is also cited extensively in Thomas Richards, Jr., *Breakaway Americas: The Unmanifest Future of the Jacksonian United States* (Baltimore: Johns Hopkins University Press, 2020), 25.
40. There is no comprehensive study of the Texas constitution. For concise summaries, see Andrew J. Torget, *Seeds of Empire: Cotton, Slavery, and the Transformation of the Texas Borderlands, 1800–1850* (Chapel Hill: University of Carolina Press, 2015),169; T. R. Fehrenbach, *Lone Star: A History of Texas and the Texans* (Cambridge, MA: Da Capo Press, 2000), 222–23.
41. Randolph B. Campbell, ed., William S. Pugsley and Marilyn P. Duncan, comps., *The Laws of Slavery in Texas: Historical Documents and Essay* (Austin: University of Texas Press, 2010), 52–53.
42. Randolph B. Campbell, *Gone to Texas: A History of the Lone Star State* (New York: Oxford University Press, 2003), 159.
43. Lamar, "Inaugural Address," 325–27.
44. Lamar, "Inaugural Address," 325–27.
45. Richards, *Breakaway Americas*, 10–11, 92, 183–84.
46. Memecum Hunt Jr., to R. A. Irion, 31 December 1837, *Diplomatic Correspondence of the Republic of Texas*, ed. George P. Garrison, 3 vols. (Washington, DC: Government Printing Office, 1908–11), 2:277–81 (hereafter *DCT*).
47. Andrés Reséndez, "Texas and the Spread of That Troublesome Secessionist Spirit," in *Secession as an International Phenomenon: From America's Civil War to Contemporary Separatist Movements*, ed. Don H. Doyle (Athens: University of Georgia Press, 2010), 193–213. While identifying the temporary and contingent nature of these movements, Reséndez still chooses to term them secessionist.
48. Richards, *Breakaway Americas*, 150–51.

49. Lanford W. Hastings, *The Emigrants' Guide to Oregon and California* (Cincinnati, 1845), 132.
50. Hubert Howe Bancroft, *History of California*, 7 vols. (San Francisco: History Company, 1884–1890), 3:470–71.
51. Richards, *Breakaway Americas*, 155.
52. Brian DeLay, *War of a Thousand Deserts: Indian Raids and the U.S.-Mexican War* (New Haven, CT: Yale University Press, 2008), 206.
53. Many northerners made an exception for Christianized tribes. See Stuart F. Voss, *On the Periphery of Nineteenth-Century Mexico: Sonora and Sinaloa, 1810–1877* (Tucson: University of Arizona Press, 1982), 90.
54. Albino Chacón, "An Account of the Chimayó Rebellion, 1837," in Janet Lecompte, *Rebellion in Río Arriba* (Albuquerque: University of New Mexico Press, 1985), 91. Also cited in DeLay, *War of a Thousand Deserts*, 167.
55. Proclamation of Juan José Esquibel in Lacompte, *Rebellion in Río Arriba*, 20.
56. Letter of Manuel Armijo, 11 October 1873, in Lecompte, *Rebellion in Río Arriba*, 139.
57. Proclamation of Manuel Armijo, 7 January 1838, in Lecompte, *Rebellion in Río Arriba*, 143.
58. For a full account of the rebellion, see DeLay, *War of a Thousand Deserts*, 168–72.
59. DeLay, *War of a Thousand Deserts*, 168–72.
60. Andrés Reséndez, *Changing National Identities at the Frontier: Texas and New Mexico, 1800–1850* (New York: Cambridge University Press, 2005), 181.
61. Ignacio Zúñiga to Anastasio Bustamante, in Voss, *On the Periphery of Nineteenth-Century Mexico*, 96; also cited in DeLay, *War of a Thousand Deserts*, 172.
62. Pronunciamiento autónomo de Sonora, 16 September 1837.
63. Voss, *On the Periphery of Nineteenth-Century Mexico*, 97; DeLay, *War of a Thousand Deserts*, 173.
64. Plan de independencia y reconciliación para los sonorenses, 1 February 1841.
65. Voss, *On the Periphery of Nineteenth-Century Mexico*, 101–2; DeLay, *War of a Thousand Deserts*, 173–74.
66. DeLay, *War of a Thousand Deserts*, 174.
67. Antonio Canales Rosillo to President *Mirabeau Buonaparte* Lamar, 7 December 1838, *DCT*, 1:430–31; also see Joseph Milton Nance, *After San Jacinto: The Texas-Mexican Frontier, 1836–1841* (Austin: University of Texas Press, 1963), 172–78.
68. *Weekly Houston Telegraph*, 10 April 1839.
69. Nance, *After San Jacinto*, 192–93.
70. Nance, *After San Jacinto*, 194–95.
71. DeLay, *War of a Thousand Deserts*, 177–82, quotes on 179 and 181; also discussed and cited in Nance, *After San Jacinto*, 256–57.
72. DeLay, *War of a Thousand Deserts*, 182.
73. "Carta del Gobernador Santiago Méndez al General Antonio López de Santa Anna, relative a la incorporación de Yucatán a la nación mexicana, 29 August 1843" in *Documentos históricos peninsulares*, ed. Michel Antochiw, vol. 1 (Mérida: Instituto de Cultura de Yucatán, 1995), 3–18; Terry Rugeley, *Rebellion Now and Forever: Mayas, Hispanics, and Caste War Violence in Yucatán, 1800–1880* (Stanford, CA: Stanford University Press, 2009), 39.

74. Terry Rugeley, *Yucatán's Maya Peasantry and the Origins of the Caste War* (Austin: University of Texas Press, 1996), xi–xiii.

75. Terry Rugeley, "The Brief, Glorious History of the Yucatecan Republic: Secession and Violence in Southeastern Mexico, 1836–1848," in Doyle, *Secession as an International Phenomenon*, 216.

76. Rugeley, *Yucatán's Mayan Peasantry*, xiv.

77. For a description of Yucatán independence and the subsequent celebration, see *El Espíritu del Siglo*, 24 May 1841, xi/481.3/1690, Archivo Histórico de la Secretaria de la Defensa Nacional, Mexico City; also see the account in Rugeley, "The Yucatán Republic," 217.

78. James Treat to Mirabeau Buonaparte Lamar, 29 February 1840, *DCT*, 2:579–80.

79. Mirabeau Buonaparte Lamar to the Senate, 1 November 1840, *Papers of Mirabeau Buonaparte Lamar*, 3:464–70.

80. Mirabeau Buonaparte Lamar to the governor of Yucatán (Santiago Imán), 20 July 1841, *DCT*, 1:792–93.

81. Miguel Brabachano to Mirabeau Buonaparte Lamar, 24 August 1841, *DCT*, 1:793–94.

82. *El Espíritu del Siglo*, 24 May 1841, xi/481.3/1690, Archivo Histórico de la Secretaria de la Defensa Nacional, Mexico City.

83. John Lloyd Stephens, *Incidents of Travel in Yucatán*, ed. Victor Wolfgang von Hagen, 2 vols. (Norman: University of Oklahoma Press, 1962), 1:53.

84. Rugeley, "A Brief, Glorious History," 220–23.

85. Stephens, *Incidents*, 2:301.

86. Stephens, *Incidents*, 2:219.

87. José Urrea to Valentín Gómez Farías, 6 April 1840, folder 47A, Valentín Gómez Farías Papers, Nettie Lee Benson Latin American Collection, University of Texas Libraries, Austin.

88. Will Fowler, *Independent Mexico: The Pronunciamiento in the Age of Santa Anna, 1821–1858* (Lincoln: University of Nebraska Press, 2016), 175–76.

89. Valentín Gómez Farías quoted in Brack, *Mexico Views Manifest Destiny*, 120.

90. Valentín Gómez Farías to Thomas F. M. Kinney, 7 October 1839, item no. GF 606 F 47A, Valentín Gómez Farías Papers, Nettie Lee Benson Latin American Collection, University of Texas Libraries, Austin.

91. Bernard E. Bee to James Webb, 24 May 1839, *DCT*, 1:447–49.

92. Richards, *Breakaway Americas*, 232–33.

93. A. James Hook to Lord Palmerston, 30 April 1841, *British Diplomatic Correspondence concerning the Republic of Texas, 1838–1846*, ed. Ephraim Douglass Adams (Austin: Texas State Historical Association, 1918), 29–39.

94. A. James Hook to Lord Palmerston, 30 April 1841, *British Diplomatic Correspondence concerning the Republic of Texas*, 29–39.

95. Karp, *This Vast Southern Empire*, 12.

96. Powhatan Ellis to John Forsythe, 19 May 1836, *Diplomatic Correspondence of the United States*, ed. William R. Manning, vol. 8 (Washington, DC: Carnegie Endowment for International Peace, 1937), 326–27.

97. John C. Calhoun, "Remarks on the Independence of Texas," *The Papers of John C. Calhoun*, ed. Clyde N. Wilson, vol. 13 (Columbia: Published by the University of South

Carolina Press for the South Caroliniana Society, 1980), 198. For slavery's significance to the British economy, see Eric Williams, *Capitalism and Slavery* (Chapel Hill: University of North Carolina Press, 1943), 81–82.

98. Karp, *This Vast Southern Empire*, 10–31.

99. Karp, *This Vast Southern Empire*, 83.

100. Henry Wise, speech in the House of Representatives, 13 April 1842, cited in Frederick Merk, *Slavery and the Annexation of Texas* (New York: Knopf, 1972), 193; also discussed in Karp, *This Vast Southern Empire*, 84.

101. Green cited in Karp, *This Vast Southern Empire*, 86.

102. Joel H. Silbey, *Storm over Texas: The Annexation Controversy and the Road to Civil War* (New York: Oxford University Press, 2005), 29.

103. Karp, *This Vast Southern Empire*, 14.

104. *Letter of Mr. Walker, of Mississippi, Relative to the Annexation of Texas* (Washington, DC: Printed at the Globe Office, 1844), 16, 18–19, 26. It is also discussed in Sam W. Haynes, *Unfinished Revolution: The Early American Republic in a British World* (Charlottesville: University of Virginia Press, 2010), 242.

105. Robert J. Walker, *Letter Relative to the Annexation of Texas* (Philadelphia: Mifflin and Parry, 1844), 3, 5, 9–10, 14..

106. Richards, *Breakaway Americas*, 214–15; Torget, *Seeds of Empire*, 219–22, 235–49.

107. Karp, *This Vast Southern Empire*, 92.

108. Karp, *This Vast Southern Empire*, 93–94.

109. Calhoun cited in Karp, *This Vast Southern Empire*, 95.

110. Michael F. Holt, *The Rise and Fall of the American Whig Party: Jacksonian Politics and the Onset of the Civil War* (New York: Oxford University Press, 1999), 176–77, 190, 196.

111. Richards, *Breakaway Americas*, 225.

112. Richards, *Breakaway Americas*, 231–33, Polk on 233.

113. George Rathbun quoted in Karp, *This Vast Southern Empire*, 98.

114. John Quincy Adams, *The Diary of John Quincy Adams, 1794–1845*, ed. Allan Nevins (New York: Longmans, Green and Co., 1929), 570–71.

115. John Quincy Adams, 26 March 1842, in *Memoirs of John Quincy Adams*, ed. Charles Francis Adams, vol. 11 (Philadelphia: L. B. Lippincott & Co., 1874), 117.

116. José María Tornel, "Relations between Texas, the United States, and Mexico," in *The Mexican Side of the Texas Revolution*, ed. and trans. Carlos E. Castañeda (Washington, DC: Documentary Publications, 1971), 346.

117. John O'Sullivan, "Annexation: 1845," in *United States Magazine and Democratic Review* 17, no. 1 (July–August 1845): 5–10.

118. O'Sullivan, "Annexation: 1845," 5–10.

119. Fowler, *Santa Anna of Mexico*, 235–36.

120. Fowler, *Santa Anna of Mexico*, 247.

121. Valentín Gómez Farías, "Federación y Téjas, artículo publicado en la Voz del Pueblo, número 29. Reimpreso con algunas notas adiciones," 3 May 1845, Mexico City.

122. Brack, *Mexico Views Manifest Destiny*, 141.

123. Brack, *Mexico Views Manifest Destiny*, 138–41.

124. Francisco Flores Alatorre, *Voto particular presentado por un individuo de la Comisión especial de la Cámara de diputados, sobre autorizar al gobierno para oir las proposiciones*

que se le han hecho relativas á Tejas (Mexico City: Impreso en papel mexicano por J. M. Lara, 1845).

125. Fowler, *Santa Anna of Mexico*, 247.
126. Manifiesto y plan de San Luis Potosí, 14 December 1845.
127. Fowler, *Santa Anna of Mexico*, 256–57.
128. James K. Polk, "War Message to Congress," 11 May 1846, in Richardson, *A Compilation of the Messages and Papers of the Presidents of the United States*, 4:437, 441–42.

Chapter 6 • Sovereignty, Secession, and the Decline of the Old Federalism

1. Ralph Waldo Emerson, *Journals and Miscellaneous Notebooks*, ed. William Gilman et al. (Cambridge, MA: Harvard University Press, 1960–1982), 9:430–31.
2. John Tutino, *The Mexican Heartland: How Communities Shaped Capitalism, a Nation, and World History, 1500–2000* (Princeton, NJ: Princeton University Press, 2018), 196.
3. Peter Guardino, *The Dead March: A History of the Mexican-American War* (Cambridge, MA: Harvard University Press, 2017), 5.
4. *El Tiempo* (Mexico City), 1 January 1846.
5. *El Siglo Diez y Nueve* (Mexico City), 13 May 1844.
6. *El Siglo Diez y Nueve* (Mexico City), 20 December 1845.
7. *La Voz del Pueblo* (Mexico City), 29 March 1845.
8. Valentín Gómez Farías cited in Gene M. Brack, *Mexico Views Manifest Destiny, 1821–1846* (Albuquerque: University of New Mexico Press, 1975), 137–38.
9. Sam W. Haynes, *James K. Polk and the Expansionist Impulse*, 3rd ed. (New York: Pearson Longman, 2006), 115–25, Manuel Peña y Peña on 124.
10. Valentín Gómez Farías to Francisco Vital Fernández, 4 June 1845, item no. GF 1194 F 48, Valentín Gómez Farías Papers, Nettie Lee Benson Latin American Collection, University of Texas Libraries, Austin.
11. *El Tiempo* (Mexico City), 31 January 1836.
12. Mariano Arista cited in Brack, *Mexico Views Manifest Destiny*, 155.
13. *El Tiempo* (Mexico City), 4 February 1846.
14. Valentín Gómez Farías to Julio Uhink, 20 April 1844, item no. GF 995 F 47B, Valentín Gómez Farías Papers, Nettie Lee Benson Latin American Collection, University of Texas Libraries, Austin.
15. *El Mosquito Mexicano* (Mexico City), 31 January and 3 February 1843; also quoted in Brack, *Mexico Views Manifest Destiny*, 120.
16. Guardino, *The Dead March*, 218–19.
17. *El Siglo Diez y Nueve* (Mexico City), 13 May 1844.
18. Pedro Ampudia, circular, 2 April 1846, cited in full in Peter F. Stevens, *The Rogue's March: John Riley and the St. Patrick's Battalion, 1846–48* (Washington, DC: Brassey's, 1999), 82.
19. Pedro Ampudia, "Mexicans to Catholic Irishmen," in Stevens, *The Rogues March*, 221–23.
20. Stevens, *The Rogues March*, 229.
21. George B. McClellan, *The Mexican War Diary and Correspondence of George B. McClellan*, ed. Thomas W. Cutrer (Baton Rouge: Louisiana State University Press, 2009), 49.

22. Franklin Smith, *Mexican War Journal of Captain Franklin Smith*, ed. Joseph E. Chance (Jackson: University Press of Mississippi, 1991), 13.

23. Thomas Barclay in *Volunteers: The Mexican War Journals of Private Richard Coulter and Sargeant Thomas Barclay*, ed. Allen Peskin (Kent, OH: Kent State University Press, 1991), 96

24. Barclay, *Volunteers*, 119.

25. James M. McCaffrey, *Army of Manifest Destiny: The American Soldier in the Mexican War* (New York: New York University Press, 1992), 107.

26. Barclay, *Volunteers*, 97.

27. Carlos María de Bustamante, *El nuevo Bernal Díaz del Castillo, ó sea, Historia de la invasión de los Anglo-Americans en México*, vol. 2 (Mexico City: Impr. de V. García Torres, 1847), 138.

28. Guardino, *The Dead March*, 89–90.

29. Samuel Chamberlain, *My Confession: Recollections of a Rogue*, ed. William H. Goetzmann (Austin: Texas State Historical Association, 1996), 176.

30. J. Jacob Oswandel, *Notes of the Mexican War, 1846–1848*, Timothy D. Johnson and Nathaniel Cheairs Hughes, Jr. (Knoxville: University of Tennessee Press, 2010), 269.

31. Barclay, *Volunteers*, 184–85.

32. Barclay, *Volunteers*, 179, 187, 192.

33. Daniel Walker Howe, *What Hath God Wrought: The Transformation of America, 1815–1848* (New York: Oxford University Press, 2007), 751.

34. *Henry Clay's Advice to His Countrymen Relative to the War with Mexico* (New York: H. R. Robinson, 1847); also cited in Amy S. Greenberg, *A Wicked War: Polk, Clay, Lincoln, and the 1846 U.S. Invasion of Mexico* (New York: Alfred A. Knopf, 2012), 229–32.

35. *Life and Speeches of Thomas Corwin: Orator, Lawyer and Statesman*, ed. Josiah Morrow (Cincinnati, OH: W. H. Anderson, 1896), 96, 379.

36. Frederick Douglass, "The War with Mexico," *North Star*, 21 January 1848.

37. John C. Calhoun, in Cong. Globe, 30th Cong., 1st Sess. 98 (1848), quoted at length in Frederick Merk, *Manifest Destiny and Mission in American History* (Cambridge: Harvard University Press, 1995), 162–63.

38. John C. Calhoun, 9 February 1847, in United States, Congress, *Abridgement of the Debates of Congress, from 1789 to 1856*, vol. 16 (New York: D. Appleton and Company, 1861), 49–51, 56–60.

39. Guardino, *The Dead March*, 324.

40. Pedro Santino, *Mexicans at Arms: Puro Federalists and the Politics of War, 1845–1848*, (Fort Worth: Texas Christian University Press, 1996), 213–21 quote on 219.

41. Santoni, *Mexicans at Arms*, 201–211.

42. Manuel Crescencio Rejón, *Observaciones del diputado saliente Manuel Crescencio Rejon, contra los tratados de paz, firmados en la ciudad Guadalup el 2 del proximo pasado febrero, precididas de la parte histórica relativa a la cuestion originaria* (Querétaro: Impr. de J. M Lara, 1848), 1 and 32. For summaries of Rejón's letter, see Santino, *Mexicans at Arms*, 227, and Richard Griswold del Castillo, *The Treaty of Guadalupe Hidalgo: A Legacy of Conflict* (Norman: University of Oklahoma Press, 1990), 49–51.

43. Suprema Corte de la Nación, "Breve impugancion a las observaciones acerca del parecer fiscal y acuerdo de la Suprema Corte, sobre el ocurso que le dirigieron once

señores disputado reclamando la inconstitucionalidad de los Tratados de paz celebrados con el gobierno Anglo-Americano," Mexico City, 10 July 1848 in Algunos documentos sobre el tratado de Gudalupe y la situación de México durante la invasion americana, (Mexico City: Publicaiones de la Secretaria de las Relaciones Exteriores: 1930); Santoni, *Mexicnas at Arms*, 229.

44. Griswold del Castillo, *The Treaty of Guadalupe Hidalgo*, 51–52.

45. Winfield Scott to Headquarters of the Army, report no. 42, 6 January 1848, in Timothy D. Johnson, ed., *Memoirs of Lieut.-General Winfield Scott* (Knoxville: University of Tennessee Press, 2015), 283–84, 287.

46. Griswold del Castillo, *The Treaty of Guadalupe Hidalgo*, 34–38.

47. Winfield Scott to Headquarters of the Army, report no. 41, 25 December 1847, in Johnson, *Memoirs of Lieut.-General Winfield Scott*, 281–83.

48. Zachary Taylor, inaugural address, 5 March 1849, in *A Compilation of the Messages and Papers of the Presidents, 1789–1897*, comp. James D. Richardson, 10 vols. (Washington, DC: Government Printing Office, 1896–99), 5:4–6.

49. James K. Polk, third annual message, 7 December 1847, in Richardson, *A Compilation of the Messages and Papers of the Presidents*, 4:532–33.

50. Polk, third annual message, 7 December 1847, in Richardson, *A Compilation of the Messages and Papers of the Presidents*, 4:532–64.

51. Douglass, "The War with Mexico," 2.

52. Stephen Douglas, in Cong. Globe, 31st Cong., 1st Sess., app., 720 (1849).

53. Speech by Lajos Kossuth, in Jackson Democratic Association, *Proceedings at the Banquet of the Jackson Democratic Association, Washington, Eighth of January, 1852* (Washington, DC: Congressional Globe Office, 1852), 4.

54. Speech by Lewis Cass, in Jackson Democratic Association, *Proceedings at the Banquet of the Jackson Democratic Association*, 7.

55. Speech by Stephen Douglas, in Jackson Democratic Association, *Proceedings at the Banquet of the Jackson Democratic Association*, 9.

56. Statement by Andrew Jackson Donelson, in Jackson Democratic Association, *Proceedings at the Banquet of the Jackson Democratic Association*, 12–14.

57. Douglas, in Jackson Democratic Association, *Proceedings at the Banquet of the Jackson Democratic Association*, 10.

58. Stephen Douglas, in Cong. Globe, 33rd Cong., 1st Sess., app., 278 (1853).

59. Douglas, in Cong. Globe, 33rd Cong., 1st Sess., app., 337–38 (1853).

60. Richard Broadhead, Cong. Globe, 33rd Cong., 1st Sess., app., 249 (1853); also cited in Michael A. Morrison, *Slavery and the American West: The Eclipse of Manifest Destiny and the Coming of the Civil War* (Chapel Hill: University of North Carolina Press, 1997), 144.

61. Richard Broadhead, Cong. Globe, 33rd Cong., 1st Sess., app., 1023.

62. Stephen A. Douglas, *Letter of Senator Douglas in Reply to the Editor of the State Capital Reporter, Concord, N.H.* (Washington, DC: Printed at the Sentinel Office, 1854), as in Morrison, *Slavery and the American West*, 146–47.

63. Charles Sumner, *The Demands of Freedom: Speech of Hon. Charles Sumner, in the Senate of the United States, on His Motion to Repeal the Fugitive Slave Bill, 23 February 1855* (Washington, DC: Printed by Buell & Blanchard). For a summary of the origin and debate around the 1850 Fugitive Slave Act and discussion of Sumner's speech, see Michael

F. Conlin, *The Constitutional Origins of the America Civil War* (Cambridge: Cambridge University Press, 2019), 62–68.

64. Henry Mayer, *All on Fire: William Lloyd Garrison and the Abolition of Slavery* (New York: W. W. Norton and Co., 1998), 143.

65. José María Tornel y Menivil, *Discurso pronunciado en la alameda de la ciudad de México en el día 27 de septiembre de 1850* (Mexico City: Imp. De I. Cumplido, 1850), 1, 12; also cited in Will Fowler, *Tornel and Santa Anna: The Writer and the Caudillo, 1795–1853* (Westport, CT: Greenwood Press, 2000), 252.

66. *La Palanca*, 3 May 1849, cited in Will Fowler, *Independent Mexico: The Pronunciamiento in the Age of Santa Anna, 1821–1858* (Lincoln: University of Nebraska Press, 2016), 194–95, and Fowler, *Tornel and Santa Anna*, 253.

67. *El Tiempo* (Mexico City), 26 January 1846.

68. *El Tiempo* (Mexico City), 4 February 1846.

69. *El Tiempo* (Mexico City), 26 February 1846.

70. Lucas Alamán cited in Fowler, *Independent Mexico*, 195.

71. *La Palanca* cited in Will Fowler, *Santa Anna of Mexico* (Lincoln: University of Nebraska Press, 2007), 292.

72. *La Palanca*, 19 June 1849; 5 June 1849; 26 May 1849; all cited in Fowler, *Tornel and Santa Anna*, 252–54.

73. Fowler, *Santa Anna of Mexico*, 292–96.

74. "Carta de Lucas Alamán a Santa Anna," in *El pensamiento de la reacción Mexicana*, vol. 1, *Historia documental 1810–1859*, ed. Gastón García Cantú (Mexico City: Universidad Nacional Autónoma de México, 1986), 313–16, quotes on 314 and 315, translations from Eric Van Young, *A Life Together: Lucas Alamán and Mexico, 1792–1853* (New Haven, CT: Yale University Press, 2021), 642–43.

75. Van Young, *A Life Together*, 643.

76. Antonio López de Santa Anna, "Bases para la administración de la República hasta la promulgación de la Constitución," 22 April 1853. The promulgation is discussed at length in Van Young, *A Life Together*, 639–40. The original is in folder 116, file 2, Archivo General de Nación.

77. Jesus Reyes Heroles, *El liberalism Méxicano*, 3 vols. (Mexico City: Fondo de Cultura Económica, 1975), 2:340–48.

78. *El Orden* (Mexico City), translated and reprinted in the *Daily Picayune*, 16 July 1853.

79. Fowler, *Santa Anna of Mexico*, 292–303.

80. Paul Neff Garber, *The Gadsden Treaty* (Philadelphia: Press of the University of Pennsylvania, 1923), 85.

81. James Gadsden to William L. Marcy, *Diplomatic Correspondence of the United States: Inter-American Affairs, 1831–1860*, ed. William R. Manning, 12 vols. (Washington, DC: Carnegie Endowment for International Peace, 1932–1939), 5 September 1853, 9:607–9; 18 September 1853, 9:616–17 (hereafter *DCIAA*).

82. Gadsden to Marcy, *DCIAA*, 3 October 1853, 9:617–19; Garber, *The Gadsden Treaty*, 87.

83. Gadsden to Marcy, *DCIAA*, 11 October 1853, 9:621–23. On the other hand, Gadsden conceded that a treaty awarding the United States more territory "will be the signal for a successful revolution against him."

84. Juan Nepomuceno Almonte to Marcy, *DCIAA*, 22 October 1853, 9:640–47. These demands were also expressed by Manuel Díaz de Bonilla in an earlier letter to James Gadsden, *DCIAA*, 18 October 1853, 9:625–40.

85. Garber, *The Gadsden Treaty*, 91.

86. James Gadsden to Manuel Díaz de Bonilla, 14 November 1853, *DCIAA*, 9:650–63.

87. Fowler, *Santa Anna of Mexico*, 305–8.

88. *Weekly Herald* (New York City), 11 February 1854.

89. Garber, *The Gadsden Treaty*, 131–34.

90. Garber, *The Gadsden Treaty*, 134

91. James Gadsden to Manuel Díaz de Bonilla, *DCIAA*, 6 June 1854, 9:713.

92. James Gadsden to William L. Marcy Marcy, *DCIAA*, 21 May 1854, 9:708.

93. Santa Anna quoted in Richard A. Johnson, *The Mexican Revolution of Ayutla, 1854–1855* (Rock Island, IL: Augustana College Library, 1939), 37.

94. *El Rayo Federal* (Mexico City), 14 May 1855, file 46, folder 11, Secretaria de Relaciones Exteriores, Mexico City.

95. Eric H. Walther, *The Fire-Eaters* (Baton Rouge: Louisiana State University Press, 1992), chap. 1.

96. Walther, *The Fire-Eaters*, chap. 1, Tucker quoted on page 44 and 46.

97. Mirabeau Buonaparte Lamar, "Address to the Southern Commercial Convention," January 1855, in *The Papers of Mirabeau Buonaparte Lamar*, 6 vols. (New York: AMS Press, 1973), 6:329–30.

98. J. M. White to Mirabeau Lamar, 1 June 1839, *The Papers of Mirabeau Buonaparte Lamar*, 3:10.

99. *Houston Telegraph*, 22 November 1849. For excerpts from the petition of Santa Fe's (mostly Hispanic) residents to Congress, see *Daily National Intelligencer* (Washington, DC) 7 November 1849. They requested permission to elect delegates to a General Convention that would be tasked with organizing a suitable government and electing a representative to Washington.

100. *The Republic* (Washington, DC), 10 January 1850, reprinted from the *Austin Gazette*.

101. Mark Joseph Stegmaier, *Texas, New Mexico, and the Compromise of 1850: Boundary Dispute and Sectional Crisis* (Ann Arbor: University of Michigan Press, 1996), 92.

102. *Daily Union* (Washington, DC), 3 January 1850.

103. *Daily National Intelligencer*, 1 March 1850.

104. For a discussion of the process by which New Mexicans declared statehood and authored their constitution, see Stegmaier, *Texas, New Mexico, and the Compromise of 1850*, chap. 6. A copy of the proposed New Mexico constitution was published in the *Daily National Intelligencer*, 7 July 1850.

105. *Houston Telegraph*, 13 June 1850.

106. *Democratic Telegraph and Texas Register*, 20 June 1850.

107. *National Era* (Washington, DC), 27 June 1850.

108. Alexander Stephens, *Daily National Intelligencer*, 4 July 1850, reprinted from the *Daily Journal of Commerce* (San Francisco), 3 July 1850.

109. *Daily National Intelligencer*, 18 July 1850.

110. *Texian Advocate*, 18 July 1850.

111. *Texian Advocate*, 14 August 1850.

112. Henry Clay, in Cong. Globe, 31st Cong., 1st Sess. 245–46 (1850).

113. Stegmaier, *Texas, New Mexico, and the Compromise of 1850*, 206–10.

114. David M. Potter, *The Impending Crisis: America before the Civil War, 1848–1861* (New York: Harper Perennial, 2011), 199–224.

115. Don E. Fehrenbacher, *The Dred Scott Case: Its Significance in American Law and Politics* (New York: Oxford University Press, 1978), 377–79; Potter, *The Impending Crisis*, 267–96.

116. Eric Foner, *Free Soil, Free Labor, Free Men: The Ideology of the Republican Party before the Civil War* (New York: Oxford University Press, 1995) 73, 85.

117. Stephen A. Douglas, "Homecoming Speech at Chicago," 9 July 1858, in *Political Debates between Abraham Lincoln and Stephen A. Douglas in the Celebrated Campaign of 1858 in Illinois* (Cleveland: O. S. Hubbell and Co., 1895), 10–25.

118. Abraham Lincoln, "Speech to the Republican State Convention," 17 June 1858, in *Political Debates between Abraham Lincoln and Stephen A. Douglas*, 109.

119. Stephen A. Douglas, "Speech of Senator Douglas," 17 July 1858, in *Political Debates between Abraham Lincoln and Stephen A. Douglas in the Celebrated Campaign of 1858 in Illinois*, 74–100.

120. "Second Joint Debate at Freeport," 27 August 1858, in *Political Debates between Abraham Lincoln and Stephen A. Douglas in the Celebrated Campaign of 1858 in Illinois*, 123–95, Lincoln on 166, Douglas on 176.

121. Greg Maxcy, *An Appeal to the States Rights Party of South Carolina: In Several Letters on the Present Condition of Public Affairs* (Columbia, SC: Printed at the Office of the Southern Guardian, 1858); also cited in Manisha Sinha, *The Counterrevolution of Slavery: Politics and Ideology in Antebellum South Carolina* (Chapel Hill: University of North Carolina Press, 2000), 193.

122. This was a view shared by South Carolinian politician and proslavery ideologue William Harper. He attacked the declaration for its "well sounding but unmeaning verbiage of natural equality and inalienable rights" and wondered if it was "not palpably nearer the truth to say that no man was ever born free, and that no two men were ever born equal?" See William Harper, "Memoir in Slavery," in *The Ideology of Slavery: Proslavery Thought in the Antebellum South, 1830–1860*, ed. Drew Gilpin Faust (Baton Rouge: Louisiana State University Press, 1981), 78–135, quote on 83; Sinha, *The Counterrevolution of Slavery*, 221–54.

123. Louis T. Wigfall, "Speech of Hon. L. T. Wigfall of Texas on Relations of the States Delivered in the Senate of the United States, 22 and 23 May 1858," (Printed by Lemuel Towers), 6 and 7.

124. Allen C. Guelzo, *Lincoln and Douglas: The Debates That Defined America* (New York: Simon & Schuster, 2008), 296.

125. Robert Barnwell Rhett, "Speech of Hon. R. B. Rhett, Delivered at Grahamville, SC, July 4, 1859," Charleston, 1859.

126. William Lowndes Yancy, "Speech of the Hon. William L. Yancy, of Alabama, Delivered in the National Democratic Convention, Charleston, April 28th, 1860: From the Report of the 'Charleston Mercury,'" from the *Charleston Mercury*, HathiTrust, https://babel.hathitrust.org/cgi/pt?id=hvd.32044011713724&seq=5.

127. *Official Proceedings of the Democratic National Convention, held in 1860, at*

Charleston and Baltimore: Proceedings at Charleston, April 23–May 3 (Cleveland: Nevin's Print, 1860), 57–60.

128. Douglas R. Egerton, *Year of Meteors: Stephen Douglas, Abraham Lincoln, and the Election that Brought on the Civil War* (New York: Bloomsbury Press, 2010), 11.

129. Jefferson Davis, "Farewell Address," 21 January 1861, *Papers of Jefferson Davis*, ed. Lynda Lasswell Crist and Mary Seaton Dix, vol. 7 (Baton Rouge: Louisiana State University Press, 1992), 18–22. For a discussion of the Confederate understanding of citizenship, see Stephanie McCurry, *Confederate Reckoning: Power and Politics in the Civil War South* (Cambridge, MA: Harvard University Press, 2010), 11–37.

130. James DeBow, *The Right of Peaceful Secession* (Charleston: Evans and Cogswell, 1860), 14 and 15.

131. Louis T. Wigfall, *Speech of Hon. Louis T. Wigfall, in Reply to Mr. Douglas and on Mr. Powell's Resolution. Delivered in the Senate of the United States, Dec. 11th and 12th, 1860* (Washington, DC: Printed by Lemuel Towers, 1860), quotes from 12, 13, and 31, https://texashistory.unt.edu/ark:/67531/metapth498862/.

132. "South Carolina's Ordinance of Secession," in *American History Leaflets: Colonial and Constitutional. No. 12, Ordinances of Secession and Other Documents, 1860–61*, ed. Albert Bushnell Hart and Edward Channing (New York: Parker P. Simmons Co., 1917), 3–6.

133. "South Carolina's Ordinance of Secession," in Hart and Channing, *American History Leaflets: Colonial and Constitutional. No. 12, Ordinances of Secession and Other Documents, 1860–61*, 5.

134. Hart and Channing, *American History Leaflets: Colonial and Constitutional. No. 12, Ordinances of Secession and Other Documents, 1860–61*, South Carolina, 6–8; Alabama, 11; Texas, 15.

135. McCurry, *Confederate Reckoning*, 1–2.

136. Alexander H. Stephens, "The Cornerstone of the Confederacy," in *The Rebellion Record*, ed. Frank Moore, vol. 1 (New York: G. P. Putnam, 1861–1868), 45–46.

Chapter 7 · Ayutla, Antislavery, and the Rise of the New Liberalism

1. For studies addressing the comparative political transformations of Mexico and the United States at mid-century, see Erika Pani, *Una serie admirables acontecimientos: México y el mundo en la época de la Reforma, 1848–1867* (Mexico City: Educación y Cultura, Asesoría y Promoción; Puebla, México: Benemérita Universidad Autónoma de Puebla, 2013); also see Erika Pani, "Constitución, ciudadanía, y guerra civil: México y los Estados Unidos en la década de 1860," in *El poder y la sangre: guerra, estado y nación en la década de 1860*, ed. Guillermo Palacios and Erika Pani (Mexico City: Colegio de México, Centro de Estudios Históricos, 2014); and Thomas Bender, "Construyendo una nación: Estados Unidos. De Unión a Estado-Nación," in Palacios and Pani, *El poder y la sangre*; Thomas Bender, *A Nation among Nations: America's Place in World History* (New York: Hill and Wang, 2006), chap. 3. For the definitive work on the rise of the Republican Party, see Erica Foner, *Free Soil, Free Labor, Free Men: The Ideology of the Republican Party before the Civil War* (Oxford: Oxford University Press, 1995).

2. For definitive studies of the Reforma, see Richard N. Sinkin, *The Mexican Reform, 1855–1876: A Study in Liberal Nation-Building* (Austin: Institute of Latin American Studies, University of Texas; distributed by University of Texas Press, 1979), 3 and 9, and for a cogent analysis of the Reforma leadership, chap. 3; Edmundo O'Gorman, "Prece-

dentes y sentido de la revolución de Ayutla," *Secuencia: Revista de historia y ciencias sociales* 16 (January–April 1990): 63–96; Jesús Reyes Heroles, "Premio" in *El liberalism mexicano*, vol. 3 (Mexico City: Universidad Nacional de México, 1961). For a brief description of the Revolution of Ayutla and the events of 1855 to 1857, see Will Fowler, *Independent Mexico: The Pronunciamiento in the Age of Santa Anna, 1821–1858* (Lincoln: University of Nebraska, 2016), 228–34.

3. For a cogent discussion of the Republican Party's ideas and their relationship to other threads of liberal thought in the United States, especially radical abolitionism, see Foner, *Free Soil, Free Labor, Free Men*, prologue and chap. 1.

4. Will Fowler, *Santa Anna of Mexico* (Lincoln: University of Nebraska Press, 2007), 293.

5. Will Fowler, *Santa Anna*, 292, 306–9.

6. Plan de Ayutla, 1 March 1854, reprinted in Felipe Tena Ramírez, *Leyes fundamentales de México, 1808–1957* (Mexico City: Editorial Porrúa, 1957), 492–94; see also, Fowler, *Independent Mexico*, 228–29; Sinkin, *The Mexican Reform*, 75–76.

7. The first article of the Organic Provisional Statute, the governing document of the provisional government issued in May 1856, stated that the Mexican nation "is and always will be one, indivisible, and independent." While this precise language did not make it into the final draft of the constitution, other clauses designed to preserve its territorial integrity did. See Ramírez, *Leyes*, 499.

8. Plan de Acapulco, 11 March 1854, in Ramírez, *Leyes fundamentales de México*, 494–99; also see Fowler, *Independent Mexico*, 229; Sinkin, *The Mexican Reform*, 76.

9. Fowler, *Independent Mexico*, 231–32.

10. Sinkin, *The Mexican Reform*, chap. 3.

11. Ramírez, *Leyes fundamentales de México*, 528–29, 541, 553.

12. José María Lafragua cited in Sinkin, *The Mexican Reform*, 56.

13. Reyes Heroles *El liberalism mexicano*, xii, wrote, "The federal idea of 1824 . . . was not even adopted by our liberals."

14. Ramírez, *Leyes fundamentales de México*, 542.

15. Sinkin, *The Mexican Reform*, 72.

16. Ramírez, *Leyes fundamentales de México*, 541.

17. Ramírez, *Leyes fundamentales de México*, 534, 541.

18. Ramírez, *Leyes fundamentales de México*, 554–55.

19. Ramírez, *Leyes fundamentales de México*, 529.

20. *Consideraciones de la situación política y social de la República Mexicana, en el año 1847* (Mexico City: Impreso Valdes y Redondas, 1848), 19, 42–43.

21. For a full transcript of the 1857 constitution, see Ramírez, *Leyes fundamentales de México*, 554–73.

22. Brian Hamnett, *Juárez* (New York: Longman, 1994), 96–98. Sinkin explains that the law originally only targeted civil cases, allowing fueros to hear the criminal cases of consenting defendants. For a discussion of the debate and controversy surrounding article 15, see Sinkin, *The Mexican Reform*, 116–31.

23. Melchor Ocampo, "Respuesta quinta a la impugnación de la representación, 1851," *Obras completas*, vol. 1, *Polémicas religiosas* (Mexico City: F. Vázquez, 1900), 320 (reprint).

24. For Arriaga's protest and more on the debate, see Francisco Zarco, *Historia del*

Congreso extraordinario constituyente, 1856–1857 (Mexico City: Colegio de México, 1956), 1220–24.

25. Ramírez, *Leyes fundamentales de México*, 555.

26. For the full text of the final draft, see Ramírez, *Leyes fundamentales de México*, 606–29.

27. Sinkin, *The Mexican Reform*, 131.

28. William H. Seward, *The Works of William H. Seward*, ed. George E. Baker, vol. 4 (Boston: Houghton, Mifflin and Company, 1884), 302 and 272 (HathiTrust). A portion of this passage is also quoted in Foner, *Free Soil, Free Labor, Free Men*, 38.

29. Zarco, *Historia del Congreso extraordinario constituyente*, 319; also cited in Sinkin, *The Mexican Reform*, 67.

30. Seward, *Works*, 253 and 268.

31. Salmon P. Chase and Charles Dexter Cleveland, *Anti-Slavery Addresses of 1844 and 1845* (Philadelphia: J. A. Bancroft and Co., 1867), 29, 44 (HathiTrust).

32. Charles Sumner, *The Works of Charles Sumner*, 15 vols. (Boston: Lee and Shepard, 1870–1883), 2:55.

33. Ocampo, *Obras completas*, 319–20.

34. Zarco, *Historia del Congreso extraordinario constituyente*, 1220–24; also cited in Sinkin, *The Mexican Reform*, 129.

35. Otero, *Consideraciones de la situación política y social*, 5–7.

36. Foner, *Free Soil, Free Labor, Free Men*, 11.

37. Seward, *Works*, 290–91.

38. Otero, *Consideraciones de la situación política y social*, 19–25, 43.

39. Ponciano Arriaga, "Derecho de propiedad: voto del Sr. Arriaga," reprinted in Ramírez, *Leyes fundamentales de México*, 573–94, quotes on 591–92.

40. Abraham Lincoln, *The Collected Works of Abraham Lincoln*, ed. Roy P. Basler, 9 vols. (New Brunswick, NJ: Rutgers University Press, 1953–1955), 7:259–69; also cited in Foner, *Free Soil, Free Labor, Free Men*, 20.

41. Arriaga, "Derecho de propiedad," 575.

42. Ramírez, *Leyes fundamentales de México*, 607 and 610.

43. Ramírez, *Leyes fundamentales de México*, 625.

44. Seward, *Works*, 290, 337.

45. Oakes, *The Crooked Path to Abolition*, 63, 108.

46. Otero, *Consideraciones de la situación política y social*, 5, 43.

47. Alice L. Baumgartner, *South to Freedom: Runaway Slaves to Mexico and the Road to Civil War* (New York: Basic Books, 2020), 147.

48. Rosalie Schwartz, *Across the Rio to Freedom: U.S. Negroes in Mexico* (El Paso: Texas Western Press, University of Texas at El Paso, 1974), 32.

49. For the precise language of the two articles see Ramírez, *Leyes fundamentales de México*, 607–8.

50. Frederick Law Olmsted quoted in Schwartz, *Across the Rio to Freedom*, 45.

51. Schwartz, *Across the Rio to Freedom*, 33.

52. Robert M. Utley, *Frontiersmen in Blue: The United States Army and the Indian, 1848–1865* (New York: Macmillan, 1967), 18–58.

53. Pekka Hämäläinen, *Comanche Empire* (New Haven, CT: Yale University Press, 2008), 292–306.

54. Guy M. Bryan to David G. Burnet, 2 April 1846, box 2N244, Guy M. Bryan Papers, Dolph Briscoe Center for American History, University of Texas at Austin.
55. "The Democratic Nominees," *Texas State Gazette*, 30 May 1857.
56. "Good Signs in the Political Zodiac," *Southern Intelligencer* (Austin), 16 March 1859.
57. *New York Herald*, 26 July 1860.
58. *New York Herald*, reprinted from the *New Orleans Picayune*, 29 July 1860.
59. *San Antonio Ledger*, reprinted in the *New York Herald*, 4 August 1860.
60. *New York Herald*, 2 August 1860.
61. *Charleston Courier*, 11 August 1860, reprinted from the *New Orleans Picayune*.
62. *San Antonio Ledger*, reprinted in *New York Herald*, 4 August 1860.
63. "Texas on Secession," *Dallas Weekly Herald*, 12 December 1860.
64. Andrew F. Lang, "Memory, the Texas Revolution, and Secession: The Birth of Confederate Nationalism in the Lone Star State," in *Lone Star Blue and Gray: Essays on Texas and the Civil War*, ed. Ralph A Wooster and Robert Wooster, 2nd ed. (Denton: Texas State Historical Association, 2015), 47–63, quotes on 51 and 57.
65. "An Ordinance to Dissolve the Union between the State of Texas and the Other States," 30 January 1861, *Journals of the Secession Convention 1861*, ed. Ernest William Winkler (Austin: Austin Printing Company, 1912), 35–36.
66. "What the Frontier has Gained by Secession," *San Antonio Ledge and Texan*, 13 March 1861.
67. "Mr. Rogers of Harris," 30 January 1861, *Journal of the Secession Convention*, 29.
68. "Mr. Rogers of Harris," 94.
69. "Mr. Rogers of Harris," 206.
70. Garrison quoted in Henry Mayer, *All on Fire: William Lloyd Garrison and the Abolition of Slavery* (New York: W. W. Norton & Company, 1998), 143.
71. Mayer, *All on Fire*, 339–43.
72. Michael A. Morrison, *Slavery and the American West: The Eclipse of Manifest Destiny and the Coming of the Civil War* (Chapel Hill: University of North Carolina Press, 1997), chap. 5; Graham A. Peck, *Making an Antislavery Nation: Lincoln, Douglas, and the Battle over Freedom* (Urbana: University of Illinois Press, 2007), chap. 5.
73. Seward, *Works*, 301.
74. Sumner, *Works*, 79.
75. Sumner, *Works*, 77; Seward, *Works*, 302.
76. Seward, *Works*, 302.
77. William Jay, *A View of the Action of the Federal Government, in Behalf of Slavery* (New York: J. S. Taylor, 1839), 2, 16, 18, 193 (HathiTrust).
78. American Anti-Slavery Society, Declaration of Sentiments of the American Anti-Slavery Society, 1835, New York, 3, 5–6, and 8.
79. William Jay quoted in Daniel W. Crofts, *Lincoln and the Politics of Slavery: The Other Thirteenth Amendment and the Struggle to Save the Union* (Chapel Hill: University of North Carolina Press, 2016), 19.
80. Abraham Lincoln, "Speech at Peoria," 16 October 1856, in Basler, *The Collected Works of Abraham Lincoln*, 2:249, 255, 26, 267, 275–76.
81. William Goodell, *Views of American Constitutional Law, in Its Bearing upon American Slavery* (Utica, NY: Lawson & Chaplin, 1845), 18.

82. Abraham Lincoln, "Fragment on Sectionalism," in Basler, *The Collected Works of Abraham Lincoln*, 2:349.

83. For a description of the Republican Party's antislavery project, see James Oakes, *The Crooked Path to Abolition: Abraham Lincoln and the Antislavery Constitution* (New York: W. W. Norton and Co., 2021), 54–56.

84. George S. Boutwell quoted in Herman Belz, *Reconstructing the Union: Theory and Policy during the Civil War* (Ithaca, NY: Cornell University Press, for the American Historical Association, 1969), 42–43.

85. Abraham Lincoln, "First Inaugural Address," 4 March 1861, in Basler, *The Collected Works of Abraham Lincoln*, 4:262–71, quote on 264.

86. For Lincoln's views on the illegitimacy of southern secession, see Peter Radan, "Lincoln, the Constitution and Secession," in *Secession as an International Phenomenon: From America's Civil War to Contemporary Separatist Movements*, ed. Don H. Doyle (Athens: University of Georgia Press, 2010), 56–75.

87. Lincoln, "First Inaugural Address," 4:265.

88. Lincoln, "Message to Congress in Special Session," 4 July 1861, in Basler, *The Collected Works of Abraham Lincoln*, 4:421–41, quote on 433.

89. For a discussion of Lincoln's reasoning on statehood status outside the Union, see Akhil Reed Amar, "Abraham Lincoln and the American Union," *University of Illinois Law Review* 5 (2001): 1109–34.

90. Lincoln, "First Inaugural Address," 4:269.

91. Francis Lieber, *An Address on Secession. Delivered in South Carolina in the Year 1851* (New York: Loyal Publication Society, 1865), 6–8 (HathiTrust).

92. Francis Lieber, *On Civil Liberty and Self-Government* (Philadelphia: Lippincott, Grambo & Co., 1853), 28, 38, 128, 304 (HathiTrust); also see Brian Schoen, "Francis Lieber on Institutional Liberty, Secession, and the Modern State," *American Political Thought: A Journal of Ideas, Institutions, and Culture* 9: 4(Fall 2020): 542–70.

93. Abraham Lincoln, "Second Annual Address," 1 December 1862, in *Speeches and Writings, 1859–1865: Speeches, Letters, and Miscellaneous Writings, Presidential Messages and Proclamations. Abraham Lincoln*, ed. Don E. Fehrenbacher (New York: Literary Classics of the United States, 1989–2012), 5:215–24.

94. Abraham Lincoln, "First Inaugural Address," 4 March 1861, in Fehrenbacher, *Speeches and Writings*, 2:215–24.

Chapter 8 · *The Birth of Two Nations*

1. Guy Thompson, introduction to *The European Revolutions of 1848 and the Americas* (London: Institute in Latin American Studies, 2002), 1.

2. See the essays in Sven Beckert and Seth Rockman, ed., *Slavery's Capitalism: A New History of American Economic Development* (Philadelphia: University of Pennsylvania Press, 2016).

3. Erika Pani, "Dreaming of a Mexican Empire: The Political Project of the 'Imperialistas,'" *Hispanic American Historical Review* 82, no. 1 (February 2002): 570–96.

4. For recent works drawing comparisons between the War of the Rebellion and contemporaneous foreign conflicts, see Andre M. Fleche, *The Revolution of 1861: The American Civil War in the Age of Nationalist Conflict* (Chapel Hill: University of North Carolina Press, 2012); Don H. Doyle, *The Cause of All Nations: An International History*

of the American Civil War (New York: Basic Books, 2015); Don H. Doyle, ed., *American Civil Wars: The United States, Latin America, Europe, and the Crisis of the 1860s* (Chapel Hill: University of North Carolina Press, 2017); Steven Hahn, *A Nation without Borders: The United States and Its world in an Age of Civil Wars, 1830–1910* (New York: Viking, an imprint of Penguin Random House, 2016). For a comparative study of the United States and Mexico, see Erika Pani, *Una serie de admirables acontecimientos: México y el mundo en la época de la Reforma, 1848–1867* (Mexico City: Educación y Cultura, Asesoría y Promoción; Puebla, Mexico: Benemérita Universidad Autónoma de Puebla, 2013), and Erika Pani, *El poder y sangre: guerra, estado y nación en la década de 1860*, ed. Guillermo Palacios and Erika Pani (Mexico City: El Colegio De México, Centro de Estudios Históricos, 2014).

5. Erika Pani, "Juárez vs. Maximiliano: Mexico's Experiment with Monarchy," in Doyle, *American Civil Wars*, 171.

6. Erika Pani, "Law, Allegiance, and Sovereignty in Civil War Mexico, 1857–1867," *Journal of the Civil War Era* 7, no. 4 (December 2017): 576.

7. Richard N. Sinkin, *The Mexican Reform, 1855–1876: A Study in Liberal Nation-Building* (Austin: Institute of Latin American Studies, University of Texas at Austin; distributed by University of Texas Press, 1979), 133–34.

8. Will Fowler, *Independent Mexico: The Pronunciamiento in the Age of Santa Anna, 1821–1858* (Lincoln: University of Nebraska Press, 2016), 234–38.

9. Sinkin, *The Mexican Reform*, 138; Brian Hamnett, *Juárez,* (New York: Longman Group, 1997), 106–7.

10. Manifiesto del gobierno constitucional a la nación, 7 July 1859, in Tena Ramírez, *Leyes fundamentales de México, 1808–1957* (Mexico City: Editorial Porrúa, 1957), 634–35. For a discussion of the manifesto, see Sinkin, *The Mexican Reform*, 137–38, Juárez on 142.

11. Erika Pani, "Dreaming of a Mexican Empire"; see also Vicente Ortigosa, *Cuatro memorias sobre puntos de administración* (Mexico City: Imp. de Ignacio Cumplido, 1866), ii, https://repositories.lib.utexas.edu/server/api/core/bitstreams/d7835217-02c3-4fec-94a1-9fb348e776ea/content >

12. "Las miras de la Providencia: el gobierno supremo de la república a los mexicanos," in *El pensamiento de la reacción*, ed. Gastón García Cantú, vol. 2 (Mexico City: Universidad Nacional Autónomo, 1987), 425–30.

13. Pani, "Juárez vs. Maximiliano," 167–68.

14. Ignacio Aguilar y Machado, "Dictamen acerca de la forma de gobierno," 10 July 1863, in Ignacio Aquilar y Marocho, *La familia enferma* (Mexico City: Editorial Jus, 1969), 165–88, quotes on 165–66, 170, 182–84; also quoted in Pani, "Juárez vs. Maximiliano," 167–68.

15. Matthew J. Karp, *This Vast Southern Empire: Slaveholders at the Helm of American Foreign Policy* (Cambridge, MA: Harvard University Press, 2016), chaps. 1, 2 and 7.

16. Alexander H. Stephens, "The Cornerstone of the Confederacy," in *The Rebellion Record*, ed. Frank H. Moore, vol. 1 (New York: G.P. Putnam, 1861–1868), 45–46.

17. Leonidas Spratt, *Speech upon the Foreign Slave Trade, before the Legislature of South Carolina* (Columbia, SC: Press Southern Guardian, 1858), 7.

18. Spratt, *Speech upon the Foreign Slave*, 8.

19. George Fitzhugh, "Southern Thought," in *The Ideology of Slavery: Proslavery*

Thought in the Antebellum South, 1830–1860, ed. Drew Gilpin Faust (Baton Rouge: Louisiana State University Press, 1981), 272–300.

20. Stephanie McCurry, *Confederate Reckoning: Power and Politics in the Civil War South* (Cambridge, MA: Harvard University Press, 2010), 11–19, Davis on 17–18.

21. Pani, "Dreaming of a Mexican Empire."

22. James Williams, *The Rise and Fall of "The Model Republic"* (London: R. Bentley, 1863), 17–32.

23. Michel Chevalier, "France, Mexico, and the Confederate States," translated and reprinted in *The New York Times*, 25 September 1863.

24. Stève Sainlaude, "France's Grand Design and the Confederacy," in Doyle, *American Civil Wars*, 107–12.

25. Patrick J. Kelly, "The Cat's-Paw: Confederate Ambitions in Latin America," in Doyle, *American Civil Wars*, 65–66.

26. Matías Romero in *A Mexican View of America in the 1860s: A Foreign Diplomat Describes the Civil War and Reconstruction*, trans. and ed. Thomas Schoonover, with Ebba Wesener Schoonover (London: Associated University Presses, 1991), 30. Two months earlier, he characterized the Republican Party as a "jealous defender of [Mexico's] rights and the integrity of its territory." Matías Romero to the minister of foreign relations, 5 September 1860, in *Benito Juárez: Documentos, discursos y correspondencia*, vol. 3, *Mexico City: 1964–71*, ed. Jorge L. Tamayo (Mexico City: Secretaría del Patrimonio Nacional, 1964–), 11–13, quote on 12.

27. Matías Romero to the minister of foreign relations, 5 September 1860, in Tamayo, *Benito Juárez*, 2.

28. Paul Finkelman, "Lincoln, Emancipation, and the Limits of Constitutional Change," *Supreme Court Review* 2008, no. 1 (2008): 383.

29. James Oakes, *Freedom National: The Destruction of Slavery in the United States, 1861–1865* (New York: W. W. Norton & Co, 2013), 99.

30. Oakes, *Freedom National*, 99.

31. Oakes, *Freedom National*, 224–55; Hahn, *Nation without Borders*, 253; Eric Foner, *The Fiery Trial: Abraham Lincoln and American Slavery* (New York: W. W. Norton & Co., 2010), 214–16.

32. Hahn, *Nation without Borders*, 354.

33. Finkelman, "Lincoln, Emancipation, and the Limits of Constitutional Change," 364.

34. Matías Romero in Schoonover and Schoonover, *A Mexican View of America in the 1860s*, 115, 125, and 130.

35. Eric Foner, "Lincoln and Colonization," in *Our Lincoln: New Perspective on Lincoln and His World*, ed. Eric Foner (New York: W.W. Norton and Co., 2008), 135–66.

36. Matías Romero, *Mexican Lobby: Matías Romero in Washington, 1861–1867*, ed. and trans. Thomas D. Schoonover, with Ebba Wesener Schoonover (Lexington: University Press of Kentucky, 1986), 17–18.

37. Oakes, *Freedom National*, 340–92; Foner, *The Fiery Trial*, 248–89.

38. Hahn, *Nation without Borders*, 256.

39. For Lincoln's evolving views on colonization and the meeting with black leaders, see Foner, "Lincoln and Colonization," 135–66; Foner, *The Fiery Trial*, 221–30; Oakes, *Freedom National*, 307–10.

40. Matías Romero to the minister of foreign relations, 19 January 1863, Mexican Legation, vol. 17, Secretaria de Relaciones Exteriores, Mexico City.

41. Matías Romero to the minister of foreign relations, 19 March 1863, Mexican Legation, vol. 17, Secretaria de Relaciones Exteriores, Mexico City.

42. "El ciudadano Benito Juárez, Presidente Constitucional de la República, a la nación, 12 April 1862," in Benito Juárez, *Discursos y manifiestos de Benito Juárez*, ed. Angel Pola, vol. 2 (Mexico City: A. Pola 1905), 262–66.

43. "El ciudadano Benito Juárez, Presidente Constitucional de la República, al ejercito de Oriente, 2 March 1863," in Juárez, *Discursos y manifiestos de Benito Juárez*, 267–69.

44. Matías Romero, speech at banquet given in New York by the Mexican Legation, 18 September 1863, Mexican Legation, vol. 17, Secretaria de Relaciones Exteriores, Mexico City.

45. Emory M. Thomas, *The Confederate Nation, 1861–1865* (New York: Harper Perennial, 2011), 260.

46. Owsley, *State Rights in the Confederacy*, 157–58.

47. Owsley, *States Rights in the Confederacy*, 60.

48. John Moretta, "Pendleton Murrah and States Rights in Civil War Texas" in *Lone Star Blue and Gray: Essays on Texas and the Civil War*, ed. Ralph A. Wooster and Robert Wooster (Denton: Texas State Historical Association., 2015) 135–59.

49. Thomas, *The Confederate Nation*, 261.

50. McCurry, *Confederate Reckoning*, 332.

51. McCurry, *Confederate Reckoning*, 333–52, quotes on 335.

52. Henry Winter Davis, *Speeches and Addresses Delivered in the United States Congress and on Several Public Occasions, 1856–1865* (New York: Harper & Brothers, 1867), 395–96.

53. Andrew Jackson Hamilton quoted in Nicholas Guyatt, "'The Future Empire of Our Freedmen': Republican Colonization Schemes in Texas and Mexico, 1861–65," in *Civil War Wests: Testing the Limits of the United States*, ed. Adam Arenson and Andrew R. Graybill (Oakland: University of California Press, 2015), 95–117.

54. Gregory P. Downs, "Three Faces of Sovereignty: Governing Confederate, Mexican, and Indian Texas in the Civil War Era," in Arenson and Graybill, *Civil War Wests*, 118.

55. Todd W. Wahlstrom, *The Southern Exodus to Mexico: Migration Across the Borderlands after the American Civil War* (Lincoln: University of Nebraska Press, 2015), 1–24, Maury on 15.

56. Guyatt, "The Future Empire of Our Freedmen," 108.

57. Guyatt, "The Future Empire of Our Freedmen," 107–8.

58. Romero, *Mexican Lobby*, 58.

59. John Mason Hart, *Empire and Revolution: The American in Mexico since the Civil War* (Berkeley, University of California Press, 2002), chap. 1.

60. Benito Juárez, *Decree of the Mexican Constitutional Government Inviting American Immigrants to Settle in the Republic of Mexico* (San Francisco: E. Payot, 1865).

61. Romero, *Mexican Lobby*, 69.

62. Romero, *Mexican Lobby*, 97–98

63. *Proceedings of a Meeting of Citizens of New York to Express Sympathy and Respect for*

the Mexican Republican Exiles, 19 July 1865 (New York: John A. Gray and Green Printers, 1865), 4–5.

64. Herman Belz, *Reconstructing the Union: Theory and Policy during the Civil War* (Westport, CT: Greenwood Press, 1969), 10–13; Hahn, *Nation without Borders*, 271–72, Bingham on 272.

65. "Proclamation of Amnesty and Reconciliation," 8 December 1862, in Roy P. Basler, *The Collected Works of Lincoln*, 9 vols. (New Brunswick, NJ: Rutgers University Press, 1953–1955), 7:54–56; Belz, *Reconstructing the Union*, 155–58; Hahn, *Nation without Borders*, 273.

66. Phillips cited in Belz, *Reconstructing the Union*, 188–89.

67. Belz, *Reconstructing the Union*, 204; Hahn, *Nation without Borders*, 274.

68. Lincoln quoted in Hahn, *Nation without Borders*, 294 and 296.

69. Eric Foner, *The Second Founding: How the Civil War and Reconstruction Remade the Constitution* (New York: W. W. Norton and Co., 2019), xiv.

70. Hahn, *Nation without Borders*, 275.

71. Lincoln "Annual Message to Congress, 1 December 1862," in *This Fiery Trial: The Speeches and Writings of Abraham Lincoln*, ed. William E. Geinapp (New York: Oxford University Press, 2002), 144–50, quote on 144.

72. Hamnett, *Juárez*, 130, 175.

73. Hamnett, *Juárez*, 175–76.

74. Hamnett, *Juárez*, 176; Pani, "Law, Allegiance, and Sovereignty," 581.

75. Hamnett, *Juárez*, 116–18.

76. Hamnett, *Juárez*, 117–20.

77. *El Restaurador de le Libertad*, 25 May 1855, microfilm no. F- J 4 N838, Nettie Lee Benson Latin American Collection, University of Texas Libraries, Austin.

78. Hamnett, *Juárez*, 103.

79. Hamnett, *Juárez*, 122.

80. Tyler, *Vidaurri*, 38.

81. Tyler, *Vidaurri*, chap. 4.

82. Pani, "Law Allegiance, and Sovereignty," 586.

83. Pani, "Law Allegiance, and Sovereignty," 582.

84. Hamnett, *Juárez*, 171–74.

85. Sinkin, *The Mexican Reform*, 166.

86. Eric Foner, *Reconstruction: America's Unfinished Revolution, 1863–1877* (New York: Harper & Row, 1988), 183.

87. Foner, *Reconstruction*, 185–97.

88. Gregory P. Downs, *After Appomattox: Military Occupation and the Ends of War* (Cambridge, MA: Harvard University Press, 2015), 48.

89. Downs, *After Appomattox*, 125.

90. Johnson quoted in Downs, *After Appomattox*, 125.

91. For Foner's discussion of birthright citizenship and the importance of the Fourteenth Amendment generally, see Foner, *Second Founding*, chap. 2.

92. Hahn, *Nation without Borders*, 313–14.

93. Schultz in Foner, *Second Founding*, xxviii.

94. Downs, *After Appomattox*, 212–36.

95. Hahn, *Nation without Borders*, 301.

96. For a primes example, see Jefferson Davis, *The Rise and Fall of the Confederate Government*, 2 vols. (New York: D. Appleton and Co., 1881).

97. Pani, "Law, Allegiance, and Sovereignty," 586–87.

98. There are inconsistencies in accounts of Vidaurri's death. See Pani, "Law, Allegiance, and Sovereignty," 586.

Epilogue

1. Abraham Lincoln, "Annual Message to Congress, 1 December 1862," in *Speeches and Writings, 1859–1865: Speeches, Letters, and Miscellaneous Writings, Presidential Messages and Proclamations*, ed. Don E. Fehrenbacher, vol. 2 (New York: Library Classics of the United States, 1989), 393–415, quote on 403; also quoted in Steven Hahn, *A Nation without Borders: The United States and Its World in an Age of Civil Wars, 1830–1910* (New York: Penguin Random House, 2016), 285–86.

2. Hahn, *Nation without Borders*, 285–91.

3. Hahn, *Nation without Borders*, 234–47.

4. Hahn, *Nation without Borders*, 318–38, 363–90.

5. John Tutino, *The Mexican Heartland: How Communities Shaped Capitalism, a Nation and World History, 1500–2000* (Princeton, NJ: Princeton University Press, 2018), chap. 8.

6. Hahn, *Nation without Borders*, 382–87.

7. John Mason Hart, *Empire and Revolution: The Americans in Mexico since the Civil War* (Berkeley: University of California Press, 2002); Thomas Davis Schoonover, *Dollars over Dominion: The Triumph of Liberalism in Mexican–United States Relations, 1861–1867* (Baton Rouge: Louisiana State University Press, 1978), chap. 9.

8. Hahn, *Nation without Borders*, chap. 11.

9. Tutino, *The Mexican Heartland*, chap. 9; Hart, *Empire and Revolution*, chaps. 9 and 10.

10. Benjamin Heber Johnson, *Revolution in Texas: How a Forgotten Rebellion and Its Bloody Suppression Turned Mexicans into Americans* (New Haven, CT: Yale University Press, 2003), chap. 3, quotes on 63.

11. Hahn, *Nation without Borders*, 510–11.

12. Johnson, *Revolution in Texas*, 64.

13. Plan de San Diego, quoted and discussed in Johnson, *Revolution in Texas*, 80–81.

14. Hahn, *Nation without Borders*, 514.

15. Hahn, *Nation without Borders*, 517.

INDEX

abolition and abolitionist movement: fanaticism of, 154; for indigenous peoples, 82; Mexican Constitution of 1857 on, 217, 222; Mexican independence movement and, 80; opposition to Texas annexation, 150–51; radical, 192, 211, 229, 230, 316n3; by Spain, 39–40, 221; on Texas rebellion, 150–52; Thirteenth Amendment and, 260; transatlantic, 167; in US, 211, 221, 260; during US civil war, 247–49

Acta Constitutiva (1824), 37–39, 44, 284n107

Adams, John, 105

Adams, John Quincy, 6, 94, 144, 149–51, 172, 304n25

Adams-Onís Treaty (1819), 1, 26, 48, 149

African Americans, 247, 255

Agricultural Wheel, 272

Aguilar y Marocho, Ignacio, 241

Ahumada, Mateo, 59, 63

Alamán, Lucas, 28, 38–39, 89–91, 94–97, 117, 144–45, 193–94

Alamo, Battle of the (1836), 133–37

Alatorre, Francisco, 175

Almonte, Juan Nepomuceno, 112–14, 121

Alvarado, Juan, 156

American Anti-Slavery Society (AASS), 230

Ampudia, Pedro, 182

Anáhuac rebellion (1831), 73, 110, 111

Anna, Timothy E., 277n3, 285n120

annexation of Texas. *See* US annexation of Texas

anti-federalism: of Alamán, 194; elite, 105, 297n5; literature review, 280n4; middling, 45, 285n2, 297n6; opposition to US Constitution, 19–20; plebian populist strain of, 285n2; of US immigrant settlers, 8

antislavery movement. *See* abolition and abolitionist movement

Apache people, 46, 55, 157, 159

Archer, Branch T., 129

Arista, Mariano, 161, 181, 194

Arizpe, Miguel Ramos, 27–28, 36–39, 44, 47–50, 52–53, 57, 75–76

Armijo, Manuel, 157–58

Arriaga, Ponciano, 213, 216, 218–20, 259, 316–17n24

Articles of Confederation, 18, 39, 106, 233

Augustín I (Mexican emperor). *See* Iturbide, Augustín de

Austin, Moses, 23–27, 31, 32, 43, 48, 224

Austin, Stephen F.: arrest and imprisonment, 112, 114, 116, 123; boundary commissioners on, 92; on customs regulations, 98–99; education of, 290n94; empresario program and, 32–34, 43, 51, 56; family background, 23–24; federalism of, 79; Fredonian rebellion and, 60–61, 128; on free trade, 86–88; on indigenous peoples, 56; Jackson and, 78–79, 131; on "Law of April 6," 95–96; loyalty to Mexico, 43–45, 61, 96; map of Texas created by, 87; middling anti-federalism and, 45, 297n6; militia formed by, 56–58; in Missouri legislature, 24; in New Orleans, 32, 129–31; Panic of 1819 and, 25, 32; petitions for tariff exemption, 294nn70–71; on religion, 45, 66–70; on republicanism, 40, 45, 61, 68, 79;

Austin, Stephen F. (*cont.*)
  on slavery, 80–84; Texas rebellion and, 121, 124, 126–31, 134
autonomist movements, 5, 6, 28, 130, 155–64
autonomy: colonial, 17, 18, 27–29; communal, 45, 270, 273; economic, 8, 21, 117–18, 154; indigenous peoples and, 46, 270, 271; local, 2, 8, 10, 16–17, 27, 57, 110, 189, 202, 213, 262; political, 2, 8, 17–18, 21, 44, 117–18, 144, 154, 155; provincial, 36, 37, 39–40, 52
Ayala, Plan de (1911), 273
Ayutla, Plan de (1854), 210, 212, 214
Ayutla, Revolution of (1854), 210, 261, 316n2
Azcarate, Juan Francisco de, 71, 102

Bank of the United States, 24–25, 74, 131
Banks, Thomas, 123, 124
Barclay, Thomas, 182–83
Barnett, Thomas, 291n100
Barragán, Miguel, 116
Bases Orgánicas (1843), 147–48, 174
battles. *See specific names of battles*
Bean, Peter Ellis, 293n50
Bee, Bernard E., 166
Bell, Peter H., 200
Benton, Thomas Hart, 25
Berlandier, Luis, 91–93
Biddle, Nicholas, 131
Bingham, John, 258
Black populations: abolitionism by, 249; African Americans, 247, 255; colonization projects for, 248, 249, 321n39; free Blacks, 139, 151, 153–54, 248–49. *See also* race and racism; slavery and enslaved persons
Blancarte, José María, 194, 211
Blanco, Victor, 81, 82
Bocanegra, José María, 115
Bogart, William, 124
Bolívar, Simón, 38, 90
Booth, John Wilkes, 255, 263
Boutwell, George S., 232
Bradburn, David, 97–100
Bradburn, Juan Davis, 110
Broadhead, Richard, 191
Brooks, John Sowers, 126, 127
Brown, James Elijah, 62–63
Brownlow, Parson, 256

Brutus (anti-federalist pseudonym), 19
Bryan, Guy M., 224–25
Bryan, James, 34
Burnet, David G., 79, 137, 224
Bustamante, Anastacio, 48–50, 63, 73, 89, 94–97, 100, 108, 159, 165
Butler, Benjamin H., 246, 247

Caddo people, 46
Cádiz Constitution (1812), 27, 28, 57, 64
Calhoun, John C., 105–7, 167, 170, 172, 185–86, 205, 297n4, 297n6
California, 49, 156, 176, 180, 184, 191
Canales Rosillo, Antonio, 160–61
capitalism, 4–5, 121, 238, 242, 270, 272
Cárdenas, Lázaro, 275
Carleton, Henry, 125–26
Carrillo, Manuel, 81
Casa Mata, Plan de (1823), 35, 38
Cass, Lewis, 190
Caste War (1847–1915), 164
Catholicism: anti-Catholic sentiment, 45, 63, 181; conversion to, 22, 43, 50–51, 63–67; *fueros* (clerical tribunals) and, 108, 147, 216, 217, 316n22; Mexico's establishment clause and, 8, 45, 51, 63–70; national identity and, 182; Plan de Iguala on, 29; in Reforma period, 216–18, 239, 240
Cazneau, Mary (pseud. John O'Sullivan), 172–73
centralism: anti-centralism, 98, 105; conservative, 144; on land distribution, 52, 73; nationalism and, 156; in New Mexico, 157–58; policy priorities and, 72, 118; popular, 115–16; pronunciamientos and, 115, 117, 176, 194; reform of, 145–52, 161, 177; response to Texas rebellion, 10, 128, 139; rise of, 73, 89; of Santa Anna, 2, 104, 117; on transfer of sovereignty, 38–39; on US expansionism, 3
centrifugalism, 2–3, 11, 22, 144, 152–55, 234
Cerro Gordo, Battle of (1847), 183, 187
Chacón, Albino, 157
Channing, William, 150
Chaplin, Chinchester, 58
Chase, Salmon P., 217, 218
Cherokee people, 54, 59, 60
Chevalier, Michel, 245

Index   327

Cheyenne people, 270
Child, David Lee, 121
Child, J., 85
Chimayó rebellion (1837), 157–58
Choctaw people, 54
Christman, Horatio, 100
Christy, William, 123, 125–26
Chust, Manuel, 288n55
citizenship: birthright, 221, 258, 265, 323n91; Confederate States of America on, 315n129; Mexican, 8, 10, 45, 51, 53, 57–58, 66–67, 88, 157, 177, 263; republicanism and, 45, 146; in Republic of Texas, 153; in Spanish Empire, 28; US, 2, 144, 221, 247, 258, 265, 269, 285n2, 323n91
Civil Rights Act of 1866, 264–65
Clay, Henry, 150, 170–71, 184–85, 202
Cleburne, Patrick, 252–53
Coahuila y Téjas (state), 52–53, 56, 67, 83, 95, 98, 120
Coahuiltecan people, 46
Comanche people, 32, 46–47, 55–56, 157, 160–61, 223, 226
Comonfort, Ignacio, 210, 212, 214, 216, 239, 270
compact theory, 3, 103, 105–8, 179, 205, 207–8, 229
confederalism, 38–39
Confederate States of America: on citizenship, 315n129; constitution of, 252, 285n120; Davis as president of, 243, 251–53, 266; establishment of, 232, 237; exiles in Mexico, 254–55; foreign policy of, 243–44; manpower challenges, 251–53; state sovereignty and, 225; surrender at Appomattox, 255; trade with Vidaurri, 262. *See also* US civil war
Connaughton, Brian, 64
Constitución de las Siete Leyes (1836), 117–18
constitutional monarchy, 27–29, 33–34
Cortes (Spanish legislature), 27–29, 47, 48
Corwin, Thomas, 185
Cos, Martín Perfecto, 118, 119, 138
cotton production, 6, 9, 29, 49, 77, 80–81, 86, 104, 121
Crittenden, John J., 236
Cuernavaca, Plan de (1834), 145

Davis, Henry Winter, 253, 259
Davis, Jefferson, 195, 207, 243, 251–53, 266
Dawes Act of 1887 (US), 271
DeBow, James, 207
debt peonage, 82–83, 217–20, 254
Declaration of Independence (US), 204, 208, 222, 230–31, 242, 314n122
Declaration of Sentiments (AASS), 230
democracy: consolidated, 206; failures of, 5, 237; federalism and, 7, 16, 148, 275–76; Jacksonian ideas of, 297n3; limited, 16, 21; majoritarian, 5, 10, 104, 236, 297n4; popular, 11, 145; religion and, 68, 69; representative, 230; Slave Power's corruption of, 218; in Spanish America, 28; states' rights as safeguard for, 190; undermining of, 97
Democratic Party: agrarian movements and, 272; on annexation of Texas, 167, 170; on decentralized governance, 3; expansionism and, 144, 148, 167, 170, 178; northern, 7, 170, 178–79, 189, 202, 206; southern, 11, 205–6, 245
De Witt, Green, 56, 62
Díaz, Porfirio, 271–73
Díaz de Bonilla, Manuel, 196, 313n84
Díaz Noriega, José María, 113
disorder thesis, 5, 277n3, 278n21
Doblado, Manuel, 262
Donelson, Andrew Jackson, 190
Douglas, Stephen, 189–90, 203–6
Douglass, Frederick, 185, 189, 247–48
Dred Scott v. Sandford (1857), 7, 203–6, 218
dual sovereignty, 20, 37–41, 105
Dunbar, James T., 290n96
Durst, John, 84

Edwards, Benjamin, 58–62
Edwards, Haden, 56, 58–62, 92
Elizondo, Dionisio, 81, 82
Ellis, Powhatan, 167
emancipation: gradual, 80, 82, 248; by Great Britain, 122–23; Guerrero's decree (1829), 9, 72, 74, 79, 83–84, 89, 118; Republic of Texas on, 153
Emancipation Proclamation (1863), 249, 251
Emerson, Ralph Waldo, 178
empresario program, 32–34, 43, 51, 56

equality: centralism and, 151; Declaration of Independence on, 314n122; Guerrero's vision for, 75–76; racial, 4, 30, 60, 186, 221, 242; in Reforma period, 210–11, 213–17, 240; Republican Party on, 203, 217; in Republic of Texas, 152, 153

fanaticism, 8, 65, 66, 68, 154
Fannin, James, 127
Farías, Valentín Gómez, 10
Farmers' Alliance, 272
Federal Farmer (anti-federalist pseudonym), 20
federalism: of Austin, 79; autonomist movements and, 155–64; centrifugal, 152–55; confederalism, 38–39; in defense of state sovereignty, 187; democracy and, 7, 16, 148, 275–76; failures of, 114–18, 144; of Gómez Farías, 10, 108, 111, 118, 174–76; of Jackson, 71, 73, 79; Mexican Constitution of 1824 and, 2, 38–39, 104; Mexican Constitution of 1857 and, 4; as national creed of Mexico, 284n100; nationalist, 73, 108, 109, 165; populism and, 8–9, 71, 73; pronunciamientos and, 52, 73, 99, 100, 121, 212; radical, 7, 90, 146, 152; reform of, 165–73, 177; of Santa Anna, 98, 110, 111, 116; self-determination and, 7; slavery and, 6–7, 72–73, 82, 104, 178; social unity for reinforcement of, 43; US Constitution and, 20. *See also* anti-federalism; *puro* federalism
federal power: in Articles of Confederation, 18; balance with local autonomy, 8, 16–17; executive, 9, 71–75, 186, 208, 238, 248; expansionism and, 171; harnessing, 3, 10, 40, 73, 109, 150, 274–76; human liberty and, 260; Jacksonian ideas of, 297n3; of Juárez and juaristas, 238, 257–58, 260–63; sectionalism and, 3
Fernando VII (king of Spain), 27, 28, 64
Fields, Richard, 62
Filisola, Vicente, 138
First Confiscation Act of 1861 (US), 246–47
First Mexican Republic (1824–35), 4–5, 35–42, 117
Fisher, George, 97, 123, 124, 300n71

Fitz, Caitlyn, 283n74
Fitzhugh, George, 242
Florida, Spanish cession to US (1819), 1, 71
Foner, Eric, 260, 323n91
Foreign Affairs Committee (US), 50, 253, 287n31
Forsyth, John, 126
France: imperial consolidation, 46; Louisiana Purchase from, 23; Mexico invaded by (1861), 243, 249; Napoleonic wars, 27, 36, 47; republican transition in, 30–31; Spain invaded by (1808), 27; Veracruz blockade, 145, 159
Fredonian rebellion (1826–27), 59–63, 70, 92, 100, 128
free Blacks, 139, 151, 153–54, 248
Freedmen's Bureau, 264
freedom of religion, 45, 63–69, 118, 216, 239, 290n97
Freeport Doctrine, 205
fueros (clerical tribunals), 108, 147, 216, 217, 316n22
fugitive enslaved persons: Fugitive Slave Act of 1793, 191; Fugitive Slave Act of 1850, 6, 191–92, 200, 202–3, 206, 208, 222, 311–12n63; in Mexico, 84–85, 151, 222–23; during US civil war, 246–47
Fulton, Ambrose Calperthwaite, 123

Gadsden Purchase, 195–98, 312n83
Gamboa, José Antonio, 218
Garrison, William Lloyd, 192, 229, 230
Gettysburg, Battle of (1863), 249–50
Gettysburg Address (1863), 250, 257
Goliad, Battle of (1836), 134, 137
Gómez, Gregorio, 128
Gómez Farías, Valentín: federalism of, 10, 108, 111, 118, 174–76; imprisonment of Austin, 112, 116; in New Orleans, 116–19, 121–23, 165; reform policies, 108–9, 115, 117, 145; return from exile, 165–66; on state sovereignty, 39; US-Mexican War and, 180–81, 186
Gómez Pedraza, Manuel, 75, 99, 145
González, José (New Mexico resident), 158
González, José Vicente (Mexican colonel), 115
González, Rafael, 56

González Cosío, Manuel, 118
Goodell, William, 231
Grant, Ulysses S., 255–56
Great Britain: economic interests in Mexico, 149; Emancipation Act of 1833, 122–23; North American colonies of, 15, 17, 288n54; Republic of Texas and, 166–67, 170
Great Society, 275
Great Southwest strike (1886), 272
Green, Duff, 167
Green, Thomas J., 155
Greenback Labor Party, 272
Groce, Jared, 80, 92, 110
Guadalajara, Plan de (1852), 211
Guadalupe Hidalgo, Treaty of (1848), 11, 178, 187, 190, 194–96, 200, 222, 233
Guerrero, Vicente: emancipation decree (1829), 9, 72, 74, 79, 83–84, 89, 118; equality as envisioned by, 75–76; overthrow by Bustamante, 71, 89; Plan de Iguala and, 29; populism and, 8–9, 71, 73; presidential elections and, 75, 145; reform policies, 75, 77–78, 89; revolts led by, 97
Gutiérrez Estrada, José María, 143–45, 148, 240, 241

hacienda system, 218–19
Hamilton, Alexander, 19, 38, 72, 90, 94
Hamilton, Andrew Jackson, 254
Harper, William, 314n122
Hasinai people, 46
Hawkins, James, 33, 34
Hayne, Robert Y., 107, 135
Henry, Patrick, 20
Herrera, José Joaquín, 174–76, 180, 187
Hidalgo, Miguel, 28
Hispanic Texans. *See* Tejanos
hombres de bien, 97, 145
Houston, Sam: on annexation of Texas, 166, 170; arrival in Mexican Texas, 111; as governor of Texas, 225, 226; Texas rebellion and, 129, 137–38; unionist views of, 223; as US Senator, 200–202
Howard, Volney, 200–201
Humboldt, Alexander von, 29–30
Hunt, Memecum, Jr., 155

identity: American, 6, 8, 60, 61, 146, 189, 209, 278n22; Mexican, 44, 64, 91, 95, 140, 143, 156, 158, 240–41, 263, 267; national, 64, 91, 140, 143, 181–82, 189, 209, 263
Iguala, Plan de (1821), 29, 31, 35, 283n75
Imán, Santiago, 162, 163
Inclán, Ignacio, 99
indigenous peoples: abolition of slavery for, 82; autonomy of, 46, 270, 271; Christianized, 306n53; in Fredonian rebellion, 59, 60; Jackson and, 9, 73, 75; land seizures from, 271; relocation of, 54, 113; Republic of Texas and, 3, 4, 153–54; in Spanish America, 47, 55; treaties with, 74; war with, 8, 32, 55–56, 221
individualism, 1, 149
Ingram, Ira, 65, 68–70, 101
Iturbide, Augustín de, 29, 31, 34–39, 43, 48–49, 51, 71, 80

Jackson, Andrew: Austin and, 78–79, 131; on democracy and federal power, 297n3; expansionism of, 71, 78; federalism of, 71, 73, 79; indigenous peoples and, 9, 73, 75; nullification crisis and, 73, 108, 135; populism and, 8–9, 71, 73; tariffs and, 73, 88–89; Texas and, 71, 78, 94, 101, 168, 292n31; on violation of state sovereignty, 74
Jalapa, Plan de (1829), 89
Jalisco, Plan de (1835), 117
Jay, William, 230
Jefferson, Thomas, 18, 21, 23, 49, 54, 105, 231, 274
Jeffersonian republicanism, 44, 90, 285n2
Johnson, Andrew, 255–56, 263–66
Juárez, Benito: assumption of presidency, 239; federal power exercised by, 238, 258, 260–63; Lincoln and, 4, 11–12, 250–51, 254, 255; manifesto issued by, 239–40, 320n10; in Reforma period, 211, 213, 217, 239–40; US and, 4, 250–51, 254–56; Vidaurri and, 258, 261–62, 267
juaristas, 255–57, 262, 271

Kadohadacho people, 46
Kansas-Nebraska Act of 1854, 191
Karankawa people, 46, 55
Kinney, Samuel, 63

Kiowa people, 55
Knights of Labor, 272
Ku Klux Klan, 266
Kuykendall, Abner, 63, 64, 67
Kuykendall, Robert, 54

labor movements, 272
Lack, Paul D., 301n85
Lafragua, José María, 214
Lamar, Mirabeau Buonaparte, 152–55, 158, 160, 163, 166, 169, 199–200, 223
land: in British North American colonies, 17; empresario program and, 32–34, 43, 51, 56; Guerrero's reform policies, 75, 77; ownership of, 8, 18, 31, 44, 50, 271–74; privatization of communal lands, 270–71; in Republic of Texas, 152–53; speculation, 20–25, 32, 44, 51, 54, 117, 121, 126, 153; squatters, 21, 24, 50, 54, 58, 91, 113, 204, 206; for US immigrant settlers, 6, 16, 22–23, 32, 48–54
Land Act of 1820 (US), 53
Landero, Pedro, 97–98
La Salle, Sieur de (René-Robert Cavelier), 46
"Law of April 6" of 1830 (Mexico), 94–96, 111, 118
Lee, Robert E., 227, 255, 257
Leftwich, Robert, 56
Lerdo de Tejada, Miguel, 213
Lerdo de Tejada, Sebastián, 213, 240, 271
Lerdo Law of 1856 (Mexico), 270
Lerma, Plan de (1832), 99
liberalism, in Reforma period, 11, 210–21, 237–41
Lieber, Francis, 6, 234–35
Lincoln, Abraham: assassination of, 255, 263; on colonization of free Blacks, 248, 249, 321n39; Emancipation Proclamation (1863), 249, 251; Gettysburg Address (1863), 250, 257; Juárez and, 4, 11–12, 250–51, 254, 255; on "one national family," 236, 260, 269, 270; Preliminary Emancipation Proclamation (1862), 248; Proclamation of Amnesty and Reconciliation (1863), 259; response to secession, 11, 211, 233–36, 319n86; Second Annual Address (1864), 269; on slavery, 203–5, 231–32; on social advancement, 220; on statehood status, 233, 238, 258, 319n89
Linn, L. F., 131
localism, 11, 52, 105, 205, 280n4, 297n4
Louisiana Purchase (1803), 23, 54, 168, 190
loyalty: economic prosperity and, 26; of Mexican citizens, 215, 219, 221; oaths of, 239, 259, 264; in post-independence US, 18, 21, 26; of US immigrant settlers, 2–9, 17, 43–45, 51, 61–62, 96, 101, 110–13
Lundy, Benjamin, 151, 152, 305n31, 305n35

Madero, Francisco, 98, 272–73
Madison, James, 20, 22, 38, 105, 169
Magón, Ricardo and Enrique Flores, 273
Maldonado, Francisco Severo, 52
manifest destiny, 173, 181
Maque, Tomás, 84
Marcy, William, 196
Martínez, Antonio, 32, 48, 54–55
Marx, Karl, 274
Mason, George, 20
Maury, Matthew Fontaine, 254, 255
Maximilian I (Mexican emperor), 11, 237–39, 253–55, 262–63, 267, 270
Mayan people, 162–64
McCall, George, 201
McClellan, George, 182
McCulloch, Ben, 227
McKinney, Thomas, 125, 129–30
McQueen, John, 228–29
Meigs, Henry, 128
Mesilla, Treaty of (1854), 197–98
Mexía, José Antonio, 111, 117–23, 129, 132
Mexican Boundary Commission, 83, 91–92
Mexican civil wars, 97–103, 108, 110, 139, 159, 238–41
Mexican Constitution (1824): Acta Constitutiva and, 37–39, 44, 284n107; demands for reinstatement, 159–62, 165; dismantling of, 9, 117–19; federalism and, 2, 38–39, 104; land policy and, 51–52; local autonomy and, 16; on property rights, 84; separation of powers in, 39; state sovereignty and, 36–40, 52, 157, 198, 285n120; Texas rebellion and, 120–21, 123, 127, 129

Mexican Constitution (1857), 4, 11, 214–22, 233, 236, 239
Mexican Constitution (1917), 275
Mexican Liberal Party (PLM), 273–74
Mexican Revolution (1910–17), 273–76
Mexican Texas: Anáhuac rebellion in, 73, 110, 111; borderlands of, 9, 70, 73; colonization of, 48–56, 72; cotton production in, 80, 86; debt peonage in, 82–83; exemption from Guerrero's emancipation decree, 79, 83–84; Fredonian rebellion in, 59–63, 70, 92, 100, 128; government of, 56–63; land for US settlers in, 6, 16, 32, 48–54; merger with Coahuila, 52–53, 56, 67, 83, 95, 98, 120; religion in, 63–70; secessionist movement in, 59, 72, 111; slavery in, 9, 50, 53, 72, 79–85, 92, 112, 139; statehood push for, 108, 110–12. *See also* Texas rebellion
Mexico: antislavery laws, 80–83, 91, 139, 217, 222; autonomist movements in, 5, 6, 28, 155–64; citizenship in, 8, 10, 45, 51, 53, 57–58, 66–67, 88, 157, 177, 263; comparative history of US and, 7, 279n31, 315n1, 320n4; Confederate exiles in, 254–55; as constitutional monarchy, 27–29, 33–34; cotton production in, 29, 49, 80, 86; empresario program, 32–34, 43, 51, 56; establishment clause, 8, 45, 51, 63–70; First Republic (1824–35), 4–5, 35–42, 117; French invasion of (1861), 243, 249; historiography of, 117, 277n3, 282n55; immigration patterns, 96, 100, 296n111; independence from Spain (1821), 26, 28–31, 48, 80, 283n74; institutional weaknesses, 75, 164; labor and agrarian resistance movements in, 272–73; as "la familia inferma" (the sick family), 241; local autonomy in, 2, 8, 16; loyalty of US settlers to, 2–9, 17, 43–45, 51, 61–62, 96, 101, 110–13; militias in, 39, 45, 56–58, 62–63, 97, 100, 109, 117–18; nationalism in, 109, 139, 176, 179, 240, 241; nation-building in, 4–5, 7, 88, 217; Reforma period, 11, 210–21, 237–41, 249, 261, 315–16n2; Second Mexican Empire (1864–67), 11, 237, 263; Spanish invasion of (1829), 73, 77, 90; territorial scope, 15–16, 280n2; Texas's secession from (1836), 2, 6, 134, 136, 147, 234, 298n13; US intervention in, 255–57. *See also* Catholicism; centralism; Mexican Texas; US-Mexican War

Michelena, José Mariano, 28
Mier, Servando Teresa de, 37–38
Mier y Terán, Manuel, 83, 91–94, 96–99, 109
Military Reconstruction Acts of 1867 (US), 265
Militia Act of 1862 (US), 247
militias: African Americans in, 247, 255; in British North American colonies, 288n54; in Mexico, 39, 45, 56–58, 62–63, 97, 100, 109, 117–18; republicanism and, 57, 288nn54–55; territorial integrity and, 31–32; Texas Rebellion and, 125–27, 133, 301n85; in US, 20, 45, 126
Miller, Howard, 290n97
Missouri Compromise (1820), 190, 236
moderados, 144–45, 148–49, 174–75, 186, 194, 212
Monroe Doctrine, 168, 256
Montesquieu, 19, 40
Mora, José Luis, 144, 146, 148, 214
Morgan, Edmund, 288n51
Mormon theocracies, 154
Muldoon, Michael, 63–64, 291n100
Murrah, Pendleton, 252
Músquiz, Ramón, 83–85, 87, 95, 103, 108, 110–11, 294n62
Mussey, R. Delevan, 256

Napoleon Bonaparte (French emperor), 27, 32, 36, 47
Napoleon III (French emperor), 237, 244–45, 253–54, 260, 263
Natchitoches people, 46
National Colonization Law of 1824 (Mexico), 52
national identity, 64, 91, 140, 143, 181–82, 189, 209, 263
nationalism: centralism and, 156; federalism and, 73, 108, 109, 165; flexibility of, 4, 16; Mexican, 109, 139, 176, 179, 240, 241;

nationalism (cont.)
  modern conceptions of, 144; racialized, 166; US, 8, 44, 177, 182
nation-building, 4–5, 7, 88, 146, 217, 251
Native Americans. See indigenous peoples
Navajo people, 157, 158
Navarro, José Antonio, 62, 133
Neighbors, Robert, 201
New Deal, 275
New Mexico, 46, 49, 86–88, 155–58, 180, 184, 200–202, 313n104
New Orleans: Austin in, 32, 129–31; cotton economy in, 9, 77, 81, 104, 121; Gómez Farías in, 116–19, 121–23, 165; Mexía in, 117–19, 121–23, 129; Texas rebellion supported by, 9, 104, 120–26, 129, 301n91; US immigrant settlers in, 22–23, 50; Zavala in, 77, 119
New Spain: border agreement with US, 26, 48; empresario program, 32–34, 43, 51; Humboldt's essay on, 29–30; independence movement in, 47; Mexico City as capital of, 30; North American land claims, 15; political and administrative oversight of, 37. See also Mexico; Spanish America
Norman, B. A., 164
Norris, Samuel, 58–59, 61
Northwest Ordinances, 231
Nuevo León, Battle of (1840), 161
nullification crisis (1832–33), 9–10, 73, 104–8, 135, 146, 229, 297n4, 297n6

Ocampo, Melchor, 213, 218, 239–40
O'Donojú, Juan, 29
Olmsted, Frederick Law, 222–23
Onís y González-Vera, Luis de, 1. See also Adams-Onís Treaty
Oregon, Republic of, 154, 171
Organic Provisional Statute of 1856 (Mexico), 316n7
Orizaba, Plan de (1835), 299n43
Ortíz de Ayala, Tadeo: on colonization of Texas, 49, 50, 72; correspondence with Alamán, 90, 94–95; death of (1833), 112, 298n30; on economic prosperity, 77–78, 85; on Guerrero as threat to the republic, 75–76; Jeffersonian republicanism and, 44;

Statistical Resume of the Mexican Empire, 49; Texas, concerns regarding, 103, 109, 112
Otero, Mariano, 10, 145–46, 148, 186, 215, 218–19, 221

Padilla, José Antonio, 83
Palmerston, Lord (Henry John Temple), 166–67
Panic of 1819, 2, 8, 24–25, 32, 44, 286n3
Panic of 1837, 153, 156, 170
Paredes y Arrillaga, Mariano, 173, 176
Pastry War (1839), 145
Peña y Peña, Manuel de la, 186, 194–95
Pennsylvania Regulation of 1794, 20, 281n33
Pérez, Albino, 157
Perry, James, 100–101
Phillips, Wendell, 259
Pickett, John, 243, 262
Pierce, Franklin, 195–97
plebian populism, 70, 285n2
Poinsett, Joel, 96
Polk, James K., 171–72, 176, 180, 184–88
popular sovereignty, 3, 27–29, 38, 189–91, 197, 202–6, 231, 288n51
populism, 8–9, 59, 70–71, 73, 153, 272, 285n2
power: centralized, 2, 16–17, 38, 94, 97, 104, 148, 168, 225, 262; congressional, 178, 191, 207; in constitutional monarchy, 34; decentralized, 28, 183; economic, 145, 156; executive, 9, 71–75, 186, 208, 238, 248; hierarchical systems of, 217; legitimacy of, 38, 134; overconcentration of, 20, 39; peaceful transference of, 5; political, 145, 156, 214; representative, 104, 189, 230; social, 44, 45. See also federal power
Preliminary Emancipation Proclamation (1862), 248
Proclamation of Amnesty and Reconciliation (1863), 259
pronunciamientos (unofficial demands): by autonomist movements, 157, 159; centralist, 115, 117, 176, 194; federalist, 52, 73, 99, 100, 121, 212; in First Mexican Republic, 35; in Mexican independence movement, 28; objectives of, 36, 284n95; on presidential election of 1828, 75; Santa

Anna and, 35, 38, 99, 100, 115, 173, 210.
  See also specific pronunciamientos
Protestantism, 68–69, 77, 147, 175, 181–82, 245
Pueblo people, 157–58
puro (pure) federalism, 10, 144, 165–66, 176, 180, 186–88, 194–95, 198, 215

Quintanar, Luis, 36, 38
Quitman, John, 297n9

Rabb family, 54–55
race and racism: in agrarian movements, 272; equality and, 4, 30, 60, 186, 221, 242; hierarchies of, 2, 7, 144, 242, 243, 274; Jim Crow, 274; liberal attitudes toward, 151; Mexican institutions and, 213; nationalism and, 166; in US South, 244; Whig tropes and, 184–86. *See also* Black populations; indigenous peoples
Ramage, James, 123, 124
Ramírez, Ignacio, 213
Reconstruction, 258, 260, 265–66, 269–70, 276
Reforma period, 11, 210–21, 237–41, 249, 261, 315–16n2
Rejón, Manuel Crescencio, 10, 187, 310n42
religion: freedom of, 45, 63–69, 118, 216, 239, 290n97; tolerance of, 53, 64, 66–70, 216, 239. *See also* Catholicism; Protestantism
republicanism: antiestablishment thread of, 69, 70; Austin on, 40, 45, 61, 68, 79; citizenship and, 45, 146; despotism vs., 123, 257; expansionism and, 169, 188; Jeffersonian, 44, 90, 285n2; limitations of, 16, 18–19, 241; Mexican unsuitability to, 132, 143, 193; militias and, 57, 288nn54–55; modern conceptions of, 7; self-determination and, 3, 203; Texas rebellion and, 128; transitions to, 30–31
Republican Party: emergence of, 203, 315n1; on equality, 203, 217; on free labor, 219, 232; radicals in, 247, 248, 264; on relations with Mexico, 253–54; on slavery, 203–4, 217–21, 232, 319n83; on wealth concentration, 11, 220, 272
Republic of Texas (1836–1846): British interest in, 166–67, 170; constitution of, 152–53; declaration of independence, 134, 136, 137; expansionism of, 154–55, 158; indigenous peoples and, 3, 4, 153–54; as inspiration for federalist movements, 144, 155–64; Mexican refusal to recognize, 139; migration of US citizens to, 153, 166; slavery in, 153, 154
Republic of the Rio Grande, 160–61
Restaurador de la Libertad, Plan de (1855), 261
Rhett, Robert Barnwell, 206
Riego, Rafael del, 28
Rio Grande, Republic of, 160–61
Roberts, O. M., 228
Rocafuerte, Vicente, 68–69
Roman Catholicism. *See* Catholicism
Romero, Matías, 245–51, 253, 255–57, 271, 321n26
Ruiz, Manuel, 239–40
runaways. *See* fugitive enslaved persons
Rusk, Thomas J., 197, 202

Salcedo, Nemesio, 32
Sambrano, Manuel, 32, 283n80
Sánchez, José María, 91, 92
San Diego, Plan de (1914), 274–75
San Jacinto, Battle of (1836), 137–39, 228
Santa Anna, Antonio López de: abdication of, 210, 214; Age of Santa Anna, 5; centralism of, 2, 104, 117; constitutional convention called by, 9; dictatorship of, 147, 194, 212; in exile, 176, 194, 211; federalism of, 98, 110, 111, 116; Gadsden Purchase and, 195–98; overthrow of Bustamante, 108, 159; Pastry War and, 145; popular views of, 5, 279n24; pronunciamientos and, 35, 38, 99, 100, 115, 173, 210; on reconquest of Texas, 139; Texas rebellion and, 132–39, 301–2n106; tyranny of, 118, 123, 127; US-Mexican War and, 182, 186
santanistas, 5, 10, 145–46, 162, 192–93, 258
Saucedo, José Antonio, 58, 61
Schultz, Charles, 266
Scott, Winfield, 182, 183, 186–88, 246
Second Bank of the United States, 74, 131
Second Confiscation Act of 1862 (US), 247

Second Mexican Empire (1864–67), 11, 237, 263
sectionalism, 3, 11, 18–19, 168, 189, 192, 226
Seguín, Erasmo, 52, 53, 81
self-determination, 3, 7, 144, 171, 178, 191, 203, 209, 235
self-government: capacity for, 90, 191, 216, 238, 241, 244; in colonial America, 17, 37; federated, 189; Lincoln on, 231; localized, 204; in Mexican Texas, 56; representative, 57
separatism, 2, 18, 20, 59, 130, 134, 158, 199–202
Sepulveda, José Antonio, 58–59
Seward, William H., 217–19, 221, 229, 255
Sheridan, Phillip H., 255–56
Sinkin, Richard N., 316n22
Sioux people, 270
Slave Power thesis, 217, 218, 305n35
slavery and enslaved persons: annexation of Texas and, 3, 149–51, 169, 170; cotton production and, 77, 80; federalism and, 6–7, 72–73, 82, 104, 178; illegal trafficking of, 114; Lincoln on, 203–5, 231–32; manumission of, 23, 84; Mexican cession and, 3, 178, 189–91; in Mexican Texas, 9, 50, 53, 72, 79–85, 92, 112, 139; Missouri Compromise on (1820), 190, 236; popular sovereignty and, 202–6; Republican Party on, 203–4, 217–21, 232, 319n83; in Republic of Texas, 153, 154; states' rights in defense of, 6–7, 9, 11, 82, 104; US Constitution and, 6–7, 11, 19, 21, 178, 192, 203, 207, 220–21, 229–32. *See also* abolition and abolitionist movement; emancipation; fugitive enslaved persons
Slidell, John Mason, 175–76, 180–81
Smith, Kirby, 252
Sosa, Mariano, 66
South (US): on annexation of Texas, 3, 167, 171; cotton production in, 6, 9, 77, 81, 104, 121; racism in, 244; Reconstruction in, 258, 260, 265–66, 269–70, 276; secessionism in, 5–6, 11, 103, 179, 199–202, 206–11, 227–28, 232–36; states' rights theory in, 6–7, 11, 104; tariffs affecting, 73, 86, 105; territorialization theory applied to, 258; Texas rebellion supported by, 2, 122. *See also* Confederate States of America; slavery and enslaved persons
sovereignty: dual system of, 20, 37–41, 105; popular, 3, 27–29, 38, 189–91, 197, 202–6, 231, 288n51; territorial, 10, 169, 198, 212, 232, 243. *See also* state sovereignty
Spain: abolition of slavery by, 39–40, 221; Cádiz Constitution, 27, 28, 57, 64; cession of Florida to US (1819), 1, 71; citizenship expansion in, 28; Cortes (legislature) of, 27–29, 47, 48; French invasion of (1808), 27; invasion of Mexico (1829), 73, 77, 90; Mexican independence from (1821), 26, 28–31, 48, 80, 283n74; Siete Partidas as law code of, 23. *See also* New Spain; Spanish America
Spanish America: administrative reforms, 46–48; borderlands of, 16, 22, 47, 50; democracy in, 28; indigenous peoples in, 47, 55; Junta Central representatives from, 27; land for US settlers in, 22–23, 48; militia tradition in, 57; nation-building in, 146. *See also* New Spain
Spratt, Leonidas, 242
state sovereignty: in Articles of Confederation, 18; Calhoun on, 105–7; commitment to, 2, 7, 40; Confederacy and, 225; executive power in undermining of, 73; federalism in defense of, 187; Jackson on violations of, 74; Mexican Constitution of 1824 and, 36–40, 52, 157, 198, 285n120; Mexican Constitution of 1857 and, 214, 233; modern conceptions of, 5; nationalist federalism and, 108; opposition to, 89–90, 146; in Reforma period, 215–17, 239; US Constitution and, 19, 20, 106–7
states' rights, 6–11, 82, 104–8, 190, 229, 297n6
Stephens, Alexander, 201, 242, 266
Story, Joseph, 106
Sumner, Charles, 191, 229, 258, 311–12n63

Taney, Roger, 203, 218
tariffs, 9–10, 23–24, 73, 78, 86–89, 103–8, 111, 294nn70–71
Taylor, John, 22
Taylor, Zachary, 176, 180, 182, 187–88, 200–201

Tejanos, 9, 53–56, 67, 72, 79–84, 91–92, 110, 274–75
territorial inalienability, 4, 11, 176, 179, 198, 211, 232–34
territorialization theory, 258
territorial sovereignty, 10, 169, 198, 212, 232, 243
Texas: admission as slave state, 200; agrarian radicalism in, 272; claims to New Mexico, 200–202; descriptions of, 15, 86; Jackson and, 71, 78, 94, 101, 168, 292n31; map created by Austin, 87; secession from Mexico (1836), 2, 6, 134, 136, 147, 234, 298n13; secession from US (1861), 5, 11, 227–28, 232–33; Spanish exploration and settlement of, 46, 47; during US civil war, 252. *See also* Mexican Texas; Republic of Texas; US annexation of Texas
Texas rebellion (1835–36): abolitionists on, 150–52; Anáhuac rebellion as rehearsal for, 73; Austin and, 121, 124, 126–31, 134; battles of, 133–39; centralist response to, 10, 128, 139; as federalist resistance, 9, 120–24, 128, 133; literature review, 4–7, 278n14; Mexican Constitution of 1824 and, 120–21, 123, 127, 129; militia recruitment, 125–27, 133, 301n85; New Orleans's support for, 9, 104, 120–26, 129, 301n91; rhetoric during, 127–28, 131, 132; Santa Anna and, 132–39, 301–2n106; separatism and, 2, 134; Tornel on, 132–33, 135–36, 139
Thompson, Buttil, 60
Thorn, Frost, 56
Toluca, Plan of (1834), 115, 299n43
Toombs, Robert, 243
Tornel, José María: on Baltimore, 76–77; Bases Orgánicas and, 147; centralist-nationalist vision of, 156; on federalism, 118, 144; "On Democracy in France and Monarchy in the United States," 148; pronunciamientos and, 115; on reconquest of Texas, 148; on secession of Texas, 234, 298n13; on Texas rebellion, 132–33, 135–36, 139; on United States, 148–50, 167; on US-Mexican War, 192
trans-Mississippi west, 22, 25, 31, 50, 55, 270, 272
treaties: with indigenous peoples, 74; on Mexican independence from Spain, 29; between Texas and Yucatán, 163; in War of 1812, 24. *See also specific names of treaties*
Trist, Nicholas, 186–88
Tucker, Nathaniel Beverly, 199
Tutino, John, 179
Twiggs, David E., 227
Tyler, John, 166–68, 170, 172, 174

Ugartechea, Domingo, 99, 100
United States: border agreement with New Spain, 26, 48; citizenship in, 2, 144, 221, 247, 258, 265, 269, 285n2, 323n91; comparative history of Mexico and, 7, 279n31, 315n1, 320n4; economic crises (1780s and 1790s), 19, 278–79n22; expansionism of, 1, 92, 93, 171–74, 181, 188; hypocrisy accusations against, 10, 124, 148, 150; institutional weaknesses, 5, 75, 179, 275–76; labor and agrarian resistance movements in, 272–73; Mexico intervention by, 255–57; militias in, 20, 45, 126; nationalism in, 8, 44, 177, 182; nation-building in, 7, 146; predictions of dissolution, 1, 18, 185; secession of states from, 5–6, 11, 103, 179, 208–11, 227–28, 232–36; "second founding," 260; Spanish cession of Florida to (1819), 1, 71
Upshur, Apel P., 106, 168, 170
Urrea, José, 159–60, 165
US annexation of Texas (1845): Houston on, 166, 170; opposition to, 3, 147, 153, 168, 170–72; slavery and, 3, 149–51, 169, 170; southern support for, 3, 167, 171; territorial expansion through, 2, 103; Tyler and, 166, 168, 174
US civil war (1861–65): abolitionism during, 247–49; constitutional ambiguity and, 279n22; events leading up to, 178, 236; fugitive enslaved persons during, 246–47; geographical and chronological boundaries of, 7; Reconstruction following, 258, 260, 265–66, 269–70, 276; secession of southern states and, 5–6, 11, 103, 179, 208–11, 227–28, 232–36; surrender at Appomattox as end to, 255. *See also* Confederate States of America

US Constitution: ambiguity of, 192, 232, 279n22; compact theory on, 106, 207, 229; Constitutional Convention (1787), 18–19, 36; extraterritoriality doctrine, 19,≈191, 192, 203; federalism and, 20; Fifteenth Amendment, 265–66; Fifth Amendment, 178, 192, 207; Fourteenth Amendment, 265, 266, 323n91; on militias, 20, 45; opposition to, 19–20, 279n22, 281n34; ratification of, 20, 106, 233; slavery and, 6–7, 11, 19, 21, 178, 192, 203, 207, 220–21, 229–32; state sovereignty and, 19, 20, 106–7; Thirteenth Amendment, 260; three-fifths clause and, 192, 203, 230; Whigs on, 146

US-Mexican War (1846–48), 3, 176, 178, 180–92, 195. *See also* Guadalupe Hidalgo, Treaty of

Van Buren, Martin, 170
Velasco, Treaty of (1836), 138–39
Veracruz, Plan de (1832), 97–98, 100
Victoria, Guadalupe, 41–42
Vidaurri, Santiago, 258, 261–62, 267, 324n98
Viesca, Agustín, 81, 83–84, 87, 116, 118, 132
Viesca, José María, 81
Villa, Francisco, 273
Villareal, Florencio, 212
voting rights, 21, 90, 152, 211, 215, 217, 221, 265–66

Wade, Benjamin, 259
Walker, Robert, 168–69, 171
Walker, William, 15, 16, 34, 35
Washington, George, 20–22, 41
Weber, David J., 286n3
Webster, Daniel, 107, 108, 135, 144, 146, 147
Wharton, John, 227
Wharton, William H., 110, 111, 125, 126, 129, 227
Whigs: in abolitionist movement, 151; comparison with santanistas, 5, 145–46; on cultural uniformity, 145, 147, 154; opposition to Texas annexation, 3, 147, 168, 171, 172; political philosophy of, 144–48; racist tropes used by, 184–86; on US-Mexican War, 185–90
Wigfall, Louis T., 206–8, 252
Wilkinson, James, 55
Williams, James, 244
Williams, John, 62
Williams, Samuel May, 96, 100, 114
Wilmot, David, 189
Wilson, Woodrow, 273
Wise, Henry, 167
Worcester v. Georgia (1832), 75

Yancey, William, 206
Yates, Richard, 219
Yucatán, Republic of, 162–64, 307n77

Zapata, Emiliano, 273
Zavala, Lorenzo de, 44, 68–69, 75–78, 87, 117–21, 133, 214